Depth Psychology, Interpretation, and the Bible

Depth Psychology, Interpretation, and the Bible

An Ontological Essay on Freud

BRAYTON POLKA

McGill-Queen's University Press

Montreal & Kingston · London · Ithaca

© McGill-Queen's University Press 2001
ISBN 0-7735-2125-9

Legal deposit first quarter 2001
Bibliothèque nationale du Québec

Printed in Canada on acid-free paper

This book has been published with the help of grants
from the Humanities and Social Sciences Federation of
Canada, using funds provided by the Social Sciences
and Humanities Research Council of Canada,
and from York University.

McGill-Queen's University Press acknowledges the
financial support of the Government of Canada through
the Book Publishing Industry Development Program
(BPIDP) for its activities. We also acknowledge the
support of the Canada Council for the Arts for our
publishing program.

Canadian Cataloguing in Publication Data

Polka, Brayton
    Depth psychology, interpretation, and the Bible: an
    ontological essay on Freud
    Includes bibliographical references and index.
    ISBN 0-7735-2125-9
    1. Freud, Sigmund, 1856–1939—Religion.
    2. Psychoanalysis and religion.   I. Title.

BF173.P58 2001   150.19'52   C00-900733-4

Typeset in 10/12 Sabon by True to Type

Table of Contents

Preface

In this book I continue my thinking about interpretation, which has been the subject of my two previous books and associated smaller studies. I am concerned, above all, with showing that a concept of interpretation, which is at once systematic and comprehensive, presupposes an ontology, a commitment to thought and existence, that is biblical in origin and structure. Basic concepts that I associate with the Bible, with the ontology of biblical interpretation, include creation (*ex nihilo*), fall (sin), covenant, golden rule, idolatry, revelation, and redemption (salvation and liberation). I hold that, whatever differences there are between the Hebrew and the Christian Bibles, and these differences are critically important, they are altogether different from the differences that separate the Bible (Hebrew and Christian) from what I call extra-biblical reality. Extra-biblical reality broadly covers the three cultural groupings conventionally known as antique (Greco-Roman, Egyptian, etc.), archaic (primitive), and Eastern (particularly, Hindu, Buddhist, and Taoist).[1]

It is my position that we shall be able to overcome the dualisms paralyzing our interpretive efforts – those between reason and faith, the secular and the religious, and philosophy and theology – only if we come to realize that the Bible is no less rational, or secular, than it is faithful, or religious. In other words, the dualisms dividing our lives between the secular and the religious and between the rational and the spiritual directly reflect those that we impose on the Bible. I have in mind such dualisms as those between human and divine, sin and salvation, individual and community, fall and redemption, time and eternity (immortality), incarnation and resurrection, internal and external, soul and body. Not only does deconstruction of the dualisms of our lives involve deconstruction of the Bible, but, as Spinoza so profoundly demonstrates, deconstruction of the Bible expresses the deconstruction of our lives. Life is too important to be surrendered to secular experts, and the Bible is too important to be surrendered to experts in belief. Perhaps even more dangerous, however, are life's gurus and the Bible's pros. If we are to be neither tyros nor aces, then it is only with an amateur's loving practice, which Kant shows to be indistinguishable from thoughtful practice, that we can resist the constant pressure of the binary thinking of dualism and save God (the divine) not so much from atheists as from believers and wo/man (the human), not so much from theologues as from anthropologues.

It takes the effort of constant vigilance to keep returning to the truth that the covenant of thought and existence, whose motive (drive!) is desire (will, love), becomes repressive and oppressive and not liberating the very moment that we surrender the dialectical tension at the heart of the undecidable difference between the divine and the human. "I know, O Lord, that the way of man is not in himself, that it is not in man who walks to direct his steps" (Jeremiah 10.23). But we misread, weakly, this passage and the Bible, generally, if we conclude that, because the way of human beings is not in themselves, it is therefore *in* God. The way of human beings is neither internal (in themselves) nor external (in God). The way of God is neither internal (in himself) nor external (in human beings). In living the redemptive passage of the golden rule, the way of God and human beings is in and through the other. God appears (at first) to be mysterious because we do not (cannot) see him. Human beings appear (ultimately) to be mysterious because we do (can) see them. It is not easy to learn the hard lesson, which we keep forgetting, that it is solely with human eyes that we can see God and that it is solely with divine eyes that we can see human beings (including ourselves). If, however, we become tempered by the lesson of dialectic in loving God above all others and our neighbour as ourselves, then we shall understand the mystery of lucidity that is vision: seeing is believing. To believe in either God or human beings is to see both at once.

The Bible is concerned, above all, with the vision, with the promulgation, of a just and loving life. To that end it engages in a ruthless critique of idolatry, of which it is itself the first and last subject, as it repels all attempts on the part of its readers to make word (*logos*) and meaning (*Logos*), letter and spirit, commensurate. Notwithstanding the fact that there is no meaning outside its incarnation in physical manifestation (verbal or otherwise), communication is not reducible to natural language. Idolatry is the reduction of the spirit of thought and existence (at once divine and human) to the natural categories of space and time. Human beings are created in the image of God, in the image of the other: the golden rule. Human beings are not created in the image of natural opposition, which is the way of extra-biblical life.

In providing a vision of life as just and loving and a critique of injustice and oppression as idolatrous, the Bible constitutes thought and existence as the interpretation to which the reader is subject, of which the reader is the subject. The Bible creates thought and existence whose interpretation expresses the reader. In making the reader the subject of its interpretation, the Bible itself becomes the subject of the reader's interpretation. The Bible becomes subject to the reader's interpretation. Interpretation is not something extrinsic to the Bible, something that we readers do to the Bible as professionals or that the Bible does to us as novices. Interpretation is the heart and soul of both the Bible and its readers, as both are the heart and soul of interpretation.[2] To love God above all others and your neighbour as yourself (the golden rule) is the heart and soul of interpretation, the interpretation of the heart and the soul.

I call the structure of values that is at once (unconsciously) presupposed and (consciously) articulated by the act of interpretation "ontology." Ontology provides me with a term which, being the dialectical other of interpretation (thought), is supraordinate, as Jung would say, to both theology and philosophy (metaphysics). The biblical ontology presupposed by interpretation is that articulated in and through the ontological argument for thought and existence, at once divine and human. Kant liberates the ontological argument of divine existence (as that which cannot be thought without existing and that which cannot exist without being thought) from the idolatrous antinomies of time and space. He shows that existence constitutes the realm of loving, thoughtful practice, the kingdom of ends, where willing the good presupposes the practical postulates of freedom, immortality, and God. The ontological argument for existence articulates, by presupposing, the dialectical relationship of thought and existence. The thoughtful *is* the actual (what actually exists), and what actually exists *is* the thoughtful. Consciousness has an object, an other, a subject, Hegel says simply and profoundly in the Introduction of the *Phenomenology of Spirit*.

This simple, yet profound presupposition is absent from Greek philosophy, according to which the law of contradiction, as the supreme law of life, fatally opposes consciousness and its object, thought and existence. The Greek world does not know the paradoxical law of ontology, which posits that nothing exists that cannot be thought and that nothing is thought that cannot exist. Greek contradiction is exemplified by Socrates. To think, Socrates demonstrates, is always to discover that what you think (oracular god, daimon, soul, form) is precisely that which is the opposite of, that which is opposed to, your thinking. Thinking is the continuous discovery that you are ignorant of what you think. Subject and object, self and other, thinking and existence are forever opposed to each other in the Greek world. To think – the law of contradiction – is to launch the heroic life whose inexorably fatal end, at once comic and tragic, is Socratic ignorance, Oedipal blindness, and Iphigenian death – all for the greater glory of Greece. To think the law of contradiction is also to discover that the contradictory opposite of contradictory law is the law of identity (together with the law of the excluded middle). Here subject and object, thought and its object, are an immediate identity where thought is and does not have an object (for, according to Plato, to know the good is to be the good).

The *sole* alternative to the law of contradiction is the ontological argument, which is applicable to human no less than to divine thought and existence. But this alternative is absolute or infinite, that is, metaphorical, difference, not the comparative or finite difference of natural simile that simply reflects the ignorant, blind, and lethal opposition of nature. According to the ontological argument, thought and existence are posited (created) in the beginning as relationship: the covenant of self and other, the golden rule, whose patient teaching is that I have to lose my life (of thought and existence) in and through the life of the other in order to find it. The ontological argument for thought and existence and the golden rule together constitute the biblical truth that interpretation at once presupposes and demonstrates. As Kierkegaard says, love is upbuilding, for it builds up love in others by presupposing love in them. The thinkers upon whom I shall call in my study to build up my interpretive ontology are, above all, Descartes, Pascal, Spinoza, Rousseau, Kant, Hegel, Kierkegaard, and Nietzsche.

In this book I extend my concept of interpretation to comprehend Freud. I also hope to take up Jung in a subsequent study. But in these prefatory observations, and also in the introductory comments that follow in chapter 1, I shall address both Freud and Jung. I want to advance a concept of interpretation that, while encompassing both of the two great founders of depth psychology, is not reducible to either of them. I want to show that it is only on the basis of the concept of interpretation that I have sketched above and have begun to work out systematically and comprehensively in my previous studies that the rich, phenomenological insight of depth psychology, both Freudian

and Jungian, can be freed from the basic contradictions of its metapsychology (Freud) and its amplificatory mythology (Jung). I undertake to
show, in other words, that the concept of interpretation can be
enriched by depth psychology only when the fundamental assumptions
shared by psychoanalysis and analytic psychology are exposed as contradictory. What I argue, therefore, is that the psychological depths
explored by Freud and Jung can be made properly interpretive only
when they are understood to presuppose the fundamental ontology of
the Bible. My aim is to show that, in their mutual interaction, depth
psychology, interpretation, and the Bible presuppose, and thus articulate, a common ontological commitment to thought and existence.
Advance in understanding depth psychology necessitates our seeing
that it presupposes a concept of interpretation whose ontology is biblical in origin and structure. But it is also the case that advance in
understanding depth psychology results in the discovery that interpretation presupposes that which gives psychology its depth, the concept
of the unconscious. The hermeneutical circle of depth psychology,
interpretation, and the Bible is complete. Each of these three critical
elements at once presupposes and articulates the other. Depth psychology is biblical and interpretive. The interpretive depths of the Bible are
unconscious. Interpretation articulates, by overcoming, the antinomies
between depth psychology and the Bible (religion).

I treat the depth psychology of Freud and Jung as a common whole,
for, notwithstanding the celebrated differences dividing them, together
they make the single, greatest contribution to twentieth-century
thought, the elaboration of the concept of the unconscious. "Depth
psychology" is a useful term for referring commonly to the psychoanalysis of Freud and the analytic psychology of Jung, for it allows me
to indicate that, notwithstanding their significant differences, Freud
and Jung stand or fall together with the concept of the unconscious.
The term "depth psychology" was coined at the very beginning of the
twentieth century by Eugen Bleuler, Jung's distinguished mentor in psychiatry at the Burghölzli Clinic in Zurich, and it is routinely used by
both Freud and Jung to describe their own particular psychology
founded on the unconscious.

The reason that it is particularly fruitful to consider Freud and Jung
together from within a common, interpretive framework is that the
concept of the unconscious that they together hold leads them to diametrically opposed positions on religion. The views of Freud and Jung
on the relationship of the unconscious to religion are not, however,
only mutually contradictory. They are also self-contradictory. In the
first place, neither Freud nor Jung develops an ontology, a concept of
interpretation, that is true to his concept of the unconscious, that is,

that reveals the truth of the unconscious. In the second place, the reason that they both fail to develop such an ontology is that neither of them is able to conceive of the unconscious as historical, as that which comes freely into existence, in the words of Kierkegaard. Both Freud and Jung persist in viewing the unconscious as that which is prior, primordial, primitive, and original. But then they are utterly unable to explain how consciousness arises from that which was (and also is and will be) originally unconscious. If, in the beginning, the unconscious is unaware that it is unconscious, how in the world does it ever *become* (historically) conscious that it is (was) unconscious? How are we ever to *make* the unconscious conscious if, in the beginning, we are unaware that we are unconscious?

For Freud, the beginning in originary unconsciousness constitutes, at once, primary process, the pleasure principle, illusion, and religion. But then Freud is powerless to explain (except as the return of the repressed) how the secondary process of the reality principle, which is exemplified, above all, by science, arises out of and undertakes to explain that which is prior to it and original. Since when does the son, the secondary principle, get away with killing and constituting the authority for the primary principle, the father, and thus with simply eliminating the Oedipus complex – unless this is the way in which Freud bypasses, in silence (repression), the mother, the pre-Oedipal (*sic*!) relationship of mother and child? For Jung, the beginning in originary unconsciousness constitutes the unity of religious truth as found in the universal archetypes of the collective unconscious. But then Jung is powerless to explain (except as the return to the mythological) how the archetypes, which are complete and perfect in themselves, can generate the process of individuation, which Jung views at once as the method and the goal of analytic psychology. How can that which is, in the beginning, collective and complete become, in the end, differentiated and individuated?

If we are to become aware of the contradictions that unconsciously dominate Freud and Jung's concept of the unconscious, it is necessary to distinguish critically between two completely different notions of contradiction. This distinction, which is the difference between the Greek law of contradiction and the biblical paradox of ontology (the ontological argument for thought and existence), marks a more fundamental difference than Derridean *différance*. For *différance* still involves a trace (archetrace) of difference that is not truly different. Indeed, the difference between Greek contradiction and biblical paradox is the only fundamental difference there is. For it is this difference that accounts for (that narrates the story of) the difference distinguishing Socratic ignorance of thought and existence from biblical self-consciousness of thought and existence. It is the difference between the contradictory nature of paradise, according to which sin is ignorance, and the paradoxical history of redemption, according to which sin is knowing (living) the good and evil of thought and existence. The contradiction of Socratic thought and existence is that they can be known (by us) only as paradox. No concept (trace) articulating Socratic difference remains, for this difference does not exist as known (thought), and it is not known (thought) to exist. Knowledge of the form is utterly contradictory, as Plato's works,[3] consistent with Greek tragedy and comedy, demonstrate from beginning to end. Knowledge of the form is always manifested in human beings as ignorance of the form. The form, identical with itself, contradicts all appearance as different from itself. Appearance is contradiction, the ignorance of thought and existence.

The distinction between difference that fatally metamorphoses into what is indifferently identical (ignorance) and difference that matters as the thought and existence of difference (the difference of thought and existence) is the difference between Greek contradiction and biblical contradiction (paradox). It is the difference between contradiction that is unknown and unknowable as contradiction, and contradiction that, in order to be known (thought), remembered, and recognized, must be worked through in the analytic situation, as paradox. The paradox of recognizing contradictory difference transforms contradictory opposition into the difference that counts, the difference that accounts for the difference that we share with each other. The paradox – from our interpretive point of view – of the Greek law of contradiction is that it operates by imposing fatal ignorance of, and blindness to, its own lethal operations on those who learn from the seductive oracle of Delphic Apollo that, to the Socratic hero, the unexamined life is not worth living.

The difference, then, between Socrates and Descartes, which is the difference not between ancient and modern but between extra-biblical and biblical, is this: Socrates knows *that* he is ignorant, but he does not know *what* he is ignorant of.[4] He knows that he is ignorant of the contradiction between thought and existence, but he does not know what that contradiction is: he does not know what it is that constitutes contradiction. Socrates does not know what contradiction is; he does not know what constitutes the contradiction of thought and existence. Descartes launches the ship of modern ontology by transforming the contradiction of thought and existence into an ignorance, an uncertainty, a doubting so radical that there emerges from the purgatorial fires threatening the meltdown of thought and existence a primal recognition that thinking expresses existence and that existence involves thinking: I think; therefore, I am. Descartes is firm in insisting against his critics, who constantly attempt to assimilate the *logos* of his ontological argument to the ancient, skeptical doubt of the law of contradiction, that the judgment, the choice, the sacrifice, the freedom, the duty embodied in the *therefore* connecting thought and existence is not deductive (just as it is not inductive). The logic embodying the relationship of thought and existence is not that of the law of contradiction. It is – Descartes is not very clear what it is. He does not know that it is (the paradox of) love, which Spinoza, his greatest disciple and his most trenchant critic, makes the basis of both biblical interpretation and ethics. But Descartes does know (unconsciously) that the *logos* sparking the connection between thought and existence involves the logic not of contradiction but of paradox, whose depths, at once human and divine, we now call the unconscious, thanks to Freud and Jung.[5]

It is only in light of distinguishing carefully between contradiction, as extra-biblical, and paradox, as biblical (and thus modern), that it becomes evident that psychoanalysis and analytic psychology together make three basic, unexamined assumptions about the unconscious and its relationship to religion. These assumptions may be summarized in the following terms: (1) The unconscious is found universally among all peoples and precedes the emergence of consciousness; (2) Religion is universal, and biblical religion is but a late version of universal religion; (3) Depth psychology and (biblical) religion are founded on different principles. Assumption 3, in reflecting the fundamental contradictions embodied in assumptions 1 and 2, is found in a number of contradictory versions, including (in schematic form) the following: (i) Depth psychology is true, and religion is illusory (Freud and classical psychoanalysis); (ii) Depth psychology, as consistent with Greek philosophy or mythology, is true – either biblical religion is illusory, or its ontological status is (left) unclear (for example, Hillman, Lear, Marcuse, and Stein); (iii) Depth psychology possesses the truth of religion but, as an empirical science, eschews all metaphysics and theology (Jung); (iv) Depth psychology is consistent with and, indeed, can significantly contribute to (biblical) religion – but, in emulating the subordinate status of philosophy in the Middle Ages, it must accept the humble status of *ancilla theologiae* (for example, Küng, Meissner, Ricoeur, and White). Since my focus here is on depth psychology, I shall not systematically evaluate the response to depth psychology on the part of theologians. I shall also not consider those who simply dismiss either depth psychology or depth psychology together with (biblical) religion (for example, D.H. Lawrence and Sartre).

Overall, I am concerned to show in the present study that the metapsychology that is central to Freud's thinking is inherently contradictory and that it falsifies his rich phenomenological insight. I argue that his metapsychology, whose core, the father complex, is composed of two fundamental elements, the Oedipus complex and the myth of the primal father, is irremediably dualistic and must be rejected as utterly false if the depth of Freudian psychology is to be truly comprehended. But I also argue that the only basis for seeing through the dualistic metapsychology of the father complex is the concept of interpretation that, true to biblical ontology, is consistent with the golden rule. It is precisely this concept of interpretation, however, that is implicit in Freud's phenomenology and that is also presupposed by the analytic situation and the "construction" that analyst and analysand reciprocally develop together. What is so deeply ironical about Freud is that, while he constantly falsifies his phenomenological insight in the name of the metapsychological dualism of the father complex, it is precisely the content of his phenomenology that supplies the critical perspective needed to expose the metapsychological impasse generated by his dualism. This irony becomes especially poignant in *Moses and Monotheism*. Here Freud shows that fundamental elements of the phenomenology of ancient Judaism – Jewish character, mind (the advance in intellectuality), and ethics, all embodying the uniqueness and universality of Jewish monotheism – supply the basis of modern life (including psychoanalysis) and cannot be comprehended on the basis of his metapsychology. Nevertheless, he continues to argue that Judaism, like all religions, including Christianity, compulsively repeats, as it represses, the murder of the primal father.

The chapter outline of my book is as follows. In chapter 1, I introduce basic ontological considerations that arise when one undertakes to think through the interpretive structure of depth psychology. In chapters 2-4, I take up the fundamental elements of Freud's metapsychology: the pleasure principle and the unconscious (chapter 2); the Oedipus complex (chapter 3); and the myth of the primal father (chapter 4). My main point in these three chapters is to show, on the basis of a detailed analysis of critical passages in major texts of Freud, that the fundamental ideas of his metapsychology, beginning with the pleasure principle, are utterly dualistic. These metapsychological ideas compromise and, indeed, falsify all attempts on his part to arrive at a coherent and cogent concept of depth psychology. Only the primal idea of depth psychology, that of the unconscious, can and must be salvaged from the debacle of Freud's metapsychology; and that is possible, I show, only on the grounds of a concept of interpretation, consistent with the Bible, that repudiates the metapsychology of the father complex.

In chapter 5, I show how ironic it is that Freud turns not just to religion but, indeed, to biblical religion, to ancient Judaism, in his last, major, innovative work, *Moses and Monotheism*. It is his express intention to show, definitively, that religion represents the return of the repressed murder of the primal father – consistent with his metapsychology of the pleasure principle, which, it turns out, embodies the death instinct. However, what Freud shows, compulsively, in spite of himself, is that it is psychoanalysis, insofar as it is dominated by the father complex, that represents the return of the repressed religious. Freud never sees the consequences of beginning with basic dualisms, those involving beginning and end, the unconscious and consciousness, id and ego, primary process and secondary process, pleasure principle and reality principle, religion and reason (science), the primitive and the modern. He does not see that, in the end, all that is secondary, rational, modern, and scientific will then only represent the return of the repressed other, that which is primary, illusory, primitive, and religious. The sole alternative to reducing reason to the illusion of religion and to elevating religion to the illusion of reason is a concept of interpretation grounded in the dialectic of self and other: the golden rule of doing unto others as you would have them do unto you. Only a concept of interpretation that is at once secular and religious, both rational and faithful and thus no less conscious than it is unconscious can be true to the depths of Freudian psychoanalysis. Freud thus becomes an exemplary modern who is unable to be true to modernity precisely because of his refusal to see that it is the Bible that constitutes modern life from beginning to end.

In chapter 6, I shall conclude my study with a general consideration of the consequences that follow from the fact that the only alternative to the dualistic structure of Freud's metapsychology (based on the father complex), as to all structures of dualisms with which modernity, together with postmodernity, is characteristically beset, is a concept of interpretation that is consistent with biblical ontology. This ontology is at once, and undecidably, secular and religious, both rational and faithful.

To keep this study to manageable size, I shall not discuss important developments in post-Freudian psychoanalysis. Nor is this the place in which to address in detail the critical attacks to which Freudian thought has been subjected in recent years. My own critique of Freud may appear similar to that of his most severe detractors, yet it ultimately bears, I think, little relationship to it. Up to now critics of Freud have failed to explain either the basis of his insight (in his phenomenology) or the reason underlying the systematic falsification of that insight (in his metapsychology). In other words, they have failed to see that his phenomenology, in paradoxically presupposing a concept of interpretation that is biblical in its ontology, ironically reveals his metapsychology to be contradictory.[6] Freud is not a scientist *manqué*. His thought stands or falls with the Bible, as he himself indicates in *Moses and Monotheism*, as we shall see. In the study that follows I shall concentrate on the texts of Freud. I shall also call upon key ideas and passages from, in addition to the Bible, Descartes, Pascal, Spinoza, Rousseau, Kant, Hegel, Kierkegaard, and Nietzsche in my elucidation of Freud's texts.

Before concluding these prefatory remarks, I want to outline the conventions of form that I adopt in this study. Citation is by page number to particular works (as indicated by author or title of the work). Information on works cited is found in References. Except as noted, citations to Freud are from The Penguin Freud Library (in fifteen volumes), which I assume is more widely available to the non-specialist reader than the Standard Edition. I occasionally modify the Strachey translation (whose general excellence is unquestionable) to ensure consistency. Publication dates are given for the works by Freud that are cited.

With regard to emphasis that is supplied within citations from Freud (and others), there are three possibilities: (1) Where there are italics with no superscript following the page reference, the emphasis is the original author's; (2) Where there are italics with a superscript following the page reference (for example: 100e), the emphasis is mine; (3) Where there are both italics and small caps with a superscript following the page reference, the italics are the original author's emphasis, and the small caps are my own emphasis. Citations of the Bible are from the Revised Standard Version (with an eye to both its great predecessor, the Authorized Version, and its not so great successor, the New Revised Standard Version).

I follow Lear in holding that, given the diversity of conventions found in different languages (for example, "girl" is neuter in German, and "person" is feminine in French), grammar is, as such, gender-neutral (4). When I use "he," "his," etc., without a concrete antecedent, in a neutral context, or in reference to God, the "person" indicated is grammar-specific, not gender-specific.

I am grateful to the Social Sciences and Humanities Research Council of Canada, the Aid to Scholarly Publications Program, and York University for funding in support of my study. It is always a pleasure to thank those without whose help the significance of one's effort would be diminished: Christopher Anderson-Irwin, Lee Danes, Marc Egnal, John Elias, Steen Halling, Grant Havers, John Hornstein, Marlene Kadar, Tom Klein, Bernard Levinson, and Bernard Lightman, plus the anonymous readers of my study for the Aid to Scholarly Publications Program. I especially want to thank Avron Kulak for his close reading of my manuscript. I also want to thank Danièle Paycha, of the Université de Cergy-Pontoise, and Bernard Zelechow, of York University. As the organizers of the biennial conference on Studies in Cultural Meaning, they graciously invited me to read from my present book at the opening of the conference, entitled The Holy and the Worldly, that was held at the Université de Cergy-Pontoise on 7–10 November 1999.

Depth Psychology, Interpretation, and the Bible

1 Introduction: In the Beginning ... Is Interpretation

In the beginning, Freud and Jung hold, is the unconscious and only the unconscious. There is no consciousness of beginning unconsciously, no (conscious) beginning of the unconscious. Does this mean, then, that all beginnings are, in themselves, unconscious, unaware of beginning unconsciously? It is Freud and Jung who mark twentieth-century thought as beginning with the unconscious. They claim, as the founders of the psychology whose depths are unconscious in the beginning, to demonstrate that in the beginning there is no consciousness of beginning but only unconsciousness – of beginning. If, however, all beginnings are unconscious, if the beginning is unconscious, of beginning, then there will never have been a beginning that is conscious of beginning, precisely because there will never have been a beginning that is (was) not unconscious. There will never have been a beginning of the unconscious. The unconscious will never have begun.

Yet we have begun to probe the uncanny, the archetypal depths of the unconscious. But how is that possible, when both Freud and Jung proclaim, from the beginning to the end of their work, that the unconscious is first, prior, primordial, original – both in time and in eternity, both phenomenologically and ontologically, both ontogenetically and phylogenetically, both personally and historically, both individually and collectively? How do Freud and Jung themselves become conscious of the fact that, in the beginning, they are (were) unconscious of beginning? How do their analysands? How do we, their readers? How is it possible, with Freud, to make the unconscious conscious? How is it possible, with Jung, to learn that what is truly sinful is to remain unconscious (of sinning)? For in the beginning, according to Freud and Jung, there is "nothing but" – to invoke Jung's critique of Freud's instinct theory – the unconscious. But whence then is sin or evil, that peculiar consciousness that represses (evades) responsibility for its own unconsciousness, for knowledge of good and evil, what Kierkegaard calls sin-consciousness? When Jung says that the greatest sin is unconsciousness, we can be sure (or, at the least, we shall see) that it is not the unconscious that is sinful; for what drives the neurotic sufferer into analysis is precisely the sin of unconsciousness. Still, if analysands were unconscious in the beginning, they would not consciously end (by beginning) in analysis. Nor would they learn that, although the analysis of the unconscious is *endlich* (there is life beyond analysis), life is *unendlich* (there is no conscious end to our beginning unconsciously).

Freud and Jung begin with the unconscious and launch thereby the most important, perhaps the only significant, movement of ideas in the twentieth century. Their influence permeates everywhere, Freud's doubtlessly more overtly (consciously), Jung's perhaps no less covertly (unconsciously). In proposing an objective science of mind, whose primary subject is the individual human being suffering the overwhelming assaults of subjectively unconscious fantasies, emotions, and meanings, Freud and Jung (together with their countless disciples, followers, dogmatizers, revisionists, reformers, popularizers) are continuously engaged in denial that depth psychology involves or expresses either philosophy (speculation) or religion (consolation). But therapeutic practice, in centering on the suffering subject, constantly challenges the efficacy of the scientific model as knowledge of objects (controlled experimentation, the hypothetico-deductive method, the replicability of quantifiable results) in the minds of both depth psychologists and their critics, whether scientific or humanistic (religious, philosophical, or spiritualist), not to mention the legion of individual analysands themselves, the vast majority of whom remain anonymous. Thus Freud and Jung find that they have to elaborate an extraordinary edifice of interpretation, at once metapsychological and mythological, to explain the suffering subject of their new science. From the Oedipus complex to the archetypes of the collective unconscious, they are compelled to construct a concept of mind that, laden with the value of human suffering, provides a fundamental critique of human unconsciousness. While Freud universalizes the neurotic subject to the whole of civilization, Jung universally amplifies the mythological contents of his subject's unconscious. Both find themselves inextricably involved in critical questions of interpretation that are centred on the relationship between the unconscious and consciousness.

But the question of how analysands become not only conscious *that* they are unconscious but also, more critically, conscious of *what* they are unconscious of turns out to be a metapsychological question about the very nature of mythology. How is it that myth that, in the beginning, is unconscious of itself as beginning in myth, becomes critically self-conscious of its mythical beginnings? Both Freud and Jung recognize that how subjects in analysis become conscious of their unconscious reflects and is reflected by our myth of the collective unconscious, by our conception of how society at large is unconsciously dominated by its collective myths (its myths of collectivity). Freud recognizes that the etiology of neurosis in sexual repression reflects patriarchal social structures. Their pervasive presence leads him, finally, to locate the ultimate antinomy of civilization in an irreconcilable opposition not between sexuality and culture but between Eros, which binds human beings together, and the death instinct, which, in demonstrating its presence as the unconscious sense of guilt, generates hostile, aggressive impulses destructive of the work of Eros and civilization. Jung finds that the spiritual alienation experienced by his analysands reflects a dissociation of consciousness caused by unconscious complexes whose autonomy is not only personal but also collective. Both Freud and Jung are thus constantly forced to elaborate a parallel between therapy and metapsychology, between individual unconsciousness and the mythology of the collective unconscious, between ontogeny and phylogeny, and between individual history and the history of the human race. Freud insists upon the parallel between the neurotic, the savage (the primitive), and the infantile. Jung emphasizes the connection between spiritual suffering and the universality of the archetypes constituting (constellating) the collective unconscious of humankind.

Notwithstanding Freud and Jung's persistent denials that their science of mind (soul) is ontological, it is clear that, just as science itself presupposes a concept of reason as human practice, consistent with Kant's critical philosophy, so depth psychology implies a concept of interpretation that is common to all the disciplines whose subject is the human mind and not objective nature. In the subsequent chapters of this study I shall examine Freud's concept of depth psychology as a science. Here I want to indicate that what I shall be arguing in this study is that depth psychology is not a science of mind, even when it is recognized that it cannot be modeled on the natural science of objects. Nor can it be an interpretive science if it does not account for the origins of the unconscious, for unconscious beginnings. What both Freud and Jung, together with their defenders and their detractors, fail to comprehend is that depth psychology presupposes a concept of interpretation that does justice to the unconscious. What, however, is the unconscious?

It is with this question that the ironies with which we began this chapter re-emerge and pullulate. But the metapsychology that Freud and the amplificatory mythology that Jung generate to explain the history of the movement, both individual and collective, both personal and universal, from unconscious to conscious, are riddled with contradictions from beginning to end. I have no doubt that their psychotherapies, in alleviating profound human suffering and in empowering individuals to act meaningfully upon the insight they gain in their lives, demonstrate, by constellating, the movement from unconscious to conscious. But it is no less the case, as I intend to show, that the metapsychology that Freud generates and the mythology that Jung amplifies in order to explain the historical transformation, both enacted in the consulting room and represented in the life stories that human beings narrate about and to each other, are neither scientific nor interpretive. They are not scientific as physics, chemistry, and biology are scientific; for mind, which is the subject of depth psychology, is not an object of nature. They are not interpretive, for they fail the test of accounting consistently and comprehensively – that is, rationally and so practically – for unconsciousness and thus consciousness, for the whole structure of what constitutes the psychical apparatus, the psyche of humankind.

Depth psychology and interpretation are two of the three central elements of this study. I shall show in subsequent chapters that the concept of the unconscious, as embodied in the psychotherapeutic practice of psychoanalysis, must be liberated from Freud's metapsychological speculations if it is to take its place as at once the creation and the creator of the psychical history of humankind. Freud, together with Jung and their gifted followers, provides insight into the vagaries and the tergiversations of the human psyche that is without parallel in the history of human thought and that is truly only complemented by the most intensely ontological reflections in art, philosophy, and theology. The masters of depth psychology give us an incomparably rich phenomenology, a term that Jung and occasionally even Freud are pleased to use. What they see, when they look deeply into the human psyche and its unconscious processes, they see, unlike most others, unerringly, courageously, intently, freshly, and originally. What they think they see, however, or how they think about or account for what they see – i.e., all that they elaborate in their metapsychology and in their amplificatory mythology – is utterly inadequate to their phenomenology, as I intend to show. My guess is that this disparity between phenomenological insight and ontological blindness is without parallel in the history of human thought, although it may well be that it is this disparity that characterizes so much of twentieth-century creativity, in both the arts and the humanistic disciplines. My aim here is neither to analyze Freud or Jung as persons, although they are fascinating characters, nor to propose a corrective to either psychoanalysis or analytic psychology, for I have training in neither. Nor is it my aim to undertake an explanation, at least not in analytic terms, of the disparity between the phenomenological insight of depth psychology and its ontological blindness. But I can, I think, point to the reasons for the failure, on the part of both Freud and Jung, to provide an ontological framework sufficient to contain their insight into the phenomenology of the unconscious.

These reasons involve the second and third elements of this study, interpretation and the Bible, the subjects of my previous studies. They also involve why I propose undertaking a critical evaluation of the metapsychology of Freud and the amplificatory mythology of Jung from a point of view which is that neither of Freudian psychoanalysis nor of Jungian analytic psychology, although I do believe that it is informed and disciplined by both. I recognize that those who are entrenched within either a Freudian or a Jungian perspective will, at least to begin with, view with healthy suspicion an undertaking such as mine that claims to discuss Freud and Jung from the perspective of a common framework that is identifiable with neither. This will also be the case, I would hazard, on the part of both those who (more in sympathy with Freud's delineation of the bedrock of sexuality) are rightly suspicious of the tendencies of Jungianism to reduce libido to spirit and those who (more in sympathy with Jung's delineation of our embeddedness in archetypes) are rightly suspicious of the tendencies of Freudianism to reduce spirit to libido. It is hard to imagine, however, that there is anyone who would not be interested in either Freud or Jung or, at the least, in the issues that arise thanks to the role they show the unconscious to play in human thought and existence: I (unconscious[ly]) think; therefore, I am ([the] unconscious).

The reason that it is of such consuming interest to treat the depth psychology of Freud and Jung as our common inheritance is because each of them generates, but cannot account for, the uncanny paradoxes that emerge in and through the unconscious. Whatever the differences between Freud and Jung, and these differences are real and important, they are equally unable to provide a metapsychology or an amplificatory mythology that unites present and past, analysand and history, individual and society, neurosis and civilization within a comprehensive and consistent framework. Neither Freud nor Jung can account for the coming into existence of that which is unconscious of itself. I invoke here the demonstration of Kierkegaard, in the Interlude of *Philosophical Fragments*, that existence, history, faith, and freedom together bear the dialectical structure of (non-neurotic, i.e., what Freud would call resigned and Jung authentic) suffering. Indeed, it will be central to my task to show that, until and unless the unconscious is shown to constitute and to be constituted by history, it will not be possible to account either for its free beginning, its beginning in and as freedom, or for its enslavement to the neurotic structures of necessity.

The fact that freedom involves both slavery and liberation, that love is both disease and cure, that neurosis embodies both blindness and insight, that suffering represents both melancholy and mourning, that psychotherapy demonstrates both dependence (transference to the other) and dialogue (autonomy), that life itself is characterized by both loss (fall) and salvation bespeaks the dialectical rhythm of life, at once driven yet salvific. It is this life that Jung and Freud capture in their phenomenology but falsify in the metapsychology and amplificatory mythology that they adduce in order to explain what they see. For what they see they do not know. They see what they do not know, and they do not know what they see. One is reminded here of a critical passage in the Cathedral chapter of *The Trial* involving the Parable of the Doorkeeper. Having originally introduced the parable by telling melancholic Joseph K. (analysand) that it describes the particular delusion about the Court from which he suffers, the mourning priest (analyst) then responds to K.'s impulse to reduce the complexities of the parable to contradiction and deception by bringing to his attention a passage from the commentators on the scriptures: "'The right perception of any matter and a misunderstanding of the same matter do not wholly exclude each other'" (216). Seeing is believing – just as the actual is the rational (and the rational is the actual). The copula, the love, uniting seeing and understanding is incommensurate, ontological, dialectical, dialogical difference.

Knock, and you will be admitted – to the door of the law. Call up and make an appointment with an analyst – who will see you (or suggest the name of another analyst whom you can call). Analysis presupposes the call – and it is this presupposition that doubtless explains the bizarre fact that, although Joseph K. hears his name called out in the doom of the Cathedral, he shows himself incapable, as always, of listening to or calling the other, notwithstanding the fact that he constantly calls upon others to help him evade making and hearing the call. It is the presupposition of the call to life that Freud and Jung incorporate into the phenomenology of their depth psychology but that they show themselves incapable of theorizing in the terms of their metapsychology or amplificatory mythology. I have no explanation of this split between phenomenological insight and theoretical blindness, just as I do not know what ails Joseph K. For it is precisely the opaque mystery at the heart of (unanalyzed) K., occluding understanding, that Kafka invokes with such profound, unsettling effect. But I do know that it is the act of recognition, the work of love, the inspired insight, the leap of faith, the moment of revelation, the gesture of kindness that is the mystery whose light shines in the darkness and is not overcome. I also know that this moment, by illuminating differences such that they can be united in the act of love that not only preserves but enhances them, can be explained – in and as the figures of relationship. This moment, as Kierkegaard understands so well, is the paradox. Explanation is not, as Freud would have it, from the unknown to the known (with the known then understood as that reversible Laplacian origin from which all future movements, all unknown motives, could, in principle, be deduced, however refractory the material may presently appear to be). Explanation is from the unknown to (known) existence only insofar as it is also from (known) existence to the unknown, and we reengage, as always, the ontological argument for existence (at once divine and human). We cannot explain existence without presupposing existence (as necessary, that is, free relationship); for the leap of faith is not a leap into some void, nor is it some supernatural act of levitation suspending the natural laws of space and time, which themselves, by the way, presuppose existence, as Kant demonstrates so magisterially against both the skepticism of Hume and the dogmatism of Leibniz (each of which is but the reverse of the other). The leap of faith is existence itself, for existence presupposes that which is found neither outside nor inside itself: the existence of the other. The leap of faith is the recognition (the revelation) of the other of existence, the recognition (the revelation) that existence is always other – either love or hell. Choose life, not death, God (in Deuteronomy 30.19) instructs Moses to instruct the Israelites in preparation for their passage to the promised land.

Credo quia absurdum. It is by virtue of the absurd, Kierkegaard says, that the knight of faith (Abraham) regains Isaac, regains the temporal, regains existence, whereas he needs only human (calculable) strength to renounce his relations to life. Freud does not comprehend the absurd truth of life, the Kierkegaardian truth of life's absurdity – which is that life presupposes life and cannot be tested

outside the absurdity of life's self-referentiality. He is unable to withstand the pull of the explanatory model of science whereby nature
(natural law) is that supernatural miracle of reversibility to which
everything can ultimately be reduced and from which ultimately
everything can be deduced. But how what is to be explained – the
explicandum – can become the explanatory principle – the *explicans*
– is the absurdity that is without explanation. Indeed, Hegel had decisively demonstrated nearly a century before Freud and Jung that
what constitutes the science of nature is the reversibility of cause and
effect, where any cause is itself the effect of yet another cause, as distinct from the science of spirit, where desire is irreversible and incommensurate. (Desire, Rousseau points out, is inalienable, even when
alienated.) But Hegel had only recapitulated the profound ontology
of Kant and Spinoza. Kant distinguishes between two orders of cau-
sation, nature and freedom. Natural causes have no (known) beginning (but they are not, therefore, unconscious); for not only are natural causes, in principle, indistinguishable from effects, but they are
also the necessary products of (yet unknown) effects, just as effects
are the necessary products of (yet unknown) causes. Freedom, on the
other hand, is that which begins spontaneously (unconsciously or
consciously?) from itself. It is that which Spinoza calls cause "in
itself," the *causa sui* (that whose essence involves existence or that
whose nature cannot be conceived without existing), as distinct from
cause "in another," i.e., nature.

The situation with which Freud and Jung jointly confront us, therefore, is this. Together they make the most significant contribution to
twentieth-century thought by showing that, from the beginning, psyche (the psychical apparatus) is unconscious. Nevertheless, both fail to
comprehend the ontological implications of their conception of
unconscious psyche and to explicate the ontology that it presupposes.
Freud (and Jung is not fundamentally different) continues to view
modernity as succeeding a premodern (antique and/or primitive) era.
The conscious succeeds the unconscious, the secular succeeds the religious, the scientific succeeds the primitive, man (but not woman?) succeeds God: the unconscious develops into consciousness, the religious
into the secular, the primitive into the scientific, and the theocentric
into the anthropocentric. Freud fails to recognize with Nietzsche that
redemption from the binary opposition between ancient and modern
involves the heaviest burden of eternal recurrence, the transformation
of the past into the future. In the section of Part II of *Thus Spoke
Zarathustra*, entitled "On Redemption," Zarathustra declares to his
disciples:

"To redeem those who lived in the past and to recreate all 'it was' into a 'thus I willed it' – that alone should I call redemption. Will – that is the name of the liberator and joy-bringer; thus I taught you, my friends. But now learn this too: the will itself is still a prisoner. Willing liberates; but what is it that puts even the liberator himself in fetters? 'It was' – that is the name of the will's gnashing of teeth and most secret melancholy. Powerless against what has been done, he is an angry spectator of all that is past. The will [when subject to 'it was'] cannot will backwards; and that he cannot break time and time's covetousness, that is the will's loneliest melancholy." (251)[1]

What the theory presupposed by depth psychology, as by modern and postmodern theory generally, fails to comprehend is that past time, "it was," is not the time of history and thus not the "time" of the unconscious. Time understood as "it was" is the irredeemable heaviness of the past, the immovable stone against which the prisoner, fettered to the burden of past time, hurls himself in *ressentiment*, as Zarathustra explains further to his disciples, only to find continuously that he cannot will backwards. Time is rendered historical only when and as the analysand breaks his shackles to the past by willing backwards, by willing the bondage to the past as the story of his own future freedom. That the paradox of willing backwards represents the archetypal experience of freedom fundamental to the analytic encounter is known to every good analysand and to every good analyst. It is the archetypal experience of life for all individuals who freely will the good, notwithstanding the heavy, even crushing, burdens of past and also future time weighing down upon them. The redemption of time, the transformation of "it was" into "thus I willed it," is nicely consonant with Descartes: I think – the past, therefore, I am – the past (I have willed the past as my own). What willing the past (backwards) means for depth psychology is that the unconscious is not given in the past, in the beginning, as the "it was," from which consciousness then miraculously (supernaturally) emerges. Rather, the unconscious belongs to the "I will," to willing backwards. It also follows, therefore, that the unconscious is not something "discovered" in the nineteenth century and then rendered the *raison d'être* of depth psychology by Freud and Jung in the earlier twentieth century. Rather, the unconscious becomes, thanks to Freud and Jung, the radically new perspective on the dialectic of thought and history that thereby is made explicitly unconscious from the beginning.

What is then so interesting about Freud and Jung is that, although they found a new depth psychology on the idea of the unconscious, they utterly fail to comprehend the ontology that is implied by and which alone explicates it. What makes this dichotomy between psychology and ontology so very informative is that, notwithstanding their common commitment to the significance of the unconscious, Freud and Jung seemingly divide on all important questions. (I refer to Freud's work beginning with the publication of *The Interpretation of Dreams* in 1900 and to Jung's work beginning with the publication of *Symbols of Transformation* in 1911–12, signaling his break with Freud.) What interests me here, above all, is the fact that, while Freud reduces religion, as premodern, to primary illusion, Jung elevates religion, as premodern, to archetypal truth. But neither is then able to explain the emergence of either modernity, in general, or his own depth psychology, in particular. Freud cannot explain how modern science, the secondary reality principle, arises out of, or is rooted in, the primacy of religious illusion. Jung cannot explain how the primacy of religious truth as found in the archetypes of the collective unconscious gives way, secondarily, to the soulless materialism of modern life. Whereas, for Freud, religious illusion is the ground of scientific truth, for Jung, religious truth is the ground of illusory materialism. Neither can avoid religion. Neither can explain religion. Neither can explain how the unconscious – religious but at one and the same time illusory and true – begins, consciously. Neither can explain himself. Neither can explain how consciousness is (was) originally unconscious and religious.

Although Freud and Jung each uphold a psychology of religion, neither provides that for which there does not even exist a proper disciplinary designation, a religion of psychology. My intention is not to reverse, and thus blindly to retain, the binary opposition between psychology and religion as found in Freud and Jung. I champion, rather, the dialectical identity of religion and psychology such that their differences are not repressed but made explicit, to the enhancement of our understanding of both.[2]

The sole ontology consistent with Nietzsche's transformation of "it was" into "thus I willed it" is the biblical story of creation, "fall," and redemption. This story is at once religious and secular, both faithful and rational, and thus equally theological and philosophical. It is this story that, in light of the concept of the unconscious on which Freud and Jung found their new depth psychology, is revealed as deeply unconscious from the beginning. Revelation is the story of providence – both providential and provisional: it supplies us (unconsciously) with provisions for the future. The authors of Genesis show God transforming the past (the "it was" of natural paganism) into a creative act of will: thus I created it, from nothing, in the beginning. They also show that creation involves and expresses the "fall" of humankind from identity with nature, with the past "it was." Man and woman are not generated in the image of nature but are created in the image of God. God is not supernatural (or even superhuman) but omnipotent, omniscient, eternal. Although (indeed, because) he is not subject to the law of contradiction, God is the paradoxical source of the most appallingly conflictual emotions, and we shall see that the attributes that Freud (like Jung) ascribes to the unconscious only repeat those traditionally ascribed to God. There are many ways of speaking about God (for God to speak), e.g., pastoral, spiritual, covenantal, legal, faithful, literary, mystical, rational, secular, religious, Jewish, Christian; and their test, the test to which God himself is subject (as their subject), is always whether the embodiments (incarnations) of God in our lives are loving or idolatrous.

The Bible is the great social charter of humankind as it narrates the story of human liberation, the freeing of the Jewish slaves from the imperial oppression of the Pharaoh. Hegel resumes this narrative as the process of mutual recognition. Fear of the (infinite) Lord, when distinguished from (finite) fear of the lord, constitutes the liberation of human dignity from subjection to the other. The freedom of spirit to recognize the other as spirit thus appropriates the ironic riposte of the Jewish subject to the Roman emperor: render unto Caesar that which is Caesar's (which is nothing) and unto God that which is God's (which is everything created from nothing: the dead past, the "it was" of Pharaoh and Caesar). The ontology of creation from nothing – according to which there is nothing prior to creation, to creativity, for it is creation which is the beginning, not the past "it was" – is revealed in human ethics as the golden rule, the undecidability on whether life begins with me or begins with you. For it begins with both of us, together. Coming into existence from nothing, the golden rule represents the redemption of self and other from the hierarchical way "it was" naturally in the beginning, when, as Spinoza says, big fishes eat little fishes in the natural state of opposition. In the beginning is relation, Buber says. There is no first person, and there is no second person, for the first will be second (last), and the second (last) will be first: you and I. Or, as Derrida would say, in his attempt to elude the consequences of divine *logos* by spinning out his ludic neologisms: every beginning involves and expresses *différance* – both difference and deferral. The paradox of divine creation from nothing is that all natural hierarchies of race, class, and gender are abolished (*aufgehoben*) as the source of idolatry than which there is none other.

With divine ontology having come into the world as that which

shows that conscious difference always involves and expresses unconscious deferral, it also follows, however, that there is nothing that
cannot be made idolatrous and spiritless – in discriminating against
the difference of others – beginning with God (himself!) and the
Bible. What this means is that the social charter of the Bible is also
the sole – the unique and the universal – source of all discrimination.
If, in the beginning, there is no beginning in nature, if there are no
differences that begin with the way "it was" naturally or originally,
then there will be no natural difference that cannot be made into an
ontological difference. It is precisely this paradox that is inconceivable in the extra-biblical (pagan) world. For, as Pascal writes in the
Pensées: "Fathers fear that the natural love children bear their parents may fade away. What is then this nature, subject to fading away?
Custom is a second nature, which destroys the first one. But what is
nature? Why is custom not natural? I greatly fear that nature may in
itself be but a first custom, as custom is a second nature. The nature
of man is completely natural, thoroughly animal. There is nothing
that he cannot make natural to him; there is nothing natural that cannot be taken away from him" (31–2). If the distinction between
nature and custom is undecidable, if human being is natural precisely because it is not natural, that is, because it is unnatural or nothing
in itself, then nature becomes subject to the biblical dialectic of creation and nihilism, good and evil. Where there is natural hierarchy –
between races, classes, and the sexes – then, although racism, slavery,
and sexism naturally exist, there is no concept of racial, class, or gender superiority and inferiority, except on the basis of nature. When,
however, the natural distinction of race, class, and gender is abolished by the biblical vision of freedom, equality, and solidarity –
"there is nothing that human beings cannot make natural to themselves; there is nothing natural that cannot be taken away from
them" – then natural hierarchy reappears as idolatry, as the sin
against the spirit that cannot be forgiven.

I do not intend this study to become an excursus in political theory,
although it is important to recognize that there is no ontology that is
not political and no politics that does not presuppose an ontology. But
it is worth reflecting for a moment on the relationship of significant
contemporary social and political developments to the Bible. I have in
mind the various black, feminist, and gay liberation movements
(which, by the way, not only contest the external power structures of
white, male, and straight society but also find themselves having to
confront internal conflicts brought into existence by their own
demands of liberation). The biblical inspiration of the black civil
rights movement under the leadership of Martin Luther King, Jr, is

clear. It is perplexing, therefore, to see leaders of the African-American community claim to locate their roots in the slave imperialism of ancient Egypt when King had inspired millions of Americans, black and white, with his dream of liberation from such cruel, dehumanizing oppression.

With regard to feminists (most of whom are women, although the majority of women do not appear to be feminists, while there are also significant numbers of male feminists), they rightly attack the patriarchal traditions of the Bible and demand inclusive language. But the religious feminists who reject the "male" God of the Bible in the name of pagan goddesses repress two fundamental points. First, their critique of patriarchy presupposes the biblical critique of idolatry, the golden rule of mutual recognition. Such feminists forget that the Bible is a repetition of its own story, according to which men and women are constantly tempted to confuse natural differences with the truth of differentiation. In other words, they forget that the Bible, as the creation of interpretation, is the subject itself of, is subject to, interpretation. Second, extra-biblical goddesses know no tradition of freedom, equality, and solidarity. To replace a (male) god with a (female) goddess is but to reduplicate (repeat) the oppression from which one seeks liberation. It is never easy, with Nietzsche, himself a misogynist, to transform the natural way "it was" into the freedom of "thus I willed it" for all human beings.

As for gay liberationists with a religious commitment, the issue is not one of deciding whether the Bible contains or does not contain passages that either condemn or license homosexuality, whether explicitly or implicitly. For what counts are not proof texts but the proof of the text. What the Bible proves, what it approves of and is the very proof to which it, too, is subject, is love: relationship with the other. The proof, the criterion of love, is not nature but love, the golden rule of doing unto others as you would have them do unto you.

The fall from the paradise of natural opposition into the creative responsibility of knowing good and evil without reference to natural origin, ground, presence, or *telos* means that the opposition between good and evil must be constantly liberated from the binary opposition into which it eternally falls. Freud and Jung see that the neurotic conflict of opposites is satisfactorily worked through in psychotherapy when the analysand, in transforming the "it was" into the redemptive act of "thus I willed it," is liberated from *ressentiment* of the past. But neither Freud in his metapsychology nor Jung in his amplificatory mythology is able to conceive of the conflict, the opposites, posed by neurosis, and thus by life, in anything but the contradictory terms that I have outlined above and that I shall be analyzing in detail in subsequent chapters. They fail to see that what constitutes the truth of the opposites of life is the ontology that construes them as paradox and not as contradiction. This is readily apparent, as I have already indicated, in their inability to explain how consciousness emerges out of that which is unconsciously primary, primordial, and primitive illusion (for Freud) and truth (for Jung).

What Freud and Jung cannot imagine is that there is no concept of the unconscious in, for example, Greek, Trobriand,[3] or Hindu thought. In other words, the unconscious – which is not to be confused, as I indicated in the Preface, with Socratic ignorance, according to which mind is generated in the image of natural opposition – is not found outside the Bible and its traditions. There is no concept of the unconscious found outside the concepts of desire, will, or love; and it is these concepts, constituting psyche or mind, which are *substantially* unknown and unknowable in the extra-biblical world. Substance, Spinoza demonstrates, is the *causa sui*, that which, enacting the ontological argument for existence, cannot be thought without existing and cannot exist (truthfully) without being thought.

The significance of the fact that Spinoza views ethics as the articulation of the ontological argument for existence cannot be too vigorously emphasized. In liberating human beings from enslavement to the affects and leading them to the intellectual love of God, ethics, in its commitment to existence, does not have its origin in the natural hierarchy of ruler and ruled, as found in Greek life, for example. Ethics does not begin unthinkingly (ignorantly, but not unconsciously) with the noble lie of Plato whose myth of the four metals explains human beginning as naturally unequal. Nor does ethics end unthinkingly (ignorantly, but not unconsciously) with Aristotle's unmoved mover, which, in moving human beings to their unequal end in nature, is naturally unmoved by the unequal nature of their end. In articulating the ontological argument for existence, ethics reveals itself to be consistent with the three ends of the *Theological-Political Treatise*: (1) To separate philosophy from theology[4] is (2) to provide a concept of interpretation[5] that shows that (3) democracy, of which Spinoza is the world's first systematic theorist, presupposes the Bible.

Not only, however, is the substance of the unconscious not found in the extra-biblical world, but – and this will doubtless appear counter-intuitive – substantial consciousness is equally absent from the extra-biblical world. For, just as the unconscious is not given in the beginning as that which is primitive, primordial, and prior to consciousness, so consciousness (self-consciousness) is not given subsequently as that which is modern, belated, and secondary to unconsciousness. The unconscious and consciousness are together given in the beginning as mutually related. They are modelled not on natural opposition but on the biblical ontology of relationship. The only concept of interpretation that is true to the paradoxical beginning of the unconscious, and thus of consciousness, is that which holds that the unconscious and consciousness, together, come into existence historically, freely, lovingly, from nothing. Indeed, the only alternative to the natural opposition between image (illusion) and truth is the ontological argument that for an image to be true it must exist and that for truth to exist it must be imagined. It then follows that, if the unconscious and consciousness are to be liberated from the natural opposition of image (illusion) and truth, they must be modelled on the ontological argument such that they incorporate existence into the dialectic of image and truth. It is not the case, as Freud holds, that the unconscious is, first, illusory and that consciousness, then, is true or, as Jung holds, that the unconscious is, first, true and that consciousness is, then, illusory. For truth and illusion describe the relationship of the unconscious and consciousness each to existence, not their opposition to each other. Consciousness, or what we should rather call self-consciousness, is not, as Freud so crudely holds, reducible to, although it naturally includes, perception and memory. Together with its dialectical other, the unconscious, consciousness is constituted by the dialectic of desire and self (undecidably divine and human), as I shall undertake to show in the chapters that follow.

We may recall that Hegel, who, together with Kierkegaard, is our most important philosophical interpreter of the Greeks, is always careful to distinguish between the immediacy of consciousness, which he attributes to the Greeks, along with all other extra-biblical peoples, and the infinite negativity of self-consciousness, which he attributes to the modern, that is, to the Christian (biblical), world. Just as consciousness (in the generic sense used by Freud and Jung, whose usage I shall generally continue to follow) does not blindly (unconsciously) arise out of some primordial unconscious, so Hegel shows (although not always consistently) that, in his precise terms, self-consciousness (spirit recognizing spirit) does not arise out of natural or extra-biblical consciousness. Hegel is vividly aware that the fundamental claim of his ontology, that spirit has its origin only in (recognizing) spirit, and not in nature, presumes (resumes) the biblical doctrine of creation *ex nihilo*.[6] From beginning to end the Bible shows nature to be the creation of spirit.

The fact that any comprehensive and consistent concept of interpretation must be able to deal with the dialectic of unconscious and conscious presupposes a radically double distinction. The first distinction is that between natural opposition and the dialectic of spirit. Natural opposition is the blind hierarchy of ruler and ruled as found in the extra-biblical world. The dialectic of spirit resumes the biblical commitment to the ontological argument for thought and existence, the golden rule of embodying the spirit of freedom, equality, and solidarity in our relations to others. The second distinction is that between dialectic and dualism. Whereas dialectic embodies the golden rule, dualism is the reduction of spirit (divine or human) to nature, the idolatry that the Bible ruthlessly opposes from beginning to end. But it is critically important to observe that it is the adherents of the biblical covenant who are sinners – i.e., those who reduce dialectic to dualism (binary opposition) – not those who live the natural opposition of consciousness and unconsciousness, of knowledge and ignorance. Once we are exposed to the demands of freedom, equality, and solidarity, are we not then compelled, with Rousseau, to become conscious that we are unconscious and thus to become unconscious in truth? It is not natural paganism that is sinful but biblical spirit in its multifarious attempts to subordinate others according to some natural hierarchy that privileges one over another. The enemy is not Plato or Aristotle – not antiquity, primitivism, or Eastern philosophy – but those who, as Spinoza says about Platonist and Aristotelian interpreters of the Bible, evade the truth by reducing the conscious to the unconscious and thus lose both at once. One cannot lose one's soul (or mind) unless and until it has been freely created from nothing, from nothing subject to the contradictions of natural space and time.

My overall aim, then, in this study is to articulate the concept of interpretation that is true to the depth psychology of Freud and Jung. But the sole concept of interpretation that brings out its truth is that which exposes and overcomes the contradictions inherent in their conception of the unconscious and thus of consciousness. It is this concept of interpretation, I argue, that presupposes the ontology of the Bible and that, although implicit in the therapeutic practice of psychoanalysis and analytic psychology, Freud evades in his metapsychology and Jung evades in his amplificatory mythology. I have already indicated why it is fruitful to treat Freud and Jung from the perspective of a common interpretive framework. At one and the same time, they stand together on the significance of the unconscious in founding depth psychology yet radically divide on how the unconscious is to be interpreted (on how the unconscious provides the very structure of interpretation). It is particularly significant that, although they reflect diametrically opposed conceptions of religion in their conception of the unconscious, neither Freud nor Jung can show how consciousness emerges from the unconscious unity of primal religion, whether conceived as the origination of illusion (Freud) or as the originality of truth

(Jung). The irony of this situation is that, if the traditional opposition between Freud and Jung – an opposition that both of them, uniquely, foster – is maintained, then the profound truth of each of them will be lost. Either/or.

Either Freud or Jung. Either Freud in opposition to Jung or Jung in opposition to Freud – and then Freud and Jung are both lost to the common contradictions of their metapsychology and amplificatory mythology. To hold to one of these great depth psychologists in opposition to the other is to lose both of them at once.

Or both Freud and Jung – and then Freud and Jung are each regained from the common contradictions of their metapsychology and amplificatory mythology. To hold to both of these depth psychologists, notwithstanding their opposition to each other, is to attain to a truth in which they are united and that neither can claim as his own in opposition to the other.

But then another irony emerges. The truth that unites Freud and Jung, although implicit in their phenomenology, is explicitly absent from their metapsychology and amplificatory mythology. This truth is the paradox that their contradictory conception of the unconscious as beginning unaware of itself can be overcome solely by a principle of interpretation that, in presupposing the ontology of the Bible, reveals that in the beginning the unconscious is the awareness of beginning unconsciously. The beginning of the unconscious is not prior to the awareness of beginning unconsciously. The paradox that the unconscious is not prior to but is the priority of consciousness articulates the ontological argument whose golden rule of thought and existence constitutes desire and self. This is what we shall now see as we take up, in the chapters to follow, the basic concepts of Freud's metapsychology in light of beginning with the unconscious.

2 The Pleasure Principle and the Unconscious

I INTRODUCTION

From the publication in 1900 of *The Interpretation of Dreams*, in which Freud, no longer a young man, launches the revolution of depth psychology and which he subsequently always views as his most significant work, to the last works of his old age, nearly forty years later, he holds to the pleasure principle and the unconscious as the fundamental concepts of psychoanalysis. The pleasure principle provides him, he maintains unwaveringly, with essential orientation in the psychoanalytic concept of mind, and he is steadfast in upholding the unconscious as constituting the very essence of mind. He initiates his third period of speculative creativity, by writing in the first sentence of *Beyond the Pleasure Principle*, published in 1920, that "in the theory of psychoanalysis we have no hesitation in assuming that the course taken by mental events is automatically regulated by the pleasure principle" (275). Three years later, at the beginning of Chapter 1 of *The Ego and the Id*, entitled "Consciousness and What Is Unconscious," Freud reaffirms his position that "the division of the psychical into what is conscious and what is unconscious is the fundamental premise of psychoanalysis" (351).

The development of psychoanalytic theory, in Freud's hands, is a fascinating story. I am omitting here the pre-psychoanalytic (pre-1900) period as inessential (it is reviewed by Freud himself many times, and it is constantly revisited by his admirers and critics). Freudian theory never deviates from the baselines set down in *The Interpretation of*

Dreams; yet, at the same time, it undergoes dramatic reversals. For example, according to his earlier theory, repression is said to be the cause of anxiety, while in his later theory anxiety is said to be the cause of repression. Earlier, libido is identified with the sexual instincts, in contrast with the ego (or self-preservative) instincts. Later, Freud holds that the ego is itself cathected with libido and is, indeed, the reservoir of all libido, a position that he will again reverse when he contends that the id is the reservoir of libido. In the meantime he has replaced his original distinction between sexual instincts (libido) and ego instincts with his final theory of the two fundamental instincts: life or sexual instincts (Eros or libido) and the death instinct.

It is also the case that the contrast between the unconscious and consciousness, which "alone makes it possible for psychoanalysis to understand the pathological processes in mental life," as Freud writes further in the passage cited above from *The Ego and the Id*, becomes rather more complicated. He now recognizes that the unconscious not only invests the id, which would bear, one might think, the same relationship to the ego as the unconscious bears to consciousness, but also invests both the ego and the superego. But here Freud's developmental theory – his theory of history or, rather, phylogenesis – also appears to complicate his concept of psychoanalytic theory even further. Not only does the ego emerge out of the id, due to what he calls the insistent exigencies of external reality. But the superego (conscience: social, moral, and religious authority), which harshly rules over the adult (male) ego as the father rules over the (male) child, is also said to have two distinct sources: the ego (externality) and the id (internality). The superego represents both the (male) child's personal history – the child introjects its helpless dependence upon the dominating father as its superego – and its phylogenetic heritage from the Oedipus complex, behind which is found the guilt reflecting the ambivalence (of love and hate) in killing the primal father. But, just as the ego (today, as always, in each individual) comes into existence due to the pressures of external reality, so the id, which, like the unconscious, is (today, as always, in all individuals) timeless and unchanging, comes into existence originally as the inherited precipitates of countless ego experiences. Today, the ego emerges out of the id due to external pressures. Originally, the id emerges out of the ego due to external pressures (the total narcissism of the primal father).

Not only are the reversals of these opposites into each other inexplicable – for each of them is explained by its opposite – but they equally reflect, as I have already indicated in my introductory comments, the inexplicable situation of the unconscious. The unconscious precedes the conscious in time (ontogenetically) and in eternity (phylogenetically). Yet, in order for the unconscious to come into existence – in order for the unconscious to be(come) aware that it is unconscious – it must have been, from (in) the beginning, always already aware that it was (is) unconscious. Indeed, just as Freud implies that neither the id nor unconsciousness is coherent in itself but must be fulfilled in or completed by its opposite – the ego (superego) and consciousness – so he explicitly holds two contradictory positions, from the beginning, on the pleasure principle. These contradictions will then drive him, ultimately, to go beyond the pleasure principle, that is, to find that the pleasure principle is already beyond itself and is the principle not of life but of death. Freud indicates that, in following the mandate of the pleasure principle, the organism seeks to avoid unpleasure and to attain pleasure. That seems simple enough. Yet, because Freud views unpleasure in terms of life (tension, stimulus, excitation), it is life (unpleasure) that brings into existence the wish of the organism to avoid unpleasure – that is, life – and to re-establish the constant stasis of things that is without tension, stimulus, excitation: to be dead to life. This is the first contradiction. The second contradiction emerges when Freud contends that in the beginning of life (*sic*!) there is only the primary process of the pleasure principle. But then he is forced to acknowledge that, since the pleasure principle governs life by reducing it to non-existence, its non-existence is a fiction that depends for its existence upon the prior existence of the reality principle of secondary process.

Perhaps the most consistent thing about Freud, as a theorist, is the conscious consistency with which he exposes, with unconscious consistency, the inconsistency of his fundamental ideas. He is utterly consistent in not renouncing (the exposé of) his primordial inconsistencies. Having begun with the primacy of the pleasure principle, Freud is then compelled to declare, in *Beyond the Pleasure Principle*, that to adhere to the pleasure principle, in the beginning, is to seek to restore an earlier state of things, that which is inorganic, lifeless, and dead. Just as the inorganic state of things is prior to life, so the only purpose of life, the purpose of the pleasure principle, is to restore the earlier (original) state of death. Freud possesses phenomenological evidence that clearly contradicts the priority of the pleasure principle in our lives. He is vividly aware, for example, of the pervasive phenomena of masochism and sadism, where pleasure is at once product and producer of pain; of the sense of guilt (the desire for self-punishment); of clinical phenomena showing compulsive repetition, on the part of analysands, of infantile memories that are dramatically painful, not pleasurable; and of common sense evidence, rendered particularly striking, it seems, thanks to the vicissitudes of World War I, of the hostility and aggressivity that are widely found in both our family and our social lives. None of these phenomena, however, was new to Freud in 1920. Since the 1890s he had been penetrating, with unparalleled canniness, the uncanny suffering that resulted from the defenses against libidinal desire, such as repression, regression, resistance, and the neurotic gain from illness, as found in both his patients and himself. It is also the case that, as the fictive primacy of the pleasure principle is secure only on the basis of the secondary process of reality, so Freud is also compelled to acknowledge that, although the death instinct is primordial, it cannot be found separate from the life or sexual instincts, Eros.

Indeed, from the beginning to the end of his career Freud is perplexed by the instincts (*Triebe:* drives). In being at once somatic in origin and psychical in representation, the instincts form the very basis of his concept of psychical life. Yet he obsessively repeats that they are and continue to remain completely unknown and unknowable. His comment in "An Autobiographical Study" of 1925 is typical of many others: "There is no more urgent need in psychology than for a securely founded theory of the instincts on which it might then be possible to build further. Nothing of the sort exists, however" (241). When Freud writes in "Instincts and their Vicissitudes" that "even the most highly developed mental apparatus is subject to the pleasure principle, i.e., is automatically regulated by feelings belonging to the pleasure-unpleasure series" (117), he must then confront how it is possible for an instinct, instead of seeking pleasurable discharge and avoiding unpleasure, to turn into its opposite. How, for instance, can an instinct suffer repression?

It is not easy in theory [Freud writes at the beginning of "Repression"] to deduce [from a general theory of the instincts] the possibility of such a thing as repression. Why should an instinctual impulse undergo a vicissitude like this? A necessary condition of its happening must clearly be that the instinct's attainment of its aim should produce unpleasure instead of pleasure. But we cannot well imagine such a contingency. There are no such instincts: satisfaction of an instinct is always pleasurable. We should have to assume certain peculiar circumstances, some sort of process by which the pleasure of satisfaction is changed into unpleasure. (145)

Is there something about pleasure, about the pleasure principle, about beginning in pleasure that is its opposite, its very own reversal? Is there something about this beginning in pleasure that leads Freud beyond the pleasure principle in 1920 with the recognition that the pleasure principle is the very basis of the death instinct, that beyond life is the lust for returning to a prior, inorganic state, that death is the end of life? Indeed, Freud's original concept of pleasure is really that of unpleasure, a principle of constancy (which, in his later work, he will also call the Nirvana principle). Stimulus is unpleasure that stimulates the organism to eliminate the stimulus or to reduce it to the lowest level possible so that, as he writes in "Instincts and their Vicissitudes," "if it were feasible, [the mental apparatus] would maintain itself in an altogether unstimulated condition" (116). But Freud's argument then takes an interesting twist. Unlike external stimuli, from which the organism can attempt to escape (or so he says), instinct is a constant, unrelenting, internal pressure that is inescapable. Where would one flee from it, except into repression? Thus, instinctual stimuli, Freud writes,

oblige the nervous system to renounce its ideal intention of keeping off stimuli, for they maintain an incessant and unavoidable afflux of stimulation. We may therefore well conclude that instincts and not external stimuli are the true motive forces behind the advances that have led the nervous system, with its unlimited capacities, to its present high level of development. There is naturally nothing to prevent our supposing that the instincts themselves are, at least in part, precipitates of the effects of external stimulation, which in the course of phylogenesis have brought about the modifications in the living substance. (116–17)

Notwithstanding Freud's observation that the instincts, as internal stimuli, are constant, incessant, and unavoidable, he then proceeds to interpret them in terms of the pleasure principle, according to which "unpleasurable feelings are connected with an increase and pleasurable feelings with a decrease of stimulus" (117). Indeed, he states that "the aim of an instinct is in every instance satisfaction, which can only be obtained by removing the state of stimulation at the source of the instinct" (119). The aim of an instinct is, therefore, to attain that satisfaction which is the removal of all stimulation. The aim of an instinct is to have no aim at all. The aim of an instinct is the utter elimination of instinct. Ultimate satisfaction, ultimate pleasure is the elimination of all stimulation, the elimination of all instinct. Pleasure, it is evident, is death, instinctual death, the death of pleasure.

It begins to become clear why Freud is never able to develop a coherent theory of instinct, of motive (moving power), or of what I shall argue should rather be called desire (expressing a notion of self, agency, or action). But what is so perplexing about Freud is that, in his instinct theory, as in his theory of the unconscious, the problem stares him in the face, yet he never sees it. He is right that instinct is an "internal" stimulus or pressure that is unceasing in its demands. But he fails to see that this concept of drive utterly contradicts his notion of the economy of pleasure-unpleasure according to which the attainment of pleasure is the attainment of perfect stasis or, in other words, instinctual death. He knows that instinct is, like the unconscious, eternal, timeless, unchanging, and deathless, its pressure for expression unrelenting. Yet, when instinct is subordinated to the pleasure principle, it becomes the very expression of death.

Two additional characteristics of Freud's metapsychology are also clearly evident here, characteristics that, at one and the same time, remain constant in his system and drive him into the kind of reversals (contradictions) that I have noted and to which I shall constantly recur. The first is his notion of internality. Freud never understands in theory, although he clearly sees in practice, that "internal," like its opposite "external," is a metaphor, a dangerous metaphor. It implies that the instincts, like the libido or the unconscious, are a finite, natural object that can be located in some physical space (and time), although he consistently eschews an anatomical location for psychical agencies, while insisting upon their topographical significance. What Freud never comprehends is that, while natural (finite) objects are located in physical space (and time) and can be internal or external to *us*, and *we* to them, instincts, as desire, express relationship – of self and other. Indeed, the fact that internality is ultimately a contradictory notion is clear when Freud indicates, in the passage cited above, that instincts, although defined in opposition to external stimuli (which can be escaped from), are said, nevertheless, to be (at least in part) the precipitates of external stimuli. This is the second, additional characteristic of his metapsychology to which I referred. Just as Freud holds that instincts are internal, in opposition to external stimuli, so he also holds that, historically (phylogenetically), they are the products of external events. Instincts are thus defined at one and the same time as the opposite, yet as the products, of external stimuli. This is the dualistic pattern that Freud compulsively repeats throughout his work. He utterly refuses to consider the one alternative to dualism, the alternative that I associate with the ontology of desire. We can, therefore, anticipate that Freud's harsh critique of the golden rule as the desire true for all human beings, in *Civilization and its Discontents*, will reflect his conception of pleasure, whose internal demands for the elimination of all stimulation make him subject desire to what he calls the unconscious sense of guilt. But in this chapter our task is to assess the two concepts fundamental to Freud's depth psychology, the pleasure principle and the unconscious. Both receive their fundamental articulation in *The Interpretation of Dreams*, where they prove to be central to Freud's conception of the dream as the disguised fulfilment of a suppressed or repressed wish. He will continue to reconfigure them in subsequent works. We shall concentrate our attention in this chapter on *The Interpretation of Dreams*, "The Unconscious," and *Beyond the Pleasure Principle*.[1]

II THE PLEASURE PRINCIPLE

The Interpretation of Dreams is a remarkable work for two closely related reasons, reasons that reveal the structure of psychoanalysis to be at once paradoxical (true) and contradictory (false). First, Freud proclaims from the beginning that dreams possess "a psychical structure which has a meaning and which can be inserted at an assignable point in the mental activities of waking life" (57). He opposes the two dominant traditions of dream interpretation, first, that of popular dream books and occultism, which, going back to antiquity, assigns dreams an esoteric meaning, and, second, that of medical psychiatry, which views dreams as somatic in origin and without psychical meaning. Freud holds not only that dreams are psychically original and meaningful but also, consistent with his asseveration in the last section of *The Interpretation of Dreams*, that "the unconscious is the true psychical reality," that "*the interpretation of dreams is the royal road to a knowledge of the unconscious activities of the mind*" (773, 769).[2] The second reason that *The Interpretation of Dreams* is so remarkable a work is that, in Freud's view, "dreams are invariably wish-fulfilments" in that "they are products of the system *Unconscious*,[3] whose activity knows no other aim than the fulfilment of wishes and which has at its command no other forces than wishful impulses" (723). But when Freud undertakes to show that wish, whose fulfilment constitutes unconscious activity, operates according to the economy of the pleasure-unpleasure principle, we find that the interpretation of dreams plunges us into the contradictory depths of his metapsychology. Dreams meaningfully express the unconscious, for they are to be assigned their place within waking mental life. Unconscious activity is constituted by wishing, according to whose principle of pleasure external stimulus produces unpleasure that it can only be the organism's wish to eliminate. The aim of wishing is to eliminate all wishing. But what happens, then, to the unconscious? In what sense are dreams meaningful but unconscious structures?

I do not know what dreams are, at least not on the basis of what Freud tells us about them. But I am confident that he is right in insisting that dreams are neither occult in meaning nor somatic in origin. Dreams are significant psychical structures whose interpretation is deeply revealing of our unconscious life. He is also right to distinguish between what he calls their manifest (distorted) form and their latent (suppressed or repressed) content, the dream thoughts, whose material is subject to the dream work of, above all, condensation and displacement. When, however, Freud comments, in a footnote added in the revised edition of 1925 (following the previous seven editions, of which four had been enlarged and revised), that the distinction between manifest and latent continues to give even his own followers difficulty, we begin to wonder if there is not a problem inherent in the distinction itself. He remarks that originally his readers had found it difficult to learn to distinguish between

the manifest content of dreams and the latent dream thoughts ... But now that analysts at least have become reconciled to replacing the manifest dream by the meaning revealed by its interpretation, many of them have become guilty of falling into another confusion which they cling to with equal obstinacy. They seek to find the essence of dreams in their latent content and in so doing they overlook the distinction between the latent dream thoughts and the dream work. At bottom, dreams are nothing other than a particular *form* of thinking, made possible by the conditions of the state of sleep. It is the *dream work* which creates that form, and it alone is the essence of dreaming – the explanation of its peculiar nature. (649–50)

Why is it apparently so difficult, even for Freud's own followers, to maintain a clear distinction between manifest (form) and latent (content), between dream work and dream thoughts? Why, as Freud writes in a footnote added in 1914, do people now make "the mistake of confusing dreams with latent dream thoughts" (736)? The answer is, surely, that the dream is the product of both an unconscious wish to escape the censorship imposed on it by consciousness and a conscious wish to distort, to suppress, to repress the unconscious wish. But is the dream work, then, a product of the unconscious that uses the mechanisms of condensation and displacement as a means of escaping conscious censorship (but thus making itself available to conscious interpretation)? Or is the dream work, rather, a product of consciousness that uses these same mechanisms as a means of disguising from itself the wishes that it does not want to recognize yet is compelled (that is, wants) at the same time to recognize?

As we are only initiating our examination of what it is that shapes the overall structure (strategy) of psychoanalysis, it may be useful to note that, from the time of his *Introductory Lectures*, Freud calls psychoanalysis both a libido psychology and an ego psychology. In his final statement on psychotherapeutic technique, published as chapter 6 in the posthumous *Outline of Psychoanalysis*, Freud remarks that the doctor's role in analysis is to aid the patient's ego when, like a country divided by internal civil war, it needs outside support to help it fight the subversive forces of both the id and the superego. Yet he immediately adds that, when, during the course of analysis, the ego resists this support, "the party divisions are to some extent reversed: for the ego struggles against our instigation, while the unconscious, which is ordinarily our opponent, comes to our help" (412–13). If the ego is also (in part) unconscious, in its resistance to the libido demands of the id (not to mention to the "instigation" of the analyst), is the unconscious also, in part, conscious (as it supports the analyst in overcoming the unconscious ego-resistance of the analysand)? In other words, if the unconscious wish (libido, sexual instinct) is legitimate (liberating) – and thus terrifying to the ego – is the dream work produced by the unconscious so that its demands can be recognized by consciousness, if only in distorted form? Or is the dream work produced by consciousness as a means of denying the real import of libidinal demands while enjoying them in distorted (disguised) form? Manifest or latent, conscious or unconscious, ego or libido (id)? Surely, the only way of appropriating these binary oppositions is in terms of a concept of desire that constitutes and is constituted by the self.

Before, however, we undertake to show what happens when Freud analyzes wish (desire) in terms of the pleasure-unpleasure calculus, it will be instructive to see what he means when he insists – reflecting the same dualism between manifest and latent, ego and libido, conscious and unconscious – that "two fundamentally different kinds of psychical process are concerned in the formation of dreams." Freud argues that, while the dream thoughts are (as preconscious and so capable of being made conscious) rational and meaningful, like "normal thinking," the form of the dream is irrational and nonsensical (756). But who then is the dreamer? Where is the dreamer within his dreams that are at once meaningful but distorted (disguised)? Not only does Freud hold that dreams are overdetermined, which means that, precisely because they are determined (meaningful), their determinate meaning is ever subject to further (unconscious) determination (desire). But he also observes that there always remains "a tangle of dream thoughts which cannot be unraveled ... This is the dream's navel, the spot where it reaches down into the unknown" (671).[4] Freud's (unconscious) metaphors are invariably instructive. Precisely because the dream's "navel" (or center) is located in the dream thoughts, which are one with the dreamer's preconscious and (thus) conscious or waking thoughts, it clearly reaches, not down into an "unplumbable," as if indeterminate, "unknown," but rather out into a world of human relations, whose meaning, both past and future, is yet to be determined (186). Indeed, Freud points out that, in interpreting any dream element, it is always doubtful whether it is to be taken positively or negatively, historically or symbolically, or in terms of its wording. Nevertheless, although "the productions of the dream work ... *are not made with the intention of being understood*," Freud declares, "[they] present no greater difficulties to their translators than do the ancient hieroglyphic scripts to those who seek to read them" (457). But how do we read the wish of the dreamer if it is divided between unconscious (libido) and conscious (ego) – when, as Freud subsequently discovers, the ego itself is also unconscious and the very source of libido? What is the relationship of the dream wish, on the one hand, to the (latent) dream thoughts and, on the other hand, to the (manifest) dream work (which is itself no more manifest than the dream thoughts are latent)?

The question of how or where the dreamer stands in relationship to his own dream is raised by Freud when, in chapter 1, he reviews how his (mainly) nineteenth-century predecessors tergiversated in assessing the moral content of dreams.[5] What, he asks, do dreams reveal about their dreamers, especially when they show them to be shamelessly involved in the most immoral acts? Do dreams disclose the inner truth of dreamers' lives, or do they simply demonstrate the obvious fact that dreamers differ from those who put such fantasies into practice in their waking lives? If moral personality ceases to operate in dreams, how will dreamers understand the immoral deeds that they enact in them? If moral personality is revealed in dreams, how will dreamers understand the fact that in their waking (but also their dreaming[6]) lives they distinguish between immoral deeds that are dreamed and immoral deeds that are enacted when awake? Surely, it is one thing for someone (a male) to dream about killing his father and sleeping with his mother and another thing to perform these deeds. But why, then, do we dream such dreams?[7]

Of the several works of predecessors that Freud cites to illustrate the problem of determining what he calls, to cite the title of section F of chapter I, "The Moral Sense in Dreams," it is a book by Hildebrandt, published in 1875, that he praises most highly. "Of all the contributions to the study of dreams which I have come across," Freud remarks, "it is the most perfect in form and the richest in ideas." According to Freud, Hildebrandt is among those who hold that dreams truly reflect the (waking) lives of dreamers. Those who are pure in spirit have pure dreams, while those who are impure in spirit have impure dreams. Freud quotes Hildebrandt as writing that in our dreams "we never lose sight of the distinction between good and evil, between right and wrong or between virtue and vice. However much of what accompanies us in the daytime may drop away in our sleeping hours, Kant's categorical imperative is a companion who follows so close at our heels that we cannot be free of it even in sleep" (135). A dream, Hildebrandt holds, never expresses a wish, desire, or impulse that has not been present in our waking mind. The dream merely presents it in dramatic form consistent with I John 3.15: "Any one who hates his brother is a murderer." Upon waking, we may brush aside the dramatic form of the dream wish, but not the content itself. "'In short,'" Hildebrandt argues, "'if we understand in this scarcely disputable sense Christ's saying that "out of the heart come evil thoughts" [Matthew 15.19], we can hardly escape the conviction that a sin committed in a dream bears with it at least an obscure minimum of guilt'" (137). In this sense, Freud observes, Hildebrandt indicates that "dreams give us an occasional glimpse into [the] depths and recesses of our nature to which we usually have no access in our waking state" (138).

While Freud does not directly express his own opinion as to the views of Hildebrandt and others on the question of how or in what sense dreams reveal the inner (moral or immoral) character of the dreamer, he does remark, in a subsequent chapter, that, of the various ideas about dreams that he surveys in chapter 1, he denies only two of them – "the view that dreaming is a meaningless process and the view that it is a somatic one. Apart from this, I have been able to find a justification for all these mutually contradictory opinions at one point or other of my complicated thesis and to show that they had lighted upon some portion of the truth" (746).

Freud also points out, in a footnote added in 1909, that the "principal feature" of his theory of dreams, his "derivation of dream distortion from the censorship" represented by the dream work, is "once more expounded" in the last part of a story entitled "Dreaming like Waking" ("*Träumen wie Wachen*"), taken from *Fantasies of a Realist* by "Lynkeus" and first published in 1899 (418). In the passage from the story that Freud then cites (without further comment), a dialogue takes place between "'a man who has the remarkable attribute of never dreaming nonsense'" and his interlocutor, who ascribes ""this splendid gift""" to the moral serenity of the man's nature, to, that is, his kindness, sense of justice, and love of truth. But the admired dreamer's response to this explanation for his "'never dreaming nonsense'" is that he """almost""" believes that everyone is like him and that no one ever dreams nonsense. So long as a dream can be remembered, he declares, it """must *always* make sense, and it cannot possibly be otherwise. For things that were mutually contradictory could not group themselves into a single whole.""" The confusion of space and time as found in dreams does not affect the true content of dreams any more than of waking life, as is evident in fairy tales and in """the many daring products of the imagination"'" that only the unintelligent would call nonsense. The admired dreamer does acknowledge, however, the difficulty that is involved in interpreting dreams, as pointed out by his interlocutor, but he adds that the only thing that is required in successfully interpreting dreams is a little attention to oneself. The reason that you other people do not succeed in interpreting your dreams, he tells his interlocutor, is that "'"there seems always to be something that lies concealed in your dreams, something unchaste in a special and higher sense, a certain secret quality in your being which it is hard to follow. And that is why your dreams so often seem to be without meaning or even to be nonsense. But in the deepest sense this is not in the least so; indeed, it cannot be so at all – for it is always the same man, whether he is awake or dreaming"'" (418–19).

Still, although Freud claims to agree with "Lynkeus," who is clearly in agreement with Hildebrandt, that the individual is always the same, whether dreaming or awake, it is not very clear what is revealed in and by the replacement of the dream work by dream interpretation. The dream work (unconscious or conscious?) distorts the (preconscious yet potentially conscious) dream thoughts; and dream interpretation (conscious or unconscious?) replaces the manifest form of the dream, wrought by the dream work, with the latent dream thoughts now rendered manifest. At the very end of *The Interpretation of Dreams* Freud is careful to note that the contribution that his study makes to dream interpretation is theoretical, not practical. If he is asked about the moral significance of dreams, his answer will be, he says, that "I do not feel justified in answering these questions. I have not considered this side of the problem of dreams further" (781–2). Although he does proceed to point out that today, unlike in Roman times, we do not judge people on the basis of their dreams, he adds: "whether we are to attribute *reality* to unconscious wishes, I cannot say." Since psychical reality, Freud continues, is not, however, to be confused with material reality, "there seems to be no justification for people's reluctance in accepting responsibility for the immorality of their dreams." When we understand how the mental apparatus, with its division between conscious and unconscious, operates, "the greater part of what is ethically objectionable in our dream and fantasy lives will be found to disappear" (782). We judge human beings in terms not of their dreams but of their actions and consciously expressed opinions; "for many impulses which force their way through to consciousness," Freud concludes, "are even then brought to nothing by *the real forces of mental life* before they can mature into deeds. In fact, such impulses often meet with no psychical obstacles to their progress, for the very reason that *the unconscious is certain* that they will be stopped at some other stage" (782–3ᵉ).⁸

It is by no means clear that the common sense distinction between psychical reality and material reality is true either to Freud's insistence that dreams are psychical and not somatic in origin and meaning or to the distinction that he makes between fantasy and reality (internal and external), and which we shall examine in chapter 4. It is also not clear how the distinction between psychical and material would relate to what Freud, in the passage cited above, calls "the real forces of mental life." Indeed, how does the unconscious, which Freud identifies with "the impulses which force their way through to consciousness," become "certain" that these impulses will be (consciously?) stopped?

The uncertainty of the distinction that Freud makes between psychical reality and material reality, between unconscious and conscious, is reflected in his claim that we are examining that dreams are composed of two separate mental functions. On the one hand, he views dream thoughts as "entirely rational" in that, although unconscious, they are capable, because preconscious, of becoming conscious. On the other hand, he holds that the dream work, which transforms unconscious thoughts into the dream proper,

is not simply more careless, more irrational, more forgetful and more incomplete than waking thought; it is completely different from it qualitatively and for that reason not immediately comparable with it. It does not think, calculate or judge in any way at all; it restricts itself to giving things a new form. It is exhaustively described by an enumeration of the conditions which it has to satisfy in producing its result. That product, the dream, has above all to evade the censorship, and with that end in view the dream work makes use of a *displacement of psychical intensities* to the point of a transvaluation of all psychical values. (650)

That the rational dream thoughts are utterly transformed by the completely different mental process represented by the dream work Freud then articulates in the penultimate section of chapter 7 of *The Interpretation of Dreams* as the distinction between primary process and secondary process. "Thus we are driven to conclude," he writes, "that two fundamentally different kinds of psychical process are concerned in the formation of dreams. One of these produces perfectly rational dream thoughts, of no less validity than normal thinking; while the other treats these thoughts in *a manner* which is in the highest degree bewildering and irrational" (756ᵉ).

Just as Freud indicates in the passage cited earlier that the dream work creates "a particular *form* of thinking," so here, it also turns out, the contrast between the two completely different mental processes rests on a distinction between rational content (dream thoughts) and irrational "manner" (dream work). Not only, however, is the distinction between content and form inherently unstable and ultimately untenable. But, as I have already pointed out, it is also not clear whether the dream work emanates from the unconscious or from consciousness. Further, this distinction itself is complicated by the fact that the dream thoughts, too, are unconscious (although part of our waking life) and that Freud will later discover that the ego (together with the superego) is also (in part) unconscious.

The uncertainty of the distinction that Freud makes between irrational dream work and rational dream thoughts, between unconscious and conscious, between primary process and secondary process, when it turns out that these distinctions are founded on a difference between irrational form and rational content, is rendered yet more uncertain when Freud proceeds to investigate the origin of the dream work itself. He now turns to his theory of neurosis to provide him with what he calls "the assumption that the dream wish which provides the motive power [for the dream] invariably originates from the unconscious" (757).[9] But how does this wish, in dominating unconscious life, involve both the rational content of the dream thoughts and the irrational form of the dream work when it expresses the same individual, whether dreaming or awake?

The only way in which light can be thrown "upon the psychical nature of wishes," Freud declares, is by means of the original development of the psychical apparatus (718). Although the apparatus originally strives to remain free of stimuli, the exigencies of life, as found, at first, in somatic needs, impel it to further development. For example, the hunger that a helpless, kicking, and screaming infant experiences can be satisfied solely by outside help. In satisfying its original need, thanks to external intervention (on the part of its mother, say), the baby establishes a link between need and satisfaction such that the

next time this need arises a psychical impulse will at once emerge which will seek to recathect the mnemic image of the perception and to re-evoke the perception itself, that is to say, to re-establish the situation of the original satisfaction. An impulse of this kind is what we call a wish; the reappearance of the perception is the fulfillment of the wish ... Nothing prevents us from assuming that there was a primitive state of the psychical apparatus in which this path was actually traversed, that is, in which wishing ended in hallucinating [the breast]. (719–20)

Since the helpless, dependent baby cannot live, however, by hallucination alone but demands real and not merely illusory satisfaction, Freud acknowledges that primitive (primary) process has to give way to secondary process. Reality preserves illusion.

When Freud returns to a discussion of the nature of the unconscious wish fulfilled in dreams, in the section on "Primary and Secondary Processes," he now acknowledges that the pleasure-unpleasure principle by which our wishing is regulated is a "fiction" that presupposes secondary process. The primitive apparatus possesses pleasure only insofar as it does not experience excitation or stimulus. A stimulus (for example, the need to satisfy hunger), in bringing the apparatus unpleasure, impels it to seek its original satisfaction as the pleasure in which all tension has been eliminated. Freud writes: "A current of this kind in the apparatus, starting from unpleasure and aiming at pleasure, we have termed a 'wish'; and we have asserted that only a wish is able to set the apparatus in motion and that the course of the excitation in it is automatically regulated by feelings of pleasure and unpleasure" (757).

But, once again, Freud has to recognize that original wishing, as brought into being by unpleasure (stimulus) and aiming at pleasure (complete cessation of stimulation), fails to attain its end (that is, it utterly contradicts itself). Either the organism (for example, the helpless infant) dies (from lack of food, etc.), or its need (for example, for food) is undying. In the second case, it becomes evident that the fiction (contradiction) of the primary process can be maintained only upon the supposition of a second psychical system, that of secondary process, what Freud subsequently calls the reality principle. "The two systems," he writes, "are the germ of what, in the fully developed apparatus, we have described as the Unconscious and Preconscious [the preconscious being that which, while unconscious, is capable of being made conscious]" (758).

The problem with which the wish presents him, Freud thus acknowledges, is that of development (or beginning). Were it not for the fact that the organism undergoes development (or begins), then it would not be disturbed by the unpleasure of need, the stimulus of excitation. In its original condition there is only pleasure and no wish. Once the organism, however, is confronted with the real stimulus of unpleasure (for example, it is hungry), it responds by generating a wish that, in following the mandate of the primary process, seeks to eliminate the unpleasure of the stimulus by reducing it back to the pleasure of stasis in which wish is satisfied by wishing for nothing whatsoever. If an organism functioned according to the program of the primary process, it would never have begun developing, for it would never have become subject to the stimuli of unpleasure. Or, if one could imagine that it somehow came into existence, it would not be able to survive a single instant. Freud therefore has to acknowledge that the primary process, regulated by the pleasure-unpleasure mechanism, is a fiction whose reality is guaranteed only by the secondary process (the reality principle). But this is not quite how Freud puts it. He sees the problem squarely, as always; and he distorts it, as always, by formulating it in dualistic or reductive (and not in dialectical or liberating) terms.

It is true [Freud writes] that, so far as we know, no psychical apparatus exists which possesses a primary process only and that such an apparatus is to that extent a theoretical fiction. But this much is a fact: the primary processes are present in the mental apparatus from the first, while it is only during the course of life that the secondary processes unfold, and come to inhibit and overlay the primary ones; it may even be that their complete domination [of the primary process] is not attained until the prime of life. In consequence of the belated appearance of the secondary processes, the core of our being, consisting of unconscious wishful impulses, remains inaccessible to the understanding and inhibition of the preconscious. (763)[10]

Freud is right that desire is fundamental. He is also right that the development (the education, the history) of desire, the desire of development, is complex and fraught with the inhibitions of not only normalcy but also inversion, perversion, neurosis, and psychosis. But there are two basic matters that he fails to comprehend. First, desire, as primary, is no less secondary in the beginning. Second, it is only in overcoming (appropriating) the dualism between primary and secondary that the self-contradiction of desire, or what Freud calls wish, can be addressed. The fundamental flaw in Freudian metapsychology is that, in insisting upon the primacy of wish, the primary process (the pleasure principle), he is then compelled to make it blindly depend upon unpleasure that is foreign to its being. It is little wonder, then, that, when he subsequently finds himself driven to go beyond the pleasure principle, he simply shows that pleasure is, in the beginning, identical with constancy, nirvana, the earlier state of things, inorganic being: death. The primary wish is for death; everything secondary is life. Reversing Shakespeare, the past is prologue.

When Freud moves from concern with the psychical mechanism underlying the dream wish in the primary process of pleasure to ask, atypically, where the person stands in his own dream, he is confronted once again with the self-contradiction of pleasure. "No doubt a wish fulfillment must bring pleasure," he writes in a footnote added in 1919 (citing a passage from the *Introductory Lectures*); "but the question then arises, 'To whom?'" Although it is clear that the pleasure belongs to the dreamer, still, it is the dreamer who repudiates and censors his wishes, since their fulfilment would bring him not pleasure but unpleasure. "Thus a dreamer in his relation to his dream wishes," Freud observes, "can only be compared to an amalgamation of two separate people who are linked by some strong element in common. Instead of enlarging on this, I will remind you of a familiar fairy tale in which you will find the same situation repeated" (737). Freud then summarizes the fairy tale in which a poor, married couple is granted the instantaneous fulfilment of their first three wishes. Smelling sausages cooking next door, the wife (it is the woman who introduces disaster by seeking illusory pleasure!) at once wishes for a couple of sausages, and there they are before her. Infuriated, the husband at once wishes the sausages hanging on his wife's nose, and there they are hanging on her nose. The third wish (but whose wish is it, the wife's or the husband's?), in undoing the previous two wishes, restores wife and husband to the reality that wishing, when governed by the pleasure principle, is illusory and contradictory. Or, in Freud's summary of the fairy tale of the three wishes: "Since after all they were in fact one – man and wife – the third wish was bound to be that the sausages should come away from the woman's nose ... If two people are not at one with each other, the fulfillment of a wish of one of them may bring nothing but unpleasure to the other" (737–8).

But is the relationship that a person has to his dream wish that of two individuals in opposition to each other or that of two individuals at one with each other? It is clear, I think, that, phenomenologically, Freud envisages the possibility of a person's being at one with his wish: his wish can express (fulfil) his true self. But it is also clear, I think, that, metapsychologically, as a result of basing his notion of wish (desire) on the primary process of avoiding unpleasure and attaining pleasure, Freud cannot imagine the alternative to a fundamental and contradictory opposition between desire (wish) and pleasure. Desire, generated by unpleasure, seeks only to reduce unpleasure back to pleasure, in which desire is eliminated. Wish, Freud holds, is governed by the primary process of pleasure; it seeks to eliminate all unpleasure and to live by pleasure alone. But the irony, the contradiction that Freud, paradoxically, never sees is that pleasure is the absence of desire, while desire is only present as (generated by) unpleasure.

Since it is pleasure that signals the absence of desire and desire the presence of unpleasure, it is not surprising that the distinction between pleasure and unpleasure becomes (reversed), in Freud's article of 1911, "Formulations on the Two Principles of Mental Functioning," (as) the distinction between the pleasure principle and the reality principle. The reality principle, in preserving, indeed, in generating tension, conflict, and change, all involving unpleasure, is the true province of desire. But, again, this is not how Freud puts it. He acknowledges that the pleasure principle is a self-contradiction from which it is rescued only by the "external world" of the reality principle. Nevertheless, he continues to maintain the "fiction" that "the unconscious mental processes," dominated by the "primary processes" of "the pleasure-unpleasure principle," or what he now, for the first time, calls "the pleasure principle," are prior, primordial, and primitive (36–7). "It will rightly be objected," Freud observes, "that an organization which was a slave to the pleasure principle and neglected the reality of the external world could not maintain itself alive for the shortest time, so that it could not have come into existence at all. The employment of a fiction like this is, however, justified when one considers that the infant – provided one *includes* with it the care it receives from its mother – does *almost* realize a psychical system of this kind" (37e).[11]

The slave-system of the pleasure principle *almost* exists but, in fact, does not exist prior to being *included* within the reality principle of its mother's liberating (good-enough) care. Because Freud, however, does not give up his metapsychological commitment to the priority of the pleasure principle, he is compelled to maintain a quite conventional dualism between desire as primordial, but illusory, and utility as secondary, but real. This real but secondary pleasure is the one that we normally call bourgeois, Philistine, and puritanical. "Actually," Freud writes, "the substitution of the reality principle for the pleasure principle implies no deposing of the pleasure principle, but only a safeguarding of it. A momentary pleasure, uncertain in its results, is given up, but only in order to gain along the new path an assured pleasure at a later time" (41).

Freud then proceeds to remark further that the transformation of the pleasure ego into the reality ego, of original autoerotism into secondary object love (the love of another), is reflected in our great socio-ideological institutions: in religion, whose renunciation of earthly pleasures, however, remains mythical; in science, whose renunciation, or conquest, of the pleasure principle (generating intellectual pleasure and practical results) is the most successful; in education,[12] where the bestowal and withdrawal of love serve as reward and punishment; and in art, which expresses dissatisfaction with the renunciation of pleasure as demanded by the reality principle (40–2).

If science, however, is, no less than religion, the product of the fiction (the myth) of the primacy of the pleasure principle, and of the resultant dualism between pleasure and reality, between fictional autoerotism and realistic object love – "in the service of procreation" (42)

– will it turn out that the science of psychoanalysis itself is only the return of the repressed religious? Or, in other words, will it prove to be the case that psychoanalysis is only as true as religion itself is true? Is it scientific fiction or religious myth that obstinately maintains, in the face of overwhelming evidence to the contrary, both ontological and phenomenological, the primacy of the pleasure principle? What will happen to our conception of psychoanalysis if we stop repressing the truth that what is real for religious (biblical) myth is neither (unreal) internal pleasure nor external (unpleasurable) reality but desire whose fictions involve and express the self of history and the history of self? Is not Freud's science of primal beginnings – at once static (the pleasure principle) and violent (the primal father) – the dualistic myth whose idolatry the dialectic of biblical critique has always (already) deconstructed, in the beginning?

III THE UNCONSCIOUS

Before pursuing the pleasure principle beyond itself – that is, before discovering that the pleasure principle begins, prior to its real or posterior existence, dead to life – it is instructive, first, to examine Freud's concept of the unconscious. We have seen that the pleasure principle is the fiction (contradiction) that, on the one hand, precedes reality in existence yet depends on reality for its existence and, on the other hand, as will be seen, precedes (as the death instinct) existence yet depends on existence (as the life instinct of Eros) for its reality. We shall now see that the unconscious repeats this contradiction. It is the prior fiction (illusion) that depends on the posterior reality of consciousness for its existence.

Freud brings *The Interpretation of Dreams* to a close with a section distinguishing between the unconscious and consciousness, consonant, apparently, with the preceding section on primary process (the pleasure principle) and secondary process (the reality principle). He re-emphasizes the sharp difference between the two psychical processes by characterizing the unconscious as "the true psychical reality" and consciousness as the close ally of censorship (repression) (773–4) – but then also of the dream work? Freud thus indicates that unconscious fantasies find expression not only in dreams and neurotic symptoms but also in intellectual and artistic productions (including *The Interpretation of Dreams*!). But what, then, is the substance of this unconscious, psychical reality if its truth rests primordially on the pleasure principle whose hallucinatory satisfaction contradicts its very existence? (We have already seen that, if the pleasure principle takes the hallucinatory image as real, it will die of starvation.) How, in other words, can the reality of the unconscious (unconscious reality) rest on the pleasure principle whose hallucinatory illusion has to be repudiated? Will the unconscious, the lynchpin of psychoanalysis, survive the later revelation of the pleasure principle as the death instinct?

In our analysis of the unconscious we shall concentrate on the essay of that title, one of several metapsychological essays that Freud writes in about 1915, for in it he greatly amplifies the sketch of the unconscious that he gives in the final section of *The Interpretation of Dreams.*[13] Freud opens his essay on "The Unconscious" by noting that, while the process of repression involves keeping an unconscious idea from becoming conscious, the repressed is but part of a larger unconscious that is not commensurate with the repressed. Not only, however, does Freud leave the subject of the repressed obscure – do we repress something because we fear its truth or its falseness? – but he also acknowledges that we can know the unconscious only after it has been translated in conscious terms. Indeed, he points out that it is precisely the fact that the gaps that we experience in our consciousness presuppose other acts that it is necessary to assume unconscious mental processes. It is characteristic of Freud, however, that he does not directly acknowledge the vicious circle that results from the dualistic opposition between the unconscious and consciousness.

What is more, having shown, while not admitting the fact, that the unconscious presupposes consciousness (and consciousness the unconscious), he then proceeds to argue for what he calls the necessity and the legitimacy of the unconscious on grounds that completely undercut his insistence on the duality of, or the difference between, unconscious and conscious mental processes. He begins by asserting that it is perfectly legitimate to assume the existence of the unconscious "inasmuch as in postulating it we are not departing a single step from our *customary and generally accepted mode of thinking.* Consciousness makes each of us aware only of his own states of mind; that other people, too, possess a consciousness is an inference which we draw by analogy from their observable utterances and actions, in order to make this behavior of theirs intelligible to us" (170e).

Freud then restates his claim that, while we have immediate knowledge of our own consciousness, we infer the consciousness of others in what he calls "psychologically more correct" terms (170). The *sine qua non* of understanding, he states, is identification with others, the attribution to everyone else of our own mode of consciousness (the inference of everyone else from our own mode of consciousness). In the beginning, Freud holds, we identify with, by extending consciousness to, not only human but also all other animate beings, not to mention inanimate objects and the world at large. Even though the relations that we have with our fellow human beings withstand the criticism that we subsequently make of our identification with organic and inorganic nature,

the assumption of a consciousness in them [Freud declares] rests upon an inference and cannot share the immediate certainty which we have of our own consciousness. Psychoanalysis demands nothing more than that we should apply this process of inference to ourselves also ... All the acts and manifestations which I notice in myself and do not know how to link up with the rest of my mental life must be judged as if they belonged to someone else: they are to be explained by a mental life ascribed to this other person. Furthermore, experience shows that we understand very well how to interpret in other people ... the same acts which we refuse to acknowledge as being mental in ourselves. (171)[14]

Freud then concludes his argument supporting the existence of the unconscious with the claim that, just as we perceive the external world by means of sense-organs, so we perceive unconscious mental processes by means of consciousness. It can be said, therefore, he remarks, that the assumption of unconscious mental activity is an expansion of two psychical moments: (1) primitive animism, according to which the other (the object) reflects consciousness (the subject); and (2) the Kantian critique, according to which the object perceived is not identical with the subject perceiving. What this means, he concludes, is that "psychoanalysis warns us not to equate perceptions by means of consciousness with the unconscious mental processes which are their object. Like the physical, the psychical is not necessarily in reality what it appears to us to be" (173).[15]

What is astonishing about this suite of ideas purporting to show that the assumption of unconscious mental processes is both necessary and legitimate is that, as always, it encapsulates genuine insight within a wholly inadequate (indeed, simply incorrect) metapsychological proof of the reality of the unconscious. Freud is obviously right that appearances are deceiving, that the psychical, like the physical, "is not necessarily in reality what it appears to us to be." Clearly more promising, however, is his dialogical notion (applicable in the therapeutic situation) that "our" relationship to the unconscious is like our relationship to other people. Things that I notice in myself and yet cannot connect with the rest of my mental life I am to view as belonging to "this other person." But in the course of his argument defending the unconscious Freud makes two epistemological errors that constitute and will continue to constitute until the end of his life the very essence of his metapsychology. He is wrong both that we have immediate knowledge of our own consciousness and that we infer (as from effect to cause) knowledge of others and thus, by extension, knowledge of our own unconscious.[16] In addition, his understanding of Kant remains pre-critical or animistic. Indeed, it is clear, I think, that his uncritical notion of inference reflects his primordial notion that human beings begin in immediate certainty of their own consciousness. This idea is reflected everywhere in his metapsychology, from the notions of original narcissism, the primal father, the primary process, and the pleasure principle to the priority of autoerotism over object relations (that is, the relationship of subjects) and of internality over externality.

It is deeply ironic that Freud, the student nonpareil (along with Jung) of the unconscious, bases his idea of the unconscious on a concept of consciousness as immediate certainty. While utterly conventional and widely held in every generation by a legion of uncritical thinkers, the concept of consciousness as immediate (self) certainty had been demonstrated for all time by Kant and Hegel[17] to be totally false. Immediate consciousness does not yield self-knowledge. Nor does inference yield knowledge either of others or of our own unconscious – when "knowledge" is understood either in the Kantian sense of practical reason, which, as will, embodies the categorical imperative, or in the Hegelian sense of knowledge of rational objects, that is, human subjects. It is true that scientific knowledge (of objects) involves causal inference. But this objective knowledge (as Kant and Hegel demonstrate) presupposes a cognition that rests neither on immediate self-certainty nor on inference involving argument from effect to cause (or from cause to effect) but on subjects in a relationship of desire. What for Kant is rational practice and for Hegel absolute knowledge involves will or desire – the relationship of self and other as articulated in and through the structure of the golden rule. There is no consciousness of the self that precedes consciousness of the other, whose consciousness, like my own unconscious, is then to be inferred. The unconscious is the discourse of the other (to recall Lacan). We do not (and cannot) infer either the consciousness of others or our own unconscious on the basis of our immediate self-consciousness. Freud is right to defend the phenomenological originality of the unconscious. But he fails to see that the independence of unconscious process is proved not by inference but by the fact that, because it involves our deepest desire (including our deepest repressions), it is always other than ourselves. Our will, our desire is never our own, for it is, always already, the other('s).

Once we have seen Freud attempt to explain the existence of the unconscious on the spurious grounds of immediate self-consciousness, it then comes as no surprise that the metapsychological description that he proceeds to give of the unconscious involves the same tergiversation. He describes the otherness of the unconscious in the dualistic terms of a psychical system that, composed of wishful impulses seeking discharge according to the primary process of the pleasure principle, is distinct from and opposed to consciousness and its reliance on reality. But, now that the pleasure principle has been exposed as a fiction whose non-contradictory existence is assured only by the reality of desire, we can anticipate that Freud will have difficulty in maintaining the priority of the unconscious over consciousness.

Freud argues that what characterizes the unconscious is the fact that it possesses wishful impulses that are subject not to mutual contradiction but to compromise. When two apparently contradictory impulses appear simultaneously, he remarks, they "do not diminish each other or cancel each other out, but combine to form an intermediate aim, a compromise" (190). Unconscious impulses, following the primary process, operate without regard for not only contradiction but also negation, doubt, degrees of certainty, time, and reality, all of which, Freud contends, are introduced at the "higher level" of consciousness, where the secondary process is dominant. "In the *Unconscious*," he declares, "there are only contents, cathected with greater or lesser strength ... To sum up: *exemption from mutual contradiction, primary process* ... , *timelessness*, and *replacement of external by psychical reality* – these are the characteristics which we may expect to find in processes belonging to the system *Unconscious*" (190–1). Freud, however, goes on to say that communication with the unconscious is made possible by consciousness, thanks to the elements of time, censorship, reality, and memory that it introduces. We are then not surprised when he proceeds to acknowledge that unconscious processes in themselves "are even incapable of carrying on their existence" and that in adults "the system *Unconscious* operates, strictly speaking, only as a preliminary stage of the higher [conscious] organization" (192–3).

Notwithstanding the fact that Freud has sharply distinguished the elements characterizing the unconscious from those of consciousness, just as he distinguishes primary process from secondary process, he has also been careful to note that the unconscious cannot be found separate from consciousness. Having thus prepared the reader for section VI of "The Unconscious," entitled "Communication between the Two Systems,"[18] he now points out that the unconscious is not simply a vestigial organ exempt from the process of development or a mere repository for what repressive consciousness dumps into it. In fact, because the relations between the two systems are characterized by what he calls cooperation and mutual interaction, no clear-cut distinction between them exists.[19] "At the roots of instinctual activity," Freud writes, "the [two] systems communicate with one another most extensively" (198). Paths lead both from the external world inwardly, that is, from perception to the unconscious, and from the internal world outwardly, that is, from the unconscious to perception, with only the latter path being that which is normally blocked by repression. Although it is a complete breakdown of these movements, a total severance of the two systems, that characterizes mental pathology, "nevertheless," Freud remarks, "psychoanalytic treatment is based upon an influencing of the *Unconscious* from the direction of the *Conscious*, and at any rate shows that this, though a laborious task, is not impossible" (199).

The metapsychological problem of how the two distinct mental systems, the unconscious and consciousness, with their opposed attributes, reflecting the opposition between the primary process of the pleasure principle and the secondary process of the reality principle, nevertheless can and do cooperate and communicate is thus reflected in psychotherapy. Although the unconscious is prior to consciousness, the psychotherapeutic priority is to make the unconscious conscious, to influence the unconscious consciously, that is, to make a real beginning in overcoming the illusion of beginning unconsciously. It is clear that the metapsychological assumption of beginning unconsciously (the assumption that the beginning is unconscious, that the unconscious is in the beginning) is not consistent with the psychotherapeutic assumption of beginning conscious of being unconscious. What Freud then proceeds to do, at one and the same time, is to clarify and to complicate this model of the unconscious in his theory of repression and his ego psychology of the 1920s and 30s.

The essence of repression, Freud writes in the opening sentence of "The Unconscious," as we have already seen, lies not in eliminating the representatives of the instincts but in preventing them from becoming conscious. This claim echoes his statement in the essay on "Repression" that, because repression presupposes a sharp cleavage between unconscious and conscious mental activity, it cannot have been present from the beginning. "*The essence of repression,*" he declares, "*lies simply in turning something away, and keeping it at a distance, from the conscious*" (147). But how consciousness, and with it repression, can come into existence, when, in the beginning, there is only the unrepressed unconscious, is and remains mysterious, Freud recognizes, when he writes, again as we have seen, that "it is not easy *in theory* to deduce the possibility of such a thing as repression." How can the satisfaction of an instinct, which is subject to the pleasure principle, involve unpleasure? "But we cannot well *imagine* such a contingency," Freud writes. "There are no such instincts: satisfaction of an instinct is always pleasurable" (145ᵉ). The mystery of repression deepens further, however, when Freud makes it clear not only that the motive and purpose of repression are the avoidance of unpleasure but also that repression makes itself known only when (because) it fails.[20] If repression succeeded in eliminating unpleasure, then the pleasure principle would reign unchallenged in the unconscious – but *we* would have no consciousness of it. The unconscious would in that case only be a fiction that had not come into existence. Repression can succeed (in revealing a conflict between consciousness and the unconscious) only when and if it fails – in eliminating this conflict and thus in serving the pleasure principle.

Thus we see that both consciousness and repression are, paradoxically, central to the concept of the unconscious. The unconscious cannot begin – it cannot be unconscious – unless repression is (consciously) unsuccessful or incomplete. Freud further indicates the complex relationship between the unconscious and consciousness when he elaborates his ego psychology in the final version of his psychical model. I am not concerned here to expose that theory in detail or even to summarize it. I want only to highlight the fact that Freud, while he remains unflagging in his efforts to address the contradictions generated by his metapsychological dualism, consistently fails to see that they reflect the contradiction to which he remains blind: that human beings are unconscious of beginning with the pleasure principle. I shall deal with the related libido theory and the concept of the superego in the next chapter in the context of the Oedipus complex.

Although Freud announces at the beginning of *The Ego and the Id* that, as we saw earlier, "the division of the psychical into what is conscious and what is unconscious is the fundamental premise of psychoanalysis," he swiftly proceeds to replace it with a new division. He argues that account must now be taken of the fact that the ego, as the source of resistance and repression (censorship), produces effects of which it is unconscious.

From the point of view of analytic practice [Freud writes], the consequence of this discovery [that the ego also possesses unconscious content] is that we land in endless obscurities and difficulties if we keep to our habitual forms of expression and try, for instance, to derive neuroses from a conflict between the conscious and the unconscious. We shall have to substitute for *this antithesis* another, taken from our insight into the structural conditions of the mind – *the antithesis* between the coherent ego and the repressed which is split off from it. (356ᵉ)

Freud is doubtlessly right that life can be fruitfully analyzed in terms of the antithesis (conflict) between the coherent ego and what the ego has repressed (split off from itself). The dialectic of conscious and unconscious would then be housed in the ego, whose self-mastery involves the paradox that its task is to become conscious that it dwells in a house (of human relations) of which it is (largely and will largely remain) unconscious. In whatever sense the uncanny may express the castration complex, as Freud holds – and that we shall see in the next chapter – what is uncanny, *unheimlich*, is that with which we are cannily at home: *heimlich*. For the *heimlich*, the familiar, the personal, the intimate, is also the *unheimlich*, that which is private, hidden, secret, forbidden, repressed – the family romance. The ego is itself the uncanny, the *unheimlich*, for, in desiring the other (willing the good), it finds that what it is, in being at home with itself, the *heimlich*, is at one and the same time other than itself, *unheimlich*.

But Freud strives, always, to reduce the uncanny to the canny, the unknown to the known, for, as he writes in the introductory section of chapter 7 of *The Interpretation of Dreams*, "to explain a thing [which is unknown] means to trace it back to something already known" (654). Thus, in *The Ego and the Id*, he portrays the id – *das Es*: the it – as the internal thing in itself from which the ego emerges due to the influence of the external world. But the problem here is to attempt to explain what is known and what unknown, what is canny and what uncanny. The id is the source, the home, of the ego; yet the id, although governed by the primary process of the pleasure principle, gives birth to the ego, which represents secondary process (consciousness and reality). But the ego, according to Freud, owes its birth to two sources, not only to the id but also to the external world (and also to a third source, its father, the superego, as we shall see in the next chapter). Although the ego is not master in its own house, given that its house is divided, it is not reducible to id or external reality (or superego), for they are explicable only on the basis of the ego. But how the ego can have its source in both the id and the external world, how the ego can be that part of the id that "endeavors to substitute the reality principle for the pleasure principle which reigns unrestrictedly in the id," remains incomprehensible. For, as Freud acknowledges, the distinction between ego and id simply reproduces the popular, familiar dualism between reason (common sense) and passion (363–4). The ego rides the id as a rider does his horse, he observes, except that, unlike the rider, the ego uses borrowed forces. "Often a rider, if he is not to be parted from his horse," Freud remarks, "is obliged to guide it where it wants to go [this is scarcely credible!]; so in the same way the ego is in the habit of transforming the id's will [*sic*!] into action as if it [the id's will] were its [the ego's] own" (364).[21] In "The Question of Lay Analysis" the impartial interlocutor asks if the id, as the stronger party, puts up with being dominated by the weaker ego. "Yes," Freud answers, "all will be well if the ego is in possession of its whole organization and efficiency, if it has access to all parts of the id and can exercise its influence on them. For there is no natural opposition between ego and id; they belong together, and under healthy conditions cannot in practice be distinguished from each other" (301).

Neurotic conflict, he continues, arises because the ego, in finding itself subject to the demands of both the id and the external world, follows its inmost nature by siding with the external world against the id. But what causes neurosis is not the unavoidable and inevitable conflict between reality and the id "but the circumstance that the ego has made use of the inefficient instrument of repression for dealing with the conflict" (304).[22] The task of therapy, then, is "to restore the ego, to free it from its restrictions, and to give it back the command over the id which it has lost owing to its early repressions" (305).[23]

Our main purpose in introducing the topics of repression and the relationship of id and ego into our discussion of Freud's concept of the unconscious has been to show that they reproduce the same problematic. Just as repression shows that the unconscious presupposes consciousness – for it keeps an unconscious trend from becoming (or remaining) conscious – so the task of the ego, although it is *unheimlich*, for its home is outside itself in the id and the external world (and also the superego), is to become at home with its other, to become conscious that it is unconscious. Consistent with the function of repression, the task of the ego is to show that the unconscious, in the beginning, presupposes that it is aware that it is unconscious. Although Freud insists, always, upon the metapsychological difference or opposition between unconscious and consciousness, as between id and ego, what he always tends to emphasize in practice, however, as we have seen, is the fact that there is no real difference between them.

In conclusion, we may say that, notwithstanding his claim to found depth psychology on the unconscious and his polemic against academic philosophy for equating the psychical with consciousness, Freud continues to adhere to the most uncritical, conventional, and naïve concept of epistemology. As I indicated earlier, this is the position that his great predecessors like Kant, Hegel, Kierkegaard, and Nietzsche had thoroughly discredited. He persists, however, in basing knowledge of the unconscious on immediate self-consciousness and on the inference of the consciousness of others. It is, however, patently absurd, although consistent with Freud's metapsychological commitments, to infer the unconscious, as that which is primordial and eternal, from the certainty of consciousness, whose ego is not master in its own house. In other words, Freud claims to infer that which is prior, the unconscious, while possessing immediate knowledge of that which is secondary, the conscious. But it is also Freud who holds that consciousness is the product of the unconscious and that the ego is the product of the id (and of the external world, not to mention the super-ego). Such, however, is always the fate of inference within the psychical sphere. The argument that begins by inferring unknown (effect) – consciousness – from known (cause) – the unconscious – ends by reversing itself and inferring the unknown (unconscious) from the known (ego).

Freud's concept of the unconscious is thus one with his concept of the pleasure principle. Both presuppose that which they purport to explain, consciousness and reality. Both presuppose concepts of desire and self that, while alive and well in the therapeutic situation, are metapsychologically distorted by the dualism between pleasure principle and reality principle, between primary process and secondary process, between the unconscious and consciousness, and between the id and the ego. We shall now take up the question, posed at the beginning of this section, whether, or in what sense, when Freud goes beyond the pleasure principle and discovers that to begin with the pleasure principle is to reduce all life to death, the unconscious can survive beginning unconsciously with the pleasure principle.

IV BEYOND THE PLEASURE PRINCIPLE

Freud recognizes that the antithesis between consciousness and the unconscious is not adequate, in psychotherapeutic terms, and replaces it with the antithesis between the ego and its repressions. He even acknowledges that ego and id are, in principle, indistinguishable. But his resistance to giving up his fundamental metapsychology is undying. He points out in "Analysis Terminable and Interminable" that, although to resolve the conflict between ego and instincts is to tame the instincts, to bring them into harmony with the ego,

if we are asked *by what methods and means this result is achieved,* it is not easy to find an answer. We can only say: "We must call the Witch to our help after all!" [Freud cites *Faust*] – the Witch Metapsychology. Without metapsychological speculation and theorizing – I had almost said "fantasying" – we shall not get another step forward. Unfortunately, here as elsewhere, what our Witch reveals is neither very clear nor very detailed. We have only a single clue to start from – though it is a clue of the highest value – namely, the antithesis between the primary and the secondary processes. (225ᵉ)

We have already seen, however, that Freud, from the beginning, admits that the antithesis between the primary process of pleasure and the secondary process of reality is a fiction. But seventeen years prior to "Analysis Terminable and Interminable," in *Beyond the Pleasure Principle*, Freud had first formulated his theory of the death and life instincts, which goes beyond (by eliminating yet again) any simple distinction between the primary and secondary processes. He initiates his unabashedly speculative work with the claim that mental events are automatically regulated by the pleasure principle and in the final paragraph concludes that "the pleasure principle seems actually to serve the death instincts" (338). In avoiding the unpleasure of tension and seeking the pleasure of stasis, in following the constancy principle, the pleasure principle "is the effort to reduce, to keep constant or to remove internal tension due to stimuli (the *Nirvana principle*)" (329).[24]

A complex contradiction in Freud's concept of the pleasure principle now emerges that is by no means easy either to articulate or to account for. What is clear, however, is that, from the beginning, the pleasure principle goes beyond itself – for two opposed reasons. On the one hand, the pleasure principle (as primary process) is the very expression of stasis or death. On the other hand, it is a fiction that, as we have seen, cannot even exist without presupposing what Freud calls the secondary process or the reality principle. Thus, what Freud demonstrates, speculatively, in *Beyond the Pleasure Principle*, is inherent in his concept of the pleasure principle from the beginning. But that is not all. Freud also points to a body of phenomenological data – centring on the repetition compulsion in the analytic situation – that, he holds, cannot be explained on the basis of the pleasure principle. "There really does exist in the mind a compulsion to repeat which overrides the pleasure principle," he writes (293).[25] The complexity involved in thinking through the implications of the pleasure principle is that, while Freud, as always, sees clearly – repetition compulsion, together with other phenomena, does override the pleasure principle and makes the analytic situation ever more demanding for both analyst and analysand – he does not understand what he sees. He is bewitched by the fantasy of metapsychology. He reverses himself – twice – without making a change in his position. First, he claims to go beyond the pleasure principle; but what he does, instead, is to show that, from the beginning, the pleasure principle coincides with the *status quo ante*. Second, he claims that there are phenomena that override the pleasure principle; but what he shows, instead, is that, in seeking to restore an earlier state of things, they fulfil the pleasure principle. Freud is right that the phenomena he discusses go beyond the pleasure principle, but he is wrong to conclude that they thereby fulfil the pleasure principle, when the pleasure principle is rightly understood as going beyond itself, as the principle of death. Freud is right to go beyond the pleasure principle, but he is wrong to adhere to the pleasure principle as the very reverse of itself. Can one imagine anything more complex or contradictory?

It is little wonder that so many post-Freudians (Harold Bloom, N.O. Brown, Derrida, Lacan, Marcuse) are attracted to the speculative excesses of *Beyond the Pleasure Principle*. But they, no more than Freud, are able to dispel the hex of metapsychology, for they fail to make an adequate response to the invitation that, at the beginning of his essay, he offers and, it is true, immediately withdraws. "We would readily express our gratitude to any philosophical or psychological theory which was able to inform us of the meaning of the feelings of pleasure and unpleasure which act so imperatively upon us," he writes. "But on this point we are, alas, offered nothing to our purpose" (275–6). We, however, may respond to Freud's invitation by noting that desire is not that which acts upon us but that through and in which *we* act (upon others, including ourselves), just as the gift of insight is not only passive but also active receiving. "'Ask, and it will be given you; seek, and you will find; knock, and it will be opened to you'" (Matthew 7.7; Luke 11.9). But Freud, in seeking the meaning of the feelings of pleasure and unpleasure that imperatively act upon human beings in the pleasure principle and in showing that the pleasure principle, through governing all mental processes, operates as the death instinct, puts in jeopardy his notions of Eros (the life instincts) and libido. If Eros and libido are guided by the primacy of the pleasure principle, they will not escape the attraction of the death instinct. If Eros and libido renounce the primacy of the death instinct, they will have to forgo their commitment to pleasure. In the second case, apparently, Eros and libido would find their ground in the unpleasure of life, in the secondary process of the reality principle. The only alternative to the pleasure of death (the death of pleasure) appears to be the unpleasure of reality (the reality of unpleasure). We shall now see what is involved in going beyond the pleasure principle.

The speculative argument at the core of *Beyond the Pleasure Principle* is composed of three elements, each surprising – in itself, in its relationship to the other two elements, and in the totality of its relationships. The three elements are: (1) the inherent tendency of the instincts to restore an earlier state of things; (2) Freud's subsequent protest on behalf of the life instincts; and (3) a restatement, on the basis of an appeal to (Greek and Hindu) myth, of the inherent tendency of the instincts to restore an earlier state of things.

It is the first element in Freud's speculative argument that is the critical one, for it takes him beyond (and thus to the ultimate core of) the pleasure principle. "*An instinct*," he writes, "*is an urge inherent in organic life to restore an earlier state of things* which the living entity has been obliged to abandon under the pressure of external disturbing forces" (308–9).[26] Since instincts in themselves have an inclination not to change but only to repeat their original condition, all modifications are imposed by external forces. "It would be in contradiction to the conservative nature of the instincts," Freud observes, "if the goal of life were a state of things which had never yet been attained. On the contrary, it must be an *old* state of things, an initial state from which the living entity has at one time or other departed and to which it is striving to return by the circuitous paths along which its development leads" (310). Since everything dies – becomes inorganic again – due to what Freud calls internal reasons, the inescapable conclusion, he holds, is that "'*the aim of all life is death*'" – that is, "'*inanimate things* EXISTED *before living ones*'" (311ᵉ).

Freud is surely right that, if inanimate things *existed* (if they were dead) before they existed in animate form, then the aim of existence would be to return to this prior (original) existence that is non-existence. Life and death would be indistinguishable. Or, put otherwise, although Freud's second claim – inanimate things "existed" before living ones – appears (banally) true, it is (banally) false. But his first claim – the aim of all life is death – although shocking, properly explicates the common sense notion that the inorganic precedes the organic as death precedes life, the internal the external, the unconscious the conscious, the primary principle the secondary principle, etc. Freud is nothing if not consistent in his metapsychology – consistently wrong. What is so brilliant about Freud is that what he demonstrates for all time is that instinct (when understood as ultimately somatic in origin) has nothing to do with life. Instinct presupposes life (the reality of whose desire cannot be equated with feelings of pleasure and unpleasure) and is the urge, true to the pleasure principle, to reduce life – tension – back to zero: nirvana. Freud writes: "The attributes of life were at some time evoked in inanimate matter by *the action of a force of whose nature we can form no conception*. It may perhaps have been a process similar in type to that which later caused the development of consciousness in a particular stratum of living matter. The tension which then arose in what had hitherto been an inanimate substance endeavored to cancel itself out. In this way the first instinct came into being: the instinct to return to the inanimate state" (311ᵉ).

Just as he conceives of wish, in *The Interpretation of Dreams*, as the urge that, coming into being in response to the unpleasure of tension, aims to reduce that tension back to its original inertia, so Freud here conceives of instinct (*Trieb*) not as life's drive or tension but as life's inertia, that is, death. What is so peculiar about instinct, as Freud sees, yet does not understand, is that it depends, blindly, upon the ontological argument for existence, upon the force that evokes, or calls into being, the attributes of life but of whose nature we can form no conception – in terms of the feelings of pleasure and unpleasure.

But Freud then protests against his conclusion that the instincts aim at death, and we reach the second element of his speculative argument. It "cannot be" the case, he asseverates, in defending Eros, that the life or sexual instincts aim, like the instincts, generally, to restore an earlier state of things (312). When, however, it becomes evident that Freud does not identify Eros with the attributes of life that, at some time, were evoked in inanimate matter (as we saw him state) by the action of a force of whose nature we can form no concept, then we should not be surprised to find that, notwithstanding his protest, he will still be unable to distinguish Eros from the death instincts in meaningful terms.[27] All he basically says, in defending the life instincts against the death instincts, is that, while they are conservative like all instincts in bringing back earlier states of living substance, they are also more highly conservative than instincts, generally, in that they are especially resistant to external influences and preserve life for a comparatively long period of time. Freud's defense of the life instincts, in other words, amounts to little more than showing that biology (the domain of life) does not explicitly contradict, contrary to expectations, the existence of the death instincts and has nothing to say about the origin of sexuality. Having thus been able to sustain what he calls his "preeminently dualistic view of instinctual life,"[28] Freud finds that his protest on behalf of the life instincts has safely brought him into what he calls "the harbor of Schopenhauer's philosophy. For him," Freud declares, quoting Schopenhauer, "death is the 'true result and to that extent the purpose of life,' while the sexual instinct is the embodiment of the will to live" (322).

In appealing to Schopenhauer, who equates life with death in his reduction of Kantian dialectic to a dualism of sexuality and life harbouring a monism anchored in Greek and eastern philosophy, Freud anticipates the third element in his speculative argument. It is Platonic and Hindu philosophy, not the science of biology, he finds, that truly supports his speculation on the inherent tendency of the instincts to restore an earlier state of things.[29] This hypothesis, he remarks, "is of so fantastic a kind – a myth rather than a scientific explanation – that I should not venture to produce it here, were it not that it fulfills precisely the one condition whose fulfillment we desire. For it traces the

origin of an instinct to *a need to restore an earlier state of things*"
(331). The fantastic myth about the origin of sexuality that Freud discovers is that attributed by Plato in the *Symposium* to Aristophanes
and equally found, Freud points out in a footnote added in 1921, in
one of the Upanishads.[30] This myth, he says, "deals not only with the
origin of the sexual instinct but also with the most important of its
variations in relation to its object" (331). Freud then summarizes the
myth of Eros in which Aristophanes indicates that in original human
nature the sexes were not two, as they are now, but three – man,
woman, and their union – and that it was Zeus who subsequently split
this whole being into its two opposite sexes, shattering their union forever. Freud omits, however, Aristophanes' explanation that what led
Zeus to divide the original unity of man and woman in two was their
assault, when a united whole, upon the gods. We learn, then, from
Aristophanes, but not from Freud, that the point of his myth of Eros is
that "we used to be complete wholes in our original nature, and now
'Love' is the name for our pursuit of wholeness, for our desire to be
complete. Long ago we were united ... ; but now the god has divided
us as punishment for the wrong we did him" (29).

What is surprising and what Freud does not directly acknowledge in
his appeal to Plato is that the definition of an instinct as a "need to
restore an earlier state of things," which he now applies to the origin
of the life or sexual instincts, is precisely his definition of the death
instincts from which he had earlier claimed, in protest, to dissociate the
life or sexual instincts of Eros. In light of the fact that he now identifies the life or sexual instincts with the death instincts, his appeal to the
myth of Aristophanes about the original unity of human sexuality and
his suppression of the fact that the loss of this unity is due to divine
punishment of human wickedness is particularly revealing. The desire
for and pursuit of an original whole that is now lost through hubris,
Aristophanes says, are called love. Love, or Eros, is precisely the need
to restore an earlier state of things that is fatally doomed to failure by
the gods. It is subject to the very fatality that it is Socrates' point to
establish in the *Symposium* (as it is Aristophanes' in his speech at the
symposium), the fatality that inexorably punishes desire and seeking as
lacking their end. You cannot seek what you lack, except in contradictory ignorance of it, as Alcibiades, in the last section of the *Symposium*,
discovers to his continuous frustration. It is equally the case that you
cannot seek what you have (or are), your unity or identity, for in that
case you are already at your end, which is the position of the gods (ultimately fate). Seeking or desire, we see, is precisely the opposite of the
whole uniting the opposites of the sexes. Socrates' demonstration to
Agathon, the next speaker after Aristophanes at the symposium, is

consistent with Aristophanes' presentation of Eros as contradictory desire that seeks its end in ignorance of it and for which Eros is punished in its ignorance. Socrates points out that "a man or anyone else who has a desire desires what is not at hand and not present, what he does not have, and what he is not, and that of which he is in need; for such are the objects of desire and love" (42-3).[31] The fact that desire (Eros) is that which one does not possess and is not formulates in apt terms what lies beyond the pleasure principle: nirvana, death, and nothing.

What is truly surprising and revealing about the speculative argument in *Beyond the Pleasure Principle* is that Freud is not prepared to give up, while he remains disturbed by the implications of, the pleasure principle. He goes beyond it to the death instinct only to find that the general definition of instinct as the inherent tendency to restore an earlier state of things – inorganic nature: death – encompasses its dualistic opposite, the life or sexual instincts of Eros. Dualism, as always, threatens to collapse into monism. According to Plato (and consistent with the Upanishads and Empedocles, as I indicate in the Appendix and note 31), Eros represents the blind and ignorant seeking after an earlier state of things that fatally generates its opposite, strife, or, following the myth of Aristophanes, the violence of Zeus as divine punishment. We shall pursue the implications of Freud's theory of the life and death instincts for his concept of libido in the next chapter.

Here we shall conclude our examination of the pleasure principle. As the fundamental myth guiding Freud's work from the beginning, it constantly threatens, in the end, to bring it into safe harbour with Schopenhauer, that is, to shipwreck it upon the shoals of dualism, which is indistinguishable, ultimately, from foundering in the deep of monism. In chapter IV of *The Ego and the Id*, entitled "The Two Classes of Instincts," Freud indicates that the relationship between the pleasure principle, "which dominates mental processes," and the two classes of instincts is still to be determined (382). But he goes on to assert, nevertheless, that "it can hardly be doubted that the pleasure principle serves the id as a compass in its struggle against the libido – the force that introduces disturbances into the process of life" (387). More unsettling, however, is "The Economic Problem of Masochism," as Freud articulates the issue in his 1924 paper. The problem is: either the pleasure principle (metapsychology) or masochism (phenomenology). Either psychical processes are governed by the pleasure principle, whose first aim is the avoidance of unpleasure (pain), and then masochism, which identifies pleasure with pain (unpleasure), does not exist. Or masochism exists, and then the pleasure principle is eliminated as "the watchman over our mental life" (413). But the same complexity, reflecting the same reversal, that we earlier observed in *Beyond the Pleasure Principle* is also present here and is equally complex to articulate in clear terms.

Once Freud demonstrates that to go beyond the pleasure principle to its foundation in inorganic substance, in death, is to reveal instinct as that which inherently aims to restore life to an earlier (dead) state of things, it is the phenomena of masochism and sadism that provide him with the best evidence for the presence of the death instinct. For the death instinct is, as he points out, largely mute and not found separate from the life or sexual instincts of Eros. When, therefore, Freud writes in "The Economic Problem of Masochism" that "mental processes are governed by the pleasure principle in such a way that their first aim is the avoidance of unpleasure and the obtaining of pleasure" (413) he fails to account for the dynamics of masochism. He does not see that, according to the inner dualism of the pleasure-unpleasure dyad, the best (the only) way of obtaining pleasure, that is, of reducing the unpleasure (the tension) of life to null, is to show that pleasure is pain. Masochism (like sadism) is diabolical precisely because, in showing pleasure to be pain, it is the most rigorous and the most logical defender of pleasure. Surely this is why the ultimate (and only) argument that the Marquis de Sade, advocate and initiate nonpareil of sadism (which he fathers) and masochism, has for the pleasure of pain and the pain of pleasure, at once erotic and destructive, is, as he pours out his venomous hatred for Christianity, that sadism and masochism are natural or instinctual. Thus the issue, it is clear, is not either/or, not either the pleasure principle or masochism. The issue is, rather, either the pleasure principle, together with masochism, or – what? Surely, desire (and the self). But Freud, in order to preserve both the pleasure principle and masochism as distinct from each other, undertakes, in "The Economic Problem of Masochism," to identify the pleasure principle with libido. But what, then, will happen to masochism, and will libido be able to survive its identification with the pleasure principle?

Once Freud has posed the problem of either masochism or the pleasure principle, he recalls that he had shown in *Beyond the Pleasure Principle* that the pleasure principle, in governing all mental processes, embodies the constancy or nirvana principle. "Every unpleasure," he writes, "ought thus to coincide with a heightening, and every pleasure with a lowering, of mental tension due to stimulus; the nirvana principle (and the pleasure principle which is supposedly identical with it) would be entirely in the service of the death instincts, whose aim is to conduct the restlessness of life into the stability of the inorganic state." Once again, however, Freud protests that this cannot be so. "There are," he now admits, "pleasurable tensions and unpleasurable relaxations of tension. The state of sexual excitation is the most striking example of a pleasurable increase of stimulus of this sort, but it is certainly not the only one" (414).[32] It can no longer be said, he declares, that pleasure and unpleasure depend on a quantitative decrease or increase (involving a "tension due to stimulus"). They depend, rather, on a qualitative characteristic that remains unknown. Freud thus proposes a new, triadic distinction: the nirvana principle (the death instinct), the pleasure principle (the life instinct or libido), and the reality principle (the external world). The nirvana principle is modified into the pleasure principle under the influence of the libido, and the pleasure principle is modified into the reality principle under the influence of the external world. None of these three principles cancels each other out, Freud contends; they generally tolerate each other, notwithstanding the conflicts that do arise between them. In any case, "the description of the pleasure principle as the watchman over our life cannot be rejected" (415).

Freud, however, has no explanation of either how the death instinct of the nirvana principle first turns into the life instinct (libido) of the pleasure principle or how the pleasure principle subsequently turns into the reality principle. It is also the case that he now has three principles instead of two. Rather, he has two incommensurate pairs – two instincts (death and life) and two principles (pleasure and reality) – with libido, as the life instinct, identified with the pleasure principle and suspended between the death instinct and the reality principle. He also maintains his basic commitment that life is regulated by the pleasure principle, although he has now completely abandoned the economic principle of quantity on which the pleasure principle is founded. In claiming that pleasure and unpleasure depend not on a quantitative factor that can be determined but on a qualitative factor that is unknown, that is, that cannot be determined (in quantitative terms), Freud renounces his most fundamental assumption.[33] The only reason that the instincts (*Triebe*, not *Instinkte*) would (or could) not be quantitatively determined is because they are not biological or somatic in origin. Their aim would then be understood to involve quality of life, not death of quantity. In acknowledging that there is, *qualitatively* and not quantitatively, increased tension that is pleasurable and decreased tension that is unpleasureable, Freud completely reverses his beginning. He reveals his theory of instinct for what it is, a mythology whose witch metapsychology, in living by the pleasure principle, and thus by the death instinct, is sheer illusion.

Still, Freud persists in holding consistently to his utterly inconsistent metapsychological principles. The reality of masochism compels him to go beyond the pleasure principle, but only in the contradictory sense that masochism, in identifying pleasure with pain (ultimately death, the death of pleasure, the pleasure of death), is said to oppose the pleasure principle, which seeks to avoid unpleasure and to obtain pleasure. But what Freud, however, refuses to see is that, in reducing everything back to a prior, old state of things, to death, it is the pleasure principle itself that is the very source and basis, the aim, of both masochism and sadism. It is true that Freud now claims to distinguish between the death instinct (the nirvana principle) and the pleasure principle (libido) – with both distinguished from the reality principle (external reality). But it is not evident how or in what sense libido will survive its identity with and as the pleasure principle. Surely, it is one of the strangest elements in Freud's thinking that he is never prepared to renounce the pleasure principle, notwithstanding his protest against its revelation as the death instinct and his momentary rejection of its quantitative basis. Yet it is precisely this renunciation that the reality principle of psychoanalytic science sternly demands. "Science is, after all," he writes in the first of the "Contributions to the Psychology of Love," "the most complete renunciation of the pleasure principle of which our mental activity is capable" (231). Nevertheless, in his final major work, *An Outline of Psychoanalysis*, he still contends that the id inexorably obeys the pleasure principle and that the ego and the superego, while modifying it, do not nullify it. The problem of how the id becomes science, whose object of study is the id, and how the pleasure principle is both renounced yet preserved by the reality principle persists. Freud himself writes in *An Outline*, both seeing and suppressing the problem, that it "remains a question of the highest theoretical importance, and one that has not yet been answered, when and how it is ever possible for the pleasure principle to be overcome. The consideration that the pleasure principle demands a reduction, at bottom the extinction perhaps, of the tensions of instinctual needs (that is, *Nirvana*) leads to the still unassessed relations between the pleasure principle and the two primal forces, Eros and the death instinct" (434).

If science, which posits the supremacy of the pleasure principle, fails to overcome the pleasure principle, that is one thing. But what about masochism? In his 1924 essay Freud discusses three types of masochism – erotogenic, feminine, and moral – and, although his phenomenological insight is as valuable as ever, he fails to acknowledge, as we noted above, that masochism, in identifying pleasure with pain, is not opposed to but fulfils the pleasure principle. And what about libido? He identifies libido with the pleasure principle when he distinguishes the pleasure principle from the death instinct. But, as we have seen from what he writes in his final work, he continues to conceive of the pleasure principle as the elimination of the unpleasure of life and its tensions. Will libido be able to hold its own against the demands of both the death instinct and the reality principle? Indeed, if libido's relationship to the pleasure principle is insecure, will its relationship to Eros be any more secure? Eros, as we shall see in the next chapter, serves civilization by promoting unity in face of the disintegrative tendencies of the death instinct. But does not Freud also hold that civilization is the domain of the superego and that the superego represents the pure culture of the death instinct?

V CONCLUSION

The pleasure principle and the unconscious are the two most critical concepts in Freud's metapsychology. They shape, as we shall see in subsequent chapters, his concepts of the Oedipus complex, phylogenesis (history), and religion (the Bible) and thus involve his notions of infantile sexuality and infantile repression. It is hard to imagine that psychoanalysis, not only as a therapeutic practice but even as a body of theory, could endure the primacy of the pleasure principle, with all its contradictions. But it is also inconceivable that psychoanalysis, not to mention modern culture in all its vastness and variety, could endure without the paradoxical priority of the unconscious. The point is not to appeal beyond the pleasure principle to the unconscious, beyond metapsychology to phenomenology (psychotherapy), although that is, in one sense, what I am doing. The point, rather, is to see that the metapsychological commitments that Freud makes and persists in making are centred in his concept of the pleasure principle and thus shape his overall concept of the unconscious, together with all his other central ideas.

When Freud goes beyond the pleasure principle, he discovers that, in the beginning, the organism's original wish is to die. The discovery that the organism originally generates a wish in order to eliminate the unpleasure of life's tensions compels him to recognize that the pleasure principle is the embodiment of the death instinct. But this discovery, as I have shown, is inherent in Freud's beginning with the pleasure-unpleasure principle as the mechanism that governs the dream wish and thus with his notion of the essential difference between primary process and secondary process. It is appropriate, then, that Freud concludes *The Interpretation of Dreams* with a section on the fundamental difference between the two psychical systems of the unconscious and consciousness, for his metapsychological concept of the unconscious directly reflects his concept of the pleasure principle. He claims that each is primordial and timeless. But in each case he is forced to admit, grudgingly, yet not such that he is prepared to rethink his metapsychological commitments from the beginning, that each depends, externally or temporally (historically), on that to which it gives rise, secondary process (the reality principle) and consciousness.

Freud consistently sees that his primary commitments are contradictory; but he is equally consistent, that is, persistently contradictory, in misunderstanding his contradictory commitments. What he is incapable of understanding is that there is, as I am calling it in this study, one alternative, and one alternative only, to the contradictory dualism that he compulsively repeats as he fears (quite rightly) being engulfed by the contradictions of monism. The one alternative to beginning with the contradiction that every beginning is a reduction back to that which has never begun, to inorganic nature, to death, is to begin with a concept of desire whose self is the creation of life. The self of desire is not brought to birth by what Freud calls external reality – contradicting his notion of internal illusion. Rather, the self is that whose desire gives birth to life as itself the very concept of creation from nothing – from nothing prior to itself in the past. There is no past prior to creation, for creation is itself the history of creation, the creation of history. The alternative that Freud cannot imagine, the alternative of which he cannot form an image, is that of life – of desire and the self. Life (existence) is not merely internal (past) or external (future) but present, historically, in the depth of its unconscious otherness. That the unconscious operates not by the mechanism of the pleasure principle but according to the concepts of history, desire, and the self – such is the alternative that Freud cannot imagine. In the beginning is the history of the self and its desire, neither past (internal) nor future (external).

It is characteristic of the genius of Freud that he knows, notwithstanding his insistence on the fundamental difference between the two psychical systems of the unconscious and consciousness, that the dream reveals the content of our rational dream thoughts to be distorted in form by the operations of the dream work. But he remains committed to the primary process of the pleasure principle, to the wish (or instinct) as seeking to maintain absolute pleasure in the absence of instinctual tension or desire. He is thus unable to indicate with any clarity how the dream wish, in rising from and expressing unconscious desire, relates to both the rational dream thoughts (of our so-called waking life) and the dream work. As I continue to ask, is the distortion in form that the dream work introduces into the dream thoughts conscious (stemming from the ego) or unconscious (stemming from the id)? Freud would apparently hold that, because the dream work is a distortion in form, it could not be a product of the dream wish, for the unconscious, he says, is pure content, without form. At the same time, however, he makes clear that the unconscious is not subject to the law of contradiction, that is, its contents are not random, undetermined, or simply contradictory. Yet it is surely the dream wish that, because of its overwhelming urgency, compels us to attempt to flee from its demands into compromise, inhibition, distortion compulsion, evasion, hypocrisy ... neurosis.

What, however, is the nature of the urgency constituting the dream wish? What *is* desire? Strangely, that is precisely the question that Freud never answers, at least not in metapsychological terms. We have seen him raise the question of morality in dreams, yet he concludes that this question is beyond his competence. He agrees with the self-conscious dreamer in the short story of "Lynkeus" that dreaming is like waking, that how we dream our desires is how we desire to live our waking (conscious) lives. But when Freud comes to waking life he subjects the desire to live to the contradictory logic of the pleasure principle, condemning life to the death instinct. To conceive of how we live our waking lives presupposes concepts of desire and self of which Freud has no understanding. He also finds himself compelled to ask whose pleasure it is that the dream wish fulfils when the dreamer repudiates it as painful and not pleasurable. His true but massively evasive answer is the fairy tale of the three wishes, which shows that a dream, in its psychical divisions, represents the dreamer as two people in conflict with or in opposition to each other. But where the dreamer stands within that division – how he is (or is committed to becoming) conscious of what it is that his unconscious contains – on that critical point Freud remains silent (unconscious).

Freud cannot imagine history as the alternative to viewing the dream wish as that which seeks to reduce the unpleasure of external stimulus to the pleasure of internal stasis – consistent with his later discovery that instinct seeks to restore an earlier state of things. This becomes particularly evident when he writes, in the final paragraph of *The Interpretation of Dreams*, that "dreams are derived from the past in every sense." Although he allows that dreams, even if they do not foretell the future, can be said, "by picturing our wishes as fulfilled," to reveal the future, Freud nevertheless insists, in the final sentence of the work, that "this future, which the dreamer pictures as the present, has been molded by his indestructible wish into a perfect likeness of the past" (783). Just as Freud thus concludes his first major work with a ringing endorsement of the past that the dream wish fulfils, so *An Outline* concludes with a resounding declaration about the role of the superego in (re)instituting the past. "In the establishment of the superego," he writes, "we have before us, as it were, an example of the way in which the present is changed into the past" (443). But what *is* the past? We shall explore Freud's concept of the past in terms of the superego, the heir of the Oedipus complex, in chapter 3, and of the phylogenetic inheritance of the primal father, in chapter 4. But it is already clear, I think, that, as fulfilled in and by the dream and insti- tuted by and through the superego, the past unconsciously represents the triumph of the pleasure principle. According to what Freud writes in *Beyond the Pleasure Principle*, it is inconceivable, given that the instincts constitute the inherent urge to restore an earlier state of things, that the goal of life could be "a state of things which had never yet been attained." The goal of life must be, instead, "an *old* state of things, an initial state" (310) from which the unpleasure of external development (history), whose seductiveness is inconceivable, leads liv- ing entities but to which, as it were, their dream of returning is fulfilled in and by the institution of the superego.

As always, Freud moves between dualistic opposites to whose inher- ent contradictions he is unable to imagine the alternative, whose desire is the self. Development, growth, change, and history he associates with external reality. "The attributes of life were at some time evoked in inanimate matter by the action of a[n external] *force* of whose nature we can form no conception" – just as, perhaps, "the develop- ment of consciousness" was later externally evoked "in a particular stratum of living matter" (311). Freud here invokes, unconsciously, the ontological argument for existence. This is the one alternative to the pleasure principle, the one alternative to which there is no alternative. This is the one alternative to going beyond the pleasure principle only to discover that you have returned to the old state of things to which there is no alternative. For Freud, however, all that is change, history, life, and existence is secondary, external reality. In sharp (dualistic) opposition to the external reality of development (the contingent, the accidental), however, is the primordial past from which everything emerges, due to the external pressure of development (reality), and to which everything returns, due to the internal pressure of the pleasure principle. In the past, internal to itself, the pleasure principle reigns supreme. For, although external exigency generates stimulus whose unpleasure calls instinctual wish (desire) into existence, the only pur- pose of wish is to eliminate the unpleasure of stimulus and thus to restore an earlier state of things: the past as stasis, constancy, and death.

For Freud the aim of desire – consistent with Schopenhauer, Plato, and the Upanishads – is to eliminate desire. Desire is called into being, contradictorily, external to itself, in order to overcome the contradic- tion of desire (the desire of contradiction) and to reduce it(self) back to the past. The contradiction of Freud's concept of pleasure and desire (wish) – as of the past – is that, in order for (past) pleasure to exist, all (future) desire must be eliminated and that, in order for (future) desire to exist, all (past) pleasure must be eliminated. Desire, if it is to come into and remain in existence, must renounce the priority of pleasure and bow its head to the stern reality of unpleasure: secondary process. But the reversals that characterize the metapsychology of Freud and thus jeopardize his phenomenological insight here become patent. It is the illusion of the pleasure principle – the pleasure principle of illusion – that we must learn to renounce, in the name of science. Yet it is science whose first principle is that life (together with inorganic matter) is governed by the primary process of the pleasure principle. The reality (science) of the pleasure principle is its contradiction. The illusion (pleasure) of the reality principle is no less its contradiction.

Without fail, however, Freud sees deeply into the reality of life's illusions. He knows the diabolical ways of sadism and masochism. He sees, for example, how, in melancholia, the individual, in repressing his hatred for a loved one until such time as the loved one dies, can himself become, by internalizing, the hated object. The result is that the love of the melancholic, in his own desire for self-punishment, in desiring to punish himself for hating the loved one, becomes suicidal self-hatred. The melancholic, in taking his own life, restores an earlier, an old, a hated state of things and thus enjoys the masochistic pleasure of inflicting pain on himself as his own internal (contradictory) enemy, the perfect, repressed reflection of the other (loved) as external. Masochism, melancholy, suicide ... represent the ultimate contradiction of reducing the external other, as hated, arbitrary, and inconceivable unpleasure, to that which is internal, unchanging pleasure, utter unconsciousness, nirvana, and death. What Freud fails to understand, however, is that masochism, in embodying the death instinct, is not the contradiction but the fulfilment, in completely contradictory fashion, of the pleasure principle. All fulfilment of the pleasure principle is contradictory. For how else can we understand a return to the past as that which is internal to ourselves, unconscious, and timeless, notwithstanding, rather, precisely because of, the fact that in the beginning the internal id is originally indebted for its existence to the external ego (of the primal father)? If the indestructible dream wish, as the true representative of the unconscious, molds the dreamer('s present) into a perfect likeness of the past, then it follows that the dream will fulfil the wish of the pleasure principle by eliminating present unpleasure and restoring past pleasure. Pleasure is always past, and the past is always pleasurable.

Still, Freud protests, as always, against the logical conclusions of his own contradictory premises that inexorably lead to the identification of the past, death, pleasure, the unconscious, and desire (the wish). As I indicated before, he does not make clear in *The Interpretation of Dreams* whose pleasure it is that the dream wish fulfills. A wish fulfilment brings pleasure, but the dreamer repudiates (represses) his unconscious wish as unpleasurable. Freud's explanation of the contradictory wish generating both pleasure and unpleasure is that "a dreamer in his relation to his dream wishes can only be compared to an amalgamation of two separate people who are linked by some strong element in common" (737). However, instead of exploring the ontology implied by the paradox that the dreamer is really two persons "linked by some strong element in common," Freud falls back on the fairy tale of the three wishes, which, while seductively exposing, does not systematically explore the contradictions at the base of his metapsychology. Freud's reliance here upon fairy tale is consistent with his statement in the *New Introductory Lectures* that "the theory of the instincts is so to say our mythology. Instincts are mythical entities, magnificent in their indefiniteness. In our work we cannot for a moment disregard them, yet we are never sure that we are seeing them clearly" (127). What Freud cannot clearly see is that his mythical instincts are centred in the wish whose basic mythology is to restore all life to an earlier state of things in which there is only the illusory pleasure of myth (the illusory myth of pleasure).

Freud is bewitched by a metapsychology that contradicts his phenomenological insight by dividing not only reality but also fantasy (myth) between primary process and secondary process. He fails to see that he will never be able to comprehend how wish (desire) expresses the common relationship of two individuals or how the unconscious is what is other to us – precisely because it is at once subject and object of willing (desire) – so long as he adheres to a concept of myth that presupposes all reality to have been given, complete, in the past. His mythical concept of desire makes all development (history) arbitrary and yet, at the same time, the origin of the reality principle whose aim is to overcome the illusions (pleasures) of past mythology. Freud sees that his concept of the pleasure principle (together with his two instincts of death and Eros) is myth. But he never understands that that is why it is illusion and that, as the creator of the reality principle, his concept of reality remains as illusory as the pleasure principle of which it is the creation. The one person who is really two persons in relation to his unconscious dream wish is not divided, except when neurotic, between illusion and reality, between pleasure and unpleasure, between primary process and secondary process, between unconscious and conscious.

Rather, the one person is also his other (unconscious), which his desire brings into existence. Desire, in bringing the unconscious into existence as the other, presupposes a concept of myth (fiction, interpretation) that is at once internal and external, both past and future, primary and secondary, real and illusory, pleasurable and unpleasurable.

Freud fails to distinguish between two contrasting concepts of myth, between myth and its mythical alternative (difference, other). He fails to distinguish between myth unaware that it begins unconsciously and myth self-conscious in the beginning that it is not unaware that it begins unconsciously. He fails to distinguish between extra-biblical myth and biblical myth, between the mythical past and the historical past. Whereas the mythical past is that which, the moment it comes into existence, contradicts itself, the historical past is also the future of history. The mythical past is the one, primordial and internal to itself, whose generation of the changing many is absolutely contradictory, as Zeno and Gorgias, profound students of Parmenides, so brilliantly demonstrate according to the law of contradiction, the law par excellence of the Greeks, as of all extra-biblical peoples.[34] Freud fails to see that the one alterative to the dualism between illusion (fiction) and reality is the myth that, self-conscious of beginning unconsciously, absolutely distinguishes itself from myth as found in Plato and the Upanishads, as in all extra-biblical myth. It is only biblical myth that, self-conscious of its unconscious desire, knows that it is fiction, real fiction, the fiction that is to be realized in the lives, at once communal and personal, of the members of the covenant, whose reality is created in and as the fiction of God. It is biblical myth that knows that there is no reality separate, or different, from (either outside or inside) this fiction. The true division, the real difference to be preserved, is not Freud's dualism between illusion (fiction) and reality (truth) but the Bible's dialectic between, on the one hand, fiction (image) and truth (reality) and, on the other hand, the idolatrous reductions of fiction to reality (externality) and of reality to fiction (internality).

The Greeks come to realize *that* their myths are lies, as we see so poignantly depicted in the narratives of Thucydides, the Socratic dialogues of Plato, and the dramas of Sophocles and Euripides. But they do not realize *what* their mythical lies (their lying myths) are. They do not realize their myths as lies (their lies as myths). They do not make their mythical lies real. What their lying myths are, they do not realize, is that which involves a concept of self whose desire is not divided between the one and the many, between reality and appearance, and that which thus expresses what Spinoza calls sovereignty, truth as its own standard, the *causa sui*. The subject of fiction and reality is the willing self whose desire universalizes (overcomes, preserves, appropriates) the difference between fiction and reality. The enemy (opposite) of fiction is not reality, and the enemy (opposite) of reality is not fiction; but the enemy of both is illusion, what the Bible opposes as idolatry. Fiction is truer than reality. Yet reality is stranger than fiction. That it is the fiction and the reality, the truth, of biblical myth that Freud does not realize in his metapsychology, although he sees it continually at work in the practice of psychotherapy – this is what we shall be taking up in our subsequent chapters.

3 Love and Guilt

In light of the metapsychological commitments that Freud makes to the priority of the pleasure principle and the unconscious in the psychical life of human beings, as explored in chapter 2, we shall now examine his concept of libido and the cluster of ideas that it involves. Libido, as sexual instinct, would appear to be the vehicle for ensuring the primacy of the pleasure in human relations; and we have seen Freud identify libido with the pleasure principle and thus with Eros, in opposition to the death instinct as centered in the Nirvana principle (the inherent tendency to restore a prior state of things). But we have also seen that it is by no means obvious that Freud gives up his position that the id is dominated by the pleasure principle, and thus by the death instinct, in opposition to libido and Eros. Would this mean, therefore, that, as the id is governed by the pleasure principle, it is the ego that is governed by libido and Eros? Is this the conclusion, while surely absurd phenomenologically, to which Freud is driven by his metapsychology? Such a conclusion would seem, however, to be barred from the outset. Can anything be clearer in Freudian theory than that the transference neuroses are based on the conflict between the ego and the demands of libido, the sexual instincts? How could libido migrate from the sexual instincts, later the id, to ego? Not only, however, does Freud assume from the beginning that libido is at first autoerotic and only later transferred to object or sexual relations. But he also comes to discover that the duality between ego instincts (the instincts of self-preservation) and sexual instincts (libido) cannot account for the role of narcissism in human life. He arrives at the position, therefore, that the ego is itself cathected with libido and is, indeed, the very source of libido, a conclusion that is thus consistent with his original positing of autoerotic libido as prior to object libido.

It is precisely when the narcissistic ego, as the source of libido, threatens to reduce Freud's dualistic theory of the instincts to monism that he is relieved to go beyond the pleasure principle to the death instinct. He discovers that the pleasure principle is the principle not of libido or life but of death. He reconstitutes the fundamental dualism of his metapsychology on the primordial opposition between the two independent and separate instincts governing human life (and death!): the death instincts of destructiveness, aggressivity, and hostility and the life instincts of Eros promoting the unity of civilization. What Freud now realizes is that it is his original principle of pleasure-unpleasure, by which, he holds, all life is governed, that constitutes the death instinct. To seek pleasure is to avoid non-pleasure (pain). To strive to avoid non-pleasure is to eliminate the tensions of life by reducing them to a constant state (nirvana). But it is this aim, he now sees, that constitutes instinct itself: the inherent tendency to restore an earlier state of things – that which is inorganic, lifeless, and dead. Life serves death. All beings strive to die. Desire is the death instinct.

At what phenomenological cost, however, will Freud maintain his metapsychological dualism between death and life, between aggressivity (guilt) and libido (love)? In what sense can the destructive tendencies of life be understood as the pursuit of pleasure, that is, as the avoidance of pain and the inherent tendency to restore an earlier (lifeless) state of things? How, we ask, can death be the origin of life? How can death be the opposite of life (Eros) if it is the very origin of life? Does that which is, for Freud, original always have the tendency to turn into its very opposite? How can Eros (life) serve any other end than the death instinct if death is its principle, origin, source, and end? How can masochism and sadism, as the demonstration that pleasure is pain, be understood as the avoidance (or the elimination) of pain? In what sense can the destructive tendencies of aggressivity and hostility be understood as seeking pleasure? If the pleasure principle is to be truly revealed as the principle of death, in life, will we not begin to suspect that this is so precisely because the death instinct itself is indistinguishable from Eros (life)? We saw Freud, once he had shown in *Beyond the Pleasure Principle* that the death instinct is intrinsic to the fatal logic of the pleasure principle, vigorously protest his conclusion that Eros serves death. Yet, he then proceeds to endorse this conclusion with his appeal to the Platonic (and Hindu) myth of Eros as embodying the inherent tendency of all instinct to restore an earlier state of things (nirvana, original unity, the utter absence of all tension: death).

It is not clear, therefore, that Eros or libido will be able to survive the dualism of Freud's metapsychology and, in particular, the identification of pleasure with the elimination of pain, with nirvana, with the extinction of life, with death, especially when it is the pleasure principle that is said to govern the id. The metapsychological relationship of id and ego makes the picture even more complex. Freud holds that the ego originates from within the id, although it is also his view that the ego emerges in response to the demands of external reality and that the id is (internally) formed from the precipitates of endless ego (external) experiences.

Freud's story of libido becomes yet even more complicated when he proposes the Oedipus complex as the matrix for understanding the vicissitudes that libido undergoes, that it is compelled to undergo, if the originally dependent, helpless, and fearful infant is to arrive at (post-puberty) maturity with its psychical apparatus articulated as id, ego, and superego. According to Freud, the male attains maturity (as a man) possessing what he originally possesses as a boy – the father('s penis) – and the female attains maturity (as a woman) desiring what she originally lacks – the father('s penis). However, it is by no means clear, then, that libido, already endangered by Freud's metapsychological commitment to the pleasure principle, will survive the Oedipus complex. Both boy and girl begin in what appears to be a primary (libidinal) relationship to the mother, but it turns out that it is not this relationship that is primary. The boy's primary relationship is that of nonlibidinal identification with the father. The boy must never change. The girl's primary relationship is that of libidinal attachment to the father. She must, therefore, undergo a double, a completely contradictory change. Not only does the girl have to give up identification with her mother, but she also has to transfer her libido: first, to her father; then, to his surrogate, her husband; and, finally, to his surrogate, her male child. Castration – the threat of castration (the loss of the penis) – causes the boy to give up his incestuous desire for his mother and thus to maintain his identification with his father('s penis). Castration – the fact that the girl is castrated (she lacks a penis) – causes her to transfer her love from her mother, whom she comes to hate for not providing her with the penis, to her father (and ultimately to his male surrogate). The boy is what he has – a penis – and does not desire. The girl is what she lacks – a penis – but desires. The boy's identification with the penis (father) is without libido. The girl's desire (lack) of the penis (father) is libido. Since libido is absent in the male in his (narcissistic) identification with the penis and since libido is present in the female in her narcissistic desire (lack) of the penis, the status of libido is metapsychologically in question.

There is no doubt that the castration complex provides Freud with a means of looking deeply into the enormous hostility and enmity to be found in the sexual relations between men and women. For men to desire (women) is to lose what they possess – the penis. For women to desire (men) is to gain what they do not possess – the penis. If men love (women), they are castrated (by women). If women love (men), they are castrators (of men). Men can be themselves only if they do not desire (lack) what they have. Women can be themselves only if they desire (lack) what they do not have. The question posed – to, for, and by feminists, who, I would hope, are all of us, whatever our gender and however we embody sexuality in our lives (our lives in sexuality) – is whether Freud's analysis of sexuality is not dependent on his metapsychology and whether this metapsychology is not fundamentally flawed. The problem is not patriarchy (which is real enough) but metapsychology (whose reality is not substantially enough comprehended). For what we find in Freudian metapsychology is that self and desire are fatally opposed to each other, both in the individual man and woman and in their (sexual) relations with each other. The male self (penis) is without desire; for to desire is to lack the penis (self). Female desire (for the penis) is without a self; for to desire is to lack the self (penis). The only way of overcoming the hostility and enmity between men and women, of appropriating the binary opposition between self and desire, is in terms of an alternative ontology, according to whose golden rule (of loving the other as yourself) self expresses desire and desire involves the self.

Not only, however, does the Oedipus complex demonstrate the opposition between self and desire. But the *telos* of mature (male) development is the resolution (the demolition) of the Oedipus complex, whose heir is the ideal self, the super-self, the superego. It is the superego, in league with the id, that punishes the ego for any attraction that it might feel towards libidinal impulses. The identification of the boy with the father (and his penis) guarantees his (penis's) survival before the Gorgon of the castrated female who fills him with horror, not with love (for incest always involves castration). It is then identification with the father that is introjected as the superego, with the same result. The superego punishes the ego with loss of identity any time it is moved by desire (for women). Because women are pure desire, without a self, Freud holds that they are also without a significant superego. As the superego keeps men subject to the castration threat – all desire is threatened with castration – so women, since their castration is original, are actually pure libido (desire), threatening men with castration, but never endangering their self, which is precisely what they lack. This naturally provides the basis for Freud's thesis that men, with their superego (self), fulfill their (homosexual) roles in social and cultural relationships outside the family, while women, lacking a self but defined by desire (for the penis), fulfill their (productive) roles in the family, seeking to gain their identity, their self, through their male child (a surrogate penis).

Two opposed results follow, then, from the split between self and desire, between civilization and sexuality, between male and female, the opposition of whose basic elements forms a closed (vicious) circle where patriarchy is indistinguishable from matriarchy. On the one hand, women, although hostile to (male) civilization, desire that on which civilization is erected, the penis. It is little wonder, then, that civilization has all the impotence of the erect penis. It is precisely the thrusting penis that undergoes castration, for to be satisfied (sexually) is to be rendered spent, flaccid, impotent, lost in the womb, like a baby, the penis repossessed by the woman as her original self. It is easy to understand that the erect phallus has been the sexual fantasy of both men and women throughout the ages. The man has the penis erect, so long as it does not express desire; for desire is the man's nemesis, the penis's defeat, its deflation, its demonstration of impotence. The woman wants the penis erect; but, once the penis is spent inside her, all she has left is the (male) child, which is what she wants, but what she wants is precisely what she is left without, the penile self.

On the other hand, men, while the erectors of civilization, fear their erection; for their relations with other men, their social and cultural connections, are homosexual, expressing their male identification with (as) the penis. What they fear, however, is that their relations with other men signify the feminine passivity of castration. While Freud says little about the relationship of women to other women,[1] we can square the circle and suggest that, consistent with his metapsychology, they could only hate each other as bearing eternal witness to their livid hole of castration. The homosexual relationship of women with each other would be pure desire, the eternal lack of the castrated self (the penis), just as the homosexual relationship of men with each other is pure self (the identification of the ego with the penis), always fearful of desire (castration).

The fact that the split between desire as castration and the self as castrated results in the superego in men, punishing the self (penis) for its desire, and the lack of a (significant) superego in women, ensuring that their desire lacks a self (the penis), has enormous implications for Freud's conception of love and guilt. Once we expose the basic elements of Freud's Oedipus complex, issuing in the (lack of the) superego, in section ii, we shall then deal with his conceptions of love and guilt in sections iii and iv. In both *Group Psychology and the Analysis of the Ego* and *Civilization and its Discontents*, Freud develops a concept of society, indeed, of civilization, on the basis of his libido theory, as articulated in and through the Oedipus complex and its castrated heir, (the lack of) the superego. In section iii we shall examine his view that groups are maintained by libidinal ties. This seems evident, except that Freud sharply distinguishes between the ties that bind members of the group, whose origin he locates in the primal horde, to their chief (the primal father) and the ties that bind group members to each other. While soldiers – Freud uses the army to exemplify the group – look upon their chief as their ideal, their comradely ties with each other are based on identification.

This distinction between relating to the leader as one's ideal and relating to one's fellow group members in terms of identification is puzzling, however, for a number of reasons. One wonders, for instance, if Freud views the army as the model of society. Although he calls himself a pacifist in the open letter "Why War?" addressed to Einstein, Freud argues at the same time for the necessity of an educated elite who, having subordinated their instinctual life to the dictatorship of reason, rule over the masses who remain subject to the pleasure principle. More important is the fact that in the Oedipal model it is identification with the father (and thus with the father's penis) that leads, by way of the castration complex, to the boy's renunciation of (incestuous) desire. In the group model, however, it is identification not with the father but with one's fellow group members that involves aim-inhibited (non-sexual) relations. Thus, identification with the father (in the Oedipal model) and identification with one's comrades (in the group model), and not with the father, produce the same result, castration of libido. It is also the case that Freud traces the origin of both the Oedipus complex (founded on identification with the father) and the group (where the tie with the father is not based on identification) to the myth of the primal father, which thus leads to opposed results: identification with the father (in the Oedipal model) and identification with others (in the group model). Although we shall continue to defer consideration of phylogenesis, the archaic heritage, until chapter 4, it is clear that Freud's libido theory is deeply implicated in his concept of beginning (origin).

What Freud understands by identification and its significance for libido becomes even more perplexing when he acknowledges, in *Group Psychology*, that the Christian church is not a group like other groups (for example, the army). The church, he points out, doubles, by mutually interrelating, the dual ties of identification (with fellow group members) and of "object love" (with the chief!), which are opposed to each other in the group model (and also in the Oedipal model). The Christian, Freud remarks, is required to identify with Christ (who is hardly a chief among other chiefs, including the pope or other ecclesiastical officials, about whom Freud remains silent) as he identifies with his fellow Christians, and he is required to love his fellow Christians as he loves Christ. In thus linking mutual (self-)identification with love (desire) of the other, Freud explicitly states that Christianity is not a group like other groups. But what, then, is it? Are we to understand that Christianity, in viewing the ties of identification and love as mutually related to each other, and not as mutually opposed to each other as they are in the group (and also in the Oedipal) model, is the very model of democratic society? Although Freud does not mention the golden rule by name or include any of its formulations in his astonishingly brief yet accurate description of the bonds constituting Christianity, it is clear that it is the golden rule that he envisages. But what, then, does Freud understand by Christianity? Does Christianity include or exclude libido? Does it include or exclude the superego? Does it include or exclude what Freud, in the final sections of *Civilization and its Discontents*, views as the greatest threat to civilization, the sense of guilt, which is the subject of section iv of this chapter?

What is particularly fascinating here is that Freud introduces the sense of guilt by way of a vigorous attack on the golden rule. He holds that the ideal of loving your neighbour as yourself not only does not account for but actually falsifies and even intensifies the violence and aggressivity of original human nature. The source of this aggressivity, as representative of the death instinct, he argues, is the castration complex. Denied an external outlet for his hostility to his father, the Oedipal boy internalizes the hostility as the sense of guilt, which thus reflects the originary ambivalence of his identification with the father('s penis). The sense of guilt results from the fact that the hostility that the boy originally directs against the (external) father he now directs (internally) against himself. The conclusion to which Freud comes in *Civilization and its Discontents* is that the superego, as the heir of the Oedipus complex, has its origin in love, that is, in the castration complex, and its end in the sense of guilt, that is, in the destructive self-aggression that it imposes on civilization. What, however, is love? What is guilt? Freud holds that love and guilt represent the eternal conflict in civilization between the two primordial instincts, the life instincts of Eros and the death instincts of destruction and hostility. But how can civilization involve an eternal conflict *between* Eros and death when the superego, whose categorical imperative constitutes the morality of social relations, begins in love (the Oedipus complex) and ends in guilt (conscience)? Do we not begin to suspect that, because the superego owes its beginning not to love but to pre-libidinal identification with the paternal penis, Eros is ultimately indistinguishable from the death instinct? Is guilt the inexorable result of the primordial identification with the paternal phallus – its presence or its absence – which, in excluding libido from life, in the beginning, castrates it, in the end?

If, however, we were to conceive of the relationship between love and guilt on the basis of the dialectic of desire and self, would we not be able to free love from its non-libidinal beginning as identification with the penis – its presence or its absence – and from its non-libidinal end (beginning) in castration as the sense of guilt destructive of civilization? Would not love, then, become not the opposite of guilt but its standard, at once its origin and its end? Does the golden rule, as Freud holds, reflect impotence to deal with the reality of the death instinct, whether it is externally expressed as aggression and hostility or internally experienced as the guilt of self-punishment? Or does the golden rule represent, rather, the one alternative there is to viewing love and guilt as the representatives of the interminably opposed, because terminably indistinguishable, life and death instincts? Is not the guilt to which love is continually subject continuously overcome when you desire the other as yourself? Is this what Freud envisions when he views Christianity as the mutual relationship, and not the mutual opposition, of identification and love, of self and desire?

II THE OEDIPUS COMPLEX

When Freud first publishes his views on "the sexual functions of human beings" in the *Three Essays on the Theory of Sexuality*, he claims to base his findings exclusively on psychoanalytical and not at all on biological research (40–1).[2] Later, however, when he begins to formulate his instinct or libido theory, he turns explicitly to biology. In his essay "On Narcissism" Freud reiterates his commitment to keeping psychology clear of all foreign, including biological, considerations, but then he admits that, "in the total absence of any theory of the instincts which would help us to find our bearings, ... the hypothesis of separate ego instincts and sexual instincts (that is to say, the libido theory) rests scarcely at all upon a psychological basis, but derives its principal support from biology" (70–1). Like all animals, Freud writes, human beings have a twofold existence: individual self-preservation (the ego instincts) and preservation of the species (the sexual instincts). But it is inherently unlikely that the distinction between ego and sexuality, between self-preservation and preservation of the species, between ego and group, between self and other is going to be of much help in sorting out the sexual (among other) desires of the individual when they involve him in relations to others and others in relations to him.

It is also the case that Freud's instinct (libido) theory shows itself to be inherently unstable. He soon discovers that he has to replace the distinction between ego instincts and sexual instincts with that between ego libido and object libido, given the role that he finds narcissism to play in human life. But this narcissism only reflects the autoerotism that Freud, from the beginning, makes central to his theory of sexuality. He characteristically holds that the id (following his later theory) overwhelms the originally weak, helpless, and dependent ego with its libidinal demands.

Still, Freud always fundamentally insists that the individual is, at first, narcissistic (autoerotic) and that the sexual instincts (together with their object relations) emerge only subsequent to and out of the ego instincts. "Originally, at the very beginning of mental life," Freud writes in "Instincts and their Vicissitudes," "the ego is cathected with instincts and is to some extent capable of satisfying them on itself. We call this condition 'narcissism' and this way of obtaining satisfaction 'autoerotic.' At this time the external world is not cathected with interest (in a general sense) and is indifferent for purposes of satisfaction ... Insofar as the ego is autoerotic, it has no need of the external world" (132–3). Freud explains in *Three Essays on Sexuality* that, when the infant sucks at its mother's breast, the instinct that it satisfies is, originally, self-preservative (hunger) and not sexual (love). "To begin with," he writes, "sexual activity attaches itself to one of the functions serving the purpose of self-preservation and does not become independent of them until later. No one who has seen a baby sinking back satiated from the breast and falling asleep with flushed cheeks and a blissful smile can escape the reflection that this picture persists as a prototype of the expression of sexual satisfaction in later life" (98).

Given his biological (or metapsychological) distinction between ego instincts and sexual instincts (and subsequently between ego libido and object libido), Freud views the child's original association with its mother as autoerotic or narcissistic, although ultimately it does serve, he says, as the prototype of (adult) sexuality. He has no explanation of how autoeroticism or the narcissism of ego libido can exist independently of the external world, just as he cannot explain how the pleasure principle can exist independently of the reality principle. He equally has no explanation of how the original ego libido can extend itself to objects (that is, to human subjects), just as he cannot explain how the reality principle can evolve out of the pleasure principle when it is presupposed by the pleasure principle. What begins in Freud as autoerotic, because self-preservative, becomes the ego libido. But the point I want to make here, as preliminary to a discussion of the basic metapsychology of the Oedipus complex, is that Freud's libido theory is fundamentally a theory of the ego, of narcissism, just as his psychotherapeutic theory of neurosis is fundamentally a theory of ego control over the impulses of the id.

What is truly outrageous is that Freud, the great theorist of sexuality, has, ultimately, no theory of libido, no theory of sexuality. For, first and foremost, what he never realizes is that sexuality is not biology but love – both sensual and spiritual – the relationship of desire constituted by self and other. Indeed, once Freud is led by his theory of narcissistic libido to formulate his final instinct theory, the place of libido in his thought remains highly problematic. In distinguishing between Eros or the life instincts, as the unifying, social forces within civilization, and death or the aggressive instincts of hostility and destruction, as the disintegrative, anti-social forces within civilization, he also acknowledges that libido, as expressed in and through adult sexual relations, is anti-social. But what is Eros if it is not erotic, and what is libido if its sexuality is not social, integrative, and life-supporting? As I continue to emphasize, libido has difficulties in escaping its origin in the pleasure principle, which is ultimately indistinguishable from narcissism, the illusion of primary process. What we shall now see is that libido is fundamentally absent from the Oedipus complex. Is this why the superego, as the heir of the Oedipus complex, generates within the ego a sense of guilt whose origin is the interiorization of aggressivity, the representative of the death instinct? Is this why Freud indicates in *The Ego and the Id* that the superego becomes "a pure culture of the death instinct" (394)? If libido is subject to the pleasure principle, in the beginning, can it help succumbing to the pleasure principle, as the death instinct, in the end?

The Oedipus complex, as conceived by Freud, embodies two critically important issues, each deeply interwoven with the other: history and the relations between the sexes. How social structures (authority, freedom) are constituted raises issues fundamentally related to family dynamics, to how children gain their identities – involving gender, history, and culture. The family, then, brings together both cultural and sexual difference, raising for us what the role of the family is in history and of history in the family. If the family is historical and if history is constituted by what Freud calls the "family romance," this will suggest that sexuality is itself historical (or what Freud would call psychical) and not biological. Rousseau, for all his ambivalence, recognizes that the citizen is not the creature of his patriarchal (social) or matriarchal (natural) family but, rather, the creation of the social contract, the general will. In the eternal transition from nature (where we argue from fact to right, from the fact that because some individuals are slaves one has a right to enslave others) to duty (where we argue from right to fact, from the right of the freedom of all to the fact that some are unfree is unconstitutional), we begin with the desire, the compulsion, to be free. Although humans are alienated from themselves, they have no right to alienation (alienation is not [a] right). Alienation is inconceivable outside of the context of the right of freedom, just as the child is inconceivable outside of the context of, not the family, but the general will (the community). Freedom is its own standard, the standard of both itself and its alienation. The paradox of the family, which Rousseau embodies in both his life and his writings with inimitably brilliant pathos, is that, although there are no children outside of families, it is not families but the community (the general will, humankind, God) that gives birth to children as "man": human beings. As Spinoza says, there is a fundamental difference between the slave, the son (the child), and the subject. The child is first and last a subject, in the care of parents, and not a slave, under the domination of parents. Children are first and last sovereign, democratic subjects.[3]

Freud loves to repeat the Roman dictum that, whereas maternity is certain, paternity is uncertain. He thereby embodies his critical distinction between perception (consciousness) and inference (the basis of our knowledge of the unconscious, it may be recalled), between animism (illusory projection based on the pleasure principle) and science (knowledge based on the reality principle). But this dictum reflects the fundamental difficulty that Freud has in dealing with the family, with history, with the psychical (historical) manifestations of male and female biology. The difference between immediate sense certainty and abstract understanding, to employ the categories of Hegel (reflecting those of Kant), is completely inadequate for portraying what is psychical (meaningful) in human beings. Further, Freud also ignores the critical question of Jesus, anticipating Kant's articulation of paradox as the synthetic a priori judgment: who is my mother?[4] It is also Jesus who tells his listeners: "'If any one comes to me and does not hate his own father and mother and wife and children and brothers and sisters, yes, and even his own life, he cannot be my disciple'" (Luke 14.26). Hate all those with whom you are familiar, and follow me. Love me, I who am the unfamiliar, the alienating, the uncanny one. Who am I? I am love. I am who I am (was and will be). I am one with the father. If you follow me, if you love me, you will be one with me, you will be one with the father. Who are you? You are love, loving God above all others and your neighbour as yourself.[5] Jesus appeals beyond his biological mother and father to the principle, the origin, the spirit, the creation of authority. The issue is neither maternal certainty, the illusory consciousness of the pleasure principle, nor paternal uncertainty, the inferred consciousness of the reality principle. The issue is how the individual is at one and the same time communal, social, and cultural, other than himself, both the self of desire and the desire of self, when self and desire are always other, historical, and unconscious.

Through the Oedipus complex Freud attempts to deal with history and the transmission of culture (phylogenesis) and with the institution of social authority (the superego). But because he is unable to separate the issue of individual and universal (self and other) from the biological bedrock of the instincts, he is unable to provide a model of the family that is true to both history and the relations between the sexes. Here we shall expose the salient details of his Oedipal model, while in chapters 4 and 5 we shall examine the issue of the "universality," the historicity, of the Oedipus complex and Freud's view that ontogeny (the individual) repeats phylogeny (the species). We shall then also have the opportunity of discussing Freud's concept of the relationship between fantasy and reality.

Freud's Oedipal model is firmly based on what he calls the duality of the sexes. It both presupposes that duality and results in that duality. It is always difficult to know whether the Oedipus complex describes the mechanism by which the duality of the sexes is maintained in both family and society (civilization) or whether it is a model for gaining critical insight into the range of possibilities open to men and women in their multiple relationships. It is thus not surprising that equivocation (dualism) marks Freud's conception of sexuality. He revolutionizes our understanding of the topic by showing, in the successive editions of the *Three Essays on Sexuality*, that there is no "natural" (normal) object or aim of sexuality and that its manifestations are infantile – that is, we are sexual beings from the beginning. In expanding our understanding of sexuality far beyond the limits of genitality or reproductivity, Freud makes sexuality psychical, not biological, in its significant dimensions. The sexual instincts or drives can have any legitimate (or illegitimate) object or aim. In principle, one would assume, there is no aim or object that is not by nature sexual; and there is no aim or object that is by nature sexual.

Still, although Freud appears to sever the connection between sexuality and nature, he, like the rest of us, is still confronted with the fact that there are (we are) men and women. He is of the opinion that, while each of us is either a man or a woman, the terms masculine and feminine are either relatively insignificant, because they describe merely obvious differences in anatomy and biological function, or absolutely significant, because they describe subtle cultural differences involving what we mean by activity and passivity (passion). Freud also holds that anatomy is destiny, that libido is masculine (active), and that the little girl is originally a little man. It is in the different Oedipal development of boys and girls, Freud writes in *An Outline*, that

the difference between the sexes finds psychological expression for the first time. We are faced here by the great enigma of the biological fact of the duality of the sexes: it is an ultimate fact for our knowledge, it defies every attempt to trace it back to something else. Psychoanalysis has contributed nothing to clearing up this problem, which clearly falls wholly within the province of biology. In mental life we only find reflections of this great antithesis; and their interpretation is made more difficult by the fact, long suspected, that no individual is limited to the modes of reaction of a single sex but always finds some room for those of the opposite one ... For distinguishing between male and female in mental life we make use of what is obviously an inadequate empirical and conventional equation: we call everything that is strong and active male, and everything that is weak and passive female. (422–3)[6]

On several occasions in his writings Freud points out the enormous ambiguity in the distinction between masculine and feminine. In a footnote added in 1915 to *Three Essays on Sexuality* he observes that, while the meaning of the concepts masculine and feminine "seems so unambiguous to ordinary people, [they] are among the most confused that occur in science." He distinguishes three uses. The first, the distinction between active and passive, he calls the most serviceable to psychoanalysis.[7] To describe libido as masculine means that it is active, "for an instinct," he observes, "is always active even when it has a passive aim in view" (141). But if all instincts are active, even when passive, it is not at all clear what remains of the active-passive or masculine-feminine distinction. Is this why there is nothing more active than passion, passive disobedience, or patience? Indeed, Freud points out in the *New Introductory Lectures* that masculine behavior does not coincide with activity or feminine behavior with passivity. We observe, he says, not only that a mother is active in caring for her child but also that, while women are active in life, men cannot relate to each other without "a large amount of passive adaptability." If you persist in connecting "active" with "masculine" and "passive" with "feminine," Freud writes, "I advise you against it. It seems to me to serve no useful purpose and adds nothing to our knowledge" (148). The second and third uses of the masculine-feminine polarity also provide little help, Freud goes on to show. The second, the biological, is contradictory, given that the females of some animal species are more aggressive than the males, while the third, the sociological, is consistent with neither psychology nor biology.

Still, it is instructive to note how Freud treats the active-passive distinction when he sums up his essay on "Instincts and their Vicissitudes" with the statement that "the essential feature in the vicissitudes undergone by instincts lies in *the subjection of the instinctual impulses to the influences of the three great polarities that dominate mental life.* Of these three polarities we might describe that of activity-passivity as the *biological*, that of ego [subject]-external world [object] as the *real*, and finally that of pleasure-unpleasure as the *economic* polarity" (138). There are two salient features in this passage that raise doubts as to whether or in what sense Freud severs the relationship between biology and sexuality and thus make us wonder whether he will persist in reading culture (sociology) in terms of biology – and thus biology in terms of culture (sociology) – even though he acknowledges in *Beyond the Pleasure Principle*, as we have seen, that biology throws not the slightest ray of light on the origins of sexuality. This is consistent with his statement, cited above, that the duality of the sexes is the ultimate biological fact that is (also) impenetrable to psychoanalysis. The first salient feature in the passage cited above is that Freud views the active-passive polarity as biological, although he explicitly calls it psychoanalytical and not biological in the passage cited from *Three Essays*. As for the other two polarities, they are no less suspect. The distinction between the ego and the external world is incongruous, for Freud normally defines the ego in opposition to libido, while later viewing it as the ally of the external world in opposition to the id.[8] As for the economic polarity of pleasure-unpleasure, we have already seen that it is precisely what Freud will go beyond when he discovers that, because pleasure is the avoidance of unpleasure, it is indistinguishable from the death instinct (the reduction of pain to pleasure). The second and more important feature in the passage cited above involves the relationship of the instincts to the polarities of life. If the instincts (drives) are themselves subject to polarities that appear yet more primordial, what is the nature of this primordial polarity? Is it psychoanalytic (psychical) or biological (somatic)?

Having seen that the aims and objects of the sexual instincts cannot be said to be natural, although the difference between male and female is an impenetrable biological substratum, while the distinction between active (masculine) and passive (feminine) is highly ambiguous, we may note that Freud provides two contexts for exposing the Oedipus complex. The first is that of what we have seen him call "the ultimate fact" of the duality of the sexes. The second is that of infantile sexuality, the subject of the second of the *Three Essays on Sexuality*, where he does not mention the Oedipus complex, except in footnotes added in 1920 and 1924. Although we shall examine Freud's concept of the infantile in the context of his concept of development and phylogenesis, of history, in chapter 4, we may wonder if infantile sexuality and its development are, for Freud, to be understood in terms of psychoanalysis or biology. At the beginning of his essay on "Some Psychical Consequences of the Anatomical Distinction between the Sexes," he writes that

in my own writings and in those of my followers more and more stress is laid on the necessity that the analyses of neurotics shall deal thoroughly with the remotest period of their childhood, the time of the early efflorescence of sexual life. It is only by examining the first manifestations of the patient's *innate instinctual constitution* and the effects of his earliest experiences that we can accurately gauge the motive forces that have led to his neurosis and can be secure against the errors into which we might be tempted by the degree to which things have become remodelled and overlaid in adult life. (331e)[9]

We are not concerned, in the present context, with the interplay between what Freud calls the innate instinctual constitution of the child and its actual experience as a family member – although it is the dynamic relationship between what is internal (inborn) and external (experienced) that, as I have already anticipated, should rather be conceived as history. What I want to expose, at present, are the salient features of the Oedipus complex and its heir the superego.[10] Freud clearly believes in the romance of the family, that the (male) child is the father of man – the human race. But the child is the father of man precisely because the father is the (male) child's ideal, first, in his pre-Oedipal identification with him and, then, in his post-Oedipal period, when the father becomes his ego ideal (superego). As we shall see, this ideal father is the primal father who is never a child and who never experiences the romance of family analysis but whom his primal sons spontaneously murder, thus expressing the hatred of their love for him. Surely we have to ponder deeply what it is that constitutes this identification with the father and this ego ideal as the father.

Identification is, for Freud, the primary, pre-Oedipal category (for males). It leads directly to the castration complex and the primary, post-Oedipal category of the superego. The fact that the Oedipus complex proper – sexual desire for the mother and rivalry with and hostility to the father – only serves as a link between the beginning (identification) and the end (the castration complex), with each the mirror image of the other, serves to raise the elemental question as to its actual status. "Identification," Freud writes in *Group Psychology*, "is known to psychoanalysis as the earliest expression of an emotional tie with another person." The little boy, in identifying with his father, takes him as his ideal: he wants to be a male like his father. Identification, Freud observes, thus "fits in very well with the Oedipus complex, for which it helps to prepare the way" (134). Because the pre-Oedipal identification with the father precedes any possible Oedipal choice of the father as a libidinal object – which would place the boy in a passive or feminine position (that is, he would wish to be loved by his father as his mother is loved by him) – identification expresses the original masculine ideal of what the boy would like to *be*, not what he would like (subsequently) to *have* (as a libidinal object). The distinction between ideal and object, between wanting to *be* like the father and wanting to *have* (the father as) an object, Freud explains, "depends upon whether the tie attaches to the [narcissistic] subject or to the [libidinal] object of the ego. The former kind of tie [i.e., that of identification] is therefore already possible before any sexual object choice has been made. *It is much more difficult to give a clear metapsychological representation of the distinction.* We can only see that identification endeavors to mold a person's *own ego* after the fashion of the one that has been taken as a model" (135e).[11]

Before indicating how, for the male child, identification with the father and (subsequent) object choice of the mother results in ambivalence – intense rivalry with the father over the mother as love object – it is important to see that the superego emerges, in the male, as the ego ideal, the repository of original identification with the father. Behind the ego ideal, Freud writes in *The Ego and the Id*, "lies hidden an individual's first and most important identification, his identification with the father in his own personal prehistory.[12] This is apparently not in the first instance the consequence or outcome of an object cathexis; it is a direct and immediate identification and takes place earlier than any object cathexis" (370). In the *New Introductory Lectures* he writes that

the installation of the superego can be described as a successful instance of identification with the parental agency. The fact that speaks decisively for this view is that this new creation of a superior agency within the ego is most intimately linked with the destiny of the Oedipus complex, so that the superego appears as the heir of that emotional attachment which is of such importance for childhood. With his abandonment of the Oedipus complex a child must, as we can see, renounce the intense object cathexes which he has deposited with his parents, and it is as a compensation for this loss of objects that there is such a strong intensification of the identifications with his parents which have probably long been present in his ego. (95–6)

Freud thus points out that the repetition of the original pre-Oedipal identification with the father in the post-Oedipal superego carries with it the ambivalence of the Oedipus complex. For the (male) child to want to be like his father, to have his father as his ideal or model, also means that he cannot have what his father has, his mother('s love). The fact that the boy's ego ideal is double, that to be like his father he must renounce what his father has,

derives from the fact [Freud writes in *The Ego and the Id*] that the ego ideal [or superego] had the task of repressing the Oedipus complex; indeed, it is to that revolutionary event that it owes its existence. Clearly the repression of the Oedipus complex was no easy task. The child's parents, and especially his father, were perceived as the obstacle to a realization of his Oedipus wishes; so his infantile ego fortified itself for the carrying out of the repression by erecting this same obstacle within itself. It borrowed strength to do this, so to speak, from the father, and this loan was an extraordinarily momentous act. The superego retains the character of the father. (374)

The authority of one's personal father is further reinforced through the interiorization of educational, social, cultural, and religious authority in and by the superego in the form of conscience, the (un)conscious sense of guilt, and the categorical imperative.

It is the identification of the boy with the father (with the paternal penis, as we shall see) that allows him to repress what the father('s penis) wants. He thus emerges in the post-Oedipal period, with desire repressed, in exactly the same position as he is in the pre-Oedipal period, in which he had no Oedipal desire. This shows, Freud observes, that superego domination over the ego is due to two factors: the original identification with the father when the ego was infantile, dependent, and helpless; and the fact that the superego "is the heir to the Oedipus complex and has thus introduced the most momentous objects into the ego." But Freud constantly elides the distinction between identification (on the part of the ego with its own subject) and object choice (the ego's relation to an object),[13] for surely the objects that the superego introduces into the ego are those whose origins are in identification. Although Freud remarks that the ego, upon maturing, may become more resistant to the influence of these identifications – how? – and that the superego is accessible to later influences – how? – he holds that the superego "nevertheless preserves throughout life the character given to it by its derivation from the father – complex – namely, the capacity to stand apart from the ego and to master it. It is a memorial of the former weakness and dependence of the ego, and the mature ego remains subject to its domination. As the child was once under a compulsion to obey its parents, so the ego submits to the categorical imperative of its superego" (389).[14]

When Freud then remarks in a footnote on the difficulty that an analyst faces in dealing with an unconscious sense of guilt in an analysand, he is pointing to the fact, although he does not directly indicate this, that all libidinal impulses violate identification with the father. But he goes on to observe that a special opportunity for unmasking the unconscious, repressed roots of guilt and gradually making guilt conscious is provided when the sense of guilt is borrowed, when, in other words, "it is the product of an identification with some other person [than the father] who was once [as in melancholia] the object of an erotic cathexis." Since what counts is the intensity of the sense of guilt and since the only effective force in counteracting it may be the personality of the analyst, success in analysis, Freud continues,

may depend, too, on whether the personality of the analyst allows of the patient's putting him in the place of his ego ideal, and this involves a temptation for the analyst to play the part of prophet, savior and redeemer to the patient. Since the rules of analysis are diametrically opposed to the physician's making use of his personality in any such manner, it must be honestly confessed that here we have another limitation to the effectiveness of analysis; after all, analysis does not set out to make pathological reactions impossible, but to give the patient's ego *freedom* to decide one way or the other. (391)

In thus surreptitiously shifting his focus from metapsychology to phenomenology (psychotherapy), Freud radically changes perspectives without acknowledgment. While suggesting that an unconscious sense of guilt that is based on love ("an erotic cathexis") can be cured by love (transference to the analyst), he remains strangely silent about the sense of guilt that is based *not* on an erotic cathexis or object choice but on (in the male, at least) the earlier, original identification with the father. Male identification precedes object choice (pre-Oedipally) and succeeds it (post-Oedipally in the superego). Because the sense of guilt that the superego imposes on the male ego is due to the original identification of the boy with his father, are we to conclude that all men are subject to an incurable sense of guilt? Is the sense of guilt irremediable (interminable)?

Freud's interesting point that the analyst might supply an ego ideal (through transference) for the analysand that is less punishing for him than his original father complex unhappily dissolves into the fear that the analyst might "play the part of prophet, savior, and redeemer to the patient." But no one, who was not neurotic, would claim to play such a role, for the legitimate heirs of the Bible have always held that those exalted figures bear (transfer, mediate) the metaphoric word of God, not their own literal word, to others. Freud, as ever, evades the question of the moral stance of the analyst in not raising the question of how the (male) analyst's superego is any less guilt-ridden than that of the (male) analysand. If the analyst has (through his training analysis) consciously resolved his Oedipus complex and become non-neurotic (normal), this can only mean that he is absolutely unconscious of his sense of guilt. For the sole (pre-Oedipal) source of and the sole (post-Oedipal) solution to the Oedipus complex is identification with, that is, domination by, the father, which involves complete guilt in experiencing any libidinal impulses (love), including any love that the analyst might feel for the analysand. All love is a threat to identification with the father. When Freud says that the analyst must give "the patient's ego *freedom* to decide" either for pathology or for health, his metapsychology continues to subvert his therapeutic insight. It is not something called an "ego" but the individual analysand who decides freely or unfreely. It is also the case that freedom, as Spinoza demonstrates with incomparable rigour, is not free will, which, suspended, can then decide to be free or not to be free. Freedom, rather, is the recognition, the appropriation, the working through of unfreedom (slavery to affect, Spinoza calls it). The analysand is not even unfree until he confronts his freedom, until he recognizes with Spinoza that freedom is its own standard, the standard both of itself and of its slavery.

There will be more to say about the superego, as the (resolved, crushed) heir of the Oedipus complex, both in the fourth section of this chapter, in regard to the sense of guilt that Freud finds to be the ultimate threat to, as the fatal product of, civilization, and in chapter 4, in regard to its role in transmitting (phylogenetically) the primal guilt of the primal father (as the murdered) to the primal sons (as the murderers). But, from what we have seen so far, the superego, as the heir – the destroyer – of the Oedipus complex, has its origin in primal, original, non-libidinal identification with the father, so long as we are discussing the male child. The boy is born into family life as a completely helpless, dependent, and fearful baby; and he, at once and actively (*sic*!), takes his father as his ideal. He is subsequently born into social life as a completely helpless, dependent, and fearful child, and he, at once and actively, confirms the domination of the father, now in the guise of the superego. What is extraordinary is that, just as his original identification with his father is non-libidinal (it does not involve object or sexual choice), so his ultimate identification with the father (in the superego) punishes him for any libidinal impulses as the unconscious sense of guilt. It is clear, then, that, just as identification leads to the Oedipus complex, as we have seen Freud say, so identification terminates (crushes) the Oedipus complex by ushering in the interminable reign of the superego. In other words, something happens to identification, or identification makes something happen, in and as the Oedipus complex. That something is the castration complex – the feared loss of the penis: that with which the little girl is born, so the little boy fervently believes (wishes), and that whose castration, when accepted, reaffirms the little boy's identification with the father('s penis and thus with his own). Here the story, a *roman* if there ever was one, can be simply told. It does not need to be supported by textual documentation, as does Freud's concept of identification, whose centrality in the Oedipal story it simply reinforces. Neurotic permutations of the Oedipus complex, fascinating in their phenomenology, as found, for example, in the Wolf Man case, will not be considered here.

Both the boy and the girl, according to the Freudian romance, begin with the mother and end with the father, as phenomenology gives way to metapsychology. The result, as I indicated in my introductory remarks, is the duality between self and desire, surely the index of the unconscious sense of guilt (at least in the boy). Freud has some important (although fairly obvious) things to say about the role of the mother in constituting the life of her children, phenomenologically. But, metapsychologically, the mother, and thus the female, is completely eliminated from life, as is, ultimately, the male, too. Rather, Freud has no metapsychological explanation of the female except as the source of the castration threat to the male. The domination of the male (as the one who is symbolically castrated) is thus purely metapsychological (contradictory). The male is also impotent in the sense that he depends, passively, on the female's active role as symbolic castrator. Contradictorily, it is the one who possesses the penis, the boy, who fears castration, while it is the girl, the one who is castrated (she lacks the penis), who, in desiring the penis, castrates the male in possessing it (her real love is for her son, not her husband). Or so it appears, at least.

The girl must pass from an originary identification with the mother to a libidinal relationship with the father. But it is the girl's non-libidinal, pre-Oedipal identification with the mother that utterly determines her sexual and thus her social life. For, while the boy clings to his pre-Oedipal identification with (to his narcissistical love for) the father – the penis – the girl's identificatory love for her mother turns into hate when she makes the momentous discovery that will also dominate the life of the boy: the absence of the penis. She hates her mother for lacking the penis, for causing her to lack the penis. She hates her own identity as a female. For, as female, she lacks, desires, and will never possess the penis, except insofar as she makes the transition from identification with her mother to a libidinal relationship with the father and from there to her husband and to her male child. What a future for a woman! What a future woman! Indeed, in holding that the child asleep upon its mother's breast is the ultimate image of satisfied sexual love and that the relationship between the mother and her male child is the only one that may be free of the hostility and rivalry of the Oedipus complex, Freud indicates that his perception of the relationship between mother and child (son) is dictated by the illusions of his metapsychology, not by the reality of his phenomenology. The fact that the realities, both the joys and the agonies, of sexuality are represented by the image of the son asleep on his mother's breast – is this a parody of the Christ child whose destiny is crucifixion (and the salvation of the world)? – is astonishing. The image is much more likely that of the phallic mother, the chthonic goddess, who castrates the male by getting from him (or reducing him to) a baby, asleep, helpless, impotent, and completely dependent on her. As regards the relationship between the mother and her son, we need to keep in mind (as the Virgin does, although in a completely different sense, in contemplating the Son of humanity on her lap or at her breast) the destiny, the future, of her son. Not only is the boy's libidinal (incestuous) love for his mother forbidden by his hated rival, the father, but, much more important, incest, like all libidinal impulses, confronts the lack of the penis, the castration threat. Thus, the boy, in order to protect the inviolability of his penis (and equally his identification with the father), comes to hate and to fear his mother for lacking the penis. It is equally the case that the daughter comes to hate and to fear her mother for lacking the penis.

The boy's story has already been basically told. We have seen that the girl passes from identification with the mother to a libidinal relationship with the father, with the result that the subsequent relationship is completely dominated by the earlier identification (the lack of a penis). The boy, for his part, passes from identification with the father to a libidinal relationship with the mother; but the later relationship, too, is completely dominated by identification (with the penis). In both cases, identification – with the penis and with the lack of the penis – totally controls the later libidinal (sexual) relationship. It is in this fundamental sense that Freud has no libido theory, indeed, no theory of sexuality at all, at least not metapsychologically. Freud has, rather, a theory of identification – with the penis, its presence or absence – and a theory of castration – of the penis. (The theory embodied in his therapeutic practice is, in contrast, profoundly libidinal or sexual, because truly loving.)

In the Oedipus complex proper, the boy, in desiring his mother (incestuously), becomes ambivalent towards his father, harbouring feelings of hostility and jealousy toward him (and even wishing him out of the way or dead). But the denouement of the family romance is always the castration complex. It is not so much the case that the parents prevent the boy from masturbating, threatening him with loss of his penis, or that the father makes it clear that the mother belongs to him. Rather, the boy is compelled to see what he does not want to see: the fact that the girl does not have a little penis but rather no penis at all. The absence of her penis threatens him with the loss of his own. He reacts violently, represses his hostility to his father, renounces his desire for his mother, and reaffirms the narcissistic identification with his father, with his father's penis, with his own penis that will one day identify him as a father.

While original identification with the father in the little boy leads to the Oedipus complex and its denouement in the castration complex and thus to reaffirmation of identification with the father, the little girl, in contrast, begins in identification with the lack of the penis. The little boy arrives at castration and the reaffirmation of identification. The little girl begins with castration (identification) and arrives at a libidinal relationship with the father, her desire for the penis now displaced onto the desire to have a baby by her father.

In girls [Freud writes in "Some Psychical Consequences of the Anatomical Distinction between the Sexes"] the Oedipus complex is a secondary formation. The operations of the castration complex precede it and prepare for it. As regards the relation between the Oedipus and castration complexes, there is a fundamental contrast between the two sexes. *Whereas in boys the Oedipus complex is destroyed by the castration complex, in girls it is made possible and led up to by the castration complex* ... The difference between the sexual development of males and females ... is an intelligible consequence of the anatomical distinction between their genitals and of the psychical situation involved in it. (340–1)[15]

It may seem strange that Freud, while holding that "Anatomy is Destiny" – "The Dissolution of the Oedipus Complex" (320) – also insists, as he puts it in the *New Introductory Lectures*, that "there is only one libido, which serves both the masculine and the feminine sexual functions" (165).[16] But sexual function (anatomy) – that is, pseudo-biology – wins out over libido. For, as we have seen, identification with the penis (its presence or absence), not libidinal relationship, fundamentally shapes the destiny of both males and females. The castration complex confirms the male in his identification with the father('s penis), thus smashing his Oedipal desire for the mother and his hostile rivalry with the father. Identification of the girl with the mother's lack of the penis confirms her in her Oedipus complex, in her libidinal relationship to the father. With the demolition of his Oedipus complex, the boy introjects his identification of his father as the punishing conscience and social morality of his superego. The girl's original identification with the lack of the penis, in confirming her in her Oedipus complex, leaves her without a significant superego, without a strong conscience or sense of social morality. The destiny of males and females is clear. Identification with the penis, in males, establishes a strong sense of the self, as brought about by the dissolution of the Oedipus complex and the establishment of its heir, the superego. Identification with the lack of the penis, in females, establishes a strong sense of desire, as confirmed by the establishment of the Oedipus complex and the relative absence of a strong superego.

The male self, in order to be a self, to *be* the penis, is without desire, for desire always brings with it the threat of castration. Possession of another, who is without a penis, is to give up possession of your penis (your being) to that castrator. (To desire another who has a penis, either another man or a woman fantasized as a man, or even yourself, is equally to fear castration, for then your relation to the other is passive and feminine.) It is ultimately the paternal penis that reigns in the superego, threatening the male, always, with the punishment of castration if he succumbs to the impulses of the id and gets an erection or, in other words, experiences desire (for the other). Even social erection, however, is fearsome, for it puts the man in a passive or feminine (homosexual) relation to other men.

Female desire lacks being or the self and wants to *have* or possess the other, the self or the penis of the other. But desire always lacks the self and can possess it only by confirming its own castration and by castrating the other. Because desire lacks a self (the penis), it is without a significant sense of conscience or morality (the superego) and accepts, in resigned bitterness, the male baby as its surrogate self. But, as I have already indicated, the mother will only confirm in her son that his identification is with the penis('s father): that he has what she lacks but desires and that the mother (women, generally) is the greatest threat to his self-identification with the penis.

The stage is thus set for the battle not only between the sexes but also within each of the sexes. Freud registers the bewilderment of men over "the enigma of women" when he asks: what does woman want? He describes with real insight the enormous hostility, anger, frustration, bitterness, jealousy, woundedness, fear, exasperation, indifference, envy ... that is experienced by modern (European, middle-class) men and women in their relationships with each other, at once personal and social, in both neurotic and normal contexts. As always, his phenomenology, in this case, concerning the battle of (and within) the sexes, provides a powerful indictment of both the officially sanctioned ideals and the actual practice of his society. But he utterly fails, as always, to see that his metapsychology does not provide either a scientific description of sexuality or a general theory from which the phenomena of sexuality can be deduced (or predicted). His metapsychology is, rather, a self-fulfilling prophecy, a pseudo-biology, and a sham history, a mirror of sexual relations in which he fails to see himself, his own phallic identity. What do women want? What do women lack? They want (lack) what men are, the penis – to their own loss. Freud does not ask what men want (lack). Men want nothing, men lack nothing – except desire – given that their identification with the (father's) penis rests on their not getting an erection and exposing their self to castration, on their not exposing their self to desire. The erect penis is the ultimate symbol of ambivalence. Men love the penis but hate it; for it suggests either castration by the female or a feminine (castrated) relationship to other males. Women love and hate the penis, for it reminds them of what they are not but what they desire. If they succeed in getting the erect penis inside themselves – and thus castrating the male – they are then fated to giving birth to their nemesis, the male child. The son is the eternal reminder for the mother that her desire is without a self. Meanwhile, he comes to fear and to hate his mother because of her selfless, that is, castrating, desire, which thus serves to reconfirm him in a desireless self: identification with the penis('s father).

At the end of "Analysis Terminable and Interminable" Freud addresses the issue of how difficult the treatment of neurosis is made by the fact that the castration complex is different in both origin and resolution for men and women. Although I am not here concerned with the history of Freud's thought or of psychoanalysis, generally, it may be pointed out that the fact that Freud finds himself compelled to refer in this context to Adler, Fliess, and Ferenczi, erstwhile friends and colleagues, even while disputing their views, suggests that his own position is tenuous, at best. We could say that all three represent "wild" psychoanalysis, the reduction of psychotherapy to sexology (the position that neurotic symptoms can be relieved by functional sex), of the psychical to the biological.[17] Indeed, the problem that Freud faces here is how to distinguish psychoanalysis from biology given that the Oedipus complex – when men fail (refuse) to repress it and women fail (refuse) to be repressed by it – is at the root of all neurosis (as of all life). The origin of the Oedipus complex is identification with the penis: men in being one with it (and lacking desire) and women in desiring it (and lacking phallic being). But the question then arises: is the difference between men and women the cause of neurosis? If so, another question emerges: is this difference psychological or biological?

What Freud is confronted with explaining at the end of "Analysis Terminable and Interminable" is how what he calls "the repudiation of femininity," which, in reflecting the castration complex, dominates the psychical life of men and women, is not simply biological. Both men and women repudiate the "feminine" absence (or lack) of the penis – men in fearing the loss of the penis through desire, women in envying what they lack but desire. But is the absence of the penis not biological? Is anatomy not destiny? Is destiny not biology? Freud holds that, because "the repudiation of femininity" plays opposite roles in the two sexes, "in both cases it is the attitude proper to the opposite sex which has succumbed to repression" (250-1). Thus Freud is concerned with accounting for the differential response of men and women to their difference, to the male and female difference that the penis makes. In other words, because the male begins life in identification with the father('s penis), he is confirmed in his identification by the repudiation of femininity, by the woman's lack of the penis. The woman, by beginning life in identification with the mother('s lack of the penis), is confirmed in her identification by the repudiation of femininity, by her desire for the father('s penis). It is Freud's view that, while the male is and remains masculine from the beginning – and so repudiates femininity from the beginning – the woman has to give up her masculinity (her desire for the penis) and to accept her femininity (the lack of the penis, the replacement of the clitoris by the vagina as her leading erotogenic zone, the acceptance of a baby as the surrogate penis). But what Freud fails to see is that, just as the boy, in repressing his Oedipus complex, sacrifices desire to the self (of the penis), so the girl, in being repressed by the Oedipus complex, sacrifices the self (of the penis) to desire. Because her repudiation of femininity is from the beginning, the girl is no less masculine than is the

boy who, since his repudiation of femininity is also from the beginning, is no less feminine than is the girl – which is precisely the contradictory conclusion to which Freud is destined to be driven by his
metapsychology, as we shall see.

Freud resolutely denies Fliess's contention that "the antithesis
between the sexes" is "the true cause and primal motive force of
repression: ... I decline to sexualize repression in this way – that is, to
explain it on biological grounds instead of on purely psychological
ones," he declares (251). Still, what weighs so heavily on the analytic
situation, he observes, is "the repudiation of femininity": the woman's
penis envy (her desire for the penis) and the man's fear of a passive
(castrating) relationship to other men. The woman will not accept
being a woman (she will not accept her desire for the penis being eternally unfulfilled); and the man fears a passive or feminine – castrated
– relationship in his social relations with other men. I cannot dispute
Freud's therapeutic experience and psychological insight.[18] But it is
clear, I think, that, in exposing the enormous difficulty that "the repudiation of femininity" creates for psychotherapy, he fails to acknowledge the *logical* (if irrational) demands of his metapsychology. He
evades seeing that "the repudiation of femininity" is equally "the repudiation of masculinity." The key contradiction in the Oedipal model
fairly leaps out at one. The fact that a man fears castration in having a
"passive" relationship to another man can only stem from originary
identification with the father – with his helpless and fearful dependence
on the father('s penis).

Indeed, Freud goes on to point out that in the analytic situation "the
rebellious overcompensation of the male produces one of the strongest
transference-resistances. He refuses to subject himself to a father-substitute, or to feel indebted to him for anything, and consequently he
refuses to accept his recovery from the doctor" (252). What Freud
acknowledges here, yet evades fully spelling out, is that psychotherapy
– "cure from the physician" – is rendered impotent when erected on
the originary ambivalence of identification with the father('s penis).
Because the male analysand's very being (self) stems from originary
identification with the father('s penis), the ambivalence of his originary
father-complex is carried over and repeated in his analytical relation
with the "father-substitute," the analyst. Just as the originary identification of the analysand with the father makes him subject to the castration complex – what he fears, above all, is loss of his penis (his very
self) – so the analytic situation simply revives this originary ambivalence, this total contradiction. What the analysand loves (his penis) is
what he hates or fears (losing). To love is to hate (to fear). To love is
to lose the penis, to be dependent on the other: helpless, impotent, and

castrated. To possess the penis, to be the penis, to begin life in and through identification with the penis is to be subject, eternally, to castration: to lose what you are. Desire – love – is the greatest threat to phallic being there is.

Such are the implications of the Oedipal model, the implications that Freud both sees and does not (wish [us] to) see. Freud is right that the impasse in analysis is created by "the repudiation of femininity," which is equally the repudiation of masculinity. What he fails to see, however, is that this impasse reflects on his metapsychology and its pre-libidinal and narcissistic beginning with identification, not on the real desire of men and women to love the other as their self. It is doubtless true that Freudian metapsychology is alive and well in the world. It is an accurate mirror of reality. But reflection is not reality – which is precisely the profound insight of depth psychology, in general, and of psychoanalysis, in particular, consistent with the depths of literary, artistic, philosophical, and religious analysis. One must look into the mirror, through the mirror, behind the mirror to discover that self-reflection (self-reflexivity, self-consciousness) is a reality that is not commensurate with its reflections.

Just as the male analysand, in fearing castration, repudiates his femininity in response to his analyst, so the female analysand, in hating her castration, repudiates her femininity in response to her analyst. The male analysand repudiates all desire for the analyst, fearing that he will lose his penis. The female analysand has only desire for the penis of Dr Freud, fearing that he will keep it to himself. But, in thus repudiating her femininity, the female analysand at the same time repudiates the other's masculinity; for, in order to possess Dr Freud's penis, she must castrate him. Freud does not face the fact that the repudiation of femininity is equally the repudiation of masculinity – in both self and other. Still, he does recognize that, because the repudiation of femininity (and no less of masculinity) is not complete – phenomenologically, that is, because it is complete, metapsychologically – analysis is not terminable but interminable. Thus, he terminates his reflections upon the interminability of the castration complex – the fact that it involves the repudiation of femininity (as of masculinity) on the part of both men and women – by observing that the castration complex

prevents any change from taking place – that everything stays as it was. We often have the impression that with the wish for a penis [on the part of women] and the masculine protest [the fear of castration on the part of men] we have penetrated through all the psychological strata and reached bedrock, and that thus our activities are at an end. This is probably true, since, for *the psychical field, the biological field does in fact play the part of the underlying bedrock.*

The repudiation of femininity can be nothing else than a biological fact, a part of the great riddle of sex. (252ᵉ)¹⁹

The repudiation of femininity – on the part of both men and women – is a profoundly terrible truth of our phenomenology, at once personal (familial) and social. But it is not biological, although it is metapsychological, and it involves no less the repudiation of masculinity. It is important to note that the bedrock in biology at which Freud arrives (to which he returns) in the end is the repudiation of femininity and not of incest, the prohibition against incest. The repudiation of femininity and the incest barrier doubtless mirror each other, however, for both are equally a figment of Freud's scientific – metapsychological – fantasy. But the repudiation of femininity, and thus of masculinity, has a psychological reality, a psychological dynamism, that the incest barrier lacks. But this psychological reality is metapsychologically based, as always, on identification with, and thus on the castration of, the penis.

For the man to identify with the penis, with the penis of the father, is, at the same time, to fear the father and his penis. As I have emphasized, the erect penis (like the limp penis) is itself the ultimate contradiction, reflecting the originary ambivalence of love and hate. Love of the father is also fear (hate) of the father. Identification with the penis is also the fear of (losing) the penis. For the woman to identify with the absent penis, for her to desire (in lacking) the penis, is for her to revenge her love for the father by bringing to birth a male child who will be the hated rival of his surrogate, the father (her husband). Identification with the penis and its originary ambivalence leads, in the case of the male child, to the castration complex whose termination of the Oedipus complex imposes the interminability of analysis. Desire for the (absent) penis and its originary ambivalence, on the part of the female child, is castration, whose end is the Oedipus complex (desire for the penis) that imposes the interminability of analysis. The Oedipus complex is, for the boy, the suspension of romance between originary identification with the penis and terminal castration of the penis. The Oedipus complex is, for the girl, the end of romance, for it demonstrates to her her originary castration: that her desire for the penis is her eternal loss. As Freud observes in the passage cited above, the repudiation of femininity (and of masculinity), the castration complex, "prevents any change from taking place – everything stays as it was." Change – history – is inconceivable when originary identification with the father('s penis) is asserted, presupposed, and left completely inexplicable – except that it reflects the illusory beginning of Freud's metapsychology.

Freud, we recall, begins with the pleasure principle whose illusion is demonstrated by the fact that it cannot begin without presupposing its beginning in and as the reality principle. But this beginning in illusion is the primary principle that Freud never repudiates, just as his analysands, male and female, do not repudiate, he finds, the illusion of beginning with identification with the father's penis – its presence or absence – whose end is the repudiation of femininity, the castration of desire and the self. The fact that it is the pleasure principle that announces the reign of the death instinct prepares us for the termination of the Oedipus complex. The Oedipus complex is terminated in and through the repudiation of femininity, which, as the castration complex, inaugurates the rule of the superego whose imposition of the interminable sense of guilt on the (male) ego embodies the interiorization of aggression, the representative of the death instinct.

The Oedipus complex, whatever its phenomenological significance, is a metapsychological catastrophe, demonstrating the impenetrable bedrock of biology: the castration of desire, in the male, and the castration of self, in the female. What is so astounding is that the Oedipus complex bears no relationship to biology but is pure myth whose telos is given in the originary identification of the past. The castration complex eliminates libido – love, desire – in the name of the father('s penis). In the next section we shall see whether, in discussing love (libidinal relations), Freud will adhere to the metapsychological demands of the Oedipus complex, according to which desire, together with the self, is castrated. Or will love, as the dialectic of self and desire, reveal the limits of a metapsychology whose reality is the illusory return of the repressed pleasure principle?

III LOVE

Having seen in section II that the Oedipus complex, based upon identification with the penis, splits, by opposing, self and desire, we shall now see that Freud's metapsychological commitments constantly subvert his phenomenology of love. Just as Freud exposes the enormous hostility that is generated by the conflict between male identification with the penis and female identification with lack of the penis, so he also recognizes that any depth psychology worthy of the name must both explicate the extraordinary range of human phenomena traditionally associated with love and provide an account of love that is consistent with his metapsychology. What, however, is love? Can love survive identification with the pleasure principle, when Freud is driven to go beyond the pleasure principle to discover that, in the beginning, the pleasure principle, in associating all stimulus or tension with unpleasure, is the inherent urge in life to restore life to an earlier state of things, to nirvana, to death? We have seen that Freud, in acknowledging that tension, such as that embodied in the sexual act, is sought as pleasurable and not avoided as painful, completely subverts the very basis of his metapsychology. Still, he adopts the mythology of the two instincts – death and Eros – with the id (the unconscious) being dominated by the pleasure principle now unveiled as the death instinct. Can love survive the Oedipus complex if the lives of men and women are dominated by the castration complex? Men fear castration – by both women and men. Women despise their castration – by both men and women. Ultimately, as I showed in the previous section, it is the penis (not only the father, in being it, but also the mother, in desiring it) that is the utter contradiction of both men and women. To be yourself the penis is to expose your self to loss. To desire yourself the penis is to expose your desire as lack. The penis is both self and desire; but, in their eternal opposition to each other – in their dualism – they are inherently antagonistic to each other. Dualism, as always, is the blind mirror of monism.

What Freud does not see is that his metapsychology, instead of accounting for Oedipal phenomena, instead of reducing the unknown (phenomena) to the known (metapsychology), reflects (embodies) the very mythology that underlies the dualism between self and desire, their monistic identification with the penis. He does not see that psychology will fail to explain love, if love – as articulated by poets, mystics, philosophers ... human beings (both children and adults) in the infinite variety of their everyday experience – is not understood to be an equally valid "explanation" of psychology. What is so strange about Freud – revealing both his real insight and his irreal blindness – is that he constantly states, as we have seen, that the basis of his system, the instincts, remains completely unknown. Indeed, he acknowledges the instincts to be mythological. In reducing the unknown (phenomenology, which he brings to light so perceptively) to the known (scientific principle of metapsychology), what he, in fact, does is to reduce the known (what he sees) to the unknown (the myths of his metapsychology).

In discussing the role that love plays in both individual and social life, Freud addresses issues that are central to his presentation of the pleasure principle and the Oedipus complex. In the three "Contributions to the Psychology of Love," *Group Psychology and the Analysis of the Ego*, and the first four sections of *Civilization and its Discontents*, Freud shows how love is both sensual and affectionate (inhibited in its aim), both narcissistic and other-directed. He shows that love involves both sexual relations (the intimate relationship of two adults) and group relations. In group relations love involves both taking the leader as one's ideal and identifying with one's fellow group members. Love involves both the ego instincts (the self-love of narcissism) and the sexual instincts, both Eros and civilization, both identification with one's ideal (Christ) and the ideal of identification with one's fellow human beings (Christians). Love involves the individual in the complex relationships of both family and society. Love, Freud argues in the latter part of *Civilization and its Discontents*, as we shall see in the next section, plays a fundamental role in the generation of the superego, of conscience and the sense of guilt, of aggressivity and hostility, and of the death instinct.

Love, it appears, is at once individual and social, social and natural, sexual and anti-social, egoist and idealist, erotic and hostile. Does this lack of congruence in configuring the rich paradoxicality of love reflect Freud's adherence to the castration complex as the mechanism shaping human life? The castration complex, as we saw in section ii, is founded on pre-libidinal identification, not on a libidinal – sexual, object or loving – relationship. The castration complex, in leading boys to the adult identification of their self with the superego centred on the public life of civilization, renders them hostile not only to women (the family) but also to men in their social role (their desirelessness). The castration complex, in leading girls to the adult identification of their desire with the absence of a significant superego (self) centred on the private life of the family, renders them hostile not only to men (civilization) but also to women in their desire for a family (their selflessness). What, then, is the role of love in the relationships of men and women if the expression of love always involves castration, not only of males by females and of females by males but also of males by males and of females by females? Is it the castration complex that explains love as the mythical creation of the pleasure principle and the Oedipus complex? Or is it love, rather, that "explains" the castration complex as the mythical creation of the pleasure principle and the Oedipus complex? Does not Freud's division of the instincts between the ego instincts of self-preservation and the sexual instincts of species-preservation express the split in love between self and desire, between man and woman, and thus also within both men and women?[20] Is an act of love individual (anti-social) or social (anti-individual), sexual or aim-inhibited? Does love express the individual or the group, when the group leader, modelled on the primal father, is the ideal of the group members with whom they cannot identify, given that their identification is with their fellow group members? But is it not strange that Freud denies that identification is the tie binding group members (as horde animals) to their leader (as primal father), since he also holds that within the Oedipal family both boy and girl are defined by their identification with the father? Yet he also denies, as we shall see, that the Christian church constitutes a group, given that the relations between group members and leader (Christ) are the same as those between group members themselves. How can Eros, as the enemy of the death instinct, be the very basis of civilization, given that it is love that, while limiting narcissism, is, as sexuality (libido), anti-social and indeed repressed by civilization (the superego)?

In his open letter "Why War?", which he addressed to Einstein in 1932, Freud writes that we have to acknowledge that life begins in violence, that the violent aggressivity of human beings expresses the originary death instincts, that the death instincts arise from the original violence of the primal father, and that our lives are governed by two instincts, death and Eros. "It may perhaps seem to you," Freud tells Einstein, "as though our theories are a kind of mythology and, in the present case, not even an agreeable one. But does not every science come in the end to a kind of mythology like this? Cannot the same be said today of your own physics?" (358). He notes that Eros can be effectively opposed to the death instincts insofar as it supports the development of two kinds of emotional ties between human beings. The first tie is like a non-sexual relationship to a loved object. "There is no need for psychoanalysis to be ashamed to speak of love in this connection," he remarks, "for religion itself uses the same words: 'Thou shalt love thy neighbor as thyself'" (359).[21] The second tie involves identification of shared feelings. Notwithstanding the fact that civilization begins in violence and is dominated by the natural warfare between the death instincts of aggressivity and the life instincts of Eros – consistent with the Hate and Love of Empedocles, to which he refers, and with biology – at the end of his letter Freud declares that, as a pacifist, he opposes war. The basis of his opposition to war is his belief that the evolution of civilization involves organic changes in the human psyche. These organic changes, he explains, "consist in a progressive displacement of instinctual aims and a restriction of instinctual impulses ... Now war is the crassest opposition to the psychical attitude imposed on us by the process of civilization, and for that reason we are bound to rebel against it; we simply cannot any longer put up with it. This is not merely an intellectual and emotional repudiation; we pacifists have a *constitutional* intolerance of war" (361–2).

However noble we may find Freud's opposition to war, to the violent nature of human aggressivity, what is striking is that it is sentimental (illusory) and not principled. He provides no account of – because he has no principle by which to account for – how constitutional pacifism arises out of originary violence, how human beings organically (naturally) progress from violence to pacifism, from aggressivity to constitutionalism, from nature to civilization. He has no understanding of the fact that the greatness of Spinoza, Rousseau, and Kant as theorists rests precisely on their principled demonstration that the state of nature – in which big fish, arguing from violent fact to right, eat little fish – is the social condition that naturally prevails in the absence of the democratic values of equality, freedom, and solidarity. Freud asserts, but has no explanation of the fact, that biology undergoes evolutionary (organic, natural) change and produces an animal – *homo sapiens* – whose instinctual aims and impulses cannot be accounted for on the basis of its biological origins. He has no understanding of the fact that there is one thing that the theory of evolution cannot explain, which is itself. This is what I am calling in this study the ontological alternative to the violence of nature that is projected illusorily as the origin of civilization.

Utterly foreign to Freud – what he remains completely unconscious of – is the paradox that the theory of evolution is not itself subject to (is not the subject of) the theory of evolution. The theory *of* evolution is not the evolution *of* theory. The theory of evolution belongs itself to a more comprehensive theory of history (ontology), whose principle of change – whose principled change – is not evolutionary, organic, or natural. In lacking the concepts of self and desire, the theory of evolution lacks the self-referentiality of desire (will), the concept of desire as its own reference. Freud is right that all accounts of life, including science, are mythologies; but he has no way of accounting for the fact that some mythologies are principled – in recognizing the paradox that life cannot begin unconscious of beginning: it has always already begun unconsciously – while other mythologies are idols of nature in holding that the first principle of life is inorganic nature. It is also striking that, when he appeals to the role that Eros plays in forming social relations on the basis of the emotional ties of non-sexual object relations – comparable, he says, to the golden rule – and identification, Freud omits sexuality. But is it the case that the golden rule excludes sexuality? Further, is there is any real or significant difference between object relations and identification? What is the basis on which human beings identify their interests if it is not in terms of what they share, of what they love? Is *partage* not love? Is not *partage* (the sharing of division/the division of sharing) at once "being," when it is not reduced to ego instincts, and "having," when it is not reduced to sexual instincts? Freud knows that love, together with guilt, is the crux of human psychology as encountered by psychoanalysis. For all his insight into the phenomenology of love, however, we shall come to see that love has more to tell us about his metapsychology than his metapsychology has to tell us about love.

At the beginning of the first of his three "Contributions to the Psychology of Love," Freud explains that it is now time for science to take over the treatment of love from poetry. "Up till now," he writes, "we have left it to the creative writer to depict for us the 'necessary conditions for loving' which govern people's choice of an object, and the way in which they bring the demands of their imagination into harmony with reality." Literary authors have both unique strengths and unique limitations, he observes. While they are sensitive to the unconscious of others and have the courage to speak from their own unconscious, they are restricted by the intellectual, aesthetic, and emotional aims of art. Not only do writers distort reality, in the name of "poetic licence," but they also portray the mental states that interest them in their finished and not in their original or developing state. It thus becomes inevitable, Freud concludes, that the materials, whose artistic treatment has brought people enjoyment for thousands of years, will now have to submit to scientific treatment, even though the approach and the results of science will be less aesthetically pleasing than those of poetry. "These observations will, it may be hoped," he writes, "serve to justify us in extending a strictly scientific treatment to the field of human love. Science is, after all, the most complete renunciation of the pleasure principle of which our mental activity is capable" (231).[22]

What we shall find, however, is that Freud's strictly scientific treatment of love reflects the contradiction that, as noted previously, science repudiates the first principle of its metapsychology, the principle that all mental life is strictly governed by the pleasure principle. For science to repudiate the primacy of the pleasure principle is to repudiate itself. Love, it is patent, is not strictly governed by either the pleasure principle or the reality principle.

In the three "Contributions to the Psychology of Love" Freud examines some of the untoward consequences that occur as the result of the failure of individuals to bring together what he calls the sensual and the affectionate trends in their lives. He finds that the split between desire (sexuality) and love results in "psychical impotence," which, he remarks, is the most common disorder, in addition to the many forms of anxiety, to be encountered today in the analytic situation. On the one hand, men debase their sexual object so that they can possess it (sexually) without loving it. On the other hand, they idealize their beloved object so that they can love it (impotently) without possessing it. A major consequence of the split between sexual desire and love is the fear that men have of women.

The man [Freud writes] is afraid of being weakened by the woman, infected with her femininity [i.e., he fears being castrated] and of then showing himself incapable. The effect which coitus has of discharging tensions and causing flaccidity may be the prototype of what the man fears; and realization of the influence which the woman gains over him through sexual intercourse, the consideration she thereby forces from him, may justify the extension of this fear[23] ... Psychoanalysis believes that it has discovered a large part of what underlies the *narcissistic* rejection of women by men, which is so much mixed up with despising them, in drawing attention to *the castration complex* and its influence on the opinion in which women are held. (271-2[e])

It is hardly surprising, given the role that, as we now know, the castration complex plays in resolving the (male) Oedipus complex on behalf of narcissistic identification with the penis('s father), that it is men's narcissistic fear of castration, by women, that underlies the split between sexual desire and love. I am not here primarily concerned with the phenomenological content of the three "Contributions." Rather, I shall examine the problem that Freud encounters, in the second of the "Contributions," in trying to account for the relationship between the two trends in libidinal life, the sensual and the affectionate. Then I shall show how this problem is repeated in a number of contradictory forms in both *Group Psychology* and *Civilization and its Discontents*. The problem, from our perspective, is, as always, to determine whether the castration complex, founded on narcissistic identification with the penis, is the solution to the problem of love, or whether love – the dialectic of desire and the self – is the solution to the problem of castration whose repudiation of femininity results from originary, non-libidinal, narcissistic identification with the penis. Does the castration complex result in impaired love, the split between sexual desire and love? Or does impaired love result in the castration complex, the castration of both sexuality and love?

When he takes up his discussion of the affectionate and the sensual trends in human life, Freud holds that the affectionate trend precedes the sensual trend, springs from the ego instincts of self-preservation, is directed to a child's parents (caregivers), and carries with it from the beginning sexual elements that attach themselves to its valuations. As for the sensual trend, although it announces its directly sexual aims only at the time of puberty, it follows, nevertheless, the paths that were laid down (by its relationship to the ego instincts) in infantile life. The object of a (male) youth's sexual desire is both socially restricted and forbidden by the prohibition against incest that continues to operate in his unconscious. The result is psychical impotence. The youth desires only degraded sexual objects (those not worthy of his mother); and he loves only idealized objects (those worthy of his mother). Psychical impotence, whose ubiquity Freud emphasizes, thus results from the combination of two factors that prevent (male) individuals from obtaining their sexual object: frustration and the incest barrier. "The whole sphere of love in such people," Freud writes, "remains divided in the two directions personified in art as sacred and profane (or animal) love. Where they love they do not desire, and where they desire they cannot love. They seek objects which they do not need to love, in order to keep their sensuality away from the objects they love ... Psychical impotence makes its appearance whenever an object which has been chosen with the aim of avoiding incest recalls the prohibited object through some feature, often an inconspicuous one" (251).

Soon, however, Freud rejects this explanation of psychical impotence as explaining too much. Although it shows why some people suffer from psychical impotence, it fails to explain why others escape it, given that our civilization, he says, frustrates all its members in obtaining their sexual object and burdens all of them with the fear of incest. Freud's solution to this dilemma is to broaden his notion of psychical impotence to characterize the way in which civilization universally restricts the sexual behavior of nearly all civilized men and women. Most men undervalue their (despised) sexual objects and overvalue their loved (idealized) objects. Their counterpart is the vast number of sexually frigid women who resent the debasement of sexual fulfilment and the idealization of respectful love. Only the few individuals who are educated, Freud holds, are able to unify the affectionate and the sensual trends in their lives. But he is still not persuaded by his argument that "the factors of intense incestuous fixation in childhood and the frustration by reality in adolescence" properly account for the universality of the psychical impotence with which modern men and women are afflicted (254).

Freud decides to try another tack altogether. He turns his attention from the inhibited objects of love to the (sexual) instincts themselves, to libido. What this shift in perspective immediately reveals to Freud, however, is the fact that unrestricted (unrepressed) libido has no advantage over restricted libido. Satisfaction of libido does not appear to be possible without inhibition of libido.

It can easily be shown [Freud observes] that the psychical value of erotic needs is reduced as soon as their satisfaction becomes easy. An obstacle is required in order to heighten libido; and where natural resistances to satisfaction have not been sufficient men have at all times erected conventional ones so as to be able to enjoy love ... In times in which there were no difficulties standing in the way of sexual satisfaction, such as perhaps during the decline of the ancient civilizations, love became worthless and life empty ... In this connection it may be claimed that *the ascetic current in Christianity created psychical values for love which pagan antiquity was never able to confer on it.* (256–7^e)[24]

Freud then proceeds to show that there is no direct (or quantitative) relationship between instinctual satisfaction and psychical value. Satisfaction of instinct does not necessarily result in the reduction of psychical value (as adherence to the pleasure principle would dictate). An alcoholic, for example, is like the connoisseur of poetry or love: the more he drinks the more happily he is wedded to his drink. "Why is the relation of the lover to his sexual object so very different?" Freud asks. "We must reckon with the possibility that something in the nature of the sexual instinct itself is unfavorable to the realization of complete satisfaction" (258). He proposes two reasons to explain why the lack of instinctual satisfaction is to be found in the nature of instinct itself – what we saw him call "organic" renunciation in "Why War?" – and not merely in civilization's restriction of sexual objects due to frustration and the incest-barrier. First, the final object of the sexual instinct is never original but only a substitute, given that the original sexual object, as an object of incest, is repressed. Second, various components of the sexual instinct later prove to be incompatible with each other and are suppressed or put to a different use.

Still, Freud does not long remain happy with the idea that the sexual instincts are in themselves self-inhibiting (or contradictory). He slides back into the position that, because the sexual instincts remain unyielding in their demands for satisfaction and are hard to educate, it may well be that their demands cannot be adjusted to the demands of instinctual renunciation that are imposed by civilization. But then he adds, in a statement grandly confounding the issue of whether the conflict central to libidinal life arises from the instincts themselves or from their repression by civilization, that "the non-satisfaction that goes with civilization is the necessary consequence of certain peculiarities which the sexual instinct has assumed under the pressure of culture" (259). This statement, however, is a *petitio principii*. While civilization is said to owe its non-satisfaction to the sexual instincts, the sexual instincts are said to owe their non-satisfaction to civilization. It is also inconsistent both with Freud's prior remark that there is "something in the nature of the sexual instinct itself [that] is unfavorable to the realization of complete satisfaction" and with his subsequent remark that civilization, given that it is built on the sublimation of instinct, would not exist if the sexual instincts could be fully satisfied.

For what motive would men have for putting sexual instinctual forces to other uses [Freud asks in the penultimate paragraph of the second "Contribution"] if, by any distribution of those forces, they could obtain fully satisfying pleasure? They would never abandon that pleasure and they would never make any further progress. It seems, therefore, that the irreconcilable difference between the demands of the two instincts – the sexual and the egoistic – has made men capable of ever higher achievements, though subject, it is true, to a constant danger, to which, in the form of neurosis, the weaker are succumbing today. (259–60)

The conflict of ideas that we find in the second "Contribution to the Psychology of Love" is one whose terms Freud will continue to transform but whose structure, simultaneously monistic and dualistic, he will never relinquish. He typically veers between locating the non-satisfaction of sexual instinct in the repressive trends of civilization and in the very nature of the instinct itself. He thus arrives back at his beginning with "the irreconcilable difference" between the sexual instincts and the ego instincts. But the fact that Freud does not accept his own initial explanation of the "psychical impotence" characterizing modern civilization is already anticipated in his conception of the two libidinal trends, affectionate and sensual. He tells us that the affectionate trend is older than and prior to the sensual trend in that it is attached to the (narcissistic) ego (self-preservative) instincts. Do we not begin to suspect, therefore, the reason that Freud tergiversates between viewing civilization as the source of sexual inhibition and the sexual instincts themselves as organically inhibited? Is it not because the conflict both between civilization and sexuality and within the sexual instincts themselves expresses not only the "irreconcilable" dualism between ego instincts and sexual instincts but yet, more fundamentally, the priority of the ego instincts (narcissism) over the sexual instincts? It will not be long before Freud further entrenches this position in the castration complex, the heir of the narcissistic identification on the part of both men and women with the penis – its presence or absence.

The problem that Freud faces in his second "Contribution to the Psychology of Love" is that the psychical impotence that he finds to be characteristic of our civilization cannot be explained on the basis of frustration or repression. They explain too much. He is then compelled to consider the possibility that, if it is not the inaccessibility of the sexual object, owing either to frustration (social inhibition) or repression (the incest barrier), which explains psychical impotence, then the explanation must lie in the sexual instincts (libido) themselves. He broaches the paradox that libido must be inhibited (frustrated,

repressed) in order to be satisfied (satisfying). For how would civilization ever have developed had the sexual instincts been able to obtain
fully satisfying pleasure on their own? Not only does libido need an
obstacle to be meaningful, but the satisfaction of the uninhibited sexual instincts results in no (permanent, real, or civilized) satisfaction at
all. Freud even suggests that Christian asceticism creates the psychical
values for love that are absent from pagan antiquity. The notion that
instinct is its own source of organic repression suggests, he points out,
that there is no direct relationship between instinctual satisfaction and
psychical value. Psychical value does not necessarily decrease, it turns
out, with either the inhibition or the attainment of instinctual satisfaction. Indeed, not only does inhibition of satisfaction increase psychical
pleasure but the pleasures of alcohol, poetry, and sex – all of life, one
assumes! – are not diminished but rather sustained or even increased
by their satisfaction. Freud is not ready, however, to relinquish the idea
that the renunciation of instinct that is demanded by civilization is not
compatible with sexual satisfaction; yet he points out, in conclusion,
that human beings would not fail to find complete satisfaction in the
instincts if they were capable of being satisfied. But the sexual instincts
are not capable of uninhibited satisfaction.

What Freud never acknowledges, as his argument veers back and
forth between the sexual instincts inhibited by civilization and the sexual instincts inhibited by their own organic nature, is the fact that the
very idea of uninhibited sexual instincts is contradictory. Indeed, the
idea of uninhibited sexual instincts shows that the fundamental principle of his metapsychology, the pleasure-unpleasure principle, is utterly
contradictory. Instead, Freud falls back on the dualism between the ego
instincts and the sexual instincts as a means of blocking the obvious
path that his phenomenological thinking is taking. Freud refuses to see
that the sexual instincts of human beings cannot be understood on the
biological (animal) model of satisfaction (need). Sexuality does not
obey the pleasure principle, the urge to eliminate the tension, the pain,
the experience, the content of life. The pleasure principle – the principle that the fundamental urge of humans beings is to reduce pain (life)
to pleasure (death) – is illusory. Indeed, it will not be long before Freud
goes beyond the pleasure principle to embrace the painful illusion that
to seek pleasure is to reduce libido to the death instinct.

Although Freud will continue to deepen his investigations into love
in *Group Psychology and the Analysis of the Ego* and in *Civilization
and its Discontents*, we shall see that he will not be able to overcome
the impasse at which he arrives in the second "Contribution to the Psychology of Love." The "irreconcilable difference" between the sexual
instincts and the ego instincts, in reflecting his metapsychological com-

mitment to the pleasure principle, makes it impossible for him to provide a coherent analysis of the relationships between sexual instinct
(libido), ego, Eros, love, the pleasure principle, individual happiness,
society, communal values, civilization, reality, and, ultimately, the
death instinct, the superego, and guilt (the last three of which we shall
take up in section iv). The fundamental problem that Freud faces
always remains that of explaining how libidinal impulses inhibited in
their aim can emerge from uninhibited sexual libido, when sexual
libido is said to arise consequent to and later than the ego instinct. The
problem of how the multiple relationships of individual and community are to be understood on the basis of the irreconcilable difference
between ego (individual) and sexuality (species) also becomes acute. Is
civilization (society) the product of the ego and not the sexual
instincts? The new instinct theory of Eros and death will also generate
new problems. How will Freud undertake to deal with the relations
between sexuality, love, civilization, and guilt (death)? We have seen
Freud suggest that sexuality without inhibition (civilization, Christianity?) is not love. Does this also suggest that sexuality without guilt is
not love?

In the first four (of the eight) sections of *Civilization and its Discontents*, Freud explores how civilization, in which love is central, is
itself the barrier to human satisfaction, to human happiness, to the
fulfilment of the pleasure principle. But it becomes clear that, as in
the second "Contribution to the Psychology of Love," Freud does
not remain satisfied with a facile opposition between love (sexuality) and civilization and ponders if there is not something in the very
nature of the instincts themselves that inhibits human happiness.
This is the hypothesis that he explores in terms of the sense of guilt
(the death instinct) in the second half of *Civilization and its Discontents* and that we shall examine in the next section only after having
first taken up his discussion, in *Group Psychology and the Analysis
of the Ego*, of the libidinal ties that bind the individual ego to the
group. In both works Freud is clearly deeply perplexed by how
libido, in order to be satisfied (satisfying), demands inhibition (frustration, unpleasure, repression, suffering, renunciation), while it is
inhibited libido that involves human beings in suffering (repression).
It is clear that Freud understands that completely satisfied (completely uninhibited) libido is a contradiction (it contradicts existence). But it is not clear that he can formulate, in adequate (ontological) terms, the paradox that love can overcome its contradictions
only by imposing paradoxical limits on itself. His insight into the
paradox of love is, we shall find, severely compromised by his contradictory metapsychology.

When, in *Civilization and its Discontents*, Freud broaches the issue of the nature of human happiness, he begins by noting that "the question of the purpose of human life has been raised countless times; it has never yet received a satisfactory answer and perhaps does not admit of one" (262). Indeed, "only *religion* can answer the question of the purpose of life. One can hardly be wrong in concluding that the idea of life having a purpose stands and falls with the religious system." His own aim, he says, will be less exalted. He will consider only what human beings reveal in their behaviour "to be the *purpose* and intention of their lives ... The answer to this can hardly be in doubt. They strive after happiness; they want to become happy and to remain so" (263ᵉ).

Before going on to see that Freud himself will show that happiness, as based on the pleasure principle, cannot be realized, it is instructive, first, to reflect upon the claims that Freud makes in leading up to it. What are we to think of Freud's observation that in their behaviour human beings reveal the purpose and intention of their lives to be the pursuit and attainment of happiness or pleasure, when the strong texts of art, literature, philosophy, and religion have always rejected so simplistic a claim? Freud adores (and writes on) Shakespeare and Dostoevsky and frequently cites Goethe and Heine. Where do these writers ever suggest that human beings see their aim in life to be happiness as the attainment of pleasure (satisfaction)? Freud writes brilliant essays on major works of art created by both Leonardo and Michelangelo, each of which is religious in subject and neither of which gives the remotest suggestion that happiness is pleasure (satisfaction). Freud frequently refers to Kant, Schopenhauer, and Nietzsche, each of whom reveals the utter hollowness of the notion that painless happiness is the purpose of human life. With regard to actual human behaviour – hardly a more tractable medium, given that all human action is mediated, in the beginning – it is clear that Freud does not learn from Dora, Little Hans, Dr Schreber, Rat Man, or Wolf Man that human beings strive after happiness as painless satisfaction. In what would a satisfactory, if painful, answer to the question of the purpose of human life consist? Surely, love – and freedom, and justice – in solidarity with suffering. What is religion (together with literature, art, philosophy, and depth psychology) if it is not the revelation, in and through human "behavior," that love, freedom, justice, and solidarity with the suffering of others are "the purpose of human life"?

Freud, however, remains oblivious to all that he has learned from human beings, in both their fiction and their reality, about love and its vicissitudes. Thus he merely states that "what decides the purpose of

life is simply the program of the pleasure principle. This principle dominates the operation of the mental apparatus from the start." He immediately goes on to say, however, that the pleasure principle, notwithstanding its efficacy, is absolutely opposed by the universe, both
microcosm and macrocosm. "There is no possibility at all of its being
carried through," he declares. "All the regulations of the universe run
counter to it. One feels inclined to say that the intention that man
should be 'happy' is not included in the plan of 'Creation.'"[25] Because
happiness results from the sudden satisfaction of dammed-up needs
and is thus episodic – that is to say, to obtain pleasure is to lose it, as
we observed earlier about the erect penis and that we have now seen
Freud himself say about coitus – "our possibilities of happiness are
already restricted by our constitution" (263–4).

Freud then proceeds to point out that we are vulnerable to three
sources of suffering: our body; the external world; and, above all, our
relations to others. "The suffering which comes from this last
source," he remarks, "is perhaps more painful to us than any other"
(264).[26] This seems surprising, Freud indicates, when we think that
sexual love "has given us our most intense experience of an overwhelming sensation of pleasure and has thus furnished us with a pattern for our search for happiness." Still, "we are never so defenseless
against suffering as when we love, never so helplessly unhappy as
when we have lost our loved object or its love" (270).[27] Only a few
people, Freud observes, are so constituted that they can find happiness in love and only then because "far-reaching mental changes in
the function of love are necessary before this can happen." It is only
when sexual instinct is transformed into an instinct with an inhibited
aim that lovers can become independent of the object loved. They
substitute loving for being loved. They universalize their love to
include all human beings. It was, perhaps, St. Francis, Freud suggests,
who "went furthest in thus exploiting love for the benefit of an inner
feeling of happiness" (291).[28]

Freud recalls that the sexual love that founds the family operates in
civilization both in its original, uninhibited form and in its modified,
inhibited form. "The careless way in which language uses the word
'love' has its genetic justification," he points out (292). Love refers to
relations that are both sexual (say, between man and woman) and
inhibited (say, between parents and children and between friends).
Love with an inhibited aim is originally uninhibited (sensual). But,
once love becomes inhibited, then opposition between sexuality and
civilization, that is, between uninhibited and inhibited love, arises.
This is evident in the conflict between the family and society (civilization); for the task of every individual is to leave the family and to

become a member of society (and, generally, the founder of another family).[29]

We get the impression [Freud writes] that these are difficulties which are inherent in all psychical – and, indeed, at bottom, in all *organic* – development. Furthermore, women soon come into opposition to civilization ... – those very women who, in the beginning, laid the foundations of civilization by the claims of their love. Women represent the interests of the family and of sexual life. The work of civilization has become increasingly the business of men, it confronts them with ever more difficult tasks and compels them to carry out instinctual sublimations of which women are little capable ... [Men, in devoting their *psychical energy*, which is limited in quantity, to cultural aims, withdraw it from women and sexual life. Women, in turn, become hostile to civilization. The social rules limiting love to monogamous legitimacy and to reproduction are highly restrictive yet are constantly breached.] The sexual life of civilized man is notwithstanding severely impaired; it sometimes gives the impression of being in process of involution as *a function*, just as our teeth and hair seem to be as organs. One is probably justified in assuming that its importance as a source of feelings of happiness, and therefore in the fulfillment of our aim in life, has sensibly diminished. Sometimes one seems to perceive that it is not only the pressure of civilization but something in *the nature of the function itself* which denies us full satisfaction and urges us along other paths. This may be wrong; it is hard to decide. (293-5ᵉ)

I have cited at length the key passages concluding the first half of *Civilization and its Discontents*, for here Freud testifies eloquently to his inability to conceptualize the problem of love in coherent terms. We have already seen him note that the fulfilment of the primordial pleasure principle is opposed in the beginning by the universe itself, by "Creation"; that happiness is restricted by our constitution; that (the sexual) love of others not only provides us with our pattern of happiness but is also our greatest source of suffering; and, finally, that, in order for love to be realized as a source of happiness, its original, foundational sexual aim must be secondarily and subsequently inhibited (universalized). Freud presupposes that it is the distinction between uninhibited (sexual) love and inhibited (social) love that becomes the opposition between sexuality and civilization. But the ontological incoherence of this dualism – whatever its phenomenological reality – is evident from the fact that Freud never explains (and is unable to explain) how or why sexuality gives rise (way) to aim-inhibited love. Surely, the family is the source of civilization, yet central to the family are both sexual love (as originary) and aim-inhibited love (as secondary). It is clear, however, that the first, uninhibited love does not precede the second, inhibited love but rather depends on it, which is what we saw Freud claim in the second "Contribution to the Psychology of Love." Indeed, he says, as we saw, that sexual love, in itself, suddenly becomes depleted (flaccid) and episodic, reminiscent of the conscious fantasy that Rousseau presents in the *Second Discourse* on natural savages, who, with their solitary life and episodic copulation, could never have existed. Thus, in the passage cited above, Freud is forced to consider, once again, that the inhibition in sexuality is not due to subsequent civilization – of which sexuality is the foundation! – but is "organic," that is, inherent in its very "function" or aim. The fact that sexuality as love must be inhibited in the beginning is also reflected in the incoherence with which Freud writes about the family. In the passage we are considering Freud indicates that the family is originally founded on sexual love and then, in generating aim-inhibited love, produces civilization. Not only, however, does he suggest in the second "Contribution to the Psychology of Love," as we saw, that Christianity gives to love the psychical values that it lacks in pagan antiquity, but he is also generally under no illusion about the inhibitions in primitive, as distinct from modern ("civilized"), society.[30] Thus, when he says that sexuality founds the family and gives birth to aim-inhibited love and that aim-inhibited love spreads beyond the family to found social relations (civilization), he is unable to show how the individual is the creation of both the family and society (civilization). There is clearly no "natural" family that precedes civilization.

Although Freud finds himself forced to acknowledge that "inhibition" is inherent within sexual instincts from the beginning and is not a subsequent, opposite product of civilization, he continues to hold that uninhibited sexuality is original. This makes it impossible for him to comprehend either how sexuality generates love as aim-inhibited or how sexuality can come into opposition with its own creation (civilization). It never dawns on Freud that sexuality no more creates civilization (or the family) than civilization (or the family) creates sexuality. Sexuality is no more originary than is civilization (or the family). Love is both sexuality and civilization (or the family); and each of the other two is equally the other two! This is both our blessing and our curse. Love is the paradoxical demand (command) that we choose both sexuality and civilization. To choose one in opposition to the other is to lose all three. We shall see that even Freudian Eros, in being unable to comprehend the sexual instincts, finds itself vulnerable to collapsing into the death instinct to which, supposedly, it is inalterably opposed as the life instinct.

Love is also, perhaps surprisingly, the central topic of *Group Psy-*

chology and the Analysis of the Ego. In arguing that earlier students of group psychology have failed to see that groups are held together by libidinal ties, Freud is then committed to analyzing the nature of the ties binding group members both to their leader and to each other. It is a work at once richly suggestive and highly perplexing. It is suggestive, for Freud calls upon a wide range of ideas central to his metapsychology to think through the dynamics of group psychology: the Oedipus complex, identification, the primal horde, narcissism, libido, aim-inhibited love, the superego (called here, in 1921, the ego ideal). The work is perplexing for two different yet closely related reasons. First, Freud is faced here, as in his earlier "Contributions to the Psychology of Love" and in the later *Civilization and its Discontents*, with the difficulty of explaining how the sexual instincts give rise (way) to affectionate or aim-inhibited love. Second, Freud is never really clear as to what he understands by a "group." He analyzes, briefly, two "artificial" groups, the (Roman Catholic) church and the army. On the one hand, he shows that the libidinal ties to be found in these groups bind members to their leader and to each other in a completely different fashion and that the church, whose head is Christ, is not even a group, although it is democratic. On the other hand, he never indicates how a group (or a non-group) relates to the two primal "groups" of civilization, the family and society – except that he claims to show, on the basis of the myth of the primal horde, that "man" is a horde, not a herd, animal. The members of the horde, while equal to one another, aspire to be ruled by one chief who is not their equal but their superior.

This conclusion is absolutely fantastic (mythological) for two reasons. First, whereas, in the Oedipus complex, as we have seen, identification is the primal (non-libidinal) relation binding children to their parents, in group psychology identification binds group members to each other but not to their primal leader. If, however, we assume, as Freud appears to assume, that the army stands for the primal group, how can the primal group (society) be founded on a relationship different from or opposed to that of the family? Second, in that democratic group that is not a group but a church, identification is the relationship not only between members but equally between members and chief (Christ). The "church" patently embodies the golden rule. What is truly extraordinary, then, is that Freud presents two startlingly different conceptions of the "group"! On the one hand, his founding myth of the primal father results in an authoritarian model of the group, which, exemplified by the army, is ultimately indistinguishable from authoritarianism (fascism). On the other hand, Freud shows that it is the group, whose libidinal relationships are found not in the group but in the church, which provides the model of democracy, of equality, freedom, and solidarity, within both family and society (civilization). Neither the family nor society appears to be modelled on the group, the putative subject of *Group Psychology*. In our examination of the work we shall take up broadly the following topics *seriatim*: how libido covers the popular meaning of love; the nature of aim-inhibited love; love's creation of civilization by the elimination of narcissism; and the role of identification in group psychology.

Freud observes that psychoanalysis comprehends by libido the quantitative ("though not at present actually measurable"!) energy of the instincts that involves what is usually understood by the word "love" – from sexual love to the love of children, friends, humanity, and universal ideals, from Platonic Eros to Pauline *agape*. The fact that psychoanalysis has thus "let loose a storm of indignation, as though it had been guilty of an act of outrageous innovation ... only shows," he observes, "that men do not always take their great thinkers seriously, even when they profess most to admire them" (119–20).[31] But we can well wonder how seriously Freud himself takes either Plato or Paul, the two "great thinkers" whom he names. It is by no means obvious that Platonic Eros has anything to do with sexual *love* or that Pauline *caritas* has to do with anything else – when each, subjected to a no-holds barred analysis, is stripped bare of the *unendliche* distortions to which they have been subjected by generations of Jewish and Christian readers and their secular heirs. We have seen Freud appeal, in *Beyond the Pleasure Principle*, to the Platonic conception of Eros (and to the equivalent conception in the Upanishads and, elsewhere, in Empedocles). Eros, as lack of the object desired, is punishment (in Aristophanes' myth) for attempting to unite with its object (and thus to topple the gods). Eros, like the death instinct, is the inherent tendency to restore an earlier state of things, eliminating all desire, stimulus, tension (unpleasure). Is Eros the love to be found in groups where non-sexual identification regulates the relations of members, whose chief is their (sexual) superior, their ideal? As for Paul, we have already seen Freud suggest (although he does not pursue the idea) that it is Christianity, not pagan antiquity, that creates the psychical values of love (including sexuality). Furthermore, we shall see Freud indicate that the church is not a group but a democratic body whose psychical spirit is loving equality (the equality of love).

Freud holds that the libido theory, like "love" commonly understood, distinguishes between sexual love (object cathexis) and instincts inhibited in their aim, between, say, the sexuality resulting in children and the resultant love between parents and children. But this distinction, as we have already seen, is shaky, and Freud himself points out that "the libidinal situation rarely remains so simple" (141). Indeed, Freud then makes the surprising admission that the reason that the "sexual impulsions that are inhibited in their aims ... achieve such lasting ties between people" is due to "the fact that they are not capable of complete satisfaction, while sexual impulsions which are uninhibited in their aims suffer an extraordinary reduction through the discharge of energy every time the sexual aim is attained. It is the fate of sensual love to become extinguished when it is satisfied; for it to be able to last, it must *from the beginning* be mixed with purely affectionate components – with such, that is, as are inhibited in their aims – or it must itself undergo a transformation of this kind" (146ᵉ).

Purely (uninhibited) sexual instincts, in other words, do not exist. If they did exist, as Greek (or Hindu) Eros, their existence would be marked by desire, by, that is, lack of unity with the one (self or object). Eros, in blindly obeying the fatal law of contradiction, according to which all appearances (lacking the one) are contradictory, is eternally punished for lacking (desiring) the one. Freud has again broached the paradox of the libido. If libido (desire) is satisfied, then it will utterly lack satisfaction as it vanishes, following the contradictory pleasure principle, into the priority of Nirvana for which all things are one and not appearance. If libido (desire) is not satisfied, then it will be able to be made satisfying (lasting) and to escape the fatal embrace of the pleasure principle that reduces everything back to the deathless one. From the beginning – *in the beginning* – the sexual instinct treats its object (the other) with affection, with respect, with love – either because it is originally mixed with "purely affectionate components" or because "it *must* undergo a transformation of this kind." What is simply astounding is the fact that Freud has to contend so mightily with the metapsychological monsters hidden in the night of his soul in order to attain to the commonplace (if profound) understanding of love as at once sexual and "inhibited" (treating others with respect, dignity, caring). But when he wakes, it is not obvious that he views his wound as libidinal, at once sexual and loving, for he remains caught within the contradictory coils of his metapsychology.

In section XII, the conclusion of *Group Psychology*, entitled Postscript but where Freud undertakes to summarize in succinct terms central points of his earlier, quite disparate discussion, he returns to the issue of the relation between the sexual instincts, uninhibited and inhibited. He states that "the *development of the libido* in children has made us acquainted with the first but also the best example of sexual instincts which are inhibited in their aims" (171ᵉ). But "development" is always Freud's Waterloo; for, when "anatomy is destiny," then castration (the defeat destined by identification with the imperious penis) is always the result. What is the nature of this libidinal, infantile development when, in the beginning, the purely (uninhibited) sexual instincts are inhibited (either mixed with the sexual impulses inhibited in their aim or transformed into them)? Freud outlines (actually, he fudges in highly discreet terms) the child's libidinal development in three distinct stages (as I shall call them). But how the child begins in stage 1 and how it then makes the transition to stages 2 and 3 – stage 3 is that of the inhibited sexual instincts – is, as always, a complete mystery (mystification). Freud asserts that the (original) feelings that a child has for its parents and/or caregivers (stage 1) "pass by an easy transition" into sexual feelings, mixed with hostility, for the parents (stage 2). When these Oedipal feelings subsequently undergo (normal) repression, what remains (in stage 3), Freud declares, is "a purely affectionate emotional tie, relating to the same people, but no longer to be described as 'sexual' ... Wherever we come across an affectionate feeling it is successor to a completely 'sensual' object tie with the person in question or rather with that person's prototype (or *imago*)" (171).[32]

In placing the Oedipus complex (stage 2) between pre-Oedipal identification with the parents (stage 1) and post-Oedipal repression due to the castration complex (stage 3), Freud has, in fact, no place for sexuality at all, as we showed when we discussed the Oedipus complex in section II. It is the pre-sexual (pre-libidinal) identification with the parents that survives. In other words, identification is the "successor" or heir to the "sensual object-tie" or, rather, Freud adds, to the parent's prototype or imago, that is, to the penis. Freud is very careful to say that the affectionate tie remaining after castration (the castrated affection) succeeds (comes after), but is not the product of, the earlier sexual (object) relation. Not only does Freud have no explanation of why non-libidinal identification is first or prior (except that identification mirrors what he considers to be the originary autoerotism or narcissism preceding object relations), but this identification in fact prevents any real (let alone an "easy") transition to Oedipal sexuality and hostility. The result in stage 3, in issuing from the castration complex, merely reimposes the original identification that both male and female children have with the penis (its presence or absence). In the beginning (it turns out) the boy, in fearing castration, gives up libido as he reaffirms his identification with the penis; and the girl, already castrated, desires the penis (for, in fact, as Freud later says, as we have seen, the girl's original castration confirms her in her Oedipus complex, making the final transition to the superego superfluous).

The result, in the present context, is that Freud has no explanation of aim-inhibited sexuality. He claims that aim-inhibited sexuality arises from uninhibited (original) sexuality; but, because sexuality succumbs to the castration complex, whose origin is pre-libidinal identification (with the father's penis), he actually has no explanation of sexual libido.

The solution to Freud's impasse is clear. If you do not begin with love – as the desire of self and the self of desire – love will never "develop." If love is not "in the beginning," your castrated end will reflect your beginning with the castrated penis whose (male) self is without desire (satisfaction) and whose (female) desire is without a self (satisfaction). If, in the beginning, there is not love that is at once sexual and affectionate, then neither sexual love nor inhibited love will ever emerge.

Freud, however, continues to adhere to both positions – that sexual instinct is originary (the source of aim-inhibited love) and that sexual instinct is not originally satisfying, precisely because, in aiming at satisfaction, it ends in extinguishing itself (it turns into the death instinct). He restates his claim that the aim-inhibited or affectionate ties have been "diverted" from the sexual aims, but he also acknowledges that "*there is some difficulty in giving a description of such a diversion of aim which will conform to the requirements of metapsychology*" (172^{e}).[33] The reason that the diversion of aim-inhibited love, its derivation from originary sexual instinct, runs into metapsychological difficulties is due to the fact that, as Freud repeats here, recalling the earlier passage that we examined, "those sexual instincts which are inhibited in their aims have a great functional advantage over those which are uninhibited. Since *they are not capable of really complete satisfaction*, they are especially adapted to create permanent ties; while those instincts which are directly sexual incur a loss of energy each time they are satisfied, and must wait to be renewed by a fresh accumulation of sexual libido, so that meanwhile *the object may have been changed*" (172–3^{e}).

Thus Freud continues to adhere to his contradictory metapsychology. If desire is satisfied, then it will not be satisfied. If desire is not satisfied, then it will be satisfied. His blatantly contradictory conception of desire, reflecting male and female identification with the castrated penis, is embodied in yet another set of terms whose dualism is equally contradictory, that between self-love (narcissism) and love of others. This dualism is itself, however, but a reflection of the original opposition between ego instincts and sexual instincts. Freud is forced by his metapsychology into having to explain how aim-inhibited sexual instincts derive from uninhibited sexual instincts, yet it is the limit (inhibition) imposed by the latter that resolves the contradiction (castration) of the former. The same pattern emerges when he has to explain how group ties can emerge from the original condition of narcissism (autoerotism).[34] Narcissism, he declares, can be limited only "by one factor, a libidinal tie with other people. Love for oneself knows only one barrier – love for others, love for objects ... In the development of mankind as a whole, just as in individuals, love alone acts as the civilizing factor in the sense that it brings a change from egoism to altruism."[35] Since group ties must obviously be sought outside narcissistic self-love but since these ties cannot involve directly sexual aims, "we are concerned here," Freud writes, "with love instincts which have been diverted from their original aims, though they do not operate with less energy on that account" (132–3). This, he observes, means that he must take up the emotional ties involving identification, to which he then devotes chapter 7.

We have already seen, and we shall momentarily take up again, the metapsychological impasse – the castration complex – to which Freud is led by his distinction between identification, sexual instincts, and aim-inhibited instincts. But we must first note that there are at least three reasons why his distinction between egoism and altruism reflects an equally suspect metapsychology. First, in the introductory chapter of *Group Psychology* Freud points out, correctly, that (in terms of phenomenology) individual psychology and group psychology are intimately related. All individuals are group (family, social) members, and all group members are individuals. Indeed, he observes that the distinction between mental acts as narcissistic (in the sense of autistic satisfaction of instincts withdrawn from the influence of other people) and mental acts as social "falls wholly within the domain of individual psychology, and is not well calculated to differentiate it from a social or group psychology" (96). Thus, when Freud argues that "love alone" constitutes the civilizing change from egoism to altruism, not only does "love" include "self-love" (the individual), but the distinction between egoism and altruism characterizes the difference not between individual and society (group) but between, on the one hand, individual or group as egoist (narcissistic, autistic) and, on the other hand, individual or group as altruistic. There is no transition from narcissism (individual) to the group (society), or vice-versa. It is equally not clear how love is civilizing when, although it limits narcissism, it also limits (inhibits) sexuality.

The second and third reasons for the inadequacy of the dualism between egoism (ego, individual) and altruism (group, species) can be succinctly stated. On the one hand, how can love limit narcissism, when, according to Freud's theory of narcissism, ego libido (narcissism) is the source of object libido? On the other hand, the distinction between egoism (narcissism, the individual) and altruism (society, the other) is hardly consistent with the distinction between sexual instincts and aim-inhibited instincts. Since Freud insists that group ties cannot be based on sexual instincts (thereby excluding both the family and society from group psychology), he is forced, in connecting aim-inhibited instincts with altruism, to identify egoism (narcissism) with the sexual instincts. In thus subverting the primary dualism between ego instincts and sexual instincts – although their identity is consistent with the originary narcissism of the primal father's sexual monopoly – he arrives, once again, at a metapsychological impasse. It is true that, when Freud formulates his theory of the death and life instincts, both ego instincts and sexual instincts appear to belong to Eros. But he also points out that sexual love is not social, leaving ego (narcissism) as the source of civilization, which is precisely the position that he opposes in *Group Psychology* in the name of love (libido)! Freud constantly struggles with the incongruities of his metapsychology, but he never sees that it is his metapsychology that is their source, not their solution.[36]

Given the difficulties that Freud has in working out a consistent conception of love in terms of both aim-inhibited instincts and narcissism, it is not obvious that he will have any more success in viewing group libidinal relations in terms of identification. Actually, his conclusion that members of a group replace their ego ideal with the same object (the leader) and identify with one another in their ego remains pretty obscure in formulation until he assimilates the group to his concept of the primal horde.[37] This concept allows Freud to describe the group in concrete terms: "many equals, who can identify themselves with one another, and a single person superior to them all – that is the situation that we find realized in groups which are capable of subsisting." "Man" is thus "a horde animal, an individual creature in a horde led by a chief" (153). In the Postscript Freud notes that the primal father, in his sexual monopoly, "compelled all his sons to be abstinent, and thus forced them into ties that were inhibited in their aims, while he reserved for himself freedom of sexual enjoyment and in this way remained without ties. All the ties upon which a group depends are of the character of instincts that are inhibited in their aims" (173). What is so extraordinary about Freud's assimilation of group psychology to his theory of the primal horde (whose treatment in *Totem and Taboo* and *Moses and Monotheism* we shall take up in chapters 4 and 5) is that it rests upon notions of identification and aim-inhibited instincts that are utterly inconsistent with those that he had already presented in *Group Psychology* (and equally inconsistent with those that we examined in section II). In the Oedipus complex identification is the pre-libidinal tie attaching the boy to his father. The father('s penis) is his ideal self: it is what he would like to *be*. Equally, identification is the pre-libidinal tie attaching the girl to her mother. In desiring the father('s penis), she lacks an ideal self: it is what she would like to *have*.[38]

In group psychology, however, identification describes the aim-inhibited ties that the primal sons and thus group members have with each other, while the (primal) chief is superior to and not bound by such ties. Thus, while identification, in the Oedipal model, precedes both sexual libido and the third stage of aim-inhibited or affectionate trends, as we saw, identification in group psychology derives from the sexual mastery of the leader. But this means that Freud also has two different and ultimately opposed accounts of aim-inhibited instincts. In both the Oedipal and the group psychological accounts, aim-inhibited instincts are said to derive from the sexual instincts. (However, to repeat, in the Oedipal account identification with the father is said to lead to the sexual instincts; and, in the group psychological account, identification, as corresponding to the aim-inhibited instincts, is said to derive from the sexual instincts as centred in the primal father.)

But we have also seen that Freud is forced to acknowledge that aim-inhibited instincts are successful because they are not satisfied, while the sexual instincts, if they are not *from the beginning* mixed with or transformed into the aim-inhibited instincts, are not successful because they are satisfied. Perhaps the ultimate confusion in Freud's theories of libido and identification is revealed in the fact that he attempts to derive both the Oedipus complex and group psychology ("man" is a horde animal) from his myth of the primal father. On the one hand, the Oedipal model shows the son to be castrated like the father (and the daughter like the mother). On the other hand, the group psychological model shows the group members (and the primal sons) to be castrated, while the leader (the primal) father, he who is the penis, is the castrator. But then the group leader as primal father is ultimately indistinguishable from the phallic mother, the primal fetish![39] Yet the contradictory result is the same (contradiction). In neither case is libido (the sexual instincts) "from the beginning" affectionate, loving, or "aim-inhibited." Indeed, in each case libido is isolated from both identification and the affectionate trend. In the Oedipal model, because original identification with the father('s penis), on the part of the male child, leads to the castration of libido, the resultant aim-inhibited impulse is simply narcissistic reidentification with the penis. (The girl's original identification with the absent penis means that, from the beginning, her narcissistic desire is castrated.) In the group psychological model, the identification that the narcissistic leader imposes on his followers is the inhibition of their mutual, libidinal aims.

In each of the two models libido is isolated from both identification and the aim-inhibited instincts. (In the Oedipal model, identification with the father imposes the aim-inhibited instincts as the castration of libido. In the group model patriarchal libido imposes identification as aim-inhibited instinct.) It is therefore arresting to see Freud, when he reviews his theory of group identification in the Postscript, envisage a model that, although not a group, links identification (and thus the aim-inhibited instincts) with the leader. According to the myth of the primal father, the leader is the font of the uninhibited sexual instincts. If, however, members of a group identify with the leader, will this not mean that the originary sexual instincts and the aim-inhibited instincts are linked "from the beginning" and together constitute the "identification" of both individual and community (at once familial and social)? Needless to say, this is not quite how Freud puts it! He does not raise the question of how his non-group, in which members and head are identified with, and so made indistinguishable from, each other, would relate to either the primal horde or the Oedipus complex. What Freud does say in one paragraph is radical and astonishing enough, however, above all because the head with whom members identify is Christ (God). In one paragraph Freud reveals a radical theology, a radical politics, and a radical ethics, which together uproot his metapsychology and along with it both the Oedipus complex (based on the castration complex) and the myth of the primal horde (based on originary narcissism). How is this possible?

When Freud undertakes to review his theory of group identification (in section XII.A), he writes that "the distinction between *identification of the ego* [of a group member] *with an object* [common to the group] and *replacement of the ego ideal* [of a group member] *by an object* [the group leader] finds an interesting illustration in the two great artificial groups" that he had earlier examined in section V, the army and the Christian church (167^e). In the army, a soldier takes his superior, the commanding officer, as his ideal, while he identifies himself with his fellow soldiers in a community of equal egos. The soldier "becomes ridiculous," Freud remarks, "if he tries to identify himself with the general" (167). It is typical of Freud, however, given his distinction between hierarchical ideal and horizontal equality, to remain silent on two fundamental questions. The social psychologist would question if all armies have been historically constituted on the basis of this distinction. The political theorist (ontologist) would question what would become of the distinction between ideal and equality when superior generals themselves have superiors, especially when those superiors themselves represent the primal horde, that is, Rousseau's general will, Spinoza's sovereign, the "people" (as embodied in democratically elected, civilian governments).

Freud's general point is that the relationship between ideal and identification as found in the church is different from that found in the army.[40] Although it is consistent with the army group model that the Christian loves Christ as his ideal and unites with his fellow Christians by the tie of identification, it is also the case, Freud observes, that "the church requires more of him [the individual Christian]. He has also to identify himself with Christ and love all other Christians as Christ loved them. At both points, therefore, the church requires that the position of *the libido* which is given by group formation should be supplemented. Identification has to be added where *object* [that is, sexual] *choice* has taken place, and *object* [that is, sexual] *love* where there is identification. *This addition evidently goes beyond the constitution of the group*" (167-8[e]).[41] Freud observes further that "a good Christian," the weak mortal that he is, hardly need put himself in Christ's place (in place of Christ) and claim "the Savior's largeness of soul and strength of love" in having, like him, "an all-embracing love for mankind." But it is "this further development in the distribution of libido in the group," he adds, as he brings his brief discussion of the church to an end, that "is probably the factor upon which Christianity bases its claim to have reached a higher ethical level" (168).

This extraordinary paragraph has, in addition to its enormous implications, two basic features that need careful elucidation in order to be properly appreciated. The first, more obvious feature is that the hierarchical opposition (in the group as army) between taking one's superior as one's ideal and identifying with one's fellow members is eliminated in the church. In the church ideal and identification are doubled, for each is the double of the other. Each becomes and is the other. There is no essential difference between ideal (group leader) and identification (of group members). It is not surprising, therefore, that Freud speaks in section V of the "democratic strain" in the church. (See note 40.)

But the essential connection between ideal and identification leads to the second, more subtle feature of this paragraph on the church. Freud here describes ideal and identification in terms utterly different from the obscure formulas that he uses earlier in *Group Psychology* to describe the ties that are operative in the group and about which he (typically) expresses very considerable dissatisfaction.[42] In writing that libido is "supplemented" and "further" distributed by adding identification (with fellow Christians) to "object choice" or "object love" (the Christian's relationship to Christ) and by adding object choice (object love) to identification, Freud makes it clear that libido is central to church relations. But, in *not* specifying what he means here by libido – does he mean uninhibited sexual instincts or the aim-inhibited instincts? – and, what is even more extraordinary, in using the language of the sexual instincts – that of object choice and object love – Freud indicates, indirectly (unconsciously), that there is no significant, metapsychological (ontological) distinction between, on the one hand, libido as uninhibited sexuality and libido as aim-inhibited sexuality and, on the other hand, libido and identification. Identification with Christ is object love, and the object love involving one's fellow Christians is identification. Or, the object love involving Christ is identification, and identification with one's fellow Christians is object love. To identify with Christ is to love other Christians as Christ loves them. To love Christ is to identify with other Christians whose identification is with Christ. To identify with other Christians is to love Christ as Christians love him. To love other Christians is to identify with Christ as Christians identify with him. It is little wonder that Freud points out that the "addition" of ideal (object choice or object love) to identification and of identification to ideal "goes beyond the constitution of the group." Assuming that by "the group" he means the primal horde, it is clear that the church (community) – whose similarity to the family Freud points out in section V (see note 40) – goes beyond what he calls just a few lines further on "the scientific myth of the father of the primal horde" (168). It is also clear that the church (community) model also goes beyond the Oedipal father (the castrator who is the castrated) and the Oedipal mother (the castrated who is the castrator). For it does not begin, in the beginning, with the violence of phallic narcissism, whether that of uninhibited sexuality (the primal father) or that of identification (the Oedipal father).

Several things in this remarkable paragraph become clear. For one, Freud is right when he argues, in *Group Psychology*, as we have seen, that libido comprehends what is popularly understood by "love." For another, Freud fails to see that it is likewise love that comprehends (explicates) libido. When Freud articulates, in a few simple and eloquent sentences, the "Pauline" or Christian (but certainly not Platonic!) relationship that the Christian has to both his ideal, Christ (God), and his fellow Christian (human being), his previous accounts of the relationship between libido and identification collapse. His highly artificial and scholastic accounts of the relationship between, on the one hand, libido as uninhibited sexual instinct and libido as inhibited sexual instinct and, on the other hand, between libido and identification are simply contradictory. In explicating the relationship of the individual Christian to both Christ and his fellow Christian in terms that are patently those of the golden rule – the love of both God and neighbour – Freud shows that libido is at once ideal and sexual. Love comprehends sexuality and sexuality comprehends love. For, as we saw him acknowledge earlier in *Group Psychology*, sexual instinct, if it is not, from the beginning, mixed with or transformed into aim-inhibited instinct, cannot be satisfied if (when) it is (merely) satisfied.

Given the limitations, however, of his metapsychology, Freud is generally unable to go beyond the language of need, satisfaction, pleasure-unpleasure, quantity, object love, aim-inhibited love – except when he deals with great cultural monuments (in this case, the New Testament tradition of the golden rule). Yet it is Freud, who, in claiming that, because the poets falsify reality, it is necessary to subject love to scientific treatment, also states that the purpose of human life has never received satisfactory expression. He remains, however, oblivious to the self-referentiality of truth. He does not see that one cannot discuss the purpose of life without assuming the purpose of life. He presents eloquent testimony to the libidinal (loving) adequacy of the golden rule. Yet he refuses to see that it is religion and not science that provides him with the truth of his libido theory. This is the ontological alternative that he never recognizes. It thus becomes clear that, when Freud in the name of science claims to go beyond the pleasure of poetry (religion) by repudiating its own first principle, the primacy of the pleasure principle in our lives, the self-contradiction of science can only represent the return of the repressed religious (poetic).

IV GUILT

In the previous section we saw the enormous difficulty that Freud faces in formulating a coherent concept of libido, of sexuality or love. We shall now conclude this chapter by examining how, in his view, the sense of guilt, in representing the intense hostility and aggressivity of the death instinct, endangers the very existence of civilization as represented by Eros. The fact that the (unconscious) sense of guilt arises from the (male) superego – that it is the superego, as heir to the (utterly smashed or repressed) Oedipus complex of the male child, that rules over the guilty (male) ego – indicates the profound relationship that Freud finds between the sense of guilt and libido (love). The superego is the direct heir of the castration complex, and the castration complex is, as we have seen, the direct heir of parental identification.

What follows from the fact that the superego is the heir of identification by way of the castration complex is that the ambivalence associated with the Oedipus complex proper – the arousal of the son's hostility to and rivalry with the father by his (incestuous) sexual desire for the mother – does not originate with the Oedipus complex. Rather, ambivalence – the boy both loves and hates his father (and also his mother) – stems from pre-Oedipal, pre-libidinal identification with the father. For it is identification with the paternal penis, on the part of the son, that both brings to life the ambivalence in the Oedipus complex proper and demolishes (represses) it in and through the castration complex. Faced with the threat of castration, the boy recoils back into narcissistic identification with the penis (both his own and his father's), as he represses his libidinal desire for the mother. Thus, the origin of Oedipal ambivalence is only indirectly incestuous desire for the mother. The real source of ambivalence is the originary (pre-Oedipal) identification with the penis('s father). For it is the original (pre-Oedipal) identification with the penis that makes the boy subject, from the beginning, to the threat of castration. Faced with the threat of castration, the boy retreats back into narcissistic identification with the penis. The reason for his retreat is not so much the external threat of parental punishment – against, say, his continued masturbation. Rather, he experiences enormous, internal anxiety as the result of his sight of the female genitals. He has to recognize and finally to accept, against his fondest wishes, that women (above all, his mother) are castrated (they lack the penis).

What identification with the father('s penis) means for the boy, above all, is that he gives up libidinal desire not just for his mother but for all women. The repression of male libido is not due to some primordial prohibition against incest (with mother and sisters) that is transmitted phylogenetically (a topic to be examined further in chapters 4 and 5) but, rather, due to fear of women. The boy's logic, following the logic of the (father's) penis, is primitive. Because women lack the penis, they are castrated; because they are castrated, they desire to have the penis that they lack; because they desire the penis that they lack, they are castrators. They desire to possess the (father's) penis – my penis, my identity, my self, my being. Since ambivalence in the Oedipus complex is initiated by the originary ambivalence inherent in identification with the father's penis, the demolition (repression) of the Oedipus complex in and through the castration complex only means that ambivalence is maintained (or reinforced) forever. From the beginning, identification with the father's penis involves the boy in the ambivalence of love and hate – for both father and mother. He loves the father('s penis). Yet this identity makes him completely vulnerable, for to love (women or men) is to risk losing the penis, his very identity. The ambivalence inherent in identification with the father's penis – the boy both loves and hates his penis('s father) – is, then, repeated in the sense of guilt that is experienced by the ego, as it is split between the libidinal desires of the id. Freud calls these desires the unconscious remnants of the repressed incestuous impulses. I would call them desire or love for the other, at once "uninhibited" (sexual) and "inhibited" (affectionate) – as prohibited by the superego. The superego demonstrates to the ego that, following its original identification with the penis, libido has been castrated from the beginning. All libidinal impulses – in men for women or men – threaten the individual male with castration. It is the superego that keeps alive the sense of guilt inherent in the originary identification with the pre-libidinal (narcissistic) penis. Castration, by both women and men, is the eternal threat to its identification. But Freud is actually yet more consistent than I have been indicating in deriving the sense of guilt from the castration complex. He argues, in fact, as we shall see, that it is the repression of the aggressive (death) instincts alone that is expressed in and by the ego's fear of the superego as the sense of guilt. It is not libido but aggressivity that is fundamental to the ambivalence of identification with the father's penis and its castration.

We need to keep in mind that, throughout his discussion of the sense of guilt and the superego, Freud is really only discussing men and not women. It is men whose identification with the penis involves them in erecting civilization. Women, with their desire for, and thus lack of, the penis, are limited to their feminine role, to the family, that is, to their role as castrators of men and their phallic civilization. Identification with the penis, on the part of men, leads to the (male) Oedipus complex, to its demolition in and through the castration complex, and to the permanent castration of libido within the ego by the superego (the ego ideal). The itinerary of women is different, however, as we know. Because women are castrated, from the beginning, their identification with the penis leads them directly to their end in the Oedipus complex. They are (personally, sexually) consumed by envy for what they do not have but can only desire, while men are (socially, aggressively) consumed by guilt for what they have but cannot desire.

The contradictions inherent in Freud's metapsychology pullulate interminably. It is women, according to Freudian theory, who are the enemies (castrators) of civilization; for, in desiring what they lack (the penis), they always lack what they desire. (Women, naturally, never give up their desire to be men, to possess the penis, which only goes to show how helplessly female they are!) But it is men, the erectors of civilization on the model of identification with the penis, in whom the internal aggression destructive of civilization is generated by the superego. Thus, it is Freud's theory of pre-libidinal identification (with the father's penis) that generates, in the beginning, the contradiction that leads through the Oedipus complex and the castration complex to their heir, the superego, whose harsh threat of punishment engenders the sense of guilt in the ego. Not only, as I emphasize, is the male the contradictory opposite of the female, for both male and female desire of the other (man or woman) is always contradictory, confirming castration. But also identification (with the father's penis) as found in the Oedipal model contradicts identification as found in the myth of the primal father (according to which the narcissistic libido of the primal father imposes aim-inhibited libido on the primal sons as their identification). Thus the model underlying the sense of guilt is contradictory both internally (the Oedipal mechanism) and externally or historically (the myth of the primal father). It is also the case that there is hostility not only, on the one hand, between men (in their social, aim-inhibited role) and women (in their family, sexual role) but also, on the other hand, between men themselves in their contradictory social roles. Although Freud often notes that the cordial, comradely, and friendly feelings that men develop for each other in their social relations rest on repressed (aim-inhibited, sublimated) homosexual impulses, he also emphasizes, as we have seen, that what men fear, above all else, is their social relations with other men. Relationships with other men imply a passive, feminine attitude, that is, castration.

It is clear that castration, reflecting originary identification with the penis, dominates both male and female relations. In his relations – with women (sexually) and with men (socially) – the male is dominated by the fear of castration. In her sexual relations – with men or women – the female is dominated by her castration envy. The male is consumed by the fear of losing what he has (to women or men). The female is consumed by the envy of never having what she desires (in men or women). Is it surprising, therefore, that Freud, in beginning with the identification of both men and women with the penis – its presence or absence – ends with the sense of guilt as the great enemy of civilization? In showing that the sense of guilt is deeply rooted in our culture and that the many forms of its destructiveness, both overt and subtle, are widely pervasive, Freud is right in holding that it cannot and does not arise independently of libido and its vicissitudes. We can well say, in the phenomenological spirit of Freud: where love was, there guilt will be. What Freud says, however, metapsychologically, is: where castration was first (as identification) and last (as the superego), there love (libido) will not be first or last, for it is guilt that will be first, last, and forever. The Freudian sense of guilt, as heir to the post-Oedipal castration of love, is the ultimate vicissitude of pre-Oedipal identification with the penis.

In the second half (chapters 5–8) of *Civilization and its Discontents* Freud develops his argument that the sense of guilt threatens the very existence of (our) civilization. His presentation consists of two fundamental – interrelated, yet discrete – elements: (1) a brilliant (if shallow) polemic against the truth, efficacy, and universality of the golden rule as the basis of ethical and social life; and (2) a complex, knotty, and ultimately contradictory discussion of the dual sources (origins) of the sense of guilt. Indeed, what Freud argues is that the sense of guilt is reflected in the aggressivity that the golden rule not only is hypocritically incapable of containing but also, in fact, blindly engenders. Since Freud, in dealing with what he acknowledges to be the contradictory (opposed) origins of the sense of guilt, calls upon his ideas of the superego (the Oedipus complex), the death instinct, and the myth of the primal father, in discussing them I shall again make use of *The Ego and the Id* (chapters 3–5). It is also worth noting that the discussion of the dual origin of the sense of guilt explicitly involves Freud in the problem of how to understand the relationship between external history (phenomenology) and internal theory (metapsychology). His perspective on the origins of civilization thus provides an apt prologue to the discussion of issues involving phylogenesis that I shall take up in chapters 4 and 5.

We saw in section III that Freud, when discussing love (libido), not only in the first half of *Civilization and its Discontents* but also in the three "Contributions to the Psychology of Love" and *Group Psychology and the Analysis of the Ego*, continuously questions whether the conflicts experienced in love can be due simply to a fundamental opposition between sexual life and civilization. Thus he has prepared us for his argument as presented in the second half of *Civilization and its Discontents*. Here he argues that the problem is not that civilization opposes (or is in conflict with) love (sexuality or libido) but that civilization, although based on Eros, generates the sense of guilt that, in embodying the death instinct of aggressivity, is destructive of civilization. Freud recalls at the beginning of chapter 5 that his theory of neurosis is based on the opposition between sexual life and social inhibitions and frustrations, even though this concept of neurosis fundamentally contradicts his basic instinct theory with its division between the self-preservative ego instincts and the sexual instincts of species (group, social!) preservation. Still, Freud is constantly forced, as we have seen, to acknowledge that the sexual instincts cannot, in the beginning, function unless they are "civilized." He writes, we may recall, of "something in the nature of the [sexual] function itself which denies us full satisfaction and urges us along other paths [than uninhibited satisfaction]" (295). He points out that the sexual instincts cannot be satisfied if they are (directly) satisfied and that the uninhibited sexual instincts are mixed up with or transformed into the aim-inhibited instincts from the beginning. He also observes that it is precisely love of others (that is, loss of others, dependence on others) that generates our greatest suffering.

Freud typically follows his basic metapsychological impulse of replacing one collapsed dualism with another. He replaces the dualism between sexuality and civilization with that between civilization (Eros) and the death instinct – even when aggressivity (the death instinct) would appear, by his own demonstration, to embody the failure of love and not to involve an independent principle. Or, to be consistent with his own metapsychology, since identification with the father('s penis) is pre-libidinal, there would appear to be no reason to think that the sense of guilt opposes libido, except in the sense that it reflects its very absence.

What is distinctly surprising, however, is that Freud introduces the topic of aggressivity, and thus of the sense of guilt, by way of the golden rule! If he can show that the concept of love (ethics) that is central to Christianity (and Judaism), to religion and modern civilization, generally, fails to account for human aggressivity, then he will have executed a brilliant, pre-emptive strike against his deadly enemy, religion, together with what he considers to be its illusory conception of reality. He will have demonstrated that civilization is characterized not by love but by the sense of guilt. He will have shown that external aggressivity against others, in being internalized and redirected against oneself, reflects identification with the (castrated) penis. Still, is it possible that what, in fact, Freud will demonstrate is the very opposite, that it is love, libido, the sexual instincts, and thus, ultimately, the golden rule that are both the origin and the end, at once the source and the appropriation, of the sense of guilt?

Freud is right that suffering presupposes loving. Because there is no hate where there is no love, Freud is astute (and ruthlessly unsentimental) in showing that it is precisely within love that one has to look for hidden (repressed, evaded) structures of hate (guilt). But, as always, he is unable to articulate his phenomenological insight in any other than the dualistic terms of his metapsychology. How can a pre-emptive strike against the golden rule (against the biblical story of creation, fall, and redemption) succeed when its success presupposes the loving arms of the enemy and not hate? Do we not begin to suspect that Freud's account of the golden rule exhibits features that the experienced analyst would view as those classically characteristic of the neurotic gain from illness: resistance; acting out instead of working through; a transference neurosis; and negation (suggesting that the professor doth protest too much)?[43] Or is Freud's account of the golden rule comparable to the analyst's construction, whose falsity is demonstrated by the analysand's indifference to it?[44] Or does it embody, finally, unconscious acknowledgment of the ontological alternative that love is its own standard, the standard both of love and of its distorted sense of guilt?

Freud initiates his discussion of the golden rule by claiming to find in it a clue indicating that the perturbations to which civilization is subject are not due solely to social restrictions on sexuality. Indeed, the clue is right under our nose, he remarks. For the discontents of civilization are traceable not to a remote source but to an ideal demand that, in being known throughout the world, is older than Christianity, although, until recently, still foreign to people: "you shall love your neighbor as yourself." In undertaking to provide what he calls a naïve reaction to such an ideal demand, Freud wonders how it can be viewed as reasonable if it does not allow you to prefer family and friends to strangers, especially since strangers often treat you without consideration. "Indeed, if this grandiose commandment had run, 'Love your neighbor as your neighbor loves you,'" Freud observes, "I should not take exception to it" (300). But he does take exception to it, especially because he finds that it is indistinguishable from the even more incomprehensible commandment: "love your enemies." Since your enemies are precisely those who hate you, he remarks, what the golden rule suppresses is the fact that human beings are not gentle creatures who want to be loved but rather aggressive, hostile beasts whose

neighbor is for them not only a potential helper or sexual object, but also someone WHO TEMPTS THEM to satisfy their aggressiveness on him [i.e., the neighbour is the aggressor!], to exploit his capacity for work without compensation, to use him sexually without his consent, to seize his possessions, to humiliate him, to cause him pain, to torture and to kill him. *Homo homini lupus*. Who, in the face of all his experience of life and of history, will have the courage to dispute this assertion? [As evidence for the assertion that "man is wolf to man" Freud refers to "the atrocities" committed "during the racial migrations," to those committed by the Huns, the Mongols, and the crusaders, and to "the horrors of the recent World War."] In consequence of this primary mutual hostility of human beings, civilized society is perpetually threatened with disintegration. (302[e])

Still, Freud's reaction to the golden rule is more nuanced and complex than these "naïve" comments might indicate. He goes on to say that "civilization has to use its utmost efforts in order to set limits to man's aggressive instincts" by employing psychical reaction-formations, identifications, aim-inhibited love relations, and "the ideal's commandment to love one's neighbor as oneself – a commandment *which is really justified* by the fact that nothing else runs so strongly counter to *the original nature of man*. In spite of every effort, these endeavors of civilization have not so far achieved very much" (302-3ᵉ). In other passages Freud criticizes the golden rule for claiming universality when happiness is individual ("there is no golden rule which applies to everyone"); for lacking discrimination ("not all men are worthy of love"); for neglecting differences; for creating intolerance towards those on the outside; for sacrificing real problems (like the disparity between rich and poor) to abstract principles; and, "in the severity of its commands and prohibitions," for troubling "itself too little about the happiness of the ego, in that it takes insufficient account of the resistances against obeying them" on the part of both the id and the external world.⁴⁵ Near the end of *Civilization and its Discontents* he concludes his observations on the golden rule by elaborating further his ambiguous statement that it is the most effective counter to our natural aggressiveness:

The commandment, "Love your neighbor as yourself," is *the strongest defense against human aggressiveness* and an excellent example of the unpsychological proceedings of the cultural superego. The commandment is impossible to fulfill ... What a potent obstacle to civilization aggressiveness must be, if the defense against it can cause as much unhappiness as aggressiveness itself! "Natural" ethics, as it is called, has nothing to offer here except the narcissistic satisfaction of being able to think oneself better than others.⁴⁶ At this point *the ethics based on religion* introduces its promises of a better after-life. But so long as virtue is not rewarded here on earth, ethics will, I fancy, preach in vain. (337ᵉ)

No one would dispute, I imagine, Freud's description (or even estimation) of wo/man's inhumanity to wo/man, at least to begin with. The issue, however, is how we think (that is, what we do) about good and evil, love and aggressivity. Since I am not writing here (except indirectly) a study in political theory, what I want to underline in the present context is that, in his comments on the golden rule, Freud exhibits the three basic elements of his depth psychology: (1) the (unsentimental, ruthless) realism of his phenomenological observations; (2) the severe check that his realism suffers due to the inadequacy of his metapsychology; and (3) an implicit (i.e., not articulated) recognition of (and uneasiness with) that inadequacy on his part. Since these elements intermingle with each other, I shall not attempt to keep them separate in the analysis that follows.

It is provoking that Freud, while pointing out the weakness of what he calls religious ethics, simply does not consider the arguments for universality, toleration of difference, etc. at their strongest. He does not take up the discussion of the golden rule as it is found in Hobbes or Kant, say. Nor does he indicate what the principles animating the action of a St Francis, a Cordelia, or an Alyosha Karamazov would be (although he has highly praised St Francis, as we saw, and he knows well the texts in which these two literary figures perform their heroic, loving tasks). Equally, he does not ask how an ethics based on individual happiness would be distinguishable from aggression against others. Freud's inability to *think* (philosophically, theologically, ethically, poetically, let alone scientifically) is simply astonishing. It is equally provoking that he does not apply his critique of the golden rule to himself, to psychoanalysis, to his relations with his own analysands, followers, colleagues, public (his listeners and readers), family, friends, and fellow citizens (many of whom would also be his "enemy"!). In his incapacity for thinking Freud is basically void of self-reflexivity (is it absent, unconscious, or repressed?).

Let us put aside, for the present, the fact that, as we have seen, Freud embodies the golden rule, although he leaves it unnamed, in his presentation, in *Group Psychology and the Analysis of the Ego*, of the Christian church as the democratic relationship of self and other. Let us also omit consideration of the fact that he fails to engage either the Bible or its rich Jewish and Christian traditions (one thinks, for instance, of the depth of Kierkegaard's psychology in *Works of Love*). The truly astonishing thing, however, is that Freud simply does not mention (does he evade?) what is fundamental to the golden rule – that you shall love your neighbour as yourself. How could a depth psychologist not be fascinated by the combination, in the golden rule, of command, love (desire, will), self, other, and the pivot on which the "rule" turns, the "as"? When one thinks about it, it becomes quite mysterious (moving) as to who it is who utters the command and to whom. But surely the turning point (the pivot) is the "as" that connects, while distinguishing (differentiating), self and other in their mutual desire. Strangely, joyously, painfully I must love the other (the neighbour) as myself, and – it is silently directed – I must love myself as the neighbour (loves me). The depth psychology revealed in and as the golden rule is explicated, for me, in the formulation that you are to do unto others as you would have them do unto you, a formulation that Freud ignores. It is astonishing, in other words, that Freud altogether omits consideration of the dynamic, the drama, the dialectic, the desire, the will of the golden rule. It is not that I do unto others as they do unto me, for that is actually the way of aggressivity, of identification with the penis. Rather, the golden rule recognizes that central to action is desire (will). It is true, naturally, that the perversions of the golden rule are sadism and masochism, but sadism and masochism cannot be recognized as perversions of love except on the basis of the golden rule. It is this unconscious recognition, as I suggested earlier, that doubtlessly underlies the Marquis de Sade's enormous hostility and aggressivity. The more he struggles against the "ideal," the more he reveals (is revealed in) its truth. The basic truth that Freud never sees is that it is only the golden rule (in whatever manifestation or revelation) that overcomes the contradictions of his metapsychology and is true to the depth of his phenomenological insight.

Freud's two comments on the golden rule as unnatural deserve especial attention. These comments reflect his notion that it is "the original nature of man" that is aggressive and violent and his view, later expressed in "Why War?", that civilization (justice) begins in violence and ends, for Freud, in constitutional pacifism. As always, it is the transition, the story connecting beginning (violence) and end (the peaceable kingdom), nature and civilization, for which Freud cannot account. Consistently, he confuses fact (human beings are aggressive and violent) with right (it is not right for big fishes to eat little fishes, as Spinoza and Rousseau would say). If it is true that our beginning is in violence, if violence is truth (if the might of fact or the fact of might is right), then Freud will not be able to explain how his concept of that violence is not merely its natural reflection. The claim that there is an "original nature of man" is one of those illusory ideas that turn up in every generation and that the strong thinkers and artists (formal and informal) of every generation have to deconstruct, constantly and patiently, yet one more time.

The thoughtless idea about "the original nature of man" is reflected, however, in the ambiguity with which Freud views the golden rule. Twice, as we have seen, he makes the statement, not apparently congruent with any easy dismissal of the golden rule, that it is justified by the fact that it is completely unnatural and that it is our best defense against our original human nature. Freud appears to mock belief in an ideal that causes as much unhappiness as aggressiveness itself and that would almost appear to be itself the source of aggressiveness. Still, he does not openly renounce the golden rule and even seems, in some sense, to embrace it. Why does he not simply reject the golden rule when he attacks it so harshly for its utter lack of realism and for its complete falsification of original human nature? There is no easy answer to this question. But I think the explanation lies in the fact that, as always, Freud does not relinquish the tension between his phenomenology and his metapsychology. While he never gives up his basic metapsychological principles presupposing an original human nature, governed by the pleasure principle, his psychoanalytic insight comes from his recognition that the twists and turns discernible within the human psyche are not reducible to a biological substratum. Human beings, it is true, often act like wolves in their relationships with each other, although this is not what we learn about the nature of wolves from scientific study of them! Wolves in their natural habitat never act like human beings – to their credit, the students of animal behavior and the critics of human nature would say. But that's the point. The profound aggressivity found in "human nature" is culturally liberated and rendered unnatural, untamed, barbaric, inhuman(e), animal-like, bestial, wolfish ... precisely because it is not natural. It is not confined or confinable to any (deductive or inductive) model of science, whether natural or social. Freud always wants to have it both ways – to his own immense confusion, not to mention to the immense confusion of his followers and critics. He knows that civilization, to survive, must be able to counter, to contain, human aggressiveness. But he has no explanation of how that which is "naturally" violent can become "civilized." What is the transition from violence (nature) to civilization (peace)? Freud recognizes that there is something compelling in the "unnaturalness" of the golden rule, in its opposition to the wolfish nature of human beings, in the enormous aggressivity of its own compulsive desire. But he is unable to see that the violence of human nature is completely "unnatural." He is unable to escape the terrible dualism between nature and civilization on which his metapsychology, rooted in the pleasure principle, is based.

Freud founds psychoanalysis by liberating its study of the psyche – the psychical apparatus – from both the medico-psychiatric model of soma and from the philosophical model of natural consciousness. But what he then fails to recognize is that he has no alternative to founding his metapsychology on the principles that animate the humanities: literature, the arts, religion, moral and social reflection, and what I might perhaps call here depth philosophy – that of, for example, Spinoza, Kant, Hegel, Kierkegaard, and Nietzsche. The reason that Freud always avoids (evades) Nietzsche, I suspect, is that, although he explicitly recognizes his profound phenomenological affinity with Nietzsche, he also implicitly realizes (but will not face the fact) that Nietzsche ruthlessly and systematically undercuts the very ground of his metapsychology. Of all the dead notions in the theologico-philosophico-politico-poetic tradition that Nietzsche relentlessly attacks, among the most prominent is that of an original human nature given in the past. That is the god that is dead. For Nietzsche, the will to power is the unconscious, the instinctual, the unnatural desire of the human race, its his-

tory, that is no more given naturally in the past than it is given positivistically in the future. Nietzsche is able, finally, to overcome
Schopenhauer's dualism – if not always consistently. Freud, however,
does not even see the problem of dualism. He knows that what makes
psychoanalysis creative is that it views the psychical as irreducible to
the somatic (or biological). But he constantly falsifies this insight by
failing to acknowledge that the principle underlying psychoanalysis is,
in Spinoza's terms, the psychical as the cause of itself: *hominem homini deum esse*. It is only when we recognize that "wo/man is god to
wo/man" that we can discern the wolfish nature of human beings. It is
only when I make myself subject to my neighbour's judgment and him
to mine (and vice-versa: he makes himself subject to my judgment and
me to his) that the wolfishness of our desire can be revealed for what
it is, unloving and hostile.

Once he has introduced aggressivity by way of the golden rule, Freud
proceeds in chapter 6 of *Civilization and its Discontents* to argue that
"the recognition of a special, independent aggressive instinct means an
alteration of the psychoanalytic theory of the instincts" (308).[47] He
recalls his speculation in *Beyond the Pleasure Principle* that "the phenomena of life could be explained from the concurrent or mutually
opposing action" of Eros, which strives to unify life, and of the death
instinct of aggressiveness and destructiveness, which seeks to restore
life to an original nature. It is "not easy, however," he points out, "to
demonstrate the activities of this supposed death instinct," since it
always appears to be attached to Eros, as is seen in the phenomena of
sadism and masochism (310). Although Freud acknowledges that even
psychoanalysts continue to resist the idea of an independent death
instinct, he declares that he is now more convinced than ever that the
two opposed instincts "are far more serviceable from a theoretical
standpoint than any other possible ones; they provide that simplifica-
tion, without either ignoring or doing violence to the facts, for which
we strive in scientific work."[48] But he is particularly chagrined by the
fact that, although the destructive instinct, when mixed with erotism,
has long been observed in sadism and masochism, he is no longer able
to understand "how we can have overlooked the ubiquity of *non-erotic* aggressivity and destructiveness and can have failed to give it its due
place in our interpretation of life" (311ᵉ).[49] Freud then concludes his
argument in favor of aggressivity as the representative of an original,
independent death instinct by declaring:

And now, I think, the meaning of the evolution of civilization is no longer
obscure to us. It must present *the struggle between Eros and Death, between
the instinct of life and the instinct of destruction*, as it works itself out in the

human species. This struggle is what all life essentially consists of, and the evolution of civilization may therefore be simply described as *the struggle for life* of the human species.[50] [Then Freud appends the following footnote.] And we may probably add more precisely, *a struggle for life* in the shape it was bound to assume after *a certain event which still remains to be discovered.* (314ᵉ)

Is civilization, however, the struggle *between* life and death or the struggle *for* life (against death)? To be or not to be? Is that the question that Freud simply never poses and thus simply refuses to understand? Hamlet, unlike his Oedipal critics (beginning with Claudius), understands that, in mocking himself with the question, in bethinking himself within the question – to be or not be? – the question is not one of deciding *between* life and death, between Eros and the death instinct. The question is, rather, of seeing, ironically, paradoxically, that you are freely compelled to give up the contradictory opposition between life and death and to discern providence not in the auguries of fatal *Ananke* but in the fall of sparrow. No one disputes the reality of aggressivity in our lives, Hamlet least of all. The question is what to think (to do) about it; and to pose and to answer that question is to overcome all binary oppositions between thinking and doing in the spirit of Kant's conception of reason as practice: thinking freely (as) the categorical imperative, the golden rule of love. Thinking through the question of existence, of ontology, means to see that that which Freud calls "the struggle *between* Eros and Death" is not the same as – indeed, is altogether different from and opposed to – that which he calls "the struggle *for* life." The struggle *for* life presupposes a concept of will or desire, a concept of self-reflexivity, worthy of Hamlet. The struggle *between* Eros and death, however, while characteristic of Claudius and Laertes, in imitation of Empedocles if not Darwin, has no place for making the unconscious conscious. Because the struggle *between* Eros and death leaves suspended the question where we (Hamlet, Freud, the reader) stand within the struggle, it is a mere battleground of abstractions without relation to the reality of human desire, which is precisely what Freud claims to object to in the golden rule.

Still more extraordinary, however, is Freud's appeal to a *certain event* that, while assumed, still remains to be discovered. It is clear, I think, that here, as in *Beyond the Pleasure Principle*, Freud recognizes that his instinct theory, including his final theory of the opposed instincts of Eros and death, cannot account for the coming into existence of life, the dialectic of desire and self. He never recognizes, following Kant's critique of the ontological argument of existence, that the origin of the perturbations experienced in human consciousness (as the unconscious) is not to be located outside (or inside) the human mind in some originary (planetary) or natural presence. Freud fails to see that the conflicts, the tensions, in our lives are to be understood on the basis not of a dualistic theory of instincts, whose mirror opposite is the *horror vacui* of what he views as Jung's monistic theory of libido, but of human beings themselves. It is human beings who are divided – both within their individual selves and between (and among) their social selves. The division or conflict in human beings is not between ego and species, between self-preservation and sexuality, between individual and society (nature!). It is not between civilization as individual (self-preservative) and civilization as social (group/species-preservative [natural!]). The division, rather, is between adequate and inadequate notions of what is at once individual and social. Adequate notions of individual and social are those that account for their opposites on the basis of how they account for themselves. This takes us back to the golden rule (and its equivalents). The only way in which the individual and the social can be understood is in terms of the mutuality of desire and the self. Desire, like the self, is no more (or less) individual than it is social.

In light of the clear indication that Freud is unable to account for human existence (love) on the basis of the struggle *between* Eros (life) and death, it is particularly instructive to see how he addresses the fact that his original concept of libido does not permit him to develop a concept of aggressivity that is social but non-erotic. Although the ego instincts, as they evolve into object libido and narcissism, allow him to begin to account for the source of social perturbations in terms that are not (directly) erotic (libidinal), the problem then emerges of how to relate the "ego" to the sphere of social (external) aggressivity. The problem that Freud faces is created (as always) by the opposition between ego (narcissism) and sexuality (the social). Yet he also comes to recognize that sexuality (love) is, in a profound sense, anti-social, because truly individual. Thus he is compelled to generate his concept of the death instinct in order to deal with the domain of aggressivity that cannot be accounted for on the basis of his contradictory libido theory.

As we have already anticipated, Freud is consistent in proceeding to connect his theory of the death instinct with the superego. This allows him to address the phenomena of non-erotic, social aggressivity; but at the same time his new theory is only a reinstatement of the original identification with the (father's) penis, the castration complex. Since the superego represents conscience and social morality, the very structure of civilization, it would appear that civilization, in being based upon the superego, represents the death instinct of aggressivity. But what, then, happens to Eros? Freud claims that Eros and death are the two separate, independent, and primordial instincts whose titanic struggle shapes the very nature of civilization. Eros, as the instinctual life force constituting the unity of civilization, is locked in a (death or life?) struggle with the death instinct whose disintegrative forces of aggressivity and hostility tear civilization apart. But, since the superego constitutes conscience, morality, and social rules, the very fabric of civilization, on the basis of the death instinct, what, then, is the relationship between the superego and Eros, between the death and the life instincts? Does civilization belong to the superego, and thus to the death instincts, or to Eros, and thus to the life instincts? What *is* civilization? Does it represent life or death? Can Eros and its struggle for the unity of civilization be distinguished from the superego, whose sense of guilt shows the castration complex and thus originary identification with the penis to be the source of the death instinct? Is civilization erotic or phallic? Or is it neither but, rather, loving, the dialectic of self and desire?

Once he has argued for the independence of the death instinct and its aggressivity – and thus its primordial opposition to Eros and civilization – Freud finally arrives at the real subject of *Civilization and its Discontents*, that of the sense of guilt, to which he devotes the last two chapters (7 and 8) of the work. He holds that the sense of guilt results from the means that civilization uses to inhibit aggressiveness in the individual. The individual's

aggressiveness is introjected, internalized [Freud writes]; it is, in point of fact, *sent back to where it came from* – that is, it is directed towards his own ego. There it is taken over by a portion of the ego, which sets itself over against the rest of the ego as superego, and which now, in the form of "conscience," is ready to put into action against the ego the same harsh aggressiveness that the ego would have liked to satisfy upon other, extraneous individuals [parental figures]. The tension between the harsh superego and the ego that is subjected to it, is called by us the sense of guilt; it expresses itself as a need for punishment. (315-16ᵉ)

I shall summarize what Freud writes about the superego, as the source of the sense of guilt, in *Civilization and its Discontents* and *The Ego and the Id* (keeping in mind, but not repeating as such, the earlier discussion of the superego in section ii). The superego represents conscience, morality, religion, tradition, history: civilization. It is the ego's sense of being watched over, the fear of a critical agency, the dread of punishment that the masochistic ego feels towards the sadistic superego. The superego, we recall, is the heir of the Oedipus complex, of the

castration complex, and, as such, it represents the categorical imperative to the ego: thou shalt obey me. Freud again reminds us, in *The Ego
and the Id*, that the superego derives "from an identification with the
father taken as a model. Every such identification is in the nature of a
desexualization or even of a sublimation" (396). But, since this desexualization involves what Freud calls an instinctual defusion, the death
instincts that were bound to (fused with) the erotic instincts are liberated to dominate the ego with the cruelty of the categorical imperative.[51] Freud also notes that the fear experienced by the ego represents
the heritage of the castration complex. "The superior being [father,
God, penis], which turned into the ego ideal [the superego], once
threatened castration, and this dread of castration is probably the
nucleus round which the subsequent fear of conscience has gathered; it
is this dread that persists as the fear of conscience" (399).

What is striking in this suite of ideas is the emphasis that Freud
places on – in addition to identification with the father (the importance
of which I underlined in my earlier presentation of the Oedipus complex, whose heir, by way of the castration complex, is the superego) –
three elements: (1) the fact that aggressiveness is "sent back to where
it came from" (to the ego) in the form of the punishing superego; (2)
the defusion of the instincts; and (3) the castration threat. He stresses,
in other words, what is non-sexual: the narcissistic, the release of the
aggressive instincts from their fusion with the erotic impulses, and the
castration of libido. What is not easy to grasp, however, and what
Freud himself does not altogether grasp, as I have been indicating, is
the role that identification with the father('s penis) plays in generating
the superego by way of the castration complex. In addressing against
the ego the aggression that the ego feels against the father, the superego creates in the ego the sense of guilt, the sense that it deserves interminable punishment for the aggressive impulses that it continues to
harbour against the father. In the simplest – the most profound and the
most perplexing – terms, the penis is the source of its own punishment.
The penis is its own castration. To establish identification of yourself
with the original penis as your father, god, origin, and ideal is to discover that any desire on your part to satisfy your libidinal or aggressive impulses is to undergo castration. Once again, women (outside the
seductive mother) are absent from Freud's model, in fact, if not in principle. For in their very absence they are the castrators of men, of civilization, given that their desire for the penis is insatiable, unassuage-
able, unrealizable, and utterly uncivilized.

Within the context of the superego understood as the heir to the
Oedipus complex, Freud's specific purpose in *Civilization and its Discontents* is, as he puts it, "to represent the sense of guilt as the most

important problem in the development of civilization and to show that the price we pay for our advance in civilization is a loss of happiness through the heightening of the sense of guilt" (327). He is concerned, above all, to show how what he calls the two pairs of contradictions inherent in the two different and opposed origins of the sense of guilt can be resolved. The sense of guilt appears to be the product of the fear both of parental authority, which demands renunciation of instinctual satisfaction, and of the superego, which, in addition, "presses for punishment [of the ego], since the continuance of the forbidden [aggressive] wishes cannot be concealed from the superego" (319).

Freud holds that the Oedipal boy, in fearing that he will no longer be loved by the father, accedes to the demand of his (external) authority to renounce instinctual satisfaction. Renunciation of instinct (the castration threat) attains its end. The boy maintains his love for – he solidifies identification with – the father by renouncing his instinctual wishes. In this case, however, no sense of guilt follows. Conscience, as fear of external authority, results in instinctual renunciation without a consequent sense of guilt.

But with fear of the superego [Freud points out] the case is different. Here, instinctual renunciation is not enough, for the [instinctual] wish persists and cannot be concealed from the superego. Thus, in spite of the renunciation that has been made, a sense of guilt comes about. (320) *A great change* takes place only when the authority is internalized through the establishment of a superego. The phenomena of conscience then reach a higher stage. Actually, it is not until now that we should speak of conscience or a sense of guilt.[52] At this point, too, the fear of being found out comes to an end; the distinction, moreover, between doing something bad and wishing to do it disappears entirely, since nothing can be hidden from the superego, not even thoughts. (317e)

The idea which "belongs entirely to psychoanalysis and which is foreign to people's ordinary way of thinking," Freud points out, is that, although it is conscience (external authority) that originally brings about instinctual renunciation, this relationship is reversed with the institution of the superego (321). Now instinctual renunciation reinforces the harshness and severity of conscience. This is the case because the aggressiveness that is renounced is internalized as the superego's aggression against the ego. In other words, when the child is confronted with renouncing his instinctual satisfactions, he internalizes his aggressiveness against the parental authority as his superego, which now exercises this same aggression against his ego. "By means of identification," Freud writes, the child "takes the unattackable authority into himself." Freud's essential point is that the severity of the superego's aggressivity against the ego is the product not of the severity with which one is treated or believes one is treated by parental authority but of one's own aggressiveness against that authority. Conscience can thus be said to arise "through the suppression of an aggressive impulse" and to be continuously reinforced by the suppression of further aggressive impulses.

Freud holds that the "child's revengeful aggressiveness will be, in part, determined by the amount of punitive aggression which he expects from his father" (322). (He does not say that he *receives* from his father!) But there is no direct relationship between the severity of parental treatment and the severity of the superego. Thus we arrive at the strange contradiction that it is not children who are unloved (abused?) by their parents but children who are loved by their parents who develop a superego with the consequent sense of guilt. Because unloved children have no fear of losing the love of their parents, they have an external outlet for the aggressiveness that is aroused in them by the parental ban on their instinctual satisfaction. They direct it outward against their parents and thus do not develop a superego that would generate in them a sense of guilt. How different are children who are loved! They fear that their parents will stop loving them and thus will punish them with aggression. Having no external outlet for the aggressiveness that the parental ban on their instinctual impulses (the castration complex) arouses, they direct it inwardly against themselves. The result is that it is they, the loved children, who develop a superego with the consequent sense of guilt. Severe conscience (the sense of guilt) thus has two sources, Freud concludes: the child's aggressiveness, which is unleashed by the parental demand for the renunciation of instinctual satisfaction; "and the experience of being loved, which turns the aggressiveness inwards and hands it over to the superego" (323).

The reader will have noticed how strained and peculiar are the locutions that Freud uses. He speaks of the boy's "being loved" by the parents, not of the boy loving the parents (and of the parents loving the boy). He speaks of the boy's (innate) aggressiveness being aroused by the parents(' ban on his instinctual satisfaction), not of the parents' aggression against the boy being responsible (at least, in part) for bringing about the boy's aggressiveness. He says that the "child's revengeful aggressiveness will be, in part, determined by the amount of punitive aggression which he *expects* from his father." He does not say that the child will develop revengeful aggressiveness, at least in part, in response to aggression (psychological and/or actual) from the father. We may recall that earlier Freud counters what he considers to be the irreality and the hypocrisy of loving your neighbour as yourself with the observation that people look upon their neighbour as "some-one who *tempts them to satisfy their aggressiveness on him*" (302ᵉ). The neighbour is not the object of aggression; he is, rather, the tempter, the seducer, the one who arouses aggression in the aggressor. The neighbour, like the child, is the aggressor. Typically, in all his writings, Freud speaks of love as dependence, helplessness, and defenselessness – before the illusion of pleasure – against which only stern adherence to the reality principle in renouncing pleasure (instinctual satisfaction) will be successful. Love is "being loved." Love is the fear of having one's love taken away, of being left dependent, helpless, and defenseless, as we saw Pascal write in chapter 1. Love, for Freud, is not loving – reciprocal relationship (in all its modalities: sexual, familial, cultural).

The debate rages on about Freud and the seduction theory. Since I am not directly concerned in this study with Freud's theory of neurosis, I do not intend to enter the debate. But this much can, however, be made clear. When Freud repudiates the seduction theory of neurosis in 1897,[53] he displaces the cause of neurosis from the external seduction of (generally female) children by (generally) male (paternal) figures to the fantasy of childhood seduction by parents as found internal to the psyche of the (generally female) subject. Still, although Freud radically shifts his focus from external to internal, he does not fundamentally alter his metapsychology with its dualistic opposition between internal (fantasy) and external (event). The issue is not whether Freud recognizes or denies that (especially male) parents or other adult figures seduce and otherwise abuse (especially female) children. The issue is the relationship between fantasy (imagination) and reality (history). Freud clearly sees from the beginning to the end of his career that tremendous harm is done by individuals to individuals – both others and themselves – in the name of love. He never denies that abuse is perpetrated by adults on children (although whether he assesses it correctly is another question). He also knows that there is no direct correlation (causal link) between abuse (which itself involves an extremely complex set of phenomena, at once psychological and actual) and the development of both character and neurosis. Not all parental abuse of children results in the children's becoming neurotic (as children or as adults). Not all neurosis (in children or adults) can be traced – directly or indirectly – to parental abuse (i.e., abuse may be absent). Freud properly wants to protect what he considers to be the unique subject of psychoanalysis, the autonomy of the psyche. He is concerned to ask not how the individual is (externally) affected by, but rather how he (internally) responds to, his experience. He is right that all children (in our culture, and taking into account significant variables in class, race, and gender) have the same developmental (historical) agenda to negotiate. But here two basic points must be made. First, the autonomy of the psyche cannot be sustained on the basis of Freudian metapsychology. Autonomy is not internality but relationship. Second, it is both fruitless and wrong to oppose the fantasy of the "internal" psyche to the reality of "external" abuse (whether psychological and/or actual). Indeed, the fundamental dichotomy between internal and external is precisely the metapsychological dualism that Freud does not give up when he abandons the seduction theory for what will ultimately become the castration complex. It is both fruitless and wrong to hold that parents are "external" to their children or that how a child responds to its parents is "internal" to itself.

What Freud lacks, in other words, is, notwithstanding his strong emphasis on development, a concept of history, which, neither internal nor external to the individual, is the story of his relationships – personal, familial, social, ontological. What Freud fails to see, therefore, is that, as I indicated earlier, history is always the history of loving and that loving is always historical. The point is not that the child "is loved" by its parents. The point, rather, is that the child loves its parents and that the parents love their child, an elemental point, it is true, but a point, nonetheless, that escapes Freud. Love can be terribly controlling and manipulative and so productive of guilt, Freud knows. But the fundamental motive of loving is not fear of not "being loved." The fundamental motive (the moving power) of love is that of loving another (including yourself) as you would have that person love you. As for aggressivity, precisely because it, too, is central to loving, it is not a fundamental instinct that is "internalized" due to the fear of not "being loved" by the parents, to the fear of becoming the object of their aggression. Aggressivity ("activity") is not primarily the opposite (although it can be the negation) of love, for it is the very force of love, its passion, its drive, it tenderness, its caring. Aggressivity and love are intimately related; and it is this relationship that Freud does not capture when he founds his metapsychology on the originary violence of the primal father and on the ambivalence of hate and love (the instincts of death and Eros) as present in the pre-libidinal identification of the (male) child with the father's penis. Ultimately, therefore, Freud no more has a theory of aggression than he has a theory of libido; for both aggression and libido are the subject of – they are subject to – love, the golden rule of self and desire.

Freud's view is that the (male) child's aggressiveness, instead of being directed externally against his parents, is internalized (as the superego) against himself. This view assumes that the child fears losing his parents' love (identification with the penis), and it follows directly from his idea that the superego is the product not of external experience (history) but of the internal mechanism of the castration complex (metapsychology). Indeed, he proceeds to argue that the aggressivity with which the child reacts to the renunciation of instinct that is demanded of him follows a phylogenetic model. "We cannot get away from the assumption," he writes, "that man's sense of guilt springs from the Oedipus complex and was acquired at the killing of the father by the brothers banded together" (324). Although phylogenesis may appear to explain, at least, in part, the aggressivity with which the child reacts to the ban on his instinctual satisfaction, it creates, nevertheless, a new dilemma for Freud. Whereas the primal sons acquire their sense of guilt from actually killing the father – they act out their aggressivity against him – their male heirs are stricken by the sense of guilt not because they kill the father but because they do not kill him and only want (intend) to kill him. The result is that, today, instead of killing the father, the son internalizes his intended aggression against the father as the superego's ever-increasing punishment of the ego for harbouring and not giving up its murderous wish. Freud then accounts for the change from external to internalized aggression on the model of the change from conscience to superego. Although conscience (anxiety) is originally the cause of the renunciation of instinct, the relationship is reversed with the institution of the superego. Conscience (as the sense of guilt) is in fact reproduced by the continuous suppression of instinct (by the superego). Thus Freud also argues that the distinction between the original murder and the inherited desire to murder the father falls away. Identification with the father leads to the castration complex, whose result is the internalization of the aggression that is felt against the father (the penis, God). The more one desires to kill the father, the more severely the ego is punished by the superego and the greater becomes its sense of guilt.

The sense of guilt originates in the ambivalence that the primal sons feel for their father – alive they hate him and so kill him and dead they love him and so celebrate his life. It is this ambivalence, Freud writes, that "set up the superego by *identification with the father*; it gave that agency the father's power, as though as a punishment for the deed of aggression they had carried out against him, and it created the restrictions which were intended to prevent a repetition of the deed" (325e). As the desire to kill the father persists in every generation, so does the suppression of the aggression against the father with its ever-increasing reinforcement of the sense of guilt. This leads Freud to declare that

now, I think, we can at last grasp two things perfectly clearly: *the part played by love in the origin of conscience* and the fatal inevitability of the sense of guilt. Whether one has killed one's father or has abstained from doing so is not really the decisive thing. One is bound to feel guilty in either case, for the sense of guilt is an expression of the conflict due to ambivalence, of the eternal struggle between Eros and the instinct of destruction or death. This conflict is set going as soon as men are faced with the task of living together ... Since civilization obeys an internal erotic impulse which causes human beings to unite in a closely-knit group, it can only achieve this aim through an ever-increasing reinforcement of the sense of guilt. *What began in relation to the father* is completed in relation to the group. (325–6ᵉ)

What are we to make of the fact that it is not the church (Christianity) but Freud who preaches a doctrine of original sin, of a sense of guilt that, following not Darwin but Lamarck, is inherited? Still more extraordinary is the fact that Freud's doctrine of original sin is the heir to the suppression not of sexuality but of aggressivity. Even the vulgar (Platonic or idolatrous) Christian notion of the natural inheritance of sin by the act of sex (concupiscence) recognizes the centrality of sexuality (love) in human life.

Freud concludes his account of the two sources of the sense of guilt by making it plain that he opposes a number of prominent theorists, whom he names. In holding that the sense of guilt arises from the thwarted satisfaction of only the aggressive and not, additionally, the libidinal instincts, he reinforces his stance against the psychoanalytic community in holding that there are two separate, primordial, and independent instincts, death and Eros. "For how," he asks, "are we to account, on dynamic and economic grounds, for an increase in the sense of guilt appearing in place of an unfulfilled *erotic* demand? ... I am convinced that many processes will admit of a simpler and clearer exposition if the findings of psychoanalysis with regard to the derivation of the sense of guilt are restricted to the aggressive instincts" (332).[54] It is striking how consistently Freud brings his contradictory account of the origin of guilt to conclusion. He had emphasized, as we saw, "the part played by love in the origin of conscience." Nevertheless, his metapsychological theory dictates that, notwithstanding the fact that "unfulfilled *erotic* demand" causes neurosis (in his earlier theory), it does not produce the sense of guilt that results from the prohibition and thus the internalization of the (male) child's aggressiveness against parental authority.

Once again, we have the strange situation that, while Freud acknowledges the centrality of love in the production of the sense of guilt, he cannot account for it. As a clinician he does not want to give up the actual experience of the analysand – that his relations with his parents are central to his psychical development. At the same time, however, he knows that the psyche is not a direct product of its experience, for it is also a creator of its experience. It is fascinating to see Freud, the humble servant of empirical phenomena, also champion the role of speculation in constructing (interpreting) data. He not only properly resists positivism – the reduction of mind to the sum total of its historical experience – but also compulsively flees to the opposite, deductive model. Thus he writes in the *New Introductory Lectures* that "a child's superego is in fact constructed on the model not of its parents but of its parents' superego" (99).[55] But the superego is, as we have seen, the product of the originary (narcissistic) identification on the part of the boy with the father('s penis), by way of the castration complex, which forces upon the boy the renunciation of all sexual (or object) relations.

Freud also connects the superego with the phylogenetic inheritance from the murder of the primal father and the consequent guilt that the primal sons inherit through the ages. The original deed – external to the psyche – creates the guilt; but, thereafter, the mechanism generating the sense of guilt operates internal to itself, without significant input from the "history" of the individual or his family. Freud recognizes that there is no guilt where there is no love; but his model of castration, combined with the myth of the primal father, forces him to deduce the aggression that the boy feels towards his father from the original ambivalence of his identification with the father('s penis). The struggle between the primordial instincts of Eros and death thus has nothing to do with the libidinal (loving) relationship that the boy has with his parents. For, as Freud insists, the superego and its sense of guilt are generated out of the prohibition and internalization of only aggressive, and not also libidinal, impulses. Freud, in fact, points out from time to time that Eros, in binding people into the social unities constituting civilization, is opposed not only to the destructive death instincts but equally to sexuality. "Sexual love is a relationship between two individuals," he writes, "whereas civilization depends on relationships between a considerable number of individuals" (298). In *Group Psychology*, he notes, consistent with his view that groups (but thus not the church, not to mention the family or society) rely for their identification on aim-inhibited, to the exclusion of sexual, ties, that, when two people come together sexually, they "are making a demonstration against the herd instinct, the group feeling" (174). In the *New Introductory Lectures* he remarks that the fact that women have weaker social interests than men derives from "the dissocial quality which unquestionably characterizes all sexual relations" (169).

The ego's sense of guilt, the superego (representing the ego's own self-punishment for its [unconscious] aggressive impulses against the

father), the castration complex, the Oedipus complex, originary identification with the father('s penis): this is the chain whose links Freud,
in his later works, continues to forge with ever-increasing adamantine
hardness. We see that, once he formulates his Oedipal model in
mature form, Freud derives "love" not from the child's relationship
with its parents but from its identification with the father('s penis), the
ambivalence of which generates the inner drama of love and hate
(aggressivity). The result, finally, is the superego and the ego's inheritance of the need to punish itself for its own aggressive instincts –
against the father, against the penis, against God (in terms of religion
and social morality), against itself. It is little wonder, then, that Freud
acknowledges that his concept of the superego, with the sense of guilt
that it imposes on the ego, is not strongly supported by clinical experience and that it is opposed by his fellow analysts. We can also understand why late in his career he sees his instinct theory become a
mythology to which history and experience contribute nothing at all.
What this means is that we should constantly be on guard against any
position that, in opposing history and theory to each other, cannot
account either for history theoretically or for theory historically. If the
history of theory is not the theory of history – if the actual is not the
rational (and vice versa) – then both history and theory vanish into
narcissistic identification with the penis or its equivalent god (idol).
Whenever history (as the relationship of self and desire) is reduced to
what is empirical, to the quantifiable and objectifiable, the inevitable
result is, as we see in Freud, data whose incoherence is then reflected
in (by being covered over by) an unhistorical myth. In Freud's case this
is the myth of the primal father, which depends on an original, narcissistic, initiating event, an event that, although said to begin history,
has no historical beginning itself. But again we are broaching the
theme of the following chapters.

What is presently germane is the fact that Freud cannot account for
love. He does not know that when love is not historical it is not love
and that when history is not loving it is not history. He does not know
that the love of history (existence) is the history (story) of love. He has
to assume, he acknowledges, a "certain event" – the coming into existence of history, as the relationship of love – that would explain the
human struggle *for* life against death. In the struggle *between* Eros and
death, however, love is sacrificed to the ambivalence of identification
with the father's penis. Indeed, it is the original ambivalence of love
and hate, as found both in the identification with the father's penis and
in the primal sons' murder of the primal father, that underlies Freud's
final theory of the dual instincts, death and Eros. What is more, since
Eros, as I pointed out above, cannot account for sexuality (love, libido)

– and putting aside its relationship to the pleasure principle (as the death instinct) – Eros itself becomes indistinguishable from the super-ego and thus from the death instinct, of whose aggressivity the super-ego is the bearer. Both Eros and the superego represent civilization – as constituted by tradition, history, social and group morality, the family, religion. Eros and death, like "love" and "hate," are both given in the original ambivalence of identification with the penis. The result of this ambivalence is the fact that Eros and the sense of guilt (whose origin is the superego, itself the product of the castration of libido or love) now face themselves as opposites that are indistinguishable from each other, at least in metapsychological terms. For both originate in narcissistic identification with the father's penis. It is ultimately the penis, there-fore, that is both Eros and death, both Eros and hate, both Eros and the superego, both Eros and the sense of guilt. Each member of each pair suppresses libido (love) and the history of the relationships that are the creation of love, the dialectic of desire and the self.

It is little wonder, then, that Freud, once he finally comes to realize that sexuality (libido, love) is, for him, too ambiguous a foundation on which to erect and to maintain his dualistic theory of ambivalence, launches what I called his preemptive strike against its very core, the golden rule. He points out in the earlier half of *Civilization and its Dis-contents* that dualistic opposition between sexuality (love) and civi-lization is untenable. Love (sexuality) is not only the contradictory sat-isfaction that cannot be satisfied if it is not aim-inhibited from the beginning but also our greatest source of suffering. Then, in the second half of the work, he argues that the golden rule as the ideal of civiliza-tion miscarries in failing to account for the aggressivity and the resul-tant sense of guilt that fatally burden civilization with destructive impulses. But there is terrible irony in Freud's facile dismissal of the golden rule as the ideal that exhibits the reality of human relations as the structure of desire and self – beyond good and evil. He eliminates not only the origin (the beginning) of but equally the solution (the end) to human guilt. He is left with castration – ultimately, self-castration; with ambivalence; with the dualism of Eros and death; with identifica-tion with the father's penis that, when erected into the civility of the superego, is shown to terrorize the ego with the sense of guilt; with the guilt of self-punishment; and, finally, with the fear, growing ever more threatening, of castration.

It is, therefore, love – sexual relations – that is the real threat to, the real source of fear for, the ego. What seduces men into an erection (sex-ual and cultural) is libidinal impulses, whether emanating from women or from men. The result, however, is, as I say, a terrible irony. Freud represses this erection – as libidinal, loving, or what Kierkegaard calls

upbuilding – and transforms it into the sense of guilt. Because he cannot see that the sense of guilt has its roots in love – in sexual relations
and their vicissitudes – he is unable to see in love the root of overcoming the sense of guilt. He does not see that love, when it is made historical – eschewing both the castration complex and the myth of the
primal father as' evasions (repressions) of the golden rule – is conflictual, in the beginning. Either/or. Either the conflict is loving, fraught
with all the tensions, the fear and trembling, of life. Or it is hateful.
Choose life, not death. Freud is dead right about the pervasiveness of
aggressivity in our lives (personal and cultural) and the sense of guilt
that it engenders. But he fails to see that it is only love as the dialectic
of desire and self that is both true history and true theory and that, as
the source of guilt, provides at once the unique and the universal way
of overcoming it. Love as the dialectic of desire and self is the golden
rule. What Freud sees but does not, however, comprehend is the fact
that the command that you love the other as yourself is the essence of
aggressivity – there is no aggressiveness outside the golden rule – and
the source of both masochism and sadism. The response to this aggressivity and to these perversions is then dependent on (I limit myself here
to theory) how we imagine the desire of both self and other, each of
whom is the history (desire) of the other.

   The fact that Freud cannot imagine the relationship of self and
other as the golden rule of civilization (history) is made eminently
clear at the very end of *Civilization and its Discontents*. Here he discusses the question whether, given his concept of the superego as
social conscience (history, tradition, the categorical imperative), the
concept of neurosis may not be just as applicable to society as a whole
as to the individual. Is it not possible, he asks, for a particular civilization, for an entire cultural epoch, indeed, for the whole of the
human race to become neurotic? While acknowledging that analysis
of social neuroses could be fruitful, Freud urges caution in using
analogies that tear concepts from the sphere of the individual, where
they were first developed, and apply them to a new and different
sphere, that of society.

Moreover [he observes further], the diagnosis of communal neuroses is faced
with a special difficulty. In an individual neurosis we take as our starting-point
the contrast that distinguishes the patient from *his environment, which is
assumed to be "normal."* For a group all of whose members are affected by one
and the same disorder no such background could exist; *it would have to be
found elsewhere.* And as regards the therapeutic application of our knowledge,
what would be the use of the most correct analysis of social neuroses, since *no
one possesses authority to impose such a therapy upon the group?* (338e)[56]

As I have already indicated, I am not primarily concerned in this study with Freud's theory of neurosis. I shall not specifically address the issue whether by neurosis Freud means here a conflict between the ego and the sexual instincts (as he continues to represent it, at least in part, in late works like "Lay Analysis" and "Analysis Terminable and Interminable"). Nor shall I discuss the issue whether such a concept of neurosis would be consistent with his view of the superego, which, as heir to the castration complex, engenders a fatal sense of guilt in the ego.[57] But what is striking in this passage is the inconsistency that Freud shows to exist between his concepts of neurosis and the superego. Freud holds that the Oedipus complex lies at the root of neurosis. He also holds that the complete resolution (the repression or demolition) of the Oedipus complex, by way of the castration complex, eliminates neurosis yet leads to the superego and the ever-increasing sense of guilt that threatens civilization with disintegration. But what, then, will be the "environment" (*Umgebung*) to which Freud will appeal as the norm (standard) to be imposed (by whom?) on the neurotic patient? The "environment" is constituted by the superego – both the individual superegos (of family and society) and the collective superegos (of individuals); and what the superego represents for the individual is the norms of society (moral, religious, social). Since nobody escapes the castration complex – except the neurotic – nobody escapes the superego – except women. The social "environment" to which one would then appeal as the norm for the individual man is thus composed of men of whom, as we have seen Freud say, the individual man has the greatest fear. For what men fear, above all else, is each other (and thus themselves) as the ultimate threat of feminization (castration).

All of this is really quite fantastic. But the reason that it is important to draw out the absurd implications of the metapsychology of Freud is that he leaves them largely in the shadows and/or does not (wish [us] to) see them at all. This is not to ridicule Freud but to ensure that we do not ourselves become risible in either merely following or merely rejecting his psychology for inadequate reasons. It is important to realize that it is precisely because of his metapsychology that Freud is, as always, incapable of seeing that neurosis (pathology) – individual or social – is discernible on the basis of a *Kontrast* not between the individual (neurotic) and the social norm but rather between neurotic and "sane" norms (ideals, concepts) of both individual and society. Freud has absolutely no concept of the norm as ideal that is applicable to both individual and society but reducible to neither. He does not see that his concept of the superego makes it impossible for him to distinguish between truth and illusion, between sanity and neurosis, between crisis (critique) and guilt (the compulsive need to maintain the punishment, the castration, of love), or between, ultimately, love and guilt. The superego no more establishes a contrast between individual (neurotic) and social norm than it makes it impossible to find a norm "elsewhere." Freud has no insight into the fact that it is precisely the golden rule that is the *Kontrast* which is to be found elsewhere – other than either in the individual or in society but thus in both as their critical conscience, at once individual and social. This *Kontrast* is what I am calling in this study the alternative ontology – of the dialectic of desire and self.

Immediately following his observation that he cannot imagine an alternative (*anderswoher*) to the superego – no *Hintergrund*, no unconscious, no depth – Freud concludes *Civilization and its Discontents* by returning (unconsciously) to the naïve spirit with which, he says, as we saw, he initiates his critique of the golden rule. He writes that he neither champions the opinion that civilization is progressive nor rejects the opinion that it makes life intolerable for the individual. But then Freud discreetly (evasively) acknowledges the fact that these seemingly sophisticated views are utterly inconsistent with his claim that civilization (the superego) provides the environmental contrast by which individual neurosis is made discernible and to which there is, as such, no alternative or background when he proceeds to write:

My impartiality is made all the easier to me by my knowing very little about all these things. *One thing only do I know for certain* and that is that man's judgments of value follow directly his wishes for happiness – that, accordingly, they are an attempt to support his illusions with arguments ... [He goes on to observe that historical trends can be viewed both as necessary and so unsurmountable and as contingent and so surmountable.] Thus I have not the courage to rise up before my fellow men as a prophet, and I bow to their reproach that I can offer them no consolation ... The fateful question for the human species seems to me to be whether and to what extent their cultural development will succeed in mastering the disturbance of their communal life by the human instinct of aggression and self-destruction. (339-40e)[58]

What is one to make of this statement? Where does Freud stand within it? Is the truth of his observation (that human aggressivity, as the product of civilization, may well be the destroyer of civilization) undercut by his claims that he does not know what he is talking about and that what he says only reflects his own individual wish for illusory happiness? Freud states that he is no prophet offering consolation to others. But who is a prophet? A prophet, it is certain, is not one who believes that our "environment" or civilization is the norm lacking, elsewhere, a background. A prophet is not one who believes in some god who imposes a consoling norm upon the group. Indeed, the prophet is the one who champions the golden rule. For it is the golden rule that provides the background for all analysis.

Yet Freud had introduced the golden rule into *Civilization and its Discontents* with the intention of knocking out his enemy with a preemptive strike. He claims that the loving ideal of civilization fails to account for, while, indeed, it even increases, aggressivity as the sense of guilt. The sense of guilt represents the revenge of the ego upon itself for its identification with the father('s penis) – as reflected in the superego, the ego ideal. But what Freud demonstrates by the end of *Civilization and its Discontents*, however, is that the sense of guilt, in reflecting the originary ambivalence of hate and love, of the death instinct and Eros, in identification with the father, is the castration of love, of libido, of the golden rule. This means that ultimately Freud has no way of distinguishing Eros from the superego as heir to the Oedipus complex and its suppression in and as the castration complex. Both Eros and the superego, in stemming from originary identification with the father('s penis), represent civilization. It is the contradictory fate of Freud's metapsychology that its dualism inevitably collapses into monism. He begins with the dualism between ego and sexuality, between the individual and society (nature!). When this dualism proves to be inadequate in accounting for the phenomena of narcissism and aggressivity, it evolves, finally, into the dualism between the two fundamental, primordial, distinct, and separate instincts of Eros and death. But this final dualism, no more than the initial dualism, can account for libido (love) as at once individual and social – "unnatural" yet civilized. Indeed, in bringing together the Oedipus complex, centred on the castration complex, and the theory of the two primordial instincts of Eros and death, Freud makes it evident that both reflect originary identification with the penis. The penis (the father, God) is its own castration, its own internalization of aggressivity, its own ambivalence of love and hate. Not only does Eros, therefore, not represent sexuality, but it also becomes indistinguishable from the death instinct, given their common source in the phallic ambivalence of love and hate.

Once the pleasure principle is unveiled as the death instinct, its revenge upon Freudian metapsychology is complete. But the loving victory of the golden rule is also complete. For what the golden rule demonstrates, to those who have ears to hear, is that you can truly oppose your enemy only by loving him. If, however, you view your enemy as your dualistic opposite who tempts you to exercise your aggression upon him as he aggresses against you, then you will become identical with him. This, precisely, is the fate of Eros in Freud's metapsychology. It is clear, then, that it is not the sense of guilt, as aggressivity, that explains the golden rule but the golden rule, in commanding you to love your enemy as yourself, that accounts for the aggressivity of guilt.

V CONCLUSION

Love and guilt. Freud clearly knows that the sense of guilt with which he finds the civilized life of human beings burdened must arise directly out of their sense of loving. Where there is no love, there guilt is not to be found. He stresses the role of love in forming the libidinal ties that bind group members both to each other and to their leader. Love, he shows, is one of the great themes of civilization. Love is, above all, we should think, the central dynamic of the Oedipus complex. As human beings love – although Freud typically says as human beings are loved (by others) – so they find themselves burdened with the (unconscious) sense of guilt. Indeed, he holds that the more Eros succeeds in civilizing human beings by binding them together into ever greater unities, the less opportunity they have for directing aggressivity outward and the more they are compelled to interiorize it in their superego as guilty conscience. The superego punishes the (male) ego for the aggressivity against the father (both personal and cultural) that it continues to harbour, unconsciously, but that it represses consciously. Although I am not primarily concerned in this study, as I have indicated, with Freud's theories of neurosis or psychotherapy, one cannot help posing an essential question that is raised by the relationship between love and guilt. Is the sense of guilt, in Freud's view, a neurotic condition – and thus, one would suppose – subject to therapeutic cure (intervention)?[59] Or does it signify a fundamental character of (modern?) civilization for which there is no cure and from which there is no exit?

When Freud indicates, in *Civilization and its Discontents*, that there are three sources of human suffering – our body, the external world, and our relationship to others, that is, love – it seems clear that he, like anyone, would distinguish between the (physical) body and the external (physical) world, on the one hand, and our (psychical) relations to others, on the other hand. We can make modifications, to a certain degree, in the conditions that affect our body (both internally and externally) and the external world; but, finally, dissolution and death succeed (by sometimes overwhelming) our restorative efforts. But what about our relationships to others? Freud indicates that it is precisely these relationships that are the source of our greatest suffering. The suffering that results from the loss of, the denial of, the betrayal by someone whom you love and who loves you is incomparable. Strangely, however, Freud says little about the incomparable joys of human relationships, although he does recall that the sex act between two human beings is the obvious model for everyone of what constitutes the most intense pleasure in life. But this is patently a highly tendentious judgment on Freud's part, given his own insight into the infinite variety of human experience. It is Freud, we recall, who criticizes the universality of the golden rule in the name of the individuality (subjectivity) of human happiness. It is also Freud who points out that sexual satisfaction is no satisfaction at all, because, in itself, it is ephemeral and unstable, ultimately non-existent. The paradox that he acknowledges, yet does not explicitly embrace, is that the sexual instincts can be satisfied from the beginning only insofar as they are inhibited from the beginning. It is clear that the sense of guilt does not (directly) arise from either the vulnerability of our body or from our vulnerability to external events and forces. The sense of guilt arises from – within the context of – our relations to others (including oneself as other to oneself, we may assume). Who are these others? What is the nature of these relationships? Why and how do they involve (us in) suffering? How is suffering related to the sense of guilt? Above all, what is the place of love in these relations? Do my relations to others – and their relations to me – constitute the very existence, the dynamic, of love? Is the sense of guilt, as produced by the suffering inherent in our loving relations to others, irremediable?

These questions are not, however, the ones that Freud asks, as we know. Does he presuppose them? Do we presuppose them in reading Freud? Does he hold them to be irrelevant, because non-scientific? We do know that Freud claims that science takes over the treatment of love from where the poets and artists leave it – in their fictional distortions of reality such that they sacrifice interest in the origin and development of the psychical states that constitute love to the finished product. But then we think of the two great works of (religious) art that Freud contemplates: Leonardo's depiction of the *Madonna and Child with Saint Anne* and Michelangelo's statue of *Moses*. Each portrays a profound moment in the biblical (Christian and Jewish) story of love: mother and son (and the mother's mother), with the son also representing the father and the spirit of life; and the lawgiver, the mediator between holy God and holy people whose love of God and people (Freud holds) involves deep, mournful, and triumphant renunciation of instinct (revenge). It is unquestionably true that Freud's analysis of these works of art deepens our sense of what he calls their origin and development (as long as we do not lose the art work for the artist's work). But is it also not true that these incomparable works of art are not yet (because always already) finished, that they are not yet finished with us, with how we are to understand our origin and development, as Freud's own interpretations of them indicate? Their future (perfect) course lies wide open, so long as they belong to our – and we belong to their – past, a past whose history is our (their) future. The child is the father of man, although now we say that the child gives birth to humanity: its crucifixion and its redemption, both past and future. The lawgiver comes down from the mountain bearing the word of God written in stone, triumphant, only to find his people worshipping the golden calf. But Freud proposes that Michelangelo proposes that Moses proposes that God proposes that the real test of the law is for Moses and God. How do Moses and God respond when they realize that it is precisely the law that brings idolatry and apostasy, the all-too-human nature of human beings, into existence? The law does not eliminate the worship of idols. Indeed, the law brings the worship of idols into existence, for it is only on the basis of the law that we are confronted with a choice of images – either true or false, either good or evil, either liberating or idolatrous. It is the law that renders problematic the relationship between image (fiction, illusion) and truth, "man" and God, nature and spirit. Do not our relations with others, which are the source of our greatest suffering, involve and express – presuppose – justice and love, law and the resurrection of the spirit, the spirit of paternal renunciation (sacrifice) and the flesh of maternal joy (selflessness)?

These questions are but infinite versions of "the question of the *purpose* of human life" that, as we saw Freud write at the beginning of *Civilization and its Discontents*, "has been raised countless times" but that, he asserts, has never been satisfactorily answered and "perhaps" never will be. "Only religion," he goes on to remark, "can answer the question of the *Zweck des Lebens*. One can hardly be wrong in concluding that the idea of life having a *purpose* stands and falls with the religious system." Freud claims to pursue the less exalted question of what human beings reveal in their actual behaviour (*Verhalten*) to be the *purpose* and intention of their lives. The answer that people give to the question of the purpose of human life "can hardly be in doubt," he declares. "They strive after happiness; they want to become happy and to remain so." Human beings aim to minimize pain and to maximize pleasure. For what "decides the *purpose* of life is simply the program of the pleasure principle" that "dominates the operation of the mental apparatus from the start." Yet Freud immediately acknowledges that in the end it is precisely the program of the pleasure principle that is rendered absolutely incapable of being carried through (*durchfürhbar*) by the universal *All*, macrocosm as well as microcosm, the plan of "Creation" itself (262–4ᵉ). I discussed this passage earlier. I shall now discuss it once again in conclusion. It casts a weird, penetrating light on Freud's concept of human relations, their *Verhalten*, and thus on his concept of the relationship between love and guilt.

As I indicated before, it is not at all obvious that we can accept as true Freud's opening gambit that, while the question of the purpose of human life has been raised countless times, it has never received a satisfactory answer. Is it not equally or, indeed, rather more likely that this question has received countless (infinite) satisfactory, that is, true answers? Does not Freud's formulation of the relationship between question and answer harbour a hidden (positivistic) assumption, widely held, that, while questions are countless and thus pluralistic, amphibolic, plastic, and indefinite – feminine (deep, mysterious, impenetrable) – answers are monopolistic, one, monolithic, and definite – masculine (obvious, clear, attainable)? One of the great images of the monolith is the erect penis, carved in stone. The penis becomes in Freud, as we have seen, the ultimate symbol of ambivalence, amphiboly, antagonism, and aggressivity, a dualism that, at once sexual and social, splits, by castration, self and desire, hate and love, death and life, action and passion, man and woman. But we also know another image carved in stone, the Mosaic law, the two tables of the ten commandments as depicted by Michelangelo in his statue of Moses and lovingly described by Freud in his remarkable essay on the statue, "The Moses of Michelangelo." Freud argues that Michelangelo deviates, "from inner motives," from the biblical depiction of Moses (in Exodus 32.7–35, which he cites), given the "glaring incongruities and contradictions" in the Bible's portrayal of Moses as irascible and subject to fits of sudden passion (276). Since, according to the reading that Freud gives of the statue, Moses is not about to fly into a rage (over the apostasy of the Israelites) and to smash the two tables, he concludes that Michelangelo's

Moses must be a quite different man, a new Moses of the artist's conception; so that Michelangelo must have had the presumption to emend the sacred text and to falsify the character of that holy man. Can we think him capable of a boldness which might almost be said to approach the act of blasphemy? (274) He has modified the theme of the broken Tables; he does not let Moses break them in his wrath, but makes him be influenced by the danger that they will be broken and makes him calm that wrath, or at any rate prevent it from becoming an act. In this way he has added *something new and more than human* to the figure of Moses; so that the giant frame with its tremendous physical power becomes only a concrete expression of the highest mental achievement that is possible in a man, that of struggling successfully against an inward passion for the sake of a cause to which he has devoted himself. (277e)

I am not here concerned with Freud's actual reading of the Bible, Moses, and Michelangelo's statue. My point is simply to suggest, by way of Michelangelo's statue and Freud's reading of it, that "the question of the purpose of human life" has been satisfactorily answered – an infinite number of times. But I also want to suggest that this answer is no more dual, broken, absent, and always to be interpreted anew, like the stone tablets of the law, than is the question ceaselessly asked monolithic: what, finally, is the purpose of life? Freud is himself careful to note that it is "perhaps" only the case that the question of the purpose of human life will never be answered – monolithically – as he protects the possibility of his being the new lawgiver, in the tradition of the blasphemous Moses sculpted in stone by Michelangelo. But it is bizarre to suppose that the purpose of life has never been satisfactorily answered and "perhaps" may never be (yet "perhaps" may be). If this statement were true, then it would be false; for there would be no criterion for knowing what a satisfactory answer would be. It is equally bizarre to suppose (as orthodox Jews and Christians are often said by others to suppose) that the answer to the question of the purpose of life is known only to Moses or to Jesus – directly revealed to them by God – and that it is not known to (other) human beings (in this life). I cannot know what it is that is known only to Moses or to Jesus (and not to me) without knowing *what* it is that I do not know. (I do not deny that Moses or Jesus, as portrayed in the Bible or by Michelangelo and Leonardo, can fruitfully represent what I do not know – the unconscious, say. But it is important not to reify these figures as idols before which I then bow down in abnegation of responsibility for my own ignorance.)

It is only religion, Freud holds, that "can answer the question of the purpose of life," and religion, he indicates just a page or two earlier, is the belief of "the common man" that consists in doctrines solving the riddles of the universe and in promises involving future compensation for earthly suffering.[60] Again, we are not presently concerned with Freud's conception of religion. Rather, what we want to know is the following: if Moses, as depicted by Michelangelo, according to Freud, is not religious, what is he? More relevant here, what is the source of Moses' "new" revelation that is blasphemous and apparently non-biblical? Not only does Freud find "purpose" in the statue of Moses, but he also proceeds, in the passage in *Civilization and its Discontents*, to argue that purpose and intentionality are discernible in the "behavior" of human beings – as they strive for happiness according to the purpose of life programed by the pleasure principle. But it is this program that Freud immediately acknowledges, as he had acknowledged in *The Interpretation of Dreams*, when discussing the pleasure principle, as we saw in chapter 2, to be blocked by the regulations of the *All*, by creation itself. What are we to make of the fact that Freud claims to discern the purpose of life in human behaviour, when, on the one hand, he acknowledges that this purpose, as dictated by the pleasure principle, is denied by the very nature of things, by creation itself, and, on the other hand, he interprets Michelangelo's statue of Moses as richly purposive?

There are two perplexing elements that are central to this fascinating passage on the question of the purpose of human life in *Civilization and its Discontents*. First, Freud suggests that "perhaps" there is no satisfactory answer to this question, since (yet?!) religion alone can answer the question of the purpose of life. The relationship between the purpose of human life and religion is highly ambiguous. Second, Freud indicates that he can (more modestly) read the answer to the question of the purpose of human life in the actual behaviour of men and women, although that purpose, as dictated by the pleasure principle, is blocked, in the beginning, by the very nature of things. What is Freud's more modest understanding of purpose, if there is no reason for his viewing purpose within the purposeless terms of the contradictory pleasure principle? I introduced Freud's discussion of Michelangelo's statue of Moses to suggest that Freud shows, brilliantly, how a revered work of art – however badly generations of its admirers may have distorted its meaning, as he suggests – answers the question of the purpose of human life. But thus our perplexities are intensified. Moses' "more than human" mental purpose is achieved by denying (overcoming, appropriating) the illusory (contradictory) satisfactions of the pleasure principle. If this suggests, however, that Moses is not a religious figure, given that it is religion, Freud holds, that obeys the pleasure principle in adhering to illusion and in denying reality, then it is little wonder that Freud finds that the purpose revealed by human behaviour cannot be that dictated by the pleasure principle.

Freud's dilemma, then, is this. He cannot retain the pleasure principle if he eschews religion. Equally, he cannot retain purpose if he eschews religion. His discussion of the purpose of human life and of Michelangelo's statue of Moses makes it clear, however, that he is not prepared to (he cannot) give up purpose. Still, when purpose is understood on the basis of the pleasure principle, he shows that it is opposed by *das All* – by creation itself. The statue of Moses suggests, Freud indicates, that the question of the purpose of human life has been satisfactorily answered. The statue, however, is not, perhaps, religious. Be that as it may. What Freud's analysis of the statue makes clear, however, is that the purpose of life that it reveals is not governed by the pleasure principle. What, then, is the purpose of life that Freud claims to discern

in human behaviour, if it is not that governed by the pleasure principle? Is it not extraordinary that Freud continues to adhere to the pleasure principle, while recognizing, from the beginning, that its "purpose" is utterly contradictory and illusory? But this is precisely the
grounds for his rejection of religion. The answer that religion gives to
the question of the purpose of life is contradictory and illusory, yet it
alone "can answer the question of the purpose of life." Do we not
begin to suspect that the reason that Freud continues to adhere to the
pleasure principle is precisely because it allows him to mask the illusions of religion? Is this not what Freud has shown in his interpretation of Michelangelo's statue of Moses? If the pleasure principle is not
true, what alternative will there be to religion, that is, to discerning the
Übermenschliches in human striving, in the behaviour not only of
Moses but also of all human beings? This is doubly bizarre, however,
given the fact that the pleasure principle is the first principle of illusory life that science must give up in order to establish the certainty of
the reality principle.

If the contradictory illusoriness of the pleasure principle cannot be
corrected in making it the contradictory, illusory basis of science, if
the alternative to the pleasure principle is not science, what, then, is
the alternative? If science does not show that the question of the purpose of human life, as it is revealed in human behaviour, is answered
by the pleasure principle – when science is understood as the secondary principle whose primary principle is illusory, the reflection of
a reflection – do we give up purpose or illusion? Freud, characteristically, gives up neither. He has no explanation of the purpose of
human "behaviour," as he both rejects religion – while acknowledging that religion alone can answer the question of the purpose of
human life – and sees the pleasure principle reduce (reduced by) science to the contradictory mythology of his metapsychology. If Freud
were ever to acknowledge that the pleasure principle is correctable –
on grounds other than science, naturally – then he would doubtless
have to admit that religion is correctable. For what is so fundamentally puzzling here is that the pleasure principle and religion are
identical, for both deny the reality principle (science) in the name of
illusory satisfaction. Yet, since science (metapsychology) is but the
illusory reflection of the pleasure principle, the pleasure principle is
not correctable, in theory, by science. If the pleasure principle is correctable, if there is purpose discernible in human behaviour, if Moses
– a lawgiver, and no Oedipus – is *übermenschlich* in mental achievement, will this not suggest that the correction of the pleasure principle, since it cannot come from science, will have to come from ...
itself?

But what is pleasure? Either pleasure is the contradictory illusion from whose metapsychological coils Freud cannot escape – the inherent tendency of instinct to restore an earlier state of things: inorganic nature, nirvana, death. Or pleasure is desire, love, will. In the second (original) alternative, pleasure is not the contradictory avoidance of unpleasure but the paradoxical, loving cause of itself. It is the dialectic of self and desire as articulated in and through the golden rule and as demonstrated in and through the works of the human spirit, including, among infinite others, *Beyond the Pleasure Principle*. Is not Freud's greatest fear not that religion is true – given his love of the works of Michelangelo and Leonardo (not to mention Dostoevsky or even Shakespeare) – but that psychoanalysis is true, that it has, always already, answered the question of the purpose of human life? For – and this is the challenge faced by anyone who brings truth down from the mountain into Zarathustra's (not Plato's) biblical cave of idolatry – if psychoanalysis is true, then its truth will be infinitely different from, because undecidably indistinguishable from, religion. Then psychoanalysis and religion, not to mention poetry, political theory, philosophy, will be among the countless satisfactory answers to the question of the purpose of human life. In evading this countless (infinite) answer, Freud makes a sacrifice (repression) of truth that is enormous, a sacrifice that is not in the renunciatory spirit of his hero, the superhuman Moses. In denying the truth of religion he makes the illusion imputed to religion the basis of the pleasure principle. He then makes the illusory first principle of pleasure the first principle of his science, whose illusory contradictions – dignified by the name metapsychology but actually mythology, as Freud himself comes to acknowledge – haunt his system from beginning to end.

But we, readers of Freud, remember that the pleasure principle turns out to be (turns into) the death instinct and that it is the death instinct, embodied in the sense of guilt, that threatens civilization with destruction. The sense of guilt represents the ego's fear of the superego (the father, the penis, God), the heir of the Oedipus complex, whose demolition is brought about by the castration complex as it confirms the originary, pre-libidinal identification, on the part of both male and female children, with the father's ambivalent penis – its presence, as male self, and its absence, as female desire. What we see, therefore, is that, although Freud recognizes that the greatest cause of suffering is our relations to others – he is silent, as I indicated above, about our relations to others as our greatest source of joy – he has no metapsychological representation of relationship. There is no relationship, no other, in the primal father('s penis), understood either as the primitive patriarch of humankind or as the individual father of every individual child. While the primitive patriarch immediately imposes identification (as aim-inhibited sexuality) on the primal sons, the individual, pre-Oedipal son immediately imposes identification with the father (his ideal) on himself. Because Freud has no concept of relationship, he has no explanation of beginning, of origin, of development, of history, notwithstanding his criticism of the love poets. Where there is relationship, there we find history, and vice versa. This is the reason that the history of relationships – of the vicissitudes of our loves – embodies our relationships as history, as love. The primal father has no father (or mother), and the individual father is taken immediately, non-libidinally, by his infant son as his ideal, while the infant daughter, in her immediate, non-libidinal identification with the mother, is destined to desire what the mother herself wants (desires/lacks) and thus what she, as woman, desires but does not have: the father's penis.

As I suggested above, it is hard not to see the myth of the primal father and the Oedipus complex as parodies of "what the common man understands by his religion," which Freud so harshly condemns in *Civilization and its Discontents* (261). He scorns what he calls illusory belief in providential consolation for present suffering. But we may ask whether the claim that Freud makes at the end of the work – that there is no "elsewhere," no background, no critical principle, no norm to which one can appeal as a prise on civilization when identified with the father('s penis) – is any less illusory. The fact that helpless dependence on the erect penis is completely illusory Freud himself demonstrates, yet without understanding his own demonstration. This demonstration is the castration complex, that with which the female child begins and that at which the male child ends – each the opposite of the other, each the contradiction of the other. The difference between male and female is thereby utterly occluded by their identification with the penis, which, as erect, is thus absent in the male and present in the female – it is castrated – and which, as flaccid, is thus present in the male and absent in the female – it is castrated. Identification with the penis – the originary ambivalence of love and hate, of the two primordial instincts of Eros and death – ensures castration of all libido understood as relationship with the other, whether, following Freudian terminology, this libido is uninhibited or inhibited. Indeed, identification with the penis is but one more confirmation of the pleasure principle, that primary illusion whose beginning is purely mythical unless and until the reality of human relations is presupposed. But Freud never abandons the mythical penis and its identification as the pleasure principle. Rather, he erects it ever more firmly as he arrives at his definitive formulation of the Oedipus complex (including his concept of female sexuality) in the final phase of his work in the 1920s and 30s.

With his concept of the castration complex, based on originary identification with the penis – itself but a ritual confirmation of the originary, illusory religion of the pleasure principle – Freud sacrifices, as I have argued, a comprehensive conception not only of libido, or love, but also of aggressivity, or activity (the intense passion of Moses actively transmuted into loving patience). The issue is not that aggressivity, guilt, hate, violence ... are not terrible forces of destruction in our lives. The issue is, rather, how they are to be comprehended (contained). If there is no beginning other than the narcissistic violence of the primal father or narcissistic identification with the patriarchal penis, then it follows that there will be no elsewhere, background, or alternative by which to distinguish between the sense of guilt as the psychical impotence of neurosis and the sense of guilt as the psychical impotence – the death instinct – of civilization, as such. But what is perplexing is that it is Freud himself, as we saw, who conjures up an alternative – that of the Christian church – where identification and libido (the ideal of love) are shown to be inextricably related. Not only does the church, as he depicts it, embody the golden rule – it is not a group, he says – but it also represents the total renunciation of both the myth of the primal father and the castration complex. Yet, in *Civilization and its Discontents* Freud denounces the golden rule as failing to account for human aggressivity, while simultaneously acknowledging, apparently, that it is the only effective counter to (natural) aggressivity (which is also a point of emphasis in "Why War?"), if not itself the very origin of aggressivity. What Freud never sees, however, is that the death instinct, aggressivity, the sense of guilt ... cannot account for themselves and cannot be accounted for in terms of what is merely their opposite. For opposition, or enmity, simply repeats the contradiction at the heart of the duality between the pleasure principle, as primary process, and the reality principle, as secondary process. He does not see that it is the golden rule that is the very source of the concept of action – the command that you love your neighbour as yourself. He does not see that it is the perversion (evasion, denial) of action that is the origin of the aggressivity that he discerns but cannot account for. He never connects his concept of aggressivity with his concept of activity – desire, love, will – which, he knows, is neither masculine nor feminine. At the same time, however, he never gives up the biological duality between the sexes as the very basis of his instinct theory – "the irreconcilable difference" between the ego instincts and sexual instincts, between death and Eros – and of the castration complex.

What Freud does not see is that the sense of guilt, the psychical impotence so widespread in (modern) civilization, has its source in love – in human relations – and not in identification with the penis (the primal father). He knows, phenomenologically, that where there is guilt, there love is to be found (and where there is love, there guilt is to be found). But he fails to see that the source of guilt is not identification with the penis – by way of the superego, the castration complex, and the Oedipus complex. The source of guilt is love, our relations with others. It is true that guilt can be and is deviously rationalized in terms of identification with the penis (etc.), but it is no less true that it can be comprehended (overcome) only in and through love – the golden rule. Surely, Moses' comprehension of the law comes not from identification with the father's penis (or its avatar the golden calf) but from love: loving the enemy, the holy, idolatrous people – as he (Moses) loves God above all others and his neighbour as himself. To love your enemy – as you would want your enemy to love you, not as he loves (or does not love) you – means to love him not insofar as he aggresses against you (or against himself or anyone else) but insofar as you refuse to treat him on the same inimical grounds of aggressivity as he treats you. To love your enemy does not mean that you are blind to his being your enemy, insofar as he is your enemy. For, behold! there are your fellow Israelites, the holy people, dancing before the golden calf, constructed for them by your brother Aaron. What the command that you are to love your enemy (as you love yourself) means is that you refuse, constitutionally, as Freud says about his own pacifist opposition to war, to see yourself reflected in the violence of his eyes as the aggressor.

The emotional dynamics involved in and expressed through the golden rule are intricate, loaded, dramatic, hidden, and unconscious. They are full of evasion, rationalization, guilt, denial, love, hurt – the real stuff of depth psychology, as of the depths of poetry, sculpture, philosophy, and religion. But they are rendered incomprehensible when based on the metapsychology of the castration complex that suspends (male) libidinal relations with the other between originary identification with the penis and final identification with the penis. The penis then becomes the monolith whose erection compulsively repeats the contradictions of the pleasure principle, the ultimate appearance of which is the sense of guilt, the representative of the death instinct. The only alternative to the non-libidinal erection of the monolith and its castration of love is love, whose images, among infinite others, are those of the son who, as the lamb of God, is the father and the spirit of humankind, and of the father who, as the superhuman bearer of the two stone tablets of the law, is the son of his people and their very spirit. Both Jesus and Moses are images of sacrifice. Both are images of truth and love. In casting aside the monoliths of premodernism, they repudiate, always already, the postmodern, postbiblical images of mere duality, amphiboly, difference, plurality, ambivalence, and relativity. They embrace the paradox, the undecidability, of freedom, love, and justice, the law of the golden rule, whose relationship of desire and self is written in the flesh of the heart. Jesus and Moses are the image of history, of our history, of how we are to relate to our past, our foreparents, our selves, our desires, our origin, our development, our future. In the next chapters we shall directly engage the confrontation that Freud enacts between the myth of the primal father and the historical Moses. Why does he (re)turn directly to the biblical account of Moses? Will we find that it is, indeed, religion, together with depth psychology, that answers the historical question of the purpose of human life?

4 The Myth of the Primal Father

I INTRODUCTION

In this chapter we shall see that Freud finds the lynchpin of his metapsychology in the myth of the primal father. He argues in *Totem and Taboo* that, in murdering the primal father, the primal sons initiate civilization by instituting the horror of incest. Thus he has what he considers to be the historical explanation of the origin of the impulses central to the Oedipus complex: the (male's) desire for the mother and hostility to the father. Still, we may recall that we saw in chapter 3 that the Oedipus complex does not survive the original identification with the penis (both its presence and its absence) and the final castration of the penis (both its presence and its absence). Will the myth of the primal father serve to explain the origin of the Oedipus complex, as Freud claims? Or will it turn out, rather, that what the myth of the primal father shows is that, just as the end of the Oedipus complex – consistent with the pleasure principle – is the castration complex, so the end of the castration complex is the father complex?

Freud presents the myth of the primal father in the fourth and last essay of *Totem and Taboo: Some Points of Agreement between the Mental Lives of Savages and Neurotics*. In the first three essays his general aim is to establish an analogy or parallel between primitive taboo and modern neurosis. Essays I–III thus prepare the way for his argument in the fourth essay that in the myth of the primal father we find the ultimate analogy or parallel between primitive and modern. *Totem and Taboo* contains the following four essays: I "The Horror of Incest" (on totemism and exogamy in primitive societies); II "Taboo and Emotional Ambivalence"; III "Animism, Magic and the Omnipotence of Thoughts" (on primitive thought); IV "The Return of Totemism in Childhood" (on the myth of the primal father).

At the end of the fourth and last essay, Freud points out that there are two "uncertainties of my premises or the difficulties involved in my conclusions" that his readers will not have failed to notice (220). Both uncertainties or difficulties stem directly from Freud's claim to establish an analogy or parallel between primitive taboo and modern neurosis or between what he calls (primitive) historical reality and (modern) psychical reality. Both problems bear closely on the myth of the primal father. For it is precisely Freud's claim that what we have in the myth of the primal father is the historical explanation of what today is psychically real. I shall focus on these two uncertainties as a way of elucidating the difficulties with which Freud is confronted in the myth of the primal father.

The first uncertainty, which I shall take up in section II, involves what Freud calls the relationship between collective and individual mind and how culture is transmitted from one generation to the next. In other words, what is the historical relationship between universal and individual? In this context I shall examine the reversal in his argument that Freud introduces near the end of essay II of *Totem and Taboo*. Although prior to this point Freud insists strongly on an analogy (or parallel) between taboo (in "primitive" society) and neurosis (in "civilized" society), he now acknowledges that taboo and neurosis are psychologically different. But how, we shall ask, can the myth of the primal father serve as the explanation of modern civilization if in fact Freud recognizes that there is a "psychological difference" between (primitive) taboo and modern (civilized) neurosis?

The fact that he calls the relationship between taboo and neurosis into question by asking how there could be a transition from primitive to modern leads Freud to what he acknowledges to be his second uncertainty or difficulty, which I shall take up in section III. What is at stake here is the relationship between what Freud calls fact and fantasy, between material reality and psychical reality, between deed and intention, between external and internal. According to Freud, primitive peoples (as represented by the primal sons) atone for historical deeds, the actual killing of the primal father (as embodied in the totem meal). In contrast, modern (male) neurotics react only to psychical realities, to internal fantasies, not to the actual facts of sleeping with their mother and killing their father. He holds that what is today the (internal) psychical reality of neurotics has its origin in the real (external) deeds of the primal horde, the murder of the primal father by the primal sons.

But how, then, will Freud explain the historical change from original (external) deed or fact to terminal (internal) fantasy or illusion? What is psychical reality? Is it internal or external, fiction or fact, thought or act?

It is in the context of the analogy between taboo and neurosis, which turns out to rest on a psychological difference, and of the difference between factual and psychical, which divides between an original deed and a terminal fantasy, that we shall repose the question of the unconscious and its relationship to history. This will involve our examining a number of works of Freud in addition to *Totem and Taboo* that bear on how we understand the constitution of psychical reality. In case studies and related works Freud is faced with the question of the status of infantile memory and thus, once again, with the problem of metapsychological dualism. He recognizes that each side of the dualism, when taken by itself, is inconceivable. He also recognizes that the two sides of the dualism, when taken together, are explicitly contradictory. But, instead of viewing the contradictory dualism to which he has been led as a challenge to reformulate the historical relationship between individual and universal, he simply embraces it.

Here is Freud's dilemma. If, on the one hand, infantile memory is based on a real (external) deed, it will be a product of the immature and weak ego and the infant's historically unformed consciousness. But it is hardly credible, Freud acknowledges, to base the Oedipus complex on incomplete, infantile experience that is so personally fragile and slight. Further, there would be no role for the unconscious. If, on the other hand, infantile memory is based on a real (internal) deed, it will be the product of the mature and strong id and its historically formed unconscious. But it is hardly credible, Freud again acknowledges, to base the Oedipus complex on complete, adult experience that eliminates the personal experience of the infant. Further, there would be no role for consciousness. Freud and his contemporaries discuss the issue of the historical relationship between individual and universal in the (pseudo-biological) terms of ontogeny (individual) and phylogeny (species), to whose contradictory dualism there is no solution when it does not rethink the relationship between the unconscious and consciousness. What does it mean for the human species, that is, for human history, to claim that ontogeny recapitulates phylogeny? We have reformulated this issue in terms of the historical or ontological (and not scientific or biological) relationship between individual and universal, between self and other, each of which is at one and the same time conscious and unconscious.

In later works Freud goes on to argue that the id (the unconscious), because it is the oldest stratum of the human psyche, serves as the basis of phylogeny, the archaic heritage of the human race. At the same time, in order to explain the origin of the id's content, he is forced to hold that the id is composed of the precipitates of innumerable ego experiences. In other words, phylogeny is based on ontogeny. The primitive id (the unconscious) is the origin of the modern ego (consciousness). Yet the id itself is the product of the ego. Once again, Freud is faced with an ontological dilemma to which his metapsychological dualism offers no solution at all. How can the unconscious (or id) be the originary (internal) principle of the human psyche when it is originally the product of external (ego) experiences? Is the unconscious originally internal (illusion) or external (fact)? When we repose this issue in terms of the myth of the primal father, we are faced with the problem of whether the (myth of the) primal father represents ego (conscious, historical, external fact) or id (unconscious, psychical, internal fantasy). We may observe here that, when Freud develops his concept of the id in the 1920s, he (typically) does not ask whether the primal father, in his original myth, represents the id or the ego.

The question of history – involving what Freud acknowledges to be the uncertain relationships between taboo and neurosis (primitive and modern) and between psyche and reality (fact and fantasy) – leads to two issues that I shall take up in section IV. First, in subsection b, I shall consider the relationship between the Oedipus of Sophocles and the Oedipus complex. I shall show that Freud misconstrues the originary ambivalence of primitive civilization by projecting what he calls the ambivalence of the Oedipus complex onto the secret of Oedipal blindness, which is central to the two plays of Sophocles, *Oedipus the King* and *Oedipus at Colonus*. He equally distorts the phenomenology of modern civilization by reprojecting primitive ambivalence back upon the Oedipus complex. Second, in subsection c, I shall ask, in terms of the debate initiated by Malinowski and carried to a new level of sophistication by Spiro, whether or in what sense the Oedipus complex is at once universal and historical. I shall indicate that the fact that Spiro succeeds in showing that Malinowski fails to establish his case against the universality of the Oedipus complex does not mean that his own case in support of its universality is any more sound. We shall see that Spiro himself is forced to acknowledge that, notwithstanding the universality of the Oedipus complex, pre-modern peoples, like the Trobianders studied by him and Malinowski, and modern peoples handle their Oedipal impulses in fundamentally different ways. But how can the Oedipus complex, if it is universal, have different historical outcomes in the premodern and modern worlds? What is the relationship between universality and historical difference?

All the issues involving the relationship between universality and historical difference and thus the relationship between beginning and end, unconscious and consciousness, id and ego, primitive (taboo) and modern (neurotic), real and psychical, external and internal re-emerge in and through the myth of the primal father. Freud seeks in external (original) history an ultimate explanation of what is today internal (original) psyche. More specifically, he seeks to explain the prohibition of incest and thus the original imposition of the Oedipus complex. But even here the analogy between primitive and modern is put in jeopardy. The reader will have noted the strange fact that there is actually no parallel between the (primitive) myth of the primal father and the (modern) Oedipus complex. It will be remembered that Freud distinguishes between primitive deed and modern fantasy. While the primal sons actually kill the father, their modern (neurotic) heirs only fantasize about sleeping with the mother and killing the father. Modern neurotics have to deal with terrifying fantasies, not with terrible realities. For modern neurotics in the grip of their Oedipus complex it is precisely desire for the mother that generates in them hostility to the father. But Freud fails to point out that there is no mention of the primal mother in the original myth. When the primal sons find themselves in the grip of their irremediable guilt over their murder of the primal father, their mourning is profoundly ambivalent. They hate him (for his sexual monopoly over the primal women). They love him (for his patriarchal penis). The ambivalent hatred (and love) of the primal sons towards the primal father is not motivated by rivalry over the mother. This suggests that what the myth of the primal father explains is not the original ban on incest and with it the Oedipus complex but rather the castration complex (identification with the penis) and with it the father complex. It appears that Freudian metapsychology has found its true basis in a myth in which there is no place for love as the historical dialectic of the golden rule expressing the relationship of self and other, each of whom is at once individual and universal.

II TABOO AND NEUROSIS: PRIMITIVE OR MODERN?

In *Totem and Taboo* Freud undertakes to apply psychoanalytic method to the rich, ethnographic materials published by (especially British) anthropologists in the later nineteenth and early twentieth centuries. He is concerned, above all, to argue for a strict analogy (parallel) between the primitive, the infantile, and the neurotic, all highly coloured concepts that constantly threaten to explode beyond merely scientific description, especially in the heyday of European penetration of the far reaches of the globe.

Freud is heir to the nineteenth century's two opposing, dualistic traditions of dealing with the relationship between civilized and primitive societies: the progressive and the primitive. He thus reflects the confusions, tergiversations, distortions, and illusions that result from, above all, the difficulty (the impossibility) of fitting biblical religion into either the progressive or the primitive tradition. He appears to represent the progressive trend when in various works he views psychoanalysis as the third blow of science against the pretensions of human consciousness, following the blows of Copernicus and Darwin against any claim on the part of human beings to enjoy privileged status within either the cosmos or nature. Psychoanalysis, he argues, demonstrates religion to be illusory – infantile, primitive, and neurotic, even delusory. But what is the nature of this progress over primitive religion, including Judaism and Christianity? In the third blow against human egoism Freud claims to show that psychoanalytic "man" is not the conscious master in his own house but is unconsciously dependent on the father of the house, the superego, which, as heir to the castration complex, is, as we have seen, heir to identification, whose master is the patriarchal penis (God). But what would it mean to render unconscious dependence conscious, if the unconscious, the id, is the heir to the savagery of the primal father whose violence, terminating in his violent murder, institutes civilization as the savage reign of the superego? Is the superego not the domain of the father complex, which is itself the heir of religious illusion? Has not the progressive Freud, who claims that primary, religious illusion is replaced by secondary, scientific reality, now demonstrated that the science of psychoanalysis rules in the name of primitive religion (and so represents the return of religion as repressed)?

In earlier works Freud already claims to have demonstrated the close parallel between the practices and attitudes of religion and obsessional neurosis.[1] He expands this parallel in *Totem and Taboo* with his argument that both the primitive savage and the modern neurotic are subject to a fundamental ambivalence whose basis is the horror of incest and whose origin is the myth of the primal father. Because ambivalence constitutes taboo as that which is at one and the same time loved and feared, desired and prohibited, it is taboo, he argues, that characterizes the lives of both the primitive and the neurotic. What for Freud constitutes taboo is, above all, the combination of totemism and exogamy. As kinship is organized in terms of totem-obligation, he observes, so there is "*a law against persons of the same totem having sexual relations with one another and consequently against their mar-*

rying" (56). (This is what is meant by exogamy.) The only possible explanation for the widespread character of totemism and the ban on incest, Freud holds, is the horror of incest, the fear that incest (especially between son and mother and between brother and sister) is natural and so must be prohibited by strict and severe taboos. The psychoanalytic interest in the primitive horror of incest, Freud observes, is that "it is essentially an *infantile* feature and that it reveals a striking agreement with the mental life of neurotic patients" (69–70). Because the first libidinal objects of the modern boy – his mother and sisters – are incestuous and thus prohibited, when he grows up he must either renounce these attachments or become neurotic and exhibit a "psychical infantalism." The individual becomes neurotic because he either fails to detach himself from incestuous fixations of libido ("developmental inhibition") or retreats to them ("regression"). "Thus incestuous fixations of libido," Freud declares, "continue to play (or begin once more to play) the principal part in his unconscious mental life. We have arrived at the point of regarding a child's relation to his parents, dominated as it is by incestuous longings, as the nuclear complex of neurosis" (70).

Once he has argued that the incest taboo functions in both primitive totemism and modern neurosis, Freud proceeds to show that the taboos dominating primitive life are at once sacred and dangerous, both desired and prohibited. He observes further that "taboo prohibitions have no grounds and are of unknown origin. Though they are unintelligible to *us*, to those who are dominated by them they are taken as a matter of course" (71). Freud concludes that, since savages are unable to give reasons for their taboo-prohibitions and are ignorant of their origin, they must be understood as unconscious. But when we (moderns) reconstruct taboos on the model of obsessional prohibitions, "we must suppose," he adds, that they "are prohibitions of primeval antiquity which *were at some time externally imposed* upon a generation of primitive men; they must, that is to say, no doubt have been impressed on them violently by the previous generation" (85e).[2] Freud does not discuss, let alone explain, how an earlier generation could have been without taboos and free to impose them on their successors. He also notes that it is impossible to tell whether taboos are transmitted from generation to generation by innate inheritance or by cultural acquisition. What is certain, however, he observes, is that, because taboos persist, the original desires that they prohibit must still persist. The tribes in which taboos are found, Freud declares,

must therefore have an ambivalent attitude towards their taboos. In their unconscious there is nothing they would like more than to violate them, but they are afraid to do so; they are afraid precisely because they would like to, and the fear is stronger than the desire. The desire is unconscious, however, in every individual member of the tribe just as it is in neurotics. The most ancient and important taboo prohibitions are the two basic laws of totemism: not to kill the totem animal and to avoid sexual intercourse with members of the totem clan of the opposite sex. These, then, must be the oldest and most powerful of human desires. (85)[3]

Freud repeats a few pages later that

taboo is a primeval prohibition forcibly imposed (by some authority) from outside, and directed against the most powerful longings to which human beings are subject. The desire to violate it persists in their unconscious; those who obey the taboo have an ambivalent attitude to what the taboo prohibits ... Our assertion that taboo originated in a primeval prohibition imposed at one time or other by some external authority is obviously incapable of demonstration. What we shall rather endeavor to confirm, therefore, are the psychological determinants of taboo, which we have learnt to know from obsessional neurosis. (89–90)

Freud then proceeds to argue at length that taboo, in being subject, like obsessional neurosis, to ambivalence, is characterized by the contrary impulses of desire and fear, of love and hate. What is desired and loved is unconscious, while what is feared and hated is conscious. He is concerned, above all, to emphasize the fact that, since there is no need to prohibit something that no one desires to do, a thing that is prohibited must be something that is desired: "where there is a prohibition there must be an underlying desire" (127). The primordial ambivalence constituting primitive taboo is thus built on the tension between the unconscious desire to possess the mother and to kill the father and the conscious fear of fulfilling these desires. The tabooed object is both desired and prohibited. Taboo is equally desire and prohibition.

Once Freud has claimed to explain the structure of primitive taboo, and especially the totemic structure of exogamy prohibiting incest, on the basis of ambivalence as found in obsessional neurosis, he typically reverses direction. The disappearance of the primitive taboo structure from modern life, he observes, shows that "there has been an extraordinary diminution in ambivalence ... *The psychical impulses of primitive peoples were characterized by a higher amount of ambivalence than is to be found in modern, civilized man.*"[4] With the declaration that we "need not discuss here how this alteration came about," he simply concludes that neurotics, in their subjection to the ambivalence of taboo, "may be said to have inherited an archaic constitution as an atavistic vestige" (122–3). But how neurotic ambivalence can represent an archaic inheritance – or how, in other words, primitive taboo can be explained in terms of the obsessional neurosis of moderns – is itself rendered questionable when Freud proceeds to state that "in maintaining the essential similarity between taboo prohibitions and moral [obsessional] prohibitions, I have not sought to dispute the fact that there *must be a psychological difference* between them. The only possible reason why the prohibitions no longer take the form of taboos must be some *change* in the circumstances governing the ambivalence underlying them" (128ᵉ).

Before taking up Freud's discussion of the "psychological difference" between taboo and neurosis and the "change in the circumstances governing the ambivalence underlying them," it is useful to note here that, of the two problems which, at the end of *Totem and Taboo*, Freud says readers would raise about the uncertainties of his premises or the difficulties involved in his conclusions, the first concerns change. He acknowledges that the transmission of culture (the sense of guilt, resulting from the murder of the primal father, which we shall take up in section III) presupposes "the existence of a collective mind, in which mental processes occur just as they do in the mind of an individual ... A part of the problem seems to be met by the inheritance of psychical dispositions which, however, need to be given some sort of impetus in the life of the individual before they can be roused into actual operation" (220–1). But how taboo, which, as we shall see, Freud views as collective (social) – but thus also individual – would become modern neurosis, which he views as anti-social (individual) – but thus no less collective – is rendered even more perplexing when he proceeds to argue that mental impulses cannot be so completely suppressed as to leave no trace behind.

Even the most ruthless suppression [Freud declares] must leave room for distorted surrogate impulses and for reactions resulting from them. If so, however, we may safely assume that no generation is able to conceal any of its more important mental processes from its successor. For psychoanalysis has shown us that *everyone possesses in his unconscious mental activity an apparatus which enables him to interpret other people's reactions, that is, to undo the distortions which other people have imposed on the expression of their feelings.* An unconscious understanding such as this of all the customs, ceremonies and dogmas left behind by the original relation to the [primal] father may have made it possible for later generations to take over their heritage of emotion. (221–2ᵉ)

This is surely one of the most extraordinary passages in all of Freud. The unconscious, understood as an interpretive instrument that recognizes and undoes distortions, is clearly not the "unconscious" of primitive ambivalence whose taboo structure of prohibition is marked by the (unchanging) opposition between "unconscious" desire and "conscious" fear.

Do we not begin to suspect that the "psychological difference" between taboo and neurosis, which Freud acknowledges, is precisely that between the primitive ambivalence of desire and prohibition – where what is desired is always what is feared or prohibited – and the modern repression of desire? For, as Freud indicates in the passage cited above, if repression ("suppression") were successful, it would not be successful: we would not know it as repression. Repression, to be successful, must fail; it must always be supplementary, revealing a trace of itself that is accessible to "unconscious" interpretation. What Freud fails to see, therefore, is that there is no transition from taboo to neurosis, from the ambivalence of the primitive mind to the depth of the modern unconscious. Indeed, as he says in precise terms, change (history) presupposes the unconscious. There is no transition from the (primitive) unconscious to (modern) consciousness. There is transition only (for moderns) from the unconscious to the unconscious through the unconscious. This is the alternative ontology to which there is no alternative.

Having noted that Freud views the unconscious as the instrument for discerning change, although he says that primitive peoples have no insight into the unconscious structure of unchanging taboo, we return to the end of essay II where he takes up the "psychological difference" between taboo and neurosis. He now proceeds to argue that there are two fundamental differences between (primitive) taboo and (modern) neurosis. First, taboo is social, while neurosis is anti-social (individual and private). Second, taboo is self-preservative, while neurosis is sexual.

Sexual needs [Freud elaborates further] are not capable of uniting men in the same way as are the demands of self-preservation [with which he connects taboo as social institution]. Sexual satisfaction is essentially the private affair of each individual. The asocial nature of neuroses has its genetic origin in their most fundamental purpose, which is to take flight from an unsatisfying reality into a more pleasurable world of fantasy. The real world, which is avoided in this way by neurotics, is under the sway of human society and of the institutions collectively created by it. To turn away from reality is at the same time to withdraw from the community of man. (131)

This is an altogether astonishing passage, reflecting two fundamental impasses in Freud's thinking: first, the dualism between the ego (self-preservative) instincts and the sexual (species-preservative) instincts; and, second, the putative parallel between (primitive) taboo and (civilized) neurosis. In the first case, Freud is compelled to connect the social or collective nature of taboos with egoism (the self-preservative instincts), not with what conduces to the preservation of the species (the group). Further, in sharply opposing the social and the sexual, not only does he have no place for sexuality in primitive life, but he is also unable to distinguish, in modern life, between neurosis and sexuality, for both are essentially private and anti-social. Is it not extraordinary that neurosis – given Freud's analogy between neurotic and religious obsessions and his later theory of the superego – does not involve what is social and collective? Is it not equally extraordinary that sexuality does not involve social relations? What does Freud then think about the family and the Oedipus complex? Is it because sexuality is individual, private, and anti-social that it is the castration of libido that, in confirming identification with the penis, founds civilization by imposing the sense of guilt, the representative of the death instinct, on everyone (male) in the name of the superego?

As for the second impasse, the putative parallel (analogy) between (primitive) taboo and (civilized) neurosis vanishes once Freud claims that taboo is social (yet centred on the ego instincts) and neurosis is sexual (individual and anti-social). He has no way of accounting for the change from social to individual or, more generally, for the relationship between self and desire as the mutual expression of what is at once social (universal) and individual. Neurosis is no more a flight from society than it is a flight from individuality, just as sexuality is no more private (personal) than it is social, whether understood as uninhibited (that is, as involving actual sexual relations) or aim-inhibited (as, found, for example, in love of children, friends, or God). Neurosis involves a distorted conception of both society and individual, while sexuality, as love, provides the most profound critique of both society and individual there is.

But it is typical of Freud that, although he is true to psychological difference, he does not give up his metapsychological analogies, however untrue they are to the difference that his phenomenological insight makes. With his demonstration that there is no meaningful parallel between neurosis and taboo, between modern and primitive, he has thrown into grave doubt his conception of desire as prohibition and the analogous presence of the tabooed horror of incest in both ambivalent savages and neurotic moderns. Notwithstanding the "psychological difference" between taboo and neurosis, however, he will propose the myth of the primal father as the means of explaining the origin of the Oedipus complex as found in both primitive and modern civilization, as we shall now see.

III PSYCHICAL REALITY: FACT OR FANTASY?

Again, at the end of *Totem and Taboo*, Freud raises a second problem about the efficacy of his analogy between primitive and neurotic. He has argued that the moral prohibitions stemming from the taboo structure of totemism – not to kill the totem animal (symbolizing the father) and not to have sexual relations with members of the totem clan who are of the opposite sex (exogamy: the incest barrier) – are analogous to the ceremonial prohibitions of obsessional neurosis. Now he acknowledges that he must clarify the relationship between action (fact) and thought (intention, wish, fantasy). As the first problem involves the question of how the transmission of what is subject to collective but non-sexual taboo can result in anti-social and individual but sexual neurosis, so the second problem involves the relationship between primitive fact and modern (neurotic) fantasy. What is psychical reality? Is it primitive or modern? Is it action or thought?

The problem, as Freud poses it, is that the prohibitions of primitive society arise in response to an actual deed, the killing of the primal father. (We shall discuss later the fact that the incest motive has dropped out.) In contrast, the reality of (modern) neurotics is psychical, not factual (actual, historical, or material). Neurotics are full of incestuous and murderous desires, yet they are inhibited in carrying them out. It is not (uninhibited) acts but (inhibited) thoughts that they bring to their analysts. "What lie behind the sense of guilt of neurotics," Freud declares, "are always *psychical* realities and never *factual* ones. What characterizes neurotics is that they prefer psychical to factual reality and react just as seriously to thoughts as normal people do to realities."[5] It is by no means obvious, however, that Freud will be able to sustain a simple opposition between psychical and factual (real), between (internal) thought and (external) action. But the main problem, as he sees it, is to explain how primitive peoples, with their narcissistic overvaluation of the psychical (the omnipotence of thoughts as projection onto reality, which we shall take up shortly), are distinguishable from neurotics and their world of psychical reality. Would "the mere hostile *impulse* against the [primal] father, the mere existence of a wishful *fantasy* of killing and devouring him [the absence of the incest motif is again noteworthy] ... have been enough to produce the moral reaction that created totemism and taboo" (222)?

The problem that Freud faces is a peculiar one. He must preserve the analogy between the primitive and the neurotic in order to argue for the analogy between the myth of the primal father and the modern Oedipus complex, between the taboos of totemism (against killing the father and marrying the mother) and the Oedipal impulses of the modern (male) child. But then he faces the question of how the omnipotence of thoughts, which, in essay III, as we shall see, he associates with primitive animism, can be distinguished from the psychical reality of the modern neurotic. If, on the one hand, in the beginning is the act founding human history, the actual murder of the primal father, then Freud will face the difficulty of maintaining an analogy between primitive deed and modern psychical reality. If, on the other hand, neurotic reality is psychical in the end – what Oedipal boys have to deal with is their incestuous and murderous desires, not the actual facts of bedding their mothers and murdering their fathers – then Freud will equally face the difficulty of maintaining an analogy between primitive deed and neurotic (modern) psychical reality. On the one hand, if Freud maintains the analogy between primitive and neurotic, he will then be threatened with the collapse either of ancient fact into neurotic fantasy (there is no original murder) or of neurotic fantasy into primitive fact (there is no psychical originality). To maintain the analogy between primitive and neurotic is to see it collapse. On the other hand, if Freud maintains the integrity of both primitive fact and neurotic fantasy, he will then be threatened with the loss of the analogy between them. In either case, the impasse is complete. Typically, however, Freud gives up neither the (phenomenological) reality of neurosis as psychical nor the (metapsychological) fantasy (myth) of an actual primitive beginning. He does not see that the phenomenology of psychical reality cannot be supported by a metapsychology that posits a beginning in external yet illusory (mythical) reality.

Freud raises the question of the relationship between primitive (originary) fact and neurotic (originary) fantasy in terms of the possibility of viewing the myth of the primal murder as reflecting not actual fact but rather wishful fantasy, like the psychical reality of the neurotic. But he actually discusses it from the point of view of the neurotic, not of the primitive and his omnipotence of thoughts. What he argues for, consequently, is the position that the psychical reality of neurotics can be viewed as having a historical (factual) foundation, not that the murder of the primal father might be viewed as psychical and not real. On this basis Freud claims to be able to preserve the actual murder of the primal father and thus the analogy between the primitive and the neurotic. But the result is that, in tilting the balance from psychical (internal) to factual (external) reality, he jeopardizes the psychical reality of neurosis – his phenomenological insight.

His simple argument, which amounts to little more than crude assertion, is that, when obsessive neurotics are weighed down by excessive morality, what they defend themselves against and punish themselves for is not only psychical reality, that is, (internal) impulses that they experience, but also (external) historical reality. In other words, when obsessive neurotics are children, they actually have the evil impulses that they experience and enact them insofar as their infantile impotence allows. Since Freud views the neurosis of obsessive morality to be the heir to infantile perversion, he concludes that "the analogy between primitive men and neurotics will therefore be far more fully established if we suppose that in the former instance, too, psychical reality – as to the form taken by which we are in no doubt – coincided at the beginning with factual reality: that primitive men actually *did* what all the evidence shows that they intended to do" (224).

Freud thus arrives at his goal: intention and act coincide in primitive civilization. He protects the historicity of the primal murder. The primal sons both want to murder and actually do murder the primal father. Yet, it is surely obvious that the analogy with the "historical" predisposition of obsessive neurosis in infantile perversion is forced and superficial. Indeed, in the next and final paragraph of *Totem and Taboo* Freud proceeds (once again) to undercut the analogy between the primitive and the neurotic. He observes that there are distinctions between them that must be borne in mind, just as earlier, at the end of essay II, as we saw, he places in question the analogy between taboo and neurosis by insisting upon their "psychological difference." Not only do *we* (who are non-neurotic and non-primitive?) make a distinction "between thinking and doing [that] is absent in both of them," Freud remarks, "but neurotics are above all *inhibited* in their actions: with them the thought is a complete substitute for the deed. Primitive men, on the other hand, are *uninhibited*: thought passes directly into action. With them it is rather the deed that is a substitute for the thought ... 'In the beginning was the Deed'" (224). *Totem and Taboo* concludes with this citation from *Faust*.

Although Freud is right that neurotics are inhibited, while primitive peoples are "uninhibited" precisely because repression, the unconscious, and neurosis are unknown to them, the distinction between neurotic thought substituting for deed and primitive deed substituting for thought begs the fundamental question. What is the nature of *our* non-neurotic, non-primitive thought and action, the thought and action characteristic of, for example, psychoanalysis? Typically, Freud elides the critical distinction among three varieties of thought and action: (1) "uninhibited" or primitive; (2) modern but non-neurotic; and (3) modern but neurotic. The critical distinction, in other words, is not between thought and action but between primitive ambivalence (the doctrine of opposites), involving both thought and action, and modern "inhibition" where the limit to which one is subject is either love – both thoughtful and active – or fear (hate) – both thoughtless and passive. Thought that passes, in a manner that is uninhibited, unmediated, and unloving, into action is not the beginning "deed" of history, the deed beginning history, as Freud indicates, in utterly distorting Goethe's refashioning of the opening of the Gospel of John. Consistent with this inept conception of the relationship between thought and action is Freud's claim that the uninhibited murder of the primal father leads to the inhibited psyche of the modern, Oedipal child.

Before taking up the myth of the primal father in essay IV, however, it is important, first, to see that Freud complicates his presentation of the analogy between taboo and neurosis even further when, in essay III, he argues for a concept of historical development in three stages, following standard nineteenth-century models. The issue, for us, is always the same. How can science, the third and last stage, in succeeding the first and second stages, those of animism (mythology or magic) and religion, explain that of which it is the result? How can science, as the effect of animism and religion, explain that by which it is caused? How, in other words, can the effect explain the cause? Another way of putting the same issue – the kind of issue that Freud never raises and seemingly never comprehends – is to ask how animism can turn into (by forming the basis of) religion and how religion can turn into (by forming the basis of) science. It is precisely transition – change or history – of which Freud typically has no conception. He has no understanding of the fact that that which explains (historically) another must, at the same time, be open itself to being explained by that other. The same, shared principle of reciprocity must belong to both. It is surely evident that it is the principle of reciprocity that structures the psychotherapeutic "explanation." The interpretation, or construction, that the analyst offers to the analysand must be equally applicable to himself (and vice-versa). This is the way of history, of democracy, of love, of the golden rule, to which there is no alternative. It is not the way of the primal father. For one party to begin in violence, in taboo, in animism is not to arrive at the psychoanalytic principle of truth (or at what Freud calls in "Why War?" the constitution of pacifism, as we saw earlier).

The difficulty that Freud has in explaining the relationship between animism and religion perfectly illustrates the impasse to which the theory of the three stages of human mentality leads him. He notes, for example, that "animism itself is not yet a religion but contains the foundations on which religions are later built" (135). A couple of pages later, however, in reference to Frazer's *Golden Bough*, he remarks that "it seems probable that the Biblical prohibition against making an image of any living thing originated, not from any objection to the plastic arts, but from a desire to deprive magic (which was abominated by the Hebrew religion) of one of its tools" (137). Freud reads the Bible accurately. Yet he fails to explain or even to ask how or on what basis the religion of the ancient Hebrews could have opposed animism (magic) when, according to his theory of the three stages of civilization, animism leads to religion, that is, religion grows out of the animism of magic.

The three-stage model of human progress allows Freud to apply the idea of "the omnipotence of thoughts," a phrase coined by Rat Man, to animism and thus to preserve his analogy between primitive and modern (obsessional neurosis). "The principle governing magic, the technique of the animistic mode of thinking," Freud declares, "is the principle of the 'omnipotence of thoughts'" (143). From the fact that, according to Freud, primitive peoples project their (internal) thoughts onto (external) reality, he concludes that "the omnipotence of thoughts, the overvaluation of mental processes as compared with reality, is seen to have unrestricted play in the emotional life of neurotic patients and in everything that derives from it ... The primary obsessive acts of these neurotics are of an entirely magical character" (145).[6]

Freud proposes three stages in the omnipotence of thoughts consistent with his model of the three mental stages of animism, religion, and science. In animism, people ascribe omnipotence to themselves. In religion, people ascribe omnipotence to their gods (while reserving for themselves the power of influencing their gods by their wishes). In science, people relinquish human pretension to omnipotence, acknowledge their smallness, and submit to the reality of death and other natural necessities. "Nonetheless," Freud adds, "some of the primitive belief in omnipotence still survives in men's faith in the power of the human mind, which grapples with the laws of reality" (146).

Freud also proposes three libidinal stages as mirroring the three stages of human mentality: (1) animism: narcissism; (2) religion: object-choice – "of which the characteristic is a child's attachment to his parents"; and (3) science: when "an individual has reached maturity, has renounced the pleasure principle, adjusted himself to reality and turned to the external world for the object of his desires" (148). It is uncanny that Freud's three stages of libidinal development, in reflecting the three stages of the development of human mentality, mirror the three stages of the Oedipus complex: (1) the beginning in narcissism (identification with the penis); (2) the attachment to the parents (the Oedipal impulses proper: desire for the mother and hostility to the father); and (3) the maturity of science (the castration of libido: the reduction of libido, of object relations, of love to the reality principle). But Freud fails to note (perhaps because his mature doctrine of the superego still lies in the future) that – for a man – to find the objects of his desire in the external world is to make himself subject to the sense of guilt as imposed by the superego, the heir of the castration complex, whose beginning is in narcissistic identification with the penis. How can a beginning in narcissism not end narcissistically? How can the penis not be the father of man?

The fact that Freud explicates the three stages of human mentality, the three stages of the omnipotence of thoughts, and the three stages of libidinal development prior to introducing, in essay IV, the myth of the primal father as the explanation of totemic organization and thus of the prohibition of incest is extraordinary. Has he not, thereby, made it clear that what we find, in the beginning, is animism and that what characterizes animism is, above all, the omnipotence of thoughts and narcissism? But if the primal father is the original animist who, presumably, represents the omnipotence of thoughts and narcissism at their zenith, will it not follow, therefore, that, if the primal father is the founder of civilization, he will at the same time have to be the father of psychoanalysis itself? Is the primal father the unanalyzed analyst? Is psychoanalysis itself founded on and thus ultimately indistinguishable from animism? Is it not the case that, if psychoanalysis claims to comprehend the return of totemism in childhood as the archaic heritage of the primal father, it will also have to recognize itself as the heir of the primal father? But does this suggest that what we have represented, therefore, in the myth of the primal father is Freud's unconscious (compulsive) demonstration that psychoanalysis is metapsychologically grounded in the castration complex and thus in originary, narcissistic identification with the penis – of the primal father?

The ultimate purpose that the myth of the primal father serves for Freud is to explain the origin of the incest taboo, the totemic prohibitions of exogamy. To this end, Freud points out, any explanation of the prohibition of incest, together with totemic organization (exogamy), "should be at once a historical and a psychological one. It should tell us under what conditions this peculiar institution developed and to what psychical needs in men it has given expression" (167). Freud is surely right that history is psychological and that psychology is historical, that history is psyche and that psyche is history. But to unite history and psychology is an exacting task, the most categorical there is. For it means that that which develops historically must be consistent with – adequate or true to – its beginning (origin, principle), in the beginning. The psychical (the rational) must be historical, in the beginning, and the historical (the actual) must be psychical (rational), in the beginning. The historical must be psychical, in the end, and the psychical must be historical, in the end. Is there an alternative to the dialectic of psyche and history? Is this not the alternative ontology to which there is no alternative?

It is clear, however, that the theory of the three stages of civilization (both mental and libidinal) is neither historical nor psychological. For the last stage, science, is the reverse of its beginning in animism. We have also seen Freud indicate that there is a "psychological difference" between primitive taboo and modern neurosis. He holds further that, whereas primitive peoples are uninhibited in their action (their thought passes straight into action, that is, their action is thoughtless), neurotics are inhibited in their action (their thought replaces action, that is, their thought is passive or, in other words, both their thought and their action are equally obsessive). The unsurpassable difference between primitive and neurotic is surely, however, the following. The primitive cannot change without giving up the very substance of his cultural self. In order to change, the savage would have to become other than he is: he would have to recognize the other. The neurotic, however, must change in order to be true to his psychical (and historical) self. He must desire to appropriate the otherness of his self. He must desire to make the unconscious other (than) his own conscious self. Yet, notwithstanding the fact that Freud acknowledges the "psychological difference" separating the inhibited neurotic from the uninhibited savage, the scientist from the animist, he insists, nonetheless, on the universality of the horror of incest as the ultimate analogy between primitive (uninhibited) culture and modern (inhibited) culture.

"What is the ultimate source of the horror of incest which must be recognized as the root of exogamy?" Freud asks (182). This is his basic question. His answer is the murder of the primal father, which, he holds, provides the key to all the hitherto unexplained mysteries of civilization. To explain the origin of the horror of incest is to explain the origin of civilization, at once primitive and modern. Freud indicates that he is in full agreement with Frazer, whose *Totemism and Exogamy* he cites, that it is inconceivable that (as Westermarck holds) there could be an innate aversion to incest. What is natural and instinctual does not need legal reinforcement. For example, we are not commanded by law but only by nature to eat or to drink or to avoid being burned by fire.

"The law only forbids men to do what their instincts incline them to do [Frazer writes, as cited by Freud]; what nature itself prohibits and punishes, it would be superfluous for the law to prohibit and punish. Accordingly, we may always safely assume that crimes forbidden by law are crimes which many men have a natural propensity to commit ... Instead of assuming, therefore, from the legal prohibition of incest that there is a natural aversion to incest, we ought rather to assume that there is a natural instinct in favor of it, and that if the law represses it, as it represses other natural instincts, it does so because *civilized* men have come to the conclusion that the satisfaction of these natural instincts is detrimental to the general interests of *society*."

Having introduced Frazer's observations with the statement that "they are in essential agreement with the arguments which I put forward in my [second] essay on taboo," Freud then goes on to say that what "the findings of psychoanalysis ... add to these excellent arguments of Frazer's" is that "the earliest sexual excitations" of children "are invariably of an incestuous character" and that they form, when repressed, the nucleus of later neurosis (183–4^e).

The remarks of Freud (reflecting the observations of Frazer) on the origin of law and civilization, here involving the origin of the horror of incest, are complex. We may note the following three points. First, Freud assumes, as always, an analogy between the primitive, the neurotic, and the infantile. Second, when, a decade later, Freud begins to arrive at his mature formulation of the Oedipus complex, he shows (in spite of himself), as we have seen, that it is not the horror of incest but the horror of castration that leads to the demolition (the utter extinction) of the Oedipal impulses (desire for the mother, hostility to the father). Neurosis occurs insofar as the Oedipal impulses are *not* repressed (demolished). Third, and more relevant in the present context, is the fact that Freud accepts the dualism that Frazer posits between nature and law (civilization, society), between (natural) incest and its (civilized) prohibition. This dualism mirrors his own view, as articulated in essay II, on the identity of desire and prohibition: "there is no need to prohibit something that no one desires to do, and a thing that is forbidden with the greatest emphasis must be a thing that is [most greatly?] desired" (126). Where there is prohibition, there is desire. Something would not be prohibited if it were not desired. But would it not thereby follow that where there is desire there we also find prohibition? Freud never poses this question.[7] But there is no doubt, I think, that he holds it to be the case that desire *is* prohibition, with the result that the responses of the ego to libidinal demands are always viewed as defensive.

The fact that desire is prohibition, that to desire is to invite retaliation – ultimately, castration – reflects Freud's primordial commitment to the pleasure-unpleasure principle as the foundation of all life. All desire is unpleasure or pain that, having been called into existence by "external reality," it is then the desire of the organism to reduce back to zero. Desire, or libido, is, for Freud, the unpleasure or pain of metapsychological contradiction. To desire is to desire to eliminate desire, to restore life to a prior state of things, to inorganic nature, to nirvana, to death. Desire generates fear – consistent with the fact that love for Freud always means "being loved," my fear that the other will withdraw his love from me or otherwise use it against me. It is striking, as always, that Freud does not conceive of desire as the expression of self and other. (The exceptions, as we saw, are his single paragraph description in *Group Psychology* of Christianity as embodying the relationships of the golden rule and his hesitant admission in "The Economic Problem of Masochism" that sexual intercourse – love – between two adults is not subject to the pleasure principle when understood as the death instinct.)

What Freud, together with Frazer, does not see is that, just as desire (for us moderns) is not primarily prohibition, consistent with the pleasure principle, so law (for us moderns) is not primarily prohibition, consistent with taboo and its totems. What is noteworthy about both desire (love, will) and law (the golden rule, the general will, the categorical imperative) is that neither is natural and that both involve, not prohibition, but compulsion, coercion, command, the categorical (must, ought, shall). People do not naturally love (desire) each other. Rather, they "naturally hate one another," as Pascal writes in the *Pensées* (17). When love is based on nature, it involves prohibition, fear, possessiveness, exclusiveness, retaliation; for, as we saw Pascal indicate in chapter 1, that which is natural can be taken away from me, and ultimately it will be taken away from me (by death). If my love is based on that which can be taken away from me, on that which is not truly and categorically (freely) mine – and yours – then desire will be indistinguishable from what is prohibited. It is for this reason that Kierkegaard argues, in both *Works of Love* and *Purity of Heart Is to Will One Thing*, that love (desire, will) involves duty (law) and that duty expresses love. If love and duty become dualistically opposed to (split off from) each other, the result will be either sentimental (romantic) love or moralistic (puritanical) duty.

The reason that Freud (like Frazer) cannot conceive of either desire or law as other than prohibition is because he posits, in the beginning, an opposition (a dualism) between desire (instinct) as natural and law (prohibition) as social. This dualistic opposition ultimately reflects the opposition between primary process and secondary process, between the pleasure principle and the reality principle. It is only when desire is conceived of as "law-like" (fictional) and law is conceived of as "instinctual" (factual or natural) that the opposition between them can be overcome. In other words, there is no alternative to viewing love as duty and duty as love. It is not that parents naturally love their children. It is, rather, that parents have the duty of loving (they must love) their children if their children are to become loving in turn.

It is striking that in the passage Freud cites from Frazer there is no reflection on how strange it is that it is only after people have become civilized – but when they are still enjoying the natural pleasures of incest, apparently – that they then (after mature deliberation) conclude that it would be wise of them to repress their incestuous instinct, their natural desire for instinctual pleasure, in the interest of the social good. But Freud (following Frazer) avoids asking the question that would reveal the dualism between nature and civilization to be completely contradictory. How is the transition made, in the beginning, from nature to society? If one begins in nature, with natural instinct, then one will never arrive, at the end, in society with a horror of and a ban on instinct. If one ends in society with a horror of and a ban on incest, then one will never begin in nature, with natural instinct. Or we could ask: does incest precede or succeed society (civilization)? If incest precedes society, then it will be natural; and one would have to ask how anything that is natural could ever become prohibited, civilized, or socialized (unnatural). If incest succeeds (is a result of) society, then it will not be a natural but a social product; and it would appear to be something about which "civilized men" could "come to the conclusion," if they so chose, that its "satisfaction" was *not* "detrimental to the general interests of society." Freud (along with Frazer) is quite right in generally wanting to eliminate all utilitarian explanations of the horror of incest (such as the threat of inbreeding). But it is striking that, given the inexplicable dualism between nature and law, incest and prohibition, Freud (together with Frazer) is compelled to accept the most utilitarian of explanations of the incest barrier: it "is detrimental to the general interests of society."

Since Rousseau demonstrates that the general will and Kant that the categorical imperative – law, society, civilization – are based on desire not as prohibition but as willing the good for all, it is not surprising that, as Freud points out, although Frazer is clear that exogamy "was devised to prevent incest," he remains in the dark about the origin of the horror of incest (185). But Freud – intrepid psychologist or foolish metapsychologist? – now proceeds to propose the myth of the primal father as the explanation for what hitherto has remained inexplicable: the origin of the horror of incest and thus the origin of desire as that which is prohibited, of law as prohibition, and, ultimately, of the pleasure-unpleasure principle.

In formulating the myth of the primal father, Freud faces two basic problems. (I am not concerned here with the fact that Freud has neither anthropological nor historical evidence for his myth.) First, he needs to be able to connect exogamy (with its rigorous delineation of sexually permitted and sexually tabooed liaisons along clan lines) with totemism (the identification of a particular clan with a particular totem: an animal, a bird, etc.). He must also provide a rigorous delineation of the taboos surrounding a particular totem. Second, he needs to be able to connect the exogamous horror of incest with the Oedipus complex as found, he holds, in all children.

Freud's first step in formulating the myth of the primal father is to adapt from Darwin the notion of the horde of great apes and to connect the expulsion of young males by the sexually dominant "father" with exogamy: the enforcement of the ban on sexual relations within the clan totem. His next step is to point out that the (male) child, like Little Hans, develops animal phobias symbolic of his unconscious fear of his father, while continuing to love his father consciously. Just as the boy's identification with his totem (phobic) animal is ambivalent – it expresses the ambivalence of his hate (fear) and love for his father – so primitive peoples, Freud remarks, "describe the totem as their common ancestor and primal father." If one assumes that the totem is the father – the common ancestor of the clan – then it follows, he holds, that "the two principal ordinances of totemism, the two taboo prohibitions which constitute its core – not to kill the totem and not to have sexual relations with a woman of the same totem – coincide in their content with the two crimes of Oedipus, who killed his father and married his mother, as well as with the two primal wishes of children, the insufficient repression or the re-awakening of which forms the nucleus of perhaps every psychoneurosis" (192).

Having connected exogamy (by way of Darwin's primal horde) with totemism (by way of the Oedipus complex), Freud's next step is to add Robertson Smith's hypothesis of the totem meal, the ritual sacrifice accompanying all religious ceremony. The totem animal, representing the father, the ancestor, and, ultimately, the god of the clan, whose injury or killing is utterly tabooed, is collectively sacrificed and devoured by the clan members: "the sacrificial animal was treated as a member of the tribe; *the sacrificing community, the god and the sacrificial animal were of the same blood and members of one clan*" (197). The members of the clan, as participants in the sacrificial meal, are consequently united in the common ambivalence of their blood sacrifice involving, at once, reverence and guilt, festival and mourning, violation and prohibition. That which is the greatest joy, the ritual of fellowship in which clan members identify with, by devouring, their totem sacrifice, is also the greatest crime: the (symbolic) killing of the totem, the very substance of the clan. Desire to be (one with) the father by killing and consuming him is the ultimate prohibition, the most fearful taboo, the greatest crime imaginable. Freud summarizes the totem sacrifice as follows: "Psychoanalysis has revealed that the totem animal is in reality a substitute for the father; and this tallies with the contradictory fact that, though the killing of the animal is as a rule forbidden, yet its killing is a festive occasion – with the fact that it is killed and yet mourned. The ambivalent emotional attitude, which to this day characterizes *the father complex in our children* and which often persists into adult life, seems to extend to the totem animal in its capacity as substitute for the father" (202ᵉ).

Freud is now ready to bring forward the myth of the primal father. But it appears that that which the myth of the primal father will explain is not so much the origin of the horror of incest as the origin of "the father complex in our children." Thus it will explain desire as what, in the beginning, is prohibited and prohibition as what, in the end, is desired.

One fine day,[8] Freud begins – just as Joseph K. unexpectedly and incongruously finds himself one fine morning under arrest: guilty or not guilty? – the primal sons collectively kill and devour the primal father. In identifying with the violence of the patriarch who had tyrannized them and frustrated their sexual satisfaction, they then re-enact the ambivalence of this originary violence in the ritual of the totem meal. As the primal father both loved and hated his sons, so the primal sons both love and hate their father. Because ambivalence, stemming from identification with the father('s penis), results in the sense of guilt (ultimately the superego), it is the sense of guilt, Freud holds, that is the source "of social organization, of moral restrictions and of religion" (203). Thus it follows, he observes, that the primal sons are filled "with the same contradictory feelings which we can see at work in the ambivalent father complexes of our children and of our neurotic patients" (204). The primal sons both hate the father's dominant aggressivity and sexuality yet crave to attain them for themselves. They do homage to the father by enacting against him the violence that he enacts against them. They create "out of their filial sense of guilt the two fundamental taboos of totemism" – those of the Oedipus complex (205).

Yet Freud is careful to point out that the two essential, totemic taboos are not equal psychologically (or, we might add, historically). The taboo that the primal sons violate in killing the father is that surrounding the totem animal – the father. They do not, however, violate the prohibition against incest, for the incest taboo does not yet exist. It is not incest that the primal father prohibits but sexual relations with his women. It is inconceivable who these women might be, although, presumably, they are his mother (?), grandmother (?), aunts (?), great aunts (?), wife (wives), and their daughters(' daughters). "Sexual desires do not unite men but divide them," Freud observes. "Though the brothers had banded together in order to overcome their father, they were all one another's rivals in regard to the women" (205). Having murdered their father in a frenzy of violent hatred and frustrated sexual desire, the primal brothers coolly conclude that their sexual desire for women divides them as men. They agree with Frazer that they must ban incest by instituting exogamy. Otherwise, the bonds of society would not be secure.

But all this is absurd – on Freud's very own terms – as he is compelled to adopt the most abject of utilitarian (*post hoc*) arguments to explain the ban on (the horror of) incest. The incestuous instinct is not primary – for either primal father or primal sons; and the ban on incest is equally not primary. The primal brothers could just as well have decided to use a complex computer program to calculate the period during which each – perhaps, at times, jointly – could have enjoyed their mother(s) and sisters and daughters – and why not also their father(s), and brothers, and sons? – sexually. Once Freud allows "rational" (utilitarian) calculus, one calculus is as good as another, except that the calculus he chooses naturally coincides with his concept of exogamy and its putative repetition in the Oedipus complex. Further, in addition to banning incest, the primal brothers also find it convenient – having murdered their sire – to ban murder. They want to avoid the repetition of their father's fate!

It is clear that what Freud explains with his myth of the primal father, whose murder by the primal sons results in the ambivalent sense of guilt, is the father complex, not the horror of incest. What goes into the primal myth is what comes out of it. Indeed, he emphasizes that what psychoanalysis shows us is that individuals form their idea of God in the image of their father with the same ambivalence that the primal sons feel towards the primal father. "God is nothing other than an exalted father," Freud declares. "As in the case of totemism, psychoanalysis recommends us to have faith in the believers who call God their father, just as the totem was called the tribal ancestor. If psychoanalysis deserves any attention, then[9] ... *the paternal element* in that concept must be a most important one. But in that case the father is represented twice over in the situation of primitive sacrifice: once as God and once as the totemic animal victim" (209e).

What an extraordinary passage! Just as psychoanalysis asks us to believe that God is the father – for religious believers – it also asks us to believe that the Father is god – for psychoanalytic believers. But this means that psychoanalysis, no less than religion, is the product of the father complex, for both are equally the creation of the murder of the primal father and the resultant sense of guilt. The fact that psychoanalysis cannot escape the fate of religion becomes even clearer when Freud summarizes the significance of the myth of the primal father (just before he brings *Totem and Taboo* to conclusion with a discussion of the two problems that, he acknowledges, his myth creates). He writes that it agrees with the psychoanalytic concept of neurosis in showing that "the beginnings of religion, morals, society and art converge in the Oedipus complex." What is most surprising, however, he continues, is that "the problems of social psychology" may also prove soluble on the basis of a *"man's relation to his father."* Further, Freud remarks, it may even be possible to explain what has hitherto remained inexplicable, the origin of ambivalence – "the simultaneous existence of love and hate towards the same object" – that "lies at the root of many important cultural institutions." What may well prove to be the case, he points out, is that ambivalence originally "formed no part of our emotional life but was acquired by the human race in connection with *their father complex*, precisely where the psychoanalytic examination of modern individuals still finds it revealed at its strongest" (219-20[c]).

Freud is utterly consistent in his inconsistency. The myth of the primal father ultimately brings him to the father complex as the explanation of the origin not of the horror of incest but of primal ambivalence. He sets out, he claims, to solve the problem of the origin of the horror of incest, which, he agrees with Frazer, exogamy was devised to prohibit but whose origin remains, nevertheless, unexplained. It is, however, incest – above all, mother-son incest – that the myth of the primal father does not explain. Indeed, the myth of the primal father has nothing to do with incest, as Freud himself makes pellucid yet does not acknowledge. The primal father exercises his violent domination over the primal sons in order to maintain his sexual monopoly over the women, not to ban his sons' incestuous longings for the mother. The sons violently murder their father in order to break his sexual monopoly and to attain their own sexual domination (consistent with Darwin's horde of great apes), not to enjoy an incestuous liaison with the mother. The taboo that they violate is murder of the father, not incest with the mother. In this context it is worth noting that one of the points that Spiro, in *Oedipus in the Trobriands*, uses to confute Malinowski's rejection of the universality of the Oedipal model of the family is that Malinowski confuses patriarchal power, and the son's resistance to it, with Oedipal hostility to the father when generated by the son's incestuous desire for the mother. Not all patriarchal domination is Oedipal, Spiro reminds us, and equally not all resistance to patriarchal domination is Oedipal. Freud is consequently left with the limp explanation that the sons, having killed and eaten their father, both glorying in their deed and feeling inconsolable grief over it, then decide to impose the incest prohibition on themselves, given their recognition that sexual desires do not unite but divide men. But the ban on incest is not, as I suggested, the only prudential calculation that the sons might have made to preserve social harmony.

The fact that Freud's explanation of the origin of incest is *ad hoc* and completely dependent on the father complex is reflected in his mature conception of the Oedipus complex. In *Totem and Taboo* Freud claims to demonstrate the analogy between, on the one hand, the taboos against killing the totem (animal, the patriarchal ancestor: God) and (the men's) having sexual relations with the women of the same totem clan and, on the other hand, the Oedipal impulses of the modern boy. But it is precisely this analogy that his myth of the primal father does not prove. It is also the case that what counts for Freud in his mature articulation of the Oedipus complex is, as we have seen, the father complex – the castration complex as confirmation of (male) identification with the father('s penis) – not incestuous desire for the mother. As Freud himself shows in the passages immediately cited above, not only does the myth of the primal father not explain the Oedipus complex, but it also suggests that both social psychology (the superego) and ambivalence (identification with the father's penis) are based on "man's relation to his [and also woman's relation to her] father." It is primary ambivalence – one both loves and hates the penis in self-identification with it (the penis is itself the love and hate of ambivalence) – that leads directly to the castration complex. It is the castration complex that leads directly to the sense of guilt – the repudiation of femininity and (also) of masculinity. It is the sense of guilt, reflecting the original ambivalence of identification with the penis – both its presence and its absence – that underlies the social psychology of civilization and its discontents (except for that group that is not a group: Christianity). The ambivalence that arises in the Oedipus complex proper – the boy desires his mother sexually and feels hostility toward his father – has its origin in prelibidinal identification with the father. It is equally the case that the ambivalence that the primal sons feel toward the primal father stems from their original identification with him. In killing and consuming their father, he becomes their – they become his – very flesh. The sense of guilt that they feel – the sense of guilt that ultimately becomes the superego – embodies the ambivalence of identification with the father('s penis) and has nothing to do with the horror of incest.

Ambivalence and the father complex – central alike to both the myth of the primal father and the Oedipus complex (identification with the penis and the castration complex) – reflect Freud's concept of desire as prohibition. Something would not be prohibited if it were not desired. Something would not be desired if it were not prohibited. Freud does not actually appear to utter the second, ambivalent (and equivalent) formulation; but it is implied in everything he says. Desire is prohibition; prohibition is desire. It is this concept of desire – utterly ambivalent and embodying the father complex as identification with the penis – that is expressed in and through the pleasure principle. Pleasure is the elimination of desire and thus identity with the death instinct. Furthermore, originary ambivalence, identification with the penis – both personal and primal – involves eternal opposition between the death instinct (pleasure) and the life instinct (unpleasure). What results is, as always, the elimination of libido, sexual relations, and love.

Perhaps the most extraordinary element of Freud's contradictory consistency is, however, the fact that, precisely because the myth of the primal father founds the father complex (and has nothing to do with incest), it is at the same time the foundation of religion. God is nothing other than the exalted father, Freud asserts. But the juxtaposition of father and God is uncanny, for what it shows us is that, just as Freud makes religion out of the father complex, so he also makes the father complex into (a) religion. His science of psychoanalysis makes a god of the father complex – identification with the penis and the castration of libido (desire is what is prohibited). The principle whose phenomenological content Freud apprehends but the metapsychological elements of which he utterly fails to understand is that the end is in your beginning. You do not get anything more (or different) out of a system than what you put into it. Freud begins with the father complex – both metapsychologically in the Oedipus complex and mythologically in the story of the primal father – and that is precisely what he gets out of it: primary ambivalence where filial desire is patriarchal prohibition.

In beginning with animism – one assumes that the primal father and the primal sons are animists – psychoanalysis does not proceed, metapsychologically, beyond the omnipotence of thoughts: male identification with the penis and female desire for the penis, the first prohibiting desire, the second desiring only what is prohibited (castrated). It is clear that, just as the inheritance of the sense of guilt is a parody of the vulgar tradition of original sin in Christianity, so psychoanalysis as the science of the father complex is a parody of the vulgar tradition of divine patriarchy in Christianity. But it should also be noted that Freud fails to see that his metapsychology is no less a mother complex. He demonstrates, *malgré lui*, that, precisely because identification with the penis involves the repudiation of femininity, it reposes on the fear of women as found in both men and women. Woman in her absence – she does not appear in the myth of the primal father – is the original castrator. Woman is absent because she is the phallic mother. Woman's absence demonstrates the absence of the penis, that is, woman's possession of it, the fear on the part of men that women, as the primal castrators, are, always already, in possession of the penis. Male repression of women is a repression of their own fear that what they see in the castrated female is their own castration. It is little wonder, then, that the most dangerous (tabooed) expression of impotence, as I noted earlier, is the erect penis, for it represents desire which is prohibited, that is, castrated. The penis with which the primal father and the primal sons identify is, in its primordial ambivalence, no more present than it is absent, no more to be loved than it is to be feared (hated). The penis is at once erotic and lethal. In representing both Eros and the death instinct, the penis signals the castration of libido, sexuality, and love. Where, however, desire is not prohibition but loving your neighbour as yourself, there – uniquely and universally – is found the alternative to metapsychology as the religion of the father complex to which there is no alternative.

What Freud achieves in and through the myth of the primal father, his murder by the primal sons, is surprising to the extreme. Although he claims to explain the inexplicable, the origin of the horror of incest, and thus to show that the incest taboo is the origin of the Oedipus complex, this is not at all what he accomplishes. Freud wants to argue for an analogy between primitive taboo – the Oedipal totems – and modern neurosis – the Oedipal impulses of the modern boy. But what he shows is, rather, that the myth of the primal father constitutes the father complex, which is precisely what dominates the Oedipus complex, as we saw in chapter 3. Just as incest has no part in the ambivalence of hate (fear) and love, which is what the primal father and the primal sons feel for each other, so the ambivalence that is central to the psychology of the modern boy is a product not of his Oedipal impulses but of his originary identification with the father('s penis).

The first surprise, then, is that Freud demonstrates the analogy between primitive and modern (neurotic) on the basis not of the incest taboo but of the father complex. It is not libido (sexuality, or love) but the ambivalence resulting from identification with the father('s penis) that is central to both Freud's primary mythology and his primary metapsychology. The second surprise is that, although Freud insists upon the reality of the primal murder as the ultimate source of the psychical reality of the modern neurotic, he cannot imagine that incest is primary. Primordial incest remains, apparently, utterly psychical, without reality in history. The third surprise is that, while ambivalence characterizes primitive society, it is not the basis of social relations (the categorical imperative, the general will) in the modern world. (I shall discuss this in the next section.) The fourth surprise is that, in establishing an analogy between primitive and neurotic, Freud sidesteps the issue of where non-neurotic but also non-primitive psychology (both psychoanalytic and lay) fits into this scheme. The primitive does not imagine an alternative to his taboo structures, which are centred, for Freud, on the two basic totemic taboos. In other words, taboos are not distorted, abnormal representations of reality. Further, neurosis is recognizable only in terms of its alternative, a non-neurotic, loving relationship to reality. We can well understand why, as always, Freud is compelled to recognize the psychological difference between uninhibited taboo and inhibited neurosis. Taboo is uninhibited precisely because, founded on ambivalence – the contradictory opposition between and identity of fear (hate) and love – it has no concept (image) of the other as the alternative to, or the deconstruction of, tabooed ambivalence. The alternative to neurosis is a return, not to uninhibited primitivity – centred on taboo – but to the right kind of inhibition, that founded on the loving limit of the golden rule.

But thus we arrive at the fifth surprise, that with which we shall conclude this section: what *is* psychical reality? What is surprising is that Freud, having imputed factual (historical) reality to the mythical murder of the primal father, then must insist upon the psychical but not the historical reality of the impulses of the neurotic who wishes, he holds, to violate the totemic taboos but actually does not. Freud wants to insist upon the role of the omnipotence of thoughts in both the primitive and the neurotic, yet he acknowledges that the first is uninhibited – animistic – while the second is inhibited (as the distortion of science, presumably). The surprising thing, then, is that, while Freud wants to preserve the integrity of (neurotic) psychical reality, he utterly compromises it by making it analogous to primitive thought while distinguishing it from the realistic thought of (psychoanalytic) science. But what is particularly surprising is that it is then psychoanalytic science, in its reliance upon external reality (what really happens), that is more closely related to primitive thought than is modern neurotic thought, unless one supposes that modern science, too, is inhibited. In other words, while Freud understands the importance of not making the psychical reality – fantasy – of the neurotic directly, phenomenologically, dependent upon "external" (material) reality, he is unable to conceive of psychical reality – fantasy – as beginning anywhere other than, metapsychologically, in external, material reality. His thought remains completely bound by the dualism between internal (psychical) and external (real), between primary process and secondary process, between pleasure principle (illusion) and reality principle, between unconscious and consciousness, between id and ego, between thought (intention, wish, desire) and action, between poetry (art, religion) and science, between phylogenesis and ontogenesis. Freud is unable to conceive of the relationship between psyche and history, the psychical and the actual, except in terms of their contradictory identity, in primitive beginning, and their contradictory opposition, in modern end.

The fact that Freud is unable to conceive either of psyche as historical or of history as psychical is particularly extraordinary, given psychoanalysis as depth psychology. Psychoanalysis attends to psychical reality; yet, in viewing psychical reality as ultimately dependent on identification with the father complex – the father's penis – two astonishing things occur. First, psychical reality is made dependent on its opposite, external reality, ultimately the murder of the primal father. Second, psychoanalysis itself, in making a god of the father complex, cannot distinguish itself, metapsychologically, from the animism of primitive thought – except that, like neurosis, its subject, too, is inhibited. What is so surprising about the myth of the primal father is that, in reducing internal (psychical) reality – myth – to external reality, in the beginning, Freud has no option but to reduce (external) reality – myth – to internal (psychical) reality, in the end. The omnipotence of mythical thought is external in its (primitive) beginning and internal in its (neurotic) end, notwithstanding the psychological difference between uninhibited taboo and inhibited neurosis.

The contradictory reversal of what is viewed by Freud as analogy is also the fate of what he calls phylogenetic or archaic inheritance. That which begins externally – with the murder of the primal father – becomes in the end internal to the unconscious or the id. That which is internal to the unconscious or the id in the beginning is the precipitate of countless (external) experiences. As we have already seen in our discussion of the sense of guilt, Freud is unable to work out a phenomenology of experience, of history, to explain the dialectic of individual (ontogenesis) and universal (phylogenesis). I shall now review critical passages in which Freud discusses the issue of phylogenesis in order to show how his concept of psychical reality cannot escape the contradiction of being at once phylogenetically (metapsychologically) internal but ontogenetically (phenomenologically) external. But what is so surprising is that phylogeny and ontogeny, the internal and the external, are separated as end and beginning are separated – by the three stages of human civilization. For, while the individual is, in the end, the product of his phylogenetic inheritance, the phylogenetic inheritance is, in the beginning, the product of the individual – the primal father.

The problem of what constitutes psychical reality meets head on the problem of phylogenesis when Freud attempts to assess the relationship between fantasy and experience in the memories of neurotic patients. He holds that infantile memories are composed, above all, of three "primal fantasies": observation of parental intercourse, seduction by a (male) adult, and the threat of castration. What counts, Freud writes in the *Introductory Lectures*, is not so much whether these events occur – although they often do[10] – but that they exist for the patient in his fantasy.

The fantasies possess *psychical* as contrasted with *material* reality [Freud declares], and we gradually learn to understand that *in the world of the neuroses it is psychical reality which is the decisive kind*. (415) The only impression we gain is that these events of childhood are somehow demanded as a necessity, that they are among the essential elements of a neurosis. If they have occurred in reality, so much to the good; but if they have been withheld by reality, they are put together from hints and supplemented by fantasy. The outcome is the same, and up to the present we have not succeeded in pointing to any difference in the consequences, whether fantasy or reality has had the greater share in these events of childhood. (417–18)

The only answer as to why and how these "primal fantasies" come about, Freud continues, is that their origin must lie in the instincts (*Triebe*), in "a phylogenetic endowment" in which "the individual reaches beyond his own experience into primeval experience at points where his own experience has been too rudimentary." It is quite possible, he says, that the primal fantasies "were once real occurrences in the primeval times of the human family, and that children in their fantasies are simply filling in the gaps in individual truth with prehistoric truth" (418).[11]

Freud claims here that the primal fantasies of childhood need not be based on individual experience so long as they can be said to repeat originary, phylogenetic, archaic, and primeval experience. But in his most famous case study, Wolf Man, he discusses at length whether his patient, at the age of eighteen months, actually observed his parents copulating *more ferarum*. This would have been the experience that the four-year-old boy later screened in his dream of the white, staring wolves. The boy's resulting animal phobia, combined with his seduction by his older sister and the threat of castration from his nurse, would have led to his childhood neurosis (the actual subject of the case study) that involved the most extraordinary interplay of autoerotic impulses and of inverted Oedipal impulses for his father.[12] At the conclusion of his case study Freud remarks that it raises two problems of especial interest involving the relationship between fantasy and reality. The first problem concerns what he calls "the phylogenetically inherited schemata, which, like *the categories of philosophy*, are concerned with the business of 'placing' the impressions derived from actual experience."[13] He indicates that he is inclined to view these schemata as

precipitates from the history of human civilization. The Oedipus complex, which comprises a child's relation to his parents, is one of them ... Wherever experiences fail to fit in with the hereditary schema, they become remodelled in the imagination ... It is precisely such cases that are calculated to convince us of the independent existence of the schema. We are often able to see the schema triumphing over the experience of the individual; as when in our present case the boy's father became the castrator and the menace of his infantile sexuality in spite of what was in other respects an inverted Oedipus complex. (363e)[14]

Freud calls the second problem, although closely related to the first, "incomparably more important" (363). He undertakes to explain what he views as the four-year-old boy's response to the reactivated primal scene that he would have presumably observed when he was a child of eighteen months and that then would have remained latent in him for two and a half years. (The analysand whom we know as Wolf Man did not verbalize his fantasy until he was twenty-four years old, having been once again in the grip of severe neurosis since the age of seventeen.) Freud remarks that "it is hard to dismiss the view that some sort of hardly definable knowledge, something, as it were, preparatory to an understanding, was at work in the child at the time. *WE CAN FORM NO CONCEPTION OF WHAT THIS MAY HAVE CONSISTED IN*; we have nothing at our disposal but the single *ANALOGY* – and it is an excellent one – of the far-reaching *instinctive* [*instinktiv;* not instinctual: *triebhaft*] knowledge of animals" (364e).

Such "an instinctive endowment," especially concerned with but not confined to sexuality, Freud continues, "would then be the nucleus of the unconscious, a primitive kind of mental activity, which would later be dethroned and overlaid by human reason." He comments further that this primitive, unconscious, mental activity would retain in some, perhaps in all, people "the power of drawing down to it the higher mental processes" (364). Repression would then represent a return to this instinctive stage, while the liability to neurosis would bear witness both to the price paid for the later acquisition of reason and to the earlier existence of an instinctive stage.[15]

Freud's explanation of the phylogenetic and instinctive endowment of humankind, although deceptively clear, is, in actuality, deeply confusing and confused. Neurosis is shown to depend upon a series of three implicit sets of contrasts, each of which is simple in itself; but, when all three are considered together, they are unmistakably contradictory. First, there is the contrast between what is earlier (unconscious, instinctive, inherited) and later (neurotic), but in this case both sides of the contrast are psychical (internal). Second, there is the contrast between what is earlier and psychical and what is earlier but not unconscious and thus real (primeval people actually enact the primal scenes). Third, there is the contrast between what is earlier and unconscious and what is later and at once conscious and rational (with the later dethroning the earlier, although the earlier often usurps the throne of the later).

The fact that Freud is unable to bring together earlier and later, unconscious and conscious, historical and individual, psychical and real, neurosis and reason into a common framework is reflected in his polemic against Jung[16] in his study of Wolf Man. He is especially concerned to defend the infantile aetiology of neurosis and thus the reality of the infantile primal scenes. Adult neurosis involves, he insists, both regression to infantile life and childhood impressions that operate forward. Childhood recollections (in adulthood) are not simply projections of adult conflicts back into infancy, as Jung holds often happens. It is for this reason that, after discussing the primal scenes in terms of phylogenetic inheritance and of the analogy with animal *Instinkt*, Freud concludes the Wolf Man case with the admonition that inherited strata are to be considered only after individually acquired strata have been properly assessed.

With Wolf Man Freud thus finds himself in a difficult position. He needs to defend psychical reality and consequently the idea of phylogenetic inheritance against those who (from outside depth psychology) assimilate the psychical (internal) to the material (the external). But he is also faced with the opposition of those like Jung who (from within depth psychology) accept the role that phylogenesis plays in explaining the origin of neurosis yet insist on viewing adult conflicts as more important than infantile sexuality.[17] He needs, therefore, to defend the reality of the infantile primal scenes. They are not merely psychical. They actually occur.

For Freud the core of his defense that primal scenes are "regressive fantasies" based on actual experience is that they are produced during treatment *not* by the analysand's direct recollection of them as infantile events but by the analyst's *construction* of them.[18] He points out that the spontaneous recollections that patients have of their childhood are not a simple reflection of reality. They can be true, untrue, or any combination of truth, lie, distortion, and fantasy. Consequently, whatever the material that the analysand makes available during analysis, childhood scenes have to be "divined – constructed – gradually and laboriously [by the analyst] from an aggregate of indications." Freud remarks additionally that dreams also result from construction, not from direct recollection. "It is this recurrence [of primal scenes] in dreams," he observes, "that I regard as the explanation of the fact that the patients themselves gradually acquire a profound conviction of the reality of these primal scenes, a conviction which is in no respect inferior to one based on recollection" (285).

Freud acknowledges that critics of psychoanalysis will be quick to attack the analyst's construction as simply reflecting the power that suggestion has over the analysand. The analyst will be accused of reducing reality not only to the patient's fantasy but also to his own. Freud, however, defends the reliability of the analyst's construction by pointing out that it is not a sudden creation. It takes shape only slowly; it develops independently of the analyst's control; it increasingly becomes the center on which everything at first converges and then from which everything later radiates; and, finally, it provides a single perspective from which to comprehend all the diverse aspects of a case history. In his study of Rat Man he points out that the aim of the analyst, in constructing a coherent story out of the materials provided him by the analysand, is not to create conviction in him but to bring his "repressed complexes into consciousness, to set the conflict going in the field of conscious mental activity, and to facilitate the emergence of fresh material from the unconscious. A sense of conviction is only attained after the patient has himself worked over the reclaimed material, and so long as he is not fully convinced the material must be considered as unexhausted" (62).

When a construction is properly developed – that is, when a primal scene is educed such that it provides a comprehensive solution to the whole – "then, in view of its content," Freud argues further of Wolf Man, "it is impossible that it can be anything else than the reproduction of a reality experienced by the child. For a child, like an adult, can produce fantasies only from material which has been acquired from some source or other." He notes, further, that the sources from which a young child can obtain the content of its primal scenes are, outside of actual observation, extremely limited. He also denies that a child can evade revealing the sources of its neurosis, for, he observes, "we discover [in a young child's life] nothing but instinctual impulses which the child cannot satisfy and which it is not old enough to master, and the sources from which these impulses arise" (289). The only possible conclusion, Freud declares, is that "either the analysis [of Wolf Man] based on the neurosis in his childhood is all a piece of nonsense from start to finish, or everything took place just as I have described it above" (290).[19]

Freud returns once again, later in the case study, to the question of whether the primal scene reactivated in the wolf dream is a fantasy or a real experience, this time to say that it does not make a great deal of difference, apparently. The primal scenes are all "unquestionably an inherited endowment, a phylogenetic heritage," he observes, yet, he adds, "they may just as easily be acquired by personal experience." Since Wolf Man was indubitably seduced by his older sister, why, Freud asks, can his fantasy of parental intercourse not equally be based on reality? Besides, he continues, "all that we find in the prehistory of neuroses is that a child catches hold of this phylogenetic experience where his own experience fails him. He fills in the gaps in individual truth with prehistoric truth; he replaces occurrences in his own life by occurrences in the life of his ancestors. I fully agree with Jung[20] in recognizing the existence of his phylogenetic heritage; but I regard it as a methodological error to seize on a phylogenetic explanation before the ontogenetic possibilities have been exhausted" (337).

It is inconsistent of Jung, Freud observes, to reject the importance of infantile prehistory while acknowledging the importance of ancestral prehistory. It is also the case, he points out, that phylogenetic elements often require elucidation by factors in the infantile life of the individual and that primal scenes that are transmitted phylogenetically re-emerge as concrete events in individual experience. What is more, he adds, he does not need others to remind him that the question of whether infantile fantasies represent real, primal scenes or later experiences that (reflecting some constitutional or phylogenetic factor) are projected back into childhood "is the most delicate question in the whole domain of psychoanalysis ... No doubt has troubled me more ... If, in spite of this, I have held to the more difficult and more improbable view, it has been as a result of arguments such as are forced upon the investigator by the case described in these pages or by any other infantile neurosis" (344).

How it can be understood that infantile scenes are shown to be real, not by direct recollection, on the part of the analysand, but by indirect construction, on the part of the analyst, Freud discusses in more detail in his late essay on "Constructions in Analysis." There he notes that, whereas it is the task of the analysand "to be induced to remember something that has been experienced by him and repressed," it is the task of the analyst "to make out what has been forgotten from the traces which it [the analytic work shared jointly by analysand and analyst] has left behind or, more correctly, to *construct* it" (258–9). Freud compares the work of construction on the part of the analyst to the work of reconstruction on the part of the archeologist. Both build up edifices from fragments that, although not randomly distributed, involve patterns that it takes experience and insight to discern. But the analyst has two advantages over the archeologist. First, his subject is alive and thus a constant source of new material (including, one supposes, new errors and distortions). Second, whereas most archeological sites have suffered such irreparable damage that no work can reconstruct them with certainty, in the construction of psychical objects, Freud contends, "all of the essentials are preserved; even things that seem completely forgotten are present somehow and somewhere, and have merely been buried and made inaccessible to the subject. Indeed, it may, as we know, be doubted whether any psychical structure can really be the victim of total destruction. It depends only upon analytic technique whether we shall succeed in bringing what is concealed completely to light." Not only is analytical construction superior to archeological reconstruction, Freud observes. But the objects of analytical construction are "incomparably more complicated" than those of archeological reconstruction, for "we have insufficient knowledge of what we may expect to find, since their finer structure contains so much that is still mysterious" (260).[21] Indeed, the real difference between the two, he points out, is that, whereas reconstruction is the sole aim of archeology, construction is only the preliminary work of analysis.[22]

Freud's main point is that, since the subject of analytical construction, like the unconscious itself, is alive and inexhaustible, psychical construction is far more reliable, notwithstanding its infinitely greater complications and mysteries, than the material reconstruction of archeology. This allows him to argue, as he also does in his study of Wolf Man, that analysts have sound reason to rely on their constructions.[23] Not only are unsuitable or simply wrong constructions greeted by analysands with indifference, but Freud also claims that the dangers of suggestion, unless the analyst is unscrupulous, are vastly overrated.[24] What counts, he holds, is not so much whether the analysand greets the construction proffered him by the analyst with a yes or a no, for whatever response he gives cannot be treated as unambiguous, since it can always hide evasion or resistance. What counts, rather, is whether the construction advances the analysis by eliciting fresh material from the analysand. "If the construction is wrong," Freud observes, "there is no change in the patient; but if it is right or gives an approximation to the truth, he reacts to it with an unmistakable aggravation of his symptoms and of his general condition" (265). It is not the particular reactions of the patient to construction, he observes, but only *the further course of the analysis* [that] enables us to decide whether our constructions are correct or unserviceable. We do not pretend that an individual construction is anything more than a conjecture which awaits examination, confirmation or rejection. We claim no authority for it, we require no direct agreement from the patient, nor do we argue with him if at first he denies it. In short, we conduct ourselves on the model of a familiar figure in one of Nestroy's farces – the manservant who has a single answer on his lips to every question or objection: *"It will all become clear in the course of future developments"* ... The path that starts from the analyst's construction ought to end in the patient's recollection; but it does not always lead so far. Quite often we do not succeed in bringing the patient to recollect what has been repressed. Instead of that, if the analysis is carried out correctly, we produce in him an assured conviction of the truth of the construction which achieves the same therapeutic result as a recaptured memory. *The problem of what the circumstances are in which this occurs and of how it is possible that what appears to be an incomplete substitute should nevertheless produce a complete result – all of this is matter for a later enquiry.* (265–6ᵉ)

Construction, it thus turns out, involves both a psychical past, which, unlike the material past of the archeologist, is alive and indestructible, and a psychical future, which, although reliably determined, still provides material for a later enquiry. While construction is incomplete, it actually produces a complete result; but how this complete result is possible is still incompletely known and itself depends upon future enquiry.

What Freud writes about construction in terms of its role in psychotherapy is insightful, for it is how all of us live our lives. In other words, construction would be properly viewed as coincident with desire, will, love, action, with the golden rule of self and other. It is in terms of the dynamics of the relationship of self and other – both past and future – that construction takes place in the analytic situation, although Freud states that how this is possible will be (positively) revealed only in future enquiry. Each of the parties involved in construction is the (de)constructor of and for the other, as they together shape and wait upon the future (for) results. To the degree, however, that Freud's concept of construction involves his metapsychological doctrine of the Oedipus (castration) complex and the myth of the primal father – phylogenesis – it falls into contradiction.

Two additional elements, involving how Freud conceives of the relationship between id and ego and of the infantile, further show the difficulty he has in reconciling metapsychological past and phenomenological future. In *An Outline* Freud calls the id (which largely replaces his earlier concept of the unconscious) the oldest of the psychical agencies. He claims that the id contains everything that is inherited and thus present at birth, above all, "the instincts, which originate from the somatic organization and which find a first psychical expression here in forms unknown to us." He adds that "this oldest portion of the psychical apparatus [the id] remains the most important throughout life; moreover, the investigations of psychoanalysis started with it" (376). In contrast to the id is the ego, which, although it emerges from the id, "owes its origin as well as the most important of its acquired characteristics to its relation to the real external world" (437). In *The Ego and the Id* Freud writes that, in attempting to replace the pleasure principle, which reigns in the id, with the reality principle, "the ego represents what may be called reason and common sense, in contrast to the id, which contains the passions. All this falls into line with *popular distinctions* which we are all familiar with" (364e).[25]

But the problem with popular distinctions is that, however acute their phenomenology, they tend to be woefully inadequate in their conceptual understanding. How is Freud going to explain the phenomenology of (historical) experience on the basis of a division between (internal, unconscious) id and (external, conscious) ego? All experience is transmitted internally in and by the id. Yet all experience is acquired externally by the ego. The id is the oldest psychical agency, yet it presupposes the ego. The ego is the youngest psychical agency, yet it precedes the id. How can the internal (the id) become external (the ego) in the end? How can the external be internal in the beginning? In *The Ego and the Id* Freud recalls his argument in *Totem and Taboo* that religion, morality, and a social sense are acquired phylogenetically out of the father complex. But the notion of phylogenesis raises the question, he acknowledges, of whether it is the ego or the id of primitive peoples that inherits religion, morality, and sociality from the father-complex. His answer is that the difference between ego and id is attributable "not only to primitive man but even to much simpler organisms, for it is the inevitable expression of the influence of the external world. The superego ... actually originated from the experiences that led to totemism." Thus the question of whether these experiences originate with the ego or the id is beside the point, Freud declares. For what "reflection at once shows," he writes, is

that no external vicissitudes can be experienced or undergone by the id, except by way of the *ego* which is the representative of the external world to the id. Nevertheless it is not possible to speak of direct inheritance in the *ego*. It is here that the gulf between an actual individual and the concept of a species becomes evident. Moreover, one must not take the difference between ego and id in too hard-and-fast a sense, nor forget that the ego is a specially differentiated part of the id. The experiences of the ego seem at first to be lost for inheritance; but, when they have been repeated often enough and with sufficient strength in many individuals in successive generations, THEY TRANSFORM THEMSELVES, SO TO SAY, INTO EXPERIENCES OF THE ID, the impressions of which are preserved by heredity. Thus in the id, which is capable of being inherited, are harbored RESIDUES OF THE EXISTENCES OF COUNTLESS EGOS; and, when the ego forms its superego out of the id, it may perhaps only be reviving shapes of former egos and be bringing them to resurrection. (378^e)

We may recall that in chapter 2 we saw that, while Freud argues for the prior existence of the pleasure principle, he is compelled to admit that it cannot exist prior to the reality principle. Similarly here, while he now argues for the prior existence of the id and its instinctual inheritance, he is forced to admit not only that it depends upon the external world for its existence but also that it is constituted by (countless) ego experiences. The id, therefore, cannot be "older" than the ego, for its (internal) instinctual inheritance totally depends upon external experience.

As for the ego, while today in the infant child it is weak and subject to three harsh masters – id, superego, and external world[26] – originally, in its guise as the primal father (who is never a child), it constitutes the origin of religion, morality, and sociality, which are then transmitted phylogenetically in and by the id. Freud unvaryingly views the infantile ego as immature, helpless, and dependent, as having to defend itself against both internal libidinal pressures and external social pressures (with the internal and external pressures later coalescing in and as the superego). In the *New Introductory Lectures* he writes that "most of our children pass through a neurotic phase in the course of their development" (183).[27] In *An Outline* he states that "the weak and immature ego of the first period of childhood is permanently damaged by the stresses put upon it in its efforts to fend off the dangers that are peculiar to that period of life" (435). When the Oedipal boy fears losing the love of his parents, "the threat to his *narcissism* by the danger of castration, reinforced from primeval sources, takes possession of him." What this means, "from a biological standpoint," Freud states, is that

the ego comes to grief over the task of mastering the excitations of the early sexual period, at a time *when its immaturity makes it incompetent* to do so. It is in *this lagging of ego development behind libidinal development* that we see the essential precondition of neurosis; and we cannot escape the conclusion that neuroses could be avoided if the childish ego were spared this task – if, that is to say, the child's sexual life were allowed free play, as happens among many primitive peoples[28] ... Nor should we forget *the phylogenetic influences, which are represented in some way in the id in forms that we are not yet able to grasp,* and which must certainly act upon the ego *more powerfully in that early period* than later. (436e)[29]

What is evident from this passage is that Freud views the "ego" exclusively in terms of metapsychology, not in terms of the child's experience, his interaction with his parents (and others). The id is fully endowed at birth – being the heir of countless egos over the ages, all equally weak in the beginning, with the exception, however, of the first ego, that of the primal father. The ego – although originating from the id, yet representing the external world – is essentially the slave of the libidinal impulses of the id. But then Freud has no explanation of how the ego subsequently becomes more competent and powerful, except to say that it must repress its sexual impulses. In what manner this is done, however, is completely a matter of metapsychology, of phylogeny. Once again, it is clear that the castration complex, heir to identification with the father, eliminates libido (love, object relations), in preparation for the superego, itself the heir of the id and its phylogenetic inheritance. Freud himself acknowledges that he is unable to account for how the "phylogenetic influences" are represented in the id, except to say that the id embodies countless repetitions of ego experiences. As always, Freud's metaphychological dualism terminates in an impasse. He is unable to account for the temporal (historical) relationships between id and ego, phylogeny and ontogeny, or species and individual. Today, the first is early (prior) and the second late (posterior). But in the beginning the second (the ego of the primal father) is first, while the first (the id as the residue of countless egos) is second.

There is still one more element, in the above suite of passages on the neurotic incompetence of the infantile ego, that is both prominent and incongruous and upon which I have not yet commented but which I emphasized when I discussed the Oedipus complex in chapter 3. This is the element of narcissism. It is prominent because the castration threat simply confirms the boy's identification with the father's penis (as it confirms the girl in her identification with the mother's lack of penis and her desire to have the father's penis). It is incongruous, for, although the boy's infantile ego is weak, immature, and incompetent, his narcissism is strong, absolute, and inviolable. The boy begins in narcissistic (pre-libidinal) identification with the father and ends there, with his object libido castrated. His primary experience is autoerotic, not object relational. Indeed, we earlier saw Freud describe the primary relationship of the child to its mother in terms of the ego instincts (self-preservation) and not of the sexual instincts (object relations). It is most extraordinary to see how Freud's account of the child's weak, incompetent ego, lagging behind its libido development, is congruent with his account of the child's originary narcissism and autoerotism.

In a long comment in his study of Rat Man Freud directly connects infantile autoerotism with the fact that it is often difficult to know whether or not a primal scene actually takes place. The reason for this, he holds, is that, when people consolidate their childhood memories, generally at the time of puberty, they rework their earlier autoerotism in terms of later object relations. Just as nations construct legends about their early history, it is evident, Freud writes,

that in his fantasies about his infancy the individual as he grows up *endeavors to efface the recollection of his autoerotic activities*; and this he does by exalt-ing their memory-traces to the level of object love, just as a real historian will view the past in the light of the present. This explains why these fantasies abound in seductions and assaults, where the facts will have been confined to autoerotic activities and the caresses or punishments that stimulated them. Fur-thermore, it becomes clear that in constructing fantasies about his childhood the individual *sexualizes his memories*; that is, he brings commonplace experi-ences into relation with his sexual activity, and extends his sexual interest to them. (87)

As I indicated earlier, I am not primarily concerned with the contro-versy surrounding Freud's seduction theory. What is important here, metapsychologically, is the emphasis that Freud puts on infantile sexu-ality as autoerotic.[30] If the memories that people later rewrite as sexu-al (involving object love) are originally autoerotic, this suggests three things. First, libido as (object) love is secondary, not primary. Second, although the child's ego is weak and incompetent and threatened by being overwhelmed by libidinal (id) impulses, the child is first and fore-most narcissistic: autoerotism mirrors its identification with the father. In other words, Freud's later emphasis on pre-libidinal identification with the father in his mature formulation of the Oedipus complex is consistent with his earlier insistence on autoerotism as primarily char-acterizing infantile sexuality. Third, the fact that infantile autoerotism mirrors the Oedipus complex and, ultimately, its demolition as the nar-cissistic reconfirmation of (autoerotic) identification is made evident when Freud goes on to write that

the content of the sexual life of infancy consists in autoerotic activity, ... in traces of object-love, and in the formation of that complex which deserves to be called *the nuclear complex of the neuroses*. It is the complex which comprises the child's earliest impulses, alike tender and hostile, towards its parents and brothers and sisters ... THE UNIFORMITY of the content of the sexual life of children, together with THE UNVARYING CHARACTER of the modifying tendencies which are later brought to bear upon it, will easily account for THE CONSTANT SAMENESS which as a rule characterizes the fantasies that are constructed around the period of childhood, irrespective of how greatly or how little real experiences have contributed towards them. It is entirely characteristic of the nuclear complex of infancy that the child's father should be assigned the part of A SEXUAL OPPONENT and of AN INTERFERER WITH AUTOEROTIC SEXUAL ACTIVITIES; and real events are usually to a large extent responsible for bringing this about. (88ᵉ)

The key elements in this passage are clear. Fantasies of infantile sexual life are constantly the same because infantile sexuality is primarily dominated by autoerotism and the Oedipus complex. Both autoerotism and the Oedipus complex are shaped internally and thus phylogenetically, and both of them are then terminated by the castration threat stemming from the father (with whom, Freud later says, the male child identifies, in the beginning). It is also the case that autoerotism and Oedipal impulses are united in a common, originary narcissism. Not only does autoerotism reflect an originary narcissism, but, as I have emphasized, the boy's Oedipal situation begins with the narcissism of identifying with the father's penis and ends with the narcissism of the castration complex. Two features thus characterize the narcissism of both autoerotism and the Oedipal impulses: (1) the absence of libido, of object relations; and (2) the domination of phylogenesis, the inheritance within the id of countless ego experiences and the Oedipal inheritance of (what Freud will come to formulate in Totem and Taboo as) the murder of the primal father. The story of infantile sexuality is unvarying because individual experience – history created by and through relations with others, above all, the parents – is insignificant in the face of the overweening narcissism of both autoerotism and identification with the father (the father complex).

It is also the case, however, that the infantile ego is not only autoerotic, Oedipal, and narcissistic but also incompetent, weak, helpless, immature, and completely dependent on – what? On the father. But the father represents the elimination of autoerotic and Oedipal impulses in the name of narcissism, which is thus but a reinstitution of pure autoerotism and identification with the penis. Just as narcissism ensures the inviolability of the phylogenetic heritage – confirmed in identification with the father – so the helpless, dependent ego and its autoeroticism also make personal experience and history irrelevant. The fact that the ego is, at one and the same time, weak and helpless (incompetent), primarily autoerotic, and absolutely narcissistic (both in original identification with the father and in ultimate identification with the penis, when threatened with castration) can be explained only by the role that the unvarying phylogenetic heritage plays in the life of the individual. There is also the additional factor that libido – relations with others – makes no significant contribution whatsoever to the development of infantile life, sexual or otherwise.

It is particularly striking that Freud compares the individual's construction of the story of infantile sexuality, at puberty, with both the nation's construction of its legendary past and the historian's view of the past in terms of the present. Not only, however, do we remember that Freud himself (much later) indicates that psychoanalytic construction has no alternative to (either the farce or the truth of) viewing both past and present in terms of the (yet unknown) future. But we also wonder if there is not a distinction to be made between legendary and historical construction, between neurotic and psychoanalytic construction, between fictional construction (masquerading as fact) and historical construction (whose fictionality is recognized in full self-consciousness). But, as Freud himself indicates, this is a matter for future research! As always, he gives no idea as to how it is possible for the present (or future) construction to take place. The past is unvaryingly given in the narcissism of autoerotism and supported by the phylogenetic inheritance of the castration of libido, to which the weak, dependent, and incompetent ego is destined to submit.

Freud thus finds himself confronted, in his study of Wolf Man, with the incongruity of defending the historical reality of the fantasized primal scenes in the face of the unvarying story of infantile sexuality, whose narcissistic inheritance is at once autoerotic and Oedipal. The consequence of this is one more instance of the contradictory impasse generated by his metapsychology. He finds that his emphasis upon the archaic heritage of phylogenesis places him in agreement with Jung. But Jung, in questioning the aetiological role of infantile sexuality in generating (adult) neurosis, challenges a key feature of psychoanalytic theory. In order to justify his conception of infantile sexuality, Freud sees no alternative to defending the historical reality of the primal scenes, as found in infantile fantasy. Yet he acknowledges that, whether or not the young (male) child actually observes the primal scene of parental intercourse, is seduced, or is subjected to an actual castration threat, it would make no real difference. For the child is inexorably shaped by the unvarying phylogenetic inheritance of the primal father. Thus, Freud is faced with an insoluble dilemma (which, although he recognizes, he never thematizes as such). If he emphasizes the role of phylogenetic inheritance in human development (history), the role played by infantile sexuality will be minimized. If he emphasizes the role of infantile sexuality in human development (history), the role played by phylogenetic inheritance – and thus the role of the primal father – will become otiose. Freud rightly indicates that it is incongruous on the part of Jung to accept the idea of phylogenetic inheritance and yet to subordinate the role of infantile sexuality to that of adult conflict and its projection into childhood in explaining the origin of neurosis. Jung, however, is equally right that it is incongruous on the part of Freud to emphasize the role of infantile conflict in shaping human development while making phylogeny so important in explaining the origin of neurosis.

Freud and Jung debate the character of psychical reality without accounting for the common phylogenetic premise of their depth psychology. In the terms posed in this section by Freud, he is faced with the problem of whether psychical reality is primitive fact or modern (neurotic) fantasy. He fails to see that the only way in which to comprehend the phenomenology of psychic reality and thus to avoid the metapsychological dualism opposing psyche and reality is to comprehend the psyche as historical and history as psychical. He does not see that the dualism between conscious end and unconscious beginning entails that between individual and universal (species), external and internal, ontogenetic and phylogenetic, reality and fantasy, ego and id. If the psychical is not real in the beginning, if the originary myth is not really psychical, then there will be no psychical reality in the end. If the historical is not real in the beginning – if the originary myth is not really historical (as the incarnations of God in the Hebrew covenant and in the person of Jesus are dialectical constructions of psyche and history) – then in the end there will be no history but only the mythology of phylogenetic inheritance. Further, as we have seen, phylogeny entails, amazingly, originary narcissism, autoerotism, and a completely weak, immature and incompetent ego that is dependent on the father complex, precisely because it is identified with it.

Consistent with the fact that Freud is unable to conceive of either psychical reality as originary history or historical reality as originary psyche is his conception of prohibition as desire. Nothing will be prohibited if it is not desired. But what this really means, as I have indicated, is that nothing will be desired if it is not prohibited. The fact that (internal) desire does not come into existence except as (external) prohibition reflects the originary pleasure principle, according to whose primary ambivalence desire is pain and the elimination of painful desire is pleasure. To be subject to the pleasure principle is to reduce all desire (pain), tension, existence – ultimately, life itself – to the originary (ambivalent) state of nature, to nirvana, to death.

The idea that desire is prohibited (that prohibition is desired) is central to the myth of the primal father, whose law prohibits all desire (on the part of the primal sons) while licensing his own. But the deep irony here is that the primal sons, in identifying with the father('s penis), reflect back upon him the very identical principle. It is precisely their prohibited desire that leads them to prohibit (eliminate) the desire of the primal father, consistent with the ambivalence of the pleasure principle. In murdering the primal father, the primal sons obey the pleasure principle, whose inherent urge is the death instinct of restoring a prior state of things, Nirvana or death. In loving the primal father the primal sons hate (fear) him. They can express their love for the father – the taboo against killing the totem – only by killing the father. It is the originary ambivalence at the heart of the pleasure principle that, when exposed as the myth of the primal father, is shown to be the death instinct, whose father complex involves desire as prohibition. Indeed, the principle that desire is prohibition not only underlies originary ambivalence and thus the father complex. But it is also central to the ambivalence that dominates both the Oedipus complex and, above all, identification on the part of both male and female children with the father('s penis) and consequently their subjection to the castration complex. The castration complex, as we have seen, is that with which the female child begins (to the ultimate grief of the boy) and that with which the male child ends (to the ultimate grief of the girl). He has what she wants – and thus all her acts are castrating. She wants what he has – and thus all his acts are castrated.

Ultimately, the idea that desire is prohibition is reflected in the concept that Freud has of psychical reality. Since he views psychical reality as desire internal to the organism, it is always subject to external prohibition – on the part of the primal father or of his avatar, the modern Oedipal father. But the primal or external father is himself absolutely impotent, like the erect penis. He has no way of transmitting internally (that is, psychically) what is external (or historical), the prohibition of desire, without being himself subject to its very ambivalence, which thus involves his original murder and his terminal castration in and as the Oedipal story. Although Freud holds that the original catastrophe generating history is the real murder of the primal father at the hands of the primal sons, the original catastrophe is (in fantasy) castration, whose origin is woman in her very absence (she is castrated). It is the absence (castration) of woman that reflects the impotent penis, the identification of desire with prohibition in the originary ambivalence of identification with the penis.

Freud is absolutely right in holding against his less resolute colleagues that the castration complex (as heir to the Oedipus complex) is entailed by and entails the myth of the primal father. To begin with the murder of the primal father is to terminate the Oedipus complex with castration. Freud recognizes, in other words, that to deny the validity of the myth of the primal father is also to reject the validity of the castration complex and with it the Oedipus complex. There is much at stake here, for the castration complex not only presupposes the (individual) myth of the primal father. But it also implies a (universal) concept of myth that is grounded in the principle of ambivalence involving the opposition between internal psyche and external history, between desire and prohibition. So long as desire is conceived of in terms of the pleasure principle of prohibition, there is no exit from the ambivalence of psyche and history. Each reflects the desire of, insofar as it is the prohibition of, the other. We have seen that the identification of desire with prohibition involves the metapsychological projection of the psychical reality of modernity onto primitive taboo and thus of primitive taboo back onto the psychical reality of modernity. That the opposition between psyche and reality results in, and is the result of, the confusion between primitive and modern is further confirmed by the reading that Freud gives of Oedipus, both mythical and historical, to which we shall now turn.

IV THE OEDIPUS COMPLEX IN MYTH AND REALITY

a Introduction

We have seen that Freud presents his myth of the primal father as the solution to explaining the enigma of the horror of incest, which, he holds, is central to primitive exogamy and totemism. It also explains, he believes, the return of totemism in childhood, the fact that the modern (civilized) boy's first libidinal impulses are Oedipal. But we have also noted two huge stumbling-blocks to Freud's primal myth and to his reconstruction of childhood life as Oedipal. First, both in his mature doctrine of the Oedipus complex, as we analyzed it in chapter 3, and in his presentation of the myth of the primal father, it becomes clear that Freud's emphasis is not on the horror of incest – the relationship with the mother – but on the father complex: identification with the penis. Second, in *Totem and Taboo* Freud raises fundamental questions about the cogency of the analogy between taboo (above all, the taboos of totemism: the prohibitions against killing the totem animal, the surrogate father, and having sexual relations with members of the opposite sex within the totemic clan) and neurosis. If taboo is not sexual but ego-centred and if neurosis is sexual but not social – and if sexuality, too, divides people instead of uniting them – what possible relation is there between primitive myth and modern myth?

Freud indicates, we saw earlier, that mental impulses, no matter how distorted (repressed), cannot be so completely suppressed as to leave no traces behind. No generation, he declares in *Totem and Taboo*, can conceal its mental processes from its successor. "For psychoanalysis has shown us that everyone possesses in his unconscious mental activity an apparatus which enables him to interpret other people's reactions, that is, to undo the distortions which other people have imposed on the expression of their feelings" (221). Neurosis, as inhibition, involves and expresses distortion, repression, and the unconscious. Yet, it is precisely the unconscious, Freud suggests, that sees through and undoes distortions. The unconscious, it is evident, comprehends itself as unconscious. Is it then the unconscious that, in constituting a notion of elsewhere or background – history – provides us with the perspective of seeing through and of undoing, of interpreting, distortions (repression)? But what would it mean to see through or to interpret a taboo? What do you see through taboo to? How could taboo, which is not inhibited, be distorted, repressed, or unconscious? Of what is taboo a distortion? Of what is taboo the repression? Of what is taboo unconscious? Of what, in other words, is taboo the interpretation?

It is clear, I think, that taboo – the taboo of animism, primitive taboo, as distinct from the return of taboo as totemism, as Oedipal desire and rivalry, in (modern) childhood – does not involve or express inhibition, distortion, repression, neurosis, the unconscious, or interpretation. Freud both sees and yet refuses to see the "psychological difference" between taboo and neurosis. He stresses the importance of seeing ambivalence in both. But he fails to see the fundamental difference between primitive and modern ambivalence. Primitive ambivalence involves the natural opposition between strife (hate) and Eros, the many and the one, appearance and reality, matter and form (substance). Modern ambivalence, in contrast, expresses active love (desire, will) that, in becoming active hatred (*ressentiment*), reflects inhibition, distortion, repression, neurosis, the unconscious, and interpretation. The difference between primitive and modern ("civilized") ambivalence is the difference between opposites or contradictories that cannot be known (or undone) and those that can be known (and undone). Opposites or contradictories that can be known and undone are those that are revealed by the interpretive process of the unconscious to be paradox. They express not the contradictory opposition between desire and self but their dialectically mutual relationship. To interpret – another, oneself, an event, history, a work of art – is to view contradictory distortions in light of paradoxical relationship, to impute, in other words, the structure of paradox to that which is interpreted (interpretable). The distortions (repressions) of neurosis can be interpreted only because they presuppose the paradoxical relationship of self and other on which psychoanalytic praxis (that equally is theory) is founded: the golden rule of treating others as you desire to be treated by others.

When the analysand, for example, expresses hate for (to) the analyst, the analyst does not deny the reality (not to mention the potential, if not real, danger of the situation) that is before him. But he does not return hatred for hatred (which does not mean that he may not be irritated or provoked by the patient or perhaps even hooked by his counter-transference). He does not hate the analysand in return – he may well feel deep compassion for, which does not mean that he excuses, the analysand's hatred – for two reasons. In the first place, he does not desire to be hated by the other. In the second place, he believes that love is healing, that, in loving (and not in hating) the other, the other will discover the freedom, the liberation, the empowerment of loving in return. To love, Kierkegaard observes, is to presuppose love in the other. Love is upbuilding, edification, above all, for the one who loves. The difference between taboo and neurosis is the difference between Socratic ignorance and psychoanalytic insight, between Oedipal blindness (which becomes Oedipus' secret at the end of *Oedipus at Colonus*, as we shall see) and what Freud calls in *Totem and Taboo* "an unconscious understanding ... of all the customs, ceremonies and dogmas left behind by the original relation to the father" (221–2).

Freud sees the "psychological difference" between taboo and neurosis, but he does not see that this difference involves a notion of depth psychology, based on the unconscious and interpretation, that is simply absent from the primitive world of taboo. *Totem and Taboo* is a typically (but not truly) modern text, for Freud fails to see that, if you posit religion (as founded on animism) in the beginning but not also in the end, then, in the end, you will repeat your beginning, but in a repressed fashion. It is only when modernity is understood as at once religious and secular, both faithful and rational, that the opposition between primitive as religious and modern as secular can be overcome. It is modernity that, precisely because it is inhibited, distorted, and repressed, is critically self-conscious and subject to (it is the subject of its own) interpretation. Modernity is unconscious and interpretive from beginning to end. Modernity is the history of the unconscious as interpretation, the redemption (liberation) of "it was" in light of Zarathustra's resolutely Cartesian "*ergo*: I willed it."

One can will only that which is subject to (is the subject of) will. One can interpret only that which bears the structure of interpretation. One can love only that which is loving. Love presupposes love. Interpretation presupposes interpretation. But what does one do when the structures one approaches do not know inhibition, distortion, repression, the unconscious, or interpretation, when they do not know the love which redeems "it was" as "thus I willed it"? This is the question that Freud, typically modern, does not pose, although he recognizes that "unconscious mental activity" is "an apparatus" that, in enabling us "to interpret other people's reactions," marks the psychological difference between taboo and neurosis. He fails to see that the difference between taboo and neurosis is the difference between Athens and Jerusalem, between the Greek and biblical worlds. He does not know that the Bible is no more religious than it is secular, that it is equally faithful and rational, as it expresses and is expressed by the golden rule, the alternative ontology to which there is no alternative. I have argued for this position extensively in earlier studies. I shall return to it in the final chapters of this study.

Reflection on the impasse at which Freud arrives through his failure to show that the myth of the primal father cannot account for the "psychological difference" between taboo and neurosis leads us to the story of Oedipus. We shall take up two topics. First, we shall ask whether the myth of Oedipus, as dramatized by Sophocles in both *Oedipus the King* and *Oedipus at Colonus*, is primitive or modern. Does Oedipus bear any more than an eponymous relationship to the Oedipus complex, to Oedipal desire and rivalry as described by Freud? Do we find in the Oedipus of Sophocles inhibition, distortion, repression, the unconscious, or interpretation? Or do we find, rather, subjugation to fate that, when revealed in the end, shows the hero to be ignorant and blind from the beginning? Is there any notion that Oedipus redeems the past by (re)creating it from nothing as "thus I willed it"? Second, is the Oedipus complex, when understood on the model of Sophocles and Freud – notwithstanding the fact that, as we shall find, they are utterly different (unrelatable) psychologically – universal, as Spiro argues in *Oedipus in the Trobriands* (1982) against Malinowski in *Sex and Repression in Savage Society* (1927)? As I have indicated, I believe that Spiro effectively counters Malinowki's arguments against the universality of the Oedipus complex. However, when he himself is then compelled to acknowledge that the Oedipus complex, while universal, leads to fundamentally different historical outcomes, his own analysis becomes interminably contradictory.

b The Mythical Oedipus

At the beginning of his psychoanalytic career, Freud writes in *The Interpretation of Dreams* that the story of Sophocles' *Oedipus the*

King depicts "the chief part" that parents play "in the mental lives of all children," both neurotic and normal (362).[31] "The action of the play," he continues, "consists in nothing other than the process of revealing, with cunning delays and ever-mounting excitement – *a process that can be likened to the work of a psychoanalysis* – that Oedipus himself is the murderer of Laius, but further that he is the son of the murdered man and of Jocasta [both Laius' former and now his own present wife]" (363ᵉ). Although Freud recognizes that the play is, as he calls it, a drama of destiny whose end is to demonstrate human impotence before the power of the gods, he asserts, nevertheless, that it moves us (male) moderns because of its tabooed content. We (males) share with Oedipus the impulse to sleep with our mother and to kill our father, as our dreams reveal (although Freud gives no examples of such dreams in *The Interpretation of Dreams*). While Freud holds that Oedipus fulfils the wishes of our own (male) childhood, he also acknowledges that we (males) are more fortunate than Oedipus. Insofar as we are not neurotic, we repress our sexual wishes for our mother and our jealousy for our father. We thus look upon Oedipus, Freud writes, as

one in whom these primeval wishes of our childhood have been fulfilled, and we shrink back from him with the whole force of the repression by which those wishes have since that time been held down within us. While the poet, as he unravels the past, brings to light the guilt of Oedipus, he is at the same time compelling us to recognize our own inner minds, in which those same impulses, though suppressed, are still to be found. The contrast with which the closing Chorus leaves us confronted ... [in citing the choral speech concluding the play, Freud omits the final two lines] strikes as a warning at ourselves and our pride, at us who since our childhood have grown so wise and so mighty in our own eyes. Like Oedipus, we live in ignorance of these wishes, repugnant to morality, which have been forced upon us by *Nature*, and after their revelation we may all of us well seek to close our eyes to the scenes of our childhood. (364–5ᵉ)

At the end of his psychoanalytic career, Freud writes in *An Outline* that the Oedipus complex is so named "because its essential substance is to be found in the Greek legend of King Oedipus" as presented in the play of Sophocles. The fact, however, that Oedipus kills his father and marries his mother in ignorance is, Freud acknowledges, "a deviation from the analytic facts which we can easily understand and which, indeed, we shall recognize as inevitable" (422). "What is overlooked in this," he declares, "is that a distortion of this kind is inevitable if an attempt is made at a poetic handling of the material ... The ignorance of Oedipus is a legitimate representation of the unconscious state into which, for adults, the whole experience has fallen; and the coercive power of the oracle, which makes or should make the hero innocent, is a recognition of the inevitability of the fate which has condemned every son to live through the Oedipus complex" (426–7).

In both these early and late works Freud also comments upon Hamlet as a latter-day Oedipus who is inhibited in taking revenge against his uncle. He observes in *The Interpretation of Dreams* that Claudius, in killing the prince's father and marrying his mother, shows Hamlet "the repressed wishes of his own childhood realized" (367). But Freud also notes that "the changed treatment of the same material [in *Hamlet*] reveals the whole difference in the mental life of these two widely separated epochs of civilization: the secular advance of repression in the emotional life of mankind." In *Oedipus the King*, the fantasy is made real, as in a dream. In *Hamlet*, it is repressed and we learn about it only "from its inhibiting consequences" (366).

Freud's treatment of *Oedipus the King* is characterized by the same ambiguity that we find in his approach to primitive civilization, generally. He indicates that Sophocles' conception of Oedipus is identical with yet different from our modern Oedipus complex. But, in failing to specify the nature of either this identity or this difference, Freud reflects the typically modern approach to the (Greek) classical world, whether learned or popular. Literary scholars and those actually involved in the theater might not agree that what moves us (males) in the Oedipus plays is the revelation, within ourselves, of repressed Oedipal desires. But nearly all of them, even when they recognize (correctly) with Freud that the play is, like all Greek plays, whether tragedy or comedy, a drama of fatal destiny, would hold that the play speaks to what is universal in human fate. Doubtless literary and theatre people would hesitate to agree with Freud that the reason that the play deviates from the analytical facts is because poetic treatment inevitably distorts them. But the vast majority of them would indubitably agree – as the interminable stream of learned and also popular commentary testifies – that the uncovering of Oedipus' ignorance symbolizes the process of analysis, the movement from deception to insight (truth).

Is Oedipal insight not then consistent with Socratic knowledge? We may recall that the Socrates whom Plato portrays in his dialogues insists upon his ignorance. He demonstrates that, unlike the poets (including Sophocles?), politicians, rhetoricians, and sophists – the other speakers in the Greek world – he knows *that* he is ignorant. Still, notwithstanding the fact that Socrates makes no claim to know *what* he is ignorant of, modern readers, both academic and non-academic, both philosophical and literary, with very few (yet critically important) exceptions, hold that Socrates exemplifies the modern search for knowledge. We continue today to characterize our conception of learning in terms of Socratic irony, Socratic method, and Socratic dialogue. Yet, is it not strange that, while Socrates, in dialogue with others, demonstrates to them that they, like him, are ignorant of the truth, Jesus, in dialogue with Pilate, tells him that he comes to bear witness to the truth? What is truth? Pilate asks Jesus, Socratically. Does not the silence of Jesus bear witness to the truth of the law and the prophets, the truth of (the) scripture?

Is it not Socrates who, at the end of the *Apology*, informs the jury, which has condemned him to death, that he never intends to stop talking and thus looks forward, although dead, to demonstrating to the heroes in the underworld that they know nothing? Is it not Socrates who shows in the *Phaedrus* that all writing (speech) contradicts the good that is known (innately) only within the soul? Is it not Socrates who demonstrates to Theaetetus the significance of the role of fatal midwife that he plays in dialogue with others? Sterile (ignorant) himself, he assists his interlocutors, who are swollen big with the appearance of knowledge, in giving birth to ideas that are, without exception, stillborn. *Any* idea that is born, Socrates demonstrates, is fatally subject to generation and corruption and so opposed to that which is formally one, unchanging, finite, immortal, and unknown to mortals. To be born, to give birth, is to demonstrate fatal ignorance of the truth. Does not the whole of the Socratic logic of *aporia* rest on the demonstration that you cannot seek *what* you do not know, for then you seek (you desire, you love) in ignorance of what you seek? Does not Socrates report to his fellow banqueters that he learned from Diotima that the gods are not philosophers precisely because to love, to seek, to desire wisdom – *philo-sophia* – is to lack wisdom? Is this position not consistent with his earlier demonstration to Agathon – as we saw in connection with Freud's appeal to the myth of Aristophanes – that to desire the good is to lack (forever) the good that you desire? Is it not equally the case that, in the second half of the *Symposium*, Alcibiades demonstrates, to his interminable frustration, that what he has learned from Socrates is that to desire the good is to lack it? In sum, what Socrates demonstrates throughout Platonic dialogue is that, like him, all Greeks are ignorant of the good. He shows with fatal logic that the good can be possessed only in the absence of desire, that the Idea of the Good can be possessed only in the absence of life.

It is a critical indication of our contemporary hermeneutical inadequacy that even today there are few thinkers, including literary and plastic artists, who do not continue to show massive resistance to acknowledging the truth of what Hegel and Kierkegaard wrote about

Socrates. These two incomparable, modern students of Socrates are typically viewed as thinkers whose ideas are diametrically opposed to each other, the one championing rational totality in the name of philosophy, the other the faithful individual in the name of religion.[32] But the truth is that they are our only two thinkers who articulate an adequate concept of history.[33] Hegel's demonstration that history is the universally rational story of individual freedom both presupposes and is presupposed by Kierkegaard's demonstration that history is the individual story of faithfully coming universally into existence. The reason that Hegel and Kierkegaard are able to develop an adequate concept of history is precisely because they systematically distinguish Greek philosophy – as embodied in Socrates, for example – from biblical revelation of the truth. It is doubtless because they formulate a concept of historical existence as the dialectic of (and not the dualistic opposition between) the secular and the religious that they remain voices crying in the hermeneutical wilderness.

What Hegel and Kierkegaard incontestably demonstrate is that Socratic ignorance is ignorance, that it hides no unconscious wisdom precisely because it is the secret, like fate itself, to which there is no conscious access.[34] Hegel and Kierkegaard show, as I indicated in my prefatory remarks, that we must learn to distinguish between knowing *that* one is ignorant and knowing *what* one is ignorant of. The first is Socratic (Greek, primitive). The second is psychoanalytic (and biblical), involving inhibition, distortion, repression, the unconscious, and interpretation.

It is significant, then, that Freud, although typically modern in uncritically reading the unconscious into Oedipal ignorance, is much more careful when he comes to Socrates. In the *Introductory Lectures* he reminds his audience that from what he has told them about neurosis it "would seem to be the result of a kind of ignorance – a not knowing about mental events that *one ought to know of*. This would be a close approximation to some well-known Socratic doctrines, according to which even vices are based on ignorance" (321ᵉ). Freud has in mind here famous Socratic conundrums such that no one knowingly does evil, that sin is ignorance, and that all evil is done in ignorance (of the good). Freud points out to his audience, however, that "knowledge is not always the same as knowledge: there are different sorts of knowledge, which are far from equivalent psychologically" (322). He is evidently concerned here to distinguish from Socratic ignorance the neurotic ignorance that involves denial, resistance, and repression, of which there is not the slightest hint in either Socrates or his interlocutors. The neurotic ignorance that psychotherapy brings to light is, as Freud says, "a not knowing about mental events that *one ought to know of.*"

The context in which Freud discusses the difference between Socratic ignorance and neurotic (or unconscious) ignorance is that of therapy. The analyst, he points out, does not simply hand the analysand the knowledge that is required to make him well. He must, rather, help him work through his resistance to the healing knowledge. He must help the analysand bring to consciousness his unconscious resistance to conscious knowledge, for that is what it means to make the unconscious conscious. The analysand must learn (to confront) *what* he is ignorant of and not merely recognize *that* he is ignorant – of he knows not what. In *An Outline* Freud points out that it is the task of the analysand to tell the analyst "what he does *not* know" (407). Ignorance in the psychoanalytic context, it is clear, is paradoxical. The analysand has to (come to) know *what* he does not know. Ignorance involves content, resistance to and denial of truth as embodied in the historical relationship of self and desire. "What are the motive forces that we work with in such a case?" Freud asks in the *Introductory Lectures*. He mentions two: "the patient's desire for recovery" and "his intelligence, to which we give support by our interpretation" (489).

That one desires to know, that one ought to know, that one has the responsibility of knowing *what* one does not know: that is the paradox that is absent from the Greek world of Socrates and Oedipus. All desire, all seeking, all effort, all trial, all analysis in the Greek world is doomed to ignorance, for all desire is lack, lack (ignorance) of the good. The contradictory opposite of ignorance (of the good) is knowledge (of the good) that is possessed by the individual, not in his mortal body but in his immortal soul (and here the Socratic teaching of Plato is no less Aristotelian): the unmoved mover – thought thinking itself. In contrast to Socrates, Freud demonstrates that knowledge is resistance, resistance that must be struggled with, worked through, overcome, and appropriated.

In the *Critique of Pure Reason* Kant shows that resistance (work) is indeed central to knowledge. When reason does not recognize its limits, when reason does not know *what* its limits are, when reason does not have limits to resist, the result, Kant points out, is that then

the demand for the extension of knowledge recognizes no limits. The light dove, cleaving the air in her free flight, and feeling its *resistance*, might imagine that its flight would be still easier in empty space. It was thus that Plato left the world of the senses, as setting too narrow limits to the understanding, and ventured out beyond it on the wings of the ideas, in the empty space of the pure understanding. He did not observe that with all his efforts he made no advance – meeting no *resistance* that might, as it were, serve as a support upon which he could take a stand, to which he could apply his powers, and so set his understanding in motion. (B 8–9ᵉ)

What is resisted in the Greek (and, generally, the primitive) world is, however, not knowledge but ignorance and always with fatal consequences. It is the resistance to ignorance of oracular, daimonic, and theistic powers that uncovers the contradictions fatally lurking within gnomic apothegms: nothing in excess, the unexamined life is not worth living, and it is better to suffer evil (from others) than to do evil (to others). All resistance to ignorance is shown to be fatally excessive. Think of Pentheus, the hero of the *Bacchae*, who is torn to pieces by his unknowing mother for resisting ignorance to the power of Dionysus. Think of Socrates, for whom the unexamined life is not worth living. It seems particularly ironic (to us) that Socrates, in resisting ignorance, in examining life, is condemned to death for exceeding (contradicting) what is knowable to mortals. What he demonstrates is that, while others ignorantly claim to possess knowledge of what they know, he, at least, knows that he is ignorant. He knows that he knows nothing. He knows that he does not know what he is ignorant of. He does not know whereof he speaks, he knows. It is precisely Socrates' fate, like that of all Greek heroes, to bring to light the fatal contradiction between mortal ignorance and immortal knowledge. To appeal to the Delphic oracle of Apollo is to be struck down by the blinding contradiction that to examine life is to exceed the life knowable to mortals. To examine life is to demonstrate that all mortals are fatally condemned to blindness, ignorance, and death.

Oedipus, both king of Thebes and exile at Colonus, is also, like Socrates, the archetypal Greek hero. In *Oedipus the King*, his resistance to ignorance, his ignorant attempt to avoid his fate, is utterly contradictory. He is propelled by that which he resists, ignorance of his fate; and, when his fate (that before he was born he was destined to kill his father and to marry and have children by his mother) is revealed to him, he is blinded by it. The act of his self-blinding does not symbolize any analytic insight on the part of Oedipus. Rather, it reflects, as in a blind mirror, the fate of which he is ignorant in the beginning. At the end of the play Oedipus, like Socrates, knows *that* he is ignorant. But he does not know *what* he is ignorant of. It is precisely his resistance to ignorance, to what he cannot and will never know, his contradictory fate, that brings him down. "Behold this Oedipus," the chorus sings in initiating the final passage of the play. Then, in the last two lines of the play, those omitted by Freud, the Chorus concludes: "Look upon that last day always. Count no mortal happy till / He has passed the final limit of his life secure from pain."

I have a crude paraphrase of the last lines of the play: the only happy man is a dead man. This is precisely Socrates' message at the end of his death trilogy – *Apology, Crito,* and *Phaedo* – and it is consistent with Plato's concept of the immortality of the soul. In the *Nicomachean Ethics* Aristotle claims to find Solon's dictum – look to your end – absurd. But to pursue the brilliant logic of Aristotle to its end is to find demonstrated, consistent with Socrates, that to resist ignorance is only to demonstrate yet more brilliantly the fatal logic of contradiction of which you have no knowledge and from which there is no exit except in and through death. What Sophocles and Solon are pointing to in saying "look upon that last day always" and "look to the end" is that the fate of human beings is not complete until they are dead. Prior to death chance can always intervene to change it. But even death, however, does not bring one to a final end in the Greek world. Natural metamorphosis, the ambivalence of nature, is unending. Although the *Gorgias* and the *Republic* conclude with myths of punishment, both those who are contradictorily punished for doing evil in ignorance of the good and those who are contradictorily rewarded for knowing and thus being identical with the good (including Socrates!) are fated to return to life, ignorant, having passed through the river Lethe to begin, once again, the natural (endless) cycle of life and death. Their fate is absolutely no different from that described in the Upanishads, as Freud astutely observes in *Beyond the Pleasure Principle*, as we saw. Such is the fate of those who know that they are ignorant – which is precisely the discovery that Oedipus, like Socrates, makes – but who do not know what they are ignorant of, who are ignorant "about mental events that one ought to know of."

The fate of the blind, exiled Oedipus is not complete, then, until he passes beyond mortal sight at Colonus. *Oedipus at Colonus*, the sequel to *Oedipus the King*, helps one see that the Oedipus plays of Sophocles are not about psychoanalytical method, the unconscious, or the totemic ban on incest and parricide. *Oedipus at Colonus*, while lacking the dramatic intensity of its predecessor, is a splendid antidote to conventional wisdom about Greek tragedy. Its hero appears to triumph in the end. The play concludes, after the final rites of purification, with the reception of the aged, blind, and exiled Oedipus by the gods. These are the very gods, presumably, who had originally fated Oedipus in the beginning to suffer the blinding ignorance of incest and parricide and thus exile, which is what has brought the fallen and disgraced king to Colonus in the first place.

Blind, old, and led by his daughter Antigone – who is also his half-sister, for they have the same mother – Oedipus, now uncanny, the tabooed, dreaded object who is also held in veneration and awe, awaits his death in Colonus. He promises a mysterious, secret blessing to Theseus and to the city of Athens of which Theseus is the ruler. In *Oedipus the King* a series of informers – Teiresias, Creon (Oedipus' brother-in-law), Jocasta (his mother and wife), the messenger, and the herdsman – assist the king in making good his promise to discover and punish the individual whose crime has polluted Thebes, the murderer of Laius, the former king of Thebes. The murderer is Oedipus himself, Laius' son. Similarly, at Colonus the exiled king receives a series of interlocutors – a stranger, the chorus of local citizens, Theseus, Creon, and his son (and half-brother) Polyneices. They provide him with the occasion of unsaying his guilt and execrating Thebes and his enemies (especially his sons) for exiling him.

In reversing (i.e. contradicting) his earlier disgrace, Oedipus repeats a pattern common to both Homer and Greek tragedy. One of the most brilliant depictions of reversal in all of Greek literature, epic and dramatic, is that with which Euripides brings his *Electra* to an end. The play concludes with the stark announcement to Orestes and Electra, the murderers of their mother Clytemnestra, by the divine brother of Clytemnestra and Helen, that Helen never went to Troy:

> Justice has claimed her [Clytemnestra] but you have not worked in justice.
> As for Phoebus, Phoebus [Apollo] – yet he is my lord,
> silence. He knows the truth but his oracles were lies.
> Compulsion is on us to accept this scene, on you
> to go complete the doom which fate and Zeus decreed. (1244–8)
> Helen ... never went to Troy.
> Zeus fashioned and dispatched a Helen-image there
> to Ilium [Troy] so men might die in hate and blood. (1280–3)

In reversing the myth that initiated the Trojan War and thus the cultural life of Greece, generally, Euripides consummately demonstrates that the very structure of Greek myth is reversal, i.e., contradiction. To learn that myth is contradiction is to reflect, blindly, your fatal contradiction (reversal) by it. Like Socrates, who demonstrates in Platonic dialogue that wisdom, justice, the good, etc. cannot be taught or learned, what Euripides demonstrates to the Greek audience is that they know that they are ignorant. But they do not know what they are ignorant of. They learn that Helen never went to Troy. They know that they are ignorant of Greek myth, that Greek myth, in its fatal reversals, reflects their contradictory ignorance. But they do not know what Greek myth is.

As the god Apollo demonstrates in *Electra* that life is fatal reversal – for, in the end, Helen did not initiate the Trojan War in the beginning

– so Oedipus, at his end in Colonus, reverses the beginning of his fated past. All the evil that he did, he now says, was done in fatal ignorance: don't blame me.[35] Antigone tells the chorus that her father (and half-brother) "never knew what he did" (240). Oedipus concurs: he suffered the deeds more than he did them. He merely acted in self-defense, ignorant that it was his father whom he killed (266ff). He denies that he chose exile and asserts that it was the city of Thebes that harshly drove him out (431ff). He swears that he is innocent of his father's death: "I did not know him; and he wished to murder me. / Before the law – before God – I am innocent!" (547–8) He tells Creon that he suffered the calamities of parricide and incest "by fate, against my will! It was God's pleasure ... / In me myself you could not find such evil." The oracular fate dictating that he kill his father occurred before he was born, before he was conceived. As for his mother-wife, neither she nor he knew the truth of their relation. "No: I shall not be judged an evil man, / Neither in that marriage nor in that death." I was "forced into it by the gods" (962ff).

In addition to heaping the blame for his calamitous life upon the gods and his political enemies, Oedipus promises to Theseus and Athens a gift of grace, a great blessing (576ff, 647, 1490). When, then, at the close of the play, divine thunder and lightning announce his fated end, he informs Theseus that the time has come to bestow upon him the blessing of knowing the fate that is appointed for him and Athens. But Theseus must agree to accompany Oedipus alone to his death and never to reveal the secret of his death to anyone until, at death, he transmits it to his appointed heir. The messenger then reports the mysterious death of Oedipus, which only Theseus observed, to the chorus. After bidding his daughters goodbye and accompanied only by Theseus, Oedipus simply vanished, leaving Theseus alone with "his hands before his face, / Shading his eyes as if from something awful, / Fearful and unendurable to see" (1650-2). Theseus returns from the awesome scene of Oedipus' death to tell Antigone that her father (and half-brother) had informed him that, if he kept secret how and where Oedipus died – "No mortal man should tell of it, / Since it is holy, and is his" – then he would preserve his lands from his enemies (1762-3).

What is the secret of Oedipus' death? Clearly, it is not the Freudian revelation that humankind is haunted by the return in childhood of totemism – the desire to possess the mother and to kill the father. It is striking that the king of Thebes, execrated for those crimes, becomes the venerated exile of Colonus, promising blessing to Theseus and Athens. Not only does Oedipus insist that the gods are to blame for his fate, of which he was totally ignorant, but the unholy deeds give him an uncanny aura. At the end of the play, divine *son et lumière* announce his reception by the very gods whom he blames for the fate of which he was blessedly ignorant. It is evident that Sophocles is not concerned to reveal, to the audiences of either his day or ours, the forbidden – incestuous and murderous – wishes of childhood. Oedipus' secret – the secret with which he goes to his death – is not that he murdered his father and married his mother. These deeds are widely known to all and, although execrable, become venerable and provide Oedipus with a blessing to bestow upon Theseus and Athens.[36]

It is also evident that Aristotle, in the *Poetics*, is not concerned with the particular content of *Oedipus the King* or of any of the other tragedies that he cites to exemplify his conception of tragic poetry. What he emphasizes is tragic reversal – the dramatic change of a situation into its opposite – and tragic recognition – the dramatic change from ignorance to knowledge. "The finest kind of recognition is accompanied by simultaneous reversals, as in the *Oedipus* [*the King*]," he writes in the *Poetics* (1452a). The pity and fear that a properly constructed tragedy arouses in the audience are due, Aristotle indicates, to the effectiveness with which the plot produces dramatic reversal and recognition. "The story should be so constructed," he remarks, "that the events make anyone who hears the story shudder and feel pity even without seeing the play. The story of Oedipus has this effect" (1453b). Pity and fear, within the Greek world, characterize the reaction on the part of members of the audience to the fatality of their lives that they see enacted in the drama before them. Everything is shown to be reversal (metamorphosis) into its opposite; and all seeking for wisdom is shown to involve the reversal from ignorance to knowledge, the recognition – on the part of Oedipus as of Socrates – that one is ignorant, from the beginning unto the end. Look to the end, for no man is happy until he has reached his end and passed beyond life's reversals as he acknowledges that the reversal from ignorance to knowledge is the recognition that he knows nothing. The end is death, the recognition that life is its fatal reversal, its blind opposite. Thus the chorus in *Oedipus at Colonus* contemplates the reversal and the recognition that are the fate of every human being:

Though he has watched a decent age pass by,
A man will sometimes still desire the world.
I swear I see no wisdom in that man.
The endless hours pile up a drift of pain
More unrelieved each day ...
The last attendant is the same for all, ...
        Death is the finish.
Not to be born surpasses thought and speech.

The second best is to have seen the light
And then to go back quickly whence we came. (1211–26)

The demonstration that Greek life is contradictory, that is, mythical appearance, is a teaching consistent with the views of both Plato and Aristotle on poetry. What the two philosophers demonstrate, from contradictory (reversed) positions, reflecting the opposed (mutually dependent) positions of Socrates and the polis, is that epic and tragic poetry, like all speech (including their own), is contradictory. It knows not whereof it speaks. It does not know what it says. The only speech that escapes (and thus fatally reinforces) contradiction is that found within the soul, speech that is dead to life, speech that is unknown to mortals: thought thinking itself.

The fact that there is no unconscious where there is no resistance and that there is no consciousness, as self-consciousness, where there is no unconscious – that is the unknown and unknowable secret that Oedipus in his death blindly bestows upon the bedazzled Theseus. It is a secret that can be revealed and spoken only in death. Oedipus ends his life, as he begins it, with a secret that fatally condemns his life to death and fatally liberates his death from life. The secret of Oedipus is the secret of fate, the secret of tragedy (as also of comedy), the secret of the law of contradiction, the secret of Greek life. The secret is that there is no secret – to those who have eyes to see and ears to hear, to those who, as Freud says, in being ignorant of what they "ought to know of," desire to know what it is, notwithstanding – indeed, precisely because of – their resistance to it. The secret, which remains Socratic ignorance and Oedipal blindness in the Greek world, is that "knowledge is not always the same as knowledge," that "there is more than one kind of ignorance." This is the secret that remains unknown to the primitive, Greek world and whose revelation, as the "unconscious" interpretation of distorted (inhibited and repressed) communication, is what is presupposed in the modern world of psychoanalysis.

The structure of secret is paradoxical, in the biblical tradition, when it is not contradictory, in the Greek (and primitive) tradition. One can have a secret only when it can be both told and repressed. There are no secrets where there is no repression; and where there is no repression, there is no knowledge of secrets. Freud knows that it is precisely the secret, resistance, which, at one and the same time, both inhibits and propels analysis. Only if the analysand resists his secret – only if the secret shows resistance – will the analyst be able to assist the analysand with constructions – interpretations – that reveal his secret. There is no working through if there is no secret to resist or if there is no resistance to keep secret. It is typical of Freud to understand the phenomenology of the secret but to be unable to provide a metapsychology that is true to the secret's paradoxical structure of resistance and recognition. Misled by the apparent similarity of content between the catastrophes of Oedipus and the libidinal life of the modern (male) child, he provides a reading of *Oedipus the King* that falsifies both the Greek world and his own phenomenology.

The fact that Freud is not a reliable guide to the mythical Oedipus is consistent with our earlier demonstration that what the Oedipus complex is really about is identification with and thus castration of the penis. In neither case are Oedipal desire and rivalry, notwithstanding Freud's claims, the central issue. As for Sophocles, he is interested in incest and parricide only as a means of demonstrating, in brilliant fashion, the reversal of life as the recognition of the fatal end whose secret cannot be mortally communicated. What Freud shows us is that the ambivalence, which characterizes identification with the penis – its presence or absence – both precedes and terminates Oedipal sexuality and aggressivity. In Sophocles, desire is the secret whose contradiction dies with the hero. The end of contradiction that the hero seeks lies beyond the grave. In Freud, desire remains subject to the contradiction of the pleasure principle. Desire is generated by posterior unpleasure in order to restore pleasure as the prior state of reality: nirvana and death.

c Oedipus in Reality

In light of the fact that neither the mythical Oedipus nor his modern successor, the little boy Oedipus (and the little girl Oedipa) of Freudian metapsychology, is Oedipal, we ponder the universality of the Oedipus complex. Are all children, in all civilizations, a little Oedipus and a little Oedipa? Malinowski, when reviewing the psychoanalytic approach to anthropology in the 1920s, says no. Spiro, when reviewing Malinowski's findings – plus additional field and clinical data, not to mention data on infrahuman primates – in the 1980s, in light of the Oedipus complex, as formulated by Freud and his followers, says yes.

As always, the issues are complex ontologically. I have already indicated that I believe Spiro successfully shows that Malinowski, on the basis of his data and of his conception of the Oedipus complex, fails to make his case against the universality of the Oedipus complex. But it does not, therefore, necessarily follow that, on the basis of his data and of his conception of the Oedipus complex, Spiro succeeds in demonstrating the universality of the Oedipus complex. While Spiro has a solid grasp of Freudian theory, he fails to take into account the conflict between psychotherapy and metapsychology in Freud. Nor does he acknowledge, let alone reflect upon, the "psychological difference" between primitive (uninhibited) taboo and modern (inhibited) neurosis that Freud recognizes, as we saw. Yet, like Freud, Spiro does acknowledge the difference between primitive (Trobriander) and modern (American, European, Israeli). But also, like Freud, he is unable to account for this difference in meaningful terms. I shall provide a brief analysis of Spiro's failure to account for the difference between primitive and modern in order to show that a case for or against the universality of the Oedipus complex cannot be made outside a firm grasp of the ontological, i.e., the historical, relation of individual and universal.

It is not necessary to summarize Spiro's case against Malinowski. What counts here is that, even as Spiro argues for the universality of the Oedipus complex, he is compelled, nevertheless, to recognize that there are important variations in how families and societies deal with their Oedipal impulses. His basic contention is that the Oedipus complex is variable, both cross-culturally and within a given society, in three dimensions: structure, intensity, and outcome. However, since Spiro holds that there is no known variation in structure and since variation in intensity is hardly recognizable outside of variation in outcome, it is only variation in outcome that he takes up in his final chapter, which is entitled "Is the Oedipus Complex Universal?" This is also the point at which his interpretation of the Oedipus complex becomes ontologically problematic. Spiro argues that there are three different outcomes possible to the Oedipus complex and that, although all three can be found in a given culture, generally only one predominates: weak or incomplete repression, repression, and extinction of the Oedipus complex. But how, we wonder, does a universal structure produce different historical outcomes?

Although Spiro argues that for primitive peoples like the Trobrianders the outcome of their Oedipus complex is its weak or incomplete repression, what he actually shows is that in their case they remain completely unconscious – that is, ignorant – of their Oedipal impulses. For the Trobrianders their libidinal and hostile impulses are natural. They have no concept of them as distorted or inhibited. Natural impulses, it is clear (to us) cannot be interpreted – the Trobrianders do not interpret them – for they simply are (reflected in their lives, as in their rituals, dreams, myths, and stories). In contrast are the two additional outcomes of the Oedipus complex, those characterizing modern society. Spiro holds that, in modernity, the Oedipus complex is either "repressed" (and so productive of neurosis) or "extinguished" (and so productive of "comfortable," that is, loving, relations between parents and children). When the Oedipus complex is partially repressed, as in primitive society, then it results in neither neurosis nor love. When the

Oedipus complex is strongly repressed or completely extinguished, then we have the interpretive matrix: either neurosis (distorted love) or love (neurosis overcome). Thus, Spiro ends in a contradiction of which he seems to have no awareness. The Oedipus complex can be known – recognized, analyzed, interpreted (constructed), appropriated – only because of the critical difference between neurosis (repression) and love (extinction), and it is precisely this difference that distinguishes modern from primitive civilization.

The interpretive impasse to which Spiro is led results from the fact that, like Freud, he has no notion of the paradoxical ontology involved in the unconscious. He does not see that, in the beginning, the unconscious cannot be unaware of being unconscious if it is to be unconscious in the beginning. The unconscious has to express the awareness of being unconscious if it is to be able to interpret the secret, hidden, unconscious, distortions of life. The only way in which to exit from the impasse to which Freudian metapsychology, as uncritically accepted by Spiro, leads is to see that primitive peoples do not have a – partially repressed but completely unconscious – Oedipus complex. Primitive peoples are dominated, rather, by an uncanny (to us) ambivalence of natural taboo, of desire as prohibition, from which unconscious interpretation (the interpretation of the unconscious) is utterly absent.

In failing to reflect upon how either the Trobrianders could view themselves or we could view them as only partially Oedipal, and thus, apparently, as also partially modern, Spiro does not indicate how he might deal with the "psychological difference" that Freud acknowledges to exist between primitive taboo and modern neurosis. What Spiro fails to see, therefore, is that all the evidence that he reinterprets to refute Malinowski should be properly understood as resulting from natural ambivalence. The irony of the debate over the universality of the Oedipus complex is that, whereas Freud's metapsychological rationale for the Oedipus complex rests on ambivalence – while Oedipal reality presupposes love between parents and children – it is ambivalence that is natural and found universally outside the biblical tradition of the golden rule. Therefore, what Spiro fails to see is that, while libidinal attraction to the mother as sexual object and aggressive hostility to the father as rival are "universal," they are neither repressed nor unconscious – although they are certainly contradictory – in primitive society. The Oedipus complex is not weak or incomplete in the Trobrianders and other primitive peoples. It is not partially repressed or partially unconscious. It is not repressed or unconscious at all. The concepts of the unconscious and repression are completely absent from the "premodern" world.

Impulses become Oedipal, the subject of resistance, only when, within the biblical tradition, they are cut across by that which is not natur-

al and so not merely ambivalent: love. It is precisely because love –
including both sexuality and aggressivity (that are inhibited from the
beginning) – is not natural (biological) that Spiro-Freud have no place
for it in their metapsychology, although they clearly perceive its phenomenological presence. The Oedipal triangle becomes problematic (as
it does not for the Trobrianders and other primitive peoples) only
because libidinous desire and hostile rivalry have to be made loving –
no easy task for either parents or children. The ontological alternative
– that of viewing the unconscious as either loving interpretation of distortion or distorted (neurotic) interpretation of love – appears only
when love is not fundamentally natural and familial (as dictated by
kinship lineage) but at once personal and social (and thus involving the
dialectic of universal and individual).

The ontological alternative to natural ambivalence is the basis of
the shocking defense of Mitya Karamazov, accused of parricide, that
his lawyer Fetyukovich mounts at the end of *The Brothers Karamazov*. This position is consistent with the active love embodied in
Alyosha, the youngest Karamazov brother, and his elder Zosima. The
Bible, Fetyukovich argues, teaches that you love your father not
because he is your biological (natural) father but because he is deserving of your love as a fellow human being. If, in loving your father, you
show him to be (he is shown to be) unloving as your father, then you
owe him nothing as your father, the one who brought you (biological)
life. You do not owe him your life. He does not own your life. The
notion that you are commanded to love the other (the father) as yourself means that you are thus the father of yourself. The notion that
you (the son) love the other (the father) as you (the son who are also
the father) would have the other (the father) love you (the son) – the
child is the father of man – is the radical notion that transforms the
ambivalence of natural love and hate into the paradox of love. It is
then undecidable who is "father" and who is "son," for each is both
to the other.

Spiro appears to support the fundamental position of Malinowski
that the natural family is the primary social unit. But it is precisely the
notion that the ambivalence of nature – the natural opposition between
love and hate – constitutes the priority of human life that the biblical
tradition deconstructs from beginning to end. For the Bible, the primary unit is not the natural family but rather, at one and the same
time, the individual as social (universal) and the social (the universal)
as individual. The shocking news of God the father is that you love him
not because he is your (natural) father but because he is deserving of
your love as the (creating) other, as your (creative) neighbour. If, in loving your father, you show him to be (he is shown to be) unloving as

your father, then you owe him nothing as your father, the one who brought you life. You do not owe him your life. He does not own your life.

In reinterpreting Malinowski's data from the Trobriands, in light of a more accurate understanding of Oedipal conflict, Spiro presents us with a paradox of whose contradictory elements he remains, apparently, unconscious. He claims that the violence and hostility, at once libidinal and aggressive, both intrapsychical and interpersonal, with which Trobriander life is filled, results from a weak or incomplete Oedipus complex, requiring yet additional means for shoring up the incest taboo. But what he, in fact, demonstrates is that Trobriander life is dominated by an originary ambivalence, of which the incest prohibition is but a particular feature. When he contrasts the weak or incomplete Oedipus complex of the Trobrianders with the extinguished or repressed Oedipus complex of modern society, he, like Freud, misconstrues the structure of both primitive and modern society. He fails to see that, in the name of the golden rule, modern (biblical) society has the eternal task of overcoming (extinguishing) the originary ambivalence of primitive society, what Pascal, Hobbes, and Spinoza call natural hatred or the natural warfare of all against all. The Oedipus complex is universal only insofar as it comes historically into existence as the individual task of transforming the natural ambivalence of hate and love into the dialectical relationship of self and desire that is universally true for all individuals. Spiro does not see that Freudian phenomenology (psychotherapy) contradicts and is contradicted by Freudian metapsychology, whose ground in originary identification with the penis is primitive. The paradox whose contradictory elements Spiro fails to comprehend is that natural ambivalence in Trobriand society is not Oedipal and that the Oedipus complex, insofar as it is founded on the natural ambivalence of originary identification with the penis, is equally not Oedipal.

Natural ambivalence is the contradictory beginning whose end can never be discerned. It is the secret whose contradictory terms cannot be recognized as ambivalent or contradictory, as *we* see both Greeks and Trobrianders eloquently testify. When Freud makes natural ambivalence – narcissistic, originary identification with the penis – the beginning of his metapsychology, mirroring his concept of the pleasure principle, he is unable to account for the phenomenology of the Oedipal conflict to which he testifies so eloquently. The fundamental contradiction that Spiro-Freud cannot explain is how the primitive Oedipus complex can exist outside a context that demands its overcoming (extinction) and how the modern Oedipus complex can exist within the metapsychology of identification, whose ambivalent penis eliminates Oedipal desire in the beginning. The only way of overcoming this double impasse is to eschew, radically, both the projection of Oedipal values on primitive (premodern, extrabiblical) cultures – whether Greek or Trobriander – and the reprojection of those primitive values back on modern (biblical) culture. In the first case, Oedipal conflict is conflated with ambivalence. In the second case, ambivalence is conflated with Oedipal conflict. Only when we steer clear of this double conflation can we see that what Spiro shows, *malgré lui*, is that Oedipal conflict is universal only insofar as it is understood as the natural ambivalence – the repudiation of both femininity and masculinity – that must be overcome in and by the golden rule of the relationship of self and desire. Oedipal conflict is absent from the primitive world – of Greeks and Trobrianders – for it comes into existence only with the paradoxical demonstration that, in the beginning, natural ambivalence is the blind, contradictory end to which human beings are fated as the secret that is incommunicable to and by mortals.

d Conclusion

I have undertaken consideration of the Oedipus complex in light both of the mythical fate of Oedipus, as dramatized by Sophocles, and of Spiro's view of its outcome as weak or incomplete repression in the real life of the Trobrianders in order to demonstrate the importance of distinguishing comprehensively between what Freud calls taboo and neurosis. This is the distinction between Socratic ignorance and Oedipal blindness, on the one hand, and the knowledge of repression, on the other, between knowing *that* one is ignorant and knowing *what* one is ignorant of. Neither Freud in his approach to the Oedipal myth nor Spiro in his application of the Oedipus complex to the reality of primitive life sees that it is not the particular taboos against incest and parricide but the natural ambivalence between love and hate that provides the structure of primitive myth and rite. What Freud views as the primal taboos of totemism are but a particularization of the general structure of taboo: natural ambivalence where the canny is both opposed to and identical with what is uncanny. Oedipus, guilty of the execrable crimes of incest and parricide, becomes the venerable object whose death bestows secret blessing: count no man happy until he has passed beyond the contradictions of life. Central to the natural ambivalence of taboo is not repression or the unconscious but ignorance, the fact that, in the beginning, the structure of taboo is unknown fate whose end is the impenetrable, uninterpretable secret the blessing of which is known only in death. As I have emphasized, the secret of Oedipus is not his all too natural deeds but the structure of his fate that is given to him before birth and remains the secret transmitted to others at death. But the Oedipal secret, consistent with Socratic ignorance and Trobriander taboo, is that there is no secret. It is the secret that cannot be known as a secret. For the only secret that can be known as a secret is the secret of the unconscious that, as Freud says in the passage that I continue to work through, allows us to penetrate the secret distortions that people unconsciously impose upon their feelings.

It is important to distinguish between ignorance and ignorance, as Freud says, between Oedipal blindness and neurotic distortion, between primitive and modern for two critical reasons, one more particular, the other more general. The more particular reason is that this distinction is essential to our distinguishing between Freud's phenomenological (psychotherapeutic) insight and its contradiction in and by his metapsychology. Above all, it is important to see that Freud's concept of identification with the penis, which underlies the castration complex and thus the superego, is central both to his reading of the Sophoclean Oedipus and to his myth of the primal father. It is not really possible to expose the utter contradictoriness of either his concept of mythical beginning or his concept of metapsychological beginning until and unless both are exposed as reflecting the same fundamental impasse.

The fact that the distinction between primitive and modern is central to Freud's fundamental notions of the unconscious, repression, distortion, inhibition, and interpretation, which are then falsified by his metapsychology, leads to our more general reason for insisting upon this distinction as the ontological alternative to which there is no alternative. The only adequate, comprehensive conception of interpretation is one that sees through the Freudian impasse of projecting Oedipal conflict onto primitive culture and then of reading natural, originary ambivalence back into modernity as the structure of Oedipal conflict. The impasse to which Spiro is led in claiming that the Oedipus complex is universal, and thus the model for interpreting primitive peoples, is typical and inevitable. Yet, because he recognizes that the anthropological data do not support the notions of either the repression of the Oedipus complex – neurosis – or the extinction of the Oedipus complex – loving family relations – he is compelled to fall back upon the weak or incomplete concept of the partial repression of the Oedipus complex to explain life in the Trobriands. But then Spiro fails to acknowledge two critical elements of Trobriander life. First, the Trobrianders have no idea that they are (only) partially repressed, for the concept of repression is clearly an interpretive construct of the anthropological theorist that is utterly alien to them. Second, they have no idea of therapy, of working through what is partial and thus making it

228 Depth Psychology, Interpretation, and the Bible

wholly repressive and so capable of complete extinction (resolution).
Spiro thus fails to take into account Freud's observation that taboo is
not (personal, anti-social, sexually generated) neurosis but social institution, to which there is, indeed, no elsewhere or background permit-
ting it to be interpreted as neurotic. We can add that neither Spiro nor
Freud takes into account the fact that the structure of taboo is that of
originary ambivalence, which, identical with the law of contradictory
fate, blindly condemns Oedipus to death before life and to life after
death. (The Trobrianders, Spiro and Malinowski point out, deeply fear
the aggressivity of the hostile and malicious spirits of their dead relatives, as do other primitive peoples reported on by Freud.)

What Freud and Spiro, typical moderns, do not see is that if the difference between taboo and neurosis is not rigorously articulated in
ontological terms, consistent with the phenomenology of human experience, then it becomes impossible to develop a concept of interpretation that is both consistently and comprehensively true. What is paradoxical – and truly dangerous, far more creative of resistance than
Freudian psychoanalysis – is the recognition that interpretation,
unconscious insight into unconscious distortion, presupposes a difference between primitive and modern that is impenetrable. This is the
limit whose resistance generates interpretation, as Kant would say, and
whose elimination leaves interpretation flapping interminably in a vac-
uum where individual and universal are indistinguishably ambivalent.
What both Freud and Spiro (and also Malinowski) fail to see is that
interpretation is structured on the principle of psychoanalytic praxis,
which is that of the golden rule. But, as I emphasize in this study, Freud
(together with his critics and followers), instead of developing a
metapsychology that is consistent with his psychotherapy, constantly
subverts his phenomenological insight on the basis of a metapsychology that falsifies both primitive and modern civilization. I can interpret
the other only as I wish the other to interpret me. The analyst can interpret the analysand – he can offer the analysand an interpretation, a
construction – only because the analysand is accessible to interpretation and equally because the analyst is accessible to interpretation or
construction (on the part of the analysand). To interpret (the other) is
to desire to be interpreted (by the other). The only secret of interpretation is that it is shared by and among the members of the interpretive
community.

The structure of primitive taboo, reflecting originary ambivalence, is
without interpretation precisely because it is without repression, the
unconscious, distortion, or inhibition. Socratic ignorance and Oedipal
blindness – both issuing in the secret that the only happy individual is
the one who has seen his end, that is, the death of his contradictory,

tabooed existence – cannot be interpreted (by the other) and do not make any claims of interpreting (the other). It is interpretation alone that can distinguish between, as Freud says, ignorance and ignorance, between knowing that one is ignorant and knowing what one is ignorant of. To know what one is ignorant of is to confront the paradox that, in the beginning, the unconscious cannot be unconscious that it is (the) unconscious. Or, rather, in the beginning the unconscious ought to know what it is that it is unconscious of – in other words, what the unconscious is. The unconscious must know itself as unconscious. Or, as Freud says, the analysand must know that of which he is (the) unconscious. The difference between knowing that one is ignorant and knowing what one is ignorant of is the difference between primitive and modern, between what I call extra-biblical and biblical. The modern is not, first, made in the premodern likeness of Oedipus, whose fate is to die before he is born and to be born after he dies. The modern is ... modern, in the beginning as in the end. The modern involves and expresses, with Zarathustra, the transformation of "it was" (neurotic) into "thus I willed it" (lovingly). This is the ontological alternative to which there is no alternative. Only when the past is interpreted individually as the universal true for all and interpreted universally as what is truly individual do we have a concept of interpretation that, congruent with historical truth (the truth of history), is modern from beginning to end.

The Oedipus complex is universally true insofar as myth and reality are individually brought together as the difference that repression and the unconscious – distortion – make. It is not found in Socratic ignorance or Oedipal blindness. It is not found in Trobriander taboo. It is not found in Freudian metapsychology. After summarizing how it is also not found in the myth of the primal father, the father complex reflecting originary identification with the ambivalent penis, we shall be in a position to argue further, in the next chapter, that the original Oedipus never went to Colonus, by way of the Trobriands, and was not fated to die there with his contradictory secret, the secret of contradiction. Rather, Oedipus begins his complex history with (as) the biblical paradox of falling from the contradictory paradise of primitivity into the golden rule of creating the world from nothing "it was" – originary ambivalence. He thus shows to all those who have eyes to see and ears to hear that when the past is willed as history it reveals the dialectic of self and desire: *ergo*, I will it – for you as I desire you to will it for me.

V CONCLUSION

The myth of the primal father, we have now seen, is consistent with – indeed, it both entails and is entailed by – the overall structure of

Freud's metapsychology as embodied in the Oedipus complex (the castration complex) and the pleasure principle (desire as prohibition). Freud claims that the myth of the primal father accounts for all beginnings, yet the beginning of the primal father is precisely that which cannot be accounted for. Beyond analysis but the very origin of analysis; beyond psyche, but the very origin of psyche; beyond analogy but the ultimate analogy; beyond beginning but the beginning of all beginning; beyond guilt but the origin of all guilt; beyond unconsciousness but the author of the unconscious; beyond construction but the constructor of all – the primal father is the founder of the father complex, the determinate explanation of primal ambivalence. The murder of the primal father represents not only, as I have suggested, male occlusion of the female, whose absence, or castration, symbolizes, always already, the castration of the male, but also the fate in store for analogy and thus for the whole of Freudian metapsychology. That which is beyond analysis, beginning, and analogy is ultimately that which itself in the end succumbs to contradiction.

The fact that Freud is constantly seeking an analogy for psychical reality reflects his assumption that the psychical is principally internal and that it can, contradictorily, be understood only in terms of what is external. He typically associates the psychical with the id, the pleasure principle, the unconscious, and the instinctual or the phylogenetic heritage. But he is then compelled to make what is internal depend on the ultimate analogy, on that which is external: the ego, the reality principle, consciousness, the ontogenetic, the primal father. The result is the emergence of unending contradictions. Not only is the internal also the illusory, as we see in the case of the pleasure principle. But also Freud has no explanation of how the external is made internal, except to assert that the id represents the precipitates of countless ego experiences, while the ultimate beginning is constituted by the primal father, that beginning whose beginning remains inexplicable.

Freud is acute in seeing that it is precisely primary ambivalence, the structure of primitive taboo, that is beyond analysis, beginning, and analogy. Indeed, it is the contradictory opposition between and the contradictory identity of beginning and end that we find in the life of Oedipus as dramatized by Sophocles and in the lives of pre-modern (pre-historic) peoples, such as the Trobrianders as interpreted by Malinowski and reinterpreted by Spiro. Freud provides real insight into the phenomenology of ambivalence, but he fails to distinguish between the primitive ambivalence of taboo and the modern ambivalence of neurosis. It is precisely primitive taboo that is beyond analysis, analogy, and beginning. Taboo is beyond interpretation because it remains this side of it. There is, as I argued above, no other for taboo. Taboo is what it is and equally what it is not. There is no dialectical reciprocity between the two sides of the tabooed opposition but only their contradiction. In contrast to the primitive taboo of ambivalence, the modern ambivalence of neurosis is the construction (the creation) of analysis. It presupposes a beginning and an analogy, a beginning in analysis and an analogy understood as the other, whose principle is that of reciprocity, the golden rule, the dialectic of self and desire. The strange irony is that identification with the primal father, as with the modern Oedipal father, has nothing to do either with Oedipal blindness, as portrayed in the plays of Sophocles, or with Oedipal conflict, as portrayed in the modern family romance. In conflating primitive (taboo) with modern (neurosis), notwithstanding their psychological difference, Freud is untrue to the reality of both.

It is also important to see that the myth of the primal father embodies desire as prohibition and that the concept of desire as what is prohibited is but another version of the pleasure principle, whose final avatar is the death instinct. The pleasure principle is the ultimate analogy and the ultimate contradiction in Freudian thought. It rests on a beginning whose beginning is forever unanalyzable. It rests on what is prior to life, the inorganic, death itself. When life, internal to itself as inorganic and so prior to life, is inexplicably called into painful existence by external reality – thus presupposing existence (the ontological argument!) – the organism, in obeying the pleasure principle, responds by generating desire whose purpose is to reduce the pain of life, life's conflicts, existence itself, back to originary constancy, to pleasure, to the prior state of things, to the inorganic, to death, to nullity. Instead of creating life from nothing, the pleasure principle reduces life to nothing. It is important to see that the principle of death, what I have called the Satanic principle in earlier studies, is phenomenologically real in the world and that much of our life is profoundly in its grips. But if this principle is unaccountably made the primary, metapsychological explanation of life, then we shall have no way of accounting either for our beginning or for our end.

To begin in pleasure – on analogy with the primal father, who begins with the illusion that sexuality is his narcissistic monopoly and not the psychical reality whose principle is reciprocity – is always to find yourself subject to the violence of the death instinct: irremediable guilt. But this is always how Freud begins, metapsychologically, and this is the beginning that he always shows to be illusory, phenomenologically. What Freud fails to see is that the only (psychical) pleasure and the only (psychical) reality that are available to us are those that are not opposed to but rather are mutually related to each other – from the beginning to the end of life. Pleasure and reality can become reciprocal only in and as they enact the golden rule, the dialectic of desire and self. As I continue to emphasize, Freud never understands, metapsychologically, the simple, yet profound, principle of psychical reality, that of the reciprocity of beginning and end, of universal and individual, of self and other, of ontogeny and phylogeny, of fact and fiction, of, ultimately, religion and psychoanalysis (depth psychology as science). In the end he cannot account for our human beginning as at once psychical and real. Not only does Freud begin with the myth – that of the primal father – that utterly contradicts his phenomenological insight. But he also represses the only myth that is true to that insight – that of creation from nothing, from nothing that, in itself, is either internal or external, either beginning or end, either psyche (pleasure) or reality, either fiction (illusion) or fact.

In the next chapter we shall see Freud directly confront the psychical reality of religion, of biblical myth. He acknowledges, like all strong thinkers, both analytical and artistic, that the God of the Bible, in the rich variety of his manifestations, is the opponent than whom there is none greater. Will the myth of the primal father allow Freud to show that the biblical God, in forming the basis of the father complex, explains the origin of the castration complex, the lynchpin of his metapsychology? Or will the biblical God allow us to show that the myth of the primal father, in forming the basis of the father complex, which is the key to Freudian metapsychology, falsifies Freud's phenomenological insight into psychical reality? Is the God of the Bible the basis of Freud's metapsychology or of his phenomenology? That is the question that will guide our reading of central Freudian texts in the next chapter.

5 *Moses and Monotheism*

I INTRODUCTION

"If Moses was an Egyptian," as Freud proposes in *Moses and Monotheism*. If, in other words, ancient Judaism, the Bible, Christianity, and the whole of modern ("western") civilization were to be understood as the repressed, deferred, traumatic, compulsive, neurotic, illusory, and helpless result of the external imposition of patriarchal authority, in the name of the father complex, then Freud, it is clear, would be vindicated. Any claim on the part of Judaism and/or Christianity to unique, let alone universal, authority would be undercut. The myth of the primal father would receive definitive justification as the fictive construction that explains the historical beginning of not only civilization, in general, but also religion, in particular. However, in constituting the origin of illusory religion, the myth of the primal father also serves as the scientific explanation of the origin of religion as illusory. The science of psychoanalysis, in other words, teaches the father complex as the truth of modernity. But this truth is also the teaching of primitive religion. How, we wonder, does the primitive truth of illusory religion become the modern truth of science that shows the primitive truth of illusory religion to be the modern truth of science? If the scientific explanation of religion depends on, and presupposes, the religious explanation of science, then science, having been posited as the opposite of religion, becomes indistinguishable from it. Such, however, is the inevitable fate of dualistic opposites.[1] If Moses was an Egyptian, if Moses was murdered as the primal father of biblical religion, then his primal sons would institute the science of the father complex as the vindication of the mourned (repressed) religious!

If, however, Moses was not an Egyptian but a nice, Jewish boy, a rather archetypal, Jewish boy, my son, the prince, who, making it in the flesh pots on the banks of the River Nile, became the greatest prophet of his people; if the prophet Moses demonstrated to his people that the divine life of living by and through the golden rule represented neither the internal coherence of illusion – fiction – nor external correspondence with reality – fact – but truth as their dialectic; then it would be possible to deconstruct the impasse that results from Freud's dualisms between science and religion, externality and internality, reality and illusion, the primitive and the modern. Freud never sees that, if, in separating science from religion, he does not overcome the opposition between religion as the beginning and science as the end of psychoanalysis, science will simply return in the end as religion repressed in the beginning. He claims that, after the death of Pharaoh Akhenaten[2] and the destruction of his enlightened monotheism by the forces of reaction in support of the old polytheism, Akhenaten's fervent follower, Moses, saves Egyptian monotheism by bringing it to and imposing it on the Israelite slaves of the Egyptians. The slaves subsequently revolt, cast off their religion, and murder Moses, with the result that the Mosaic religion later returns as the guilt repressing knowledge of the murder of Moses as the primal father. The irony here is that, in viewing biblical religion as the repressed return of the murder of the primal father, Freudian psychoanalysis, the science of the father complex, turns out to represent the real return of repressed religion. Precisely because Freud views religion as illusory, he renders science – the truth of religion – no less illusory. He does not see that science will be as true or false as its subject. The truth of science (as the explanation of religion) depends on the truth of religion.

We shall discover, therefore, in *Moses and Monotheism* the same phenomenological insight and the same metapsychological impasse that we found in Freud's prior work and ideas. But here the rupture between phenomenology and metapsychology becomes especially poignant. Freud subjects the authority of Judaism – the father of the Jewish people, both human and divine: *der Mann Moses* and the God of monotheism – to the father complex, as found in both the castration complex and the myth of the primal father. However, in *Moses and Monotheism* Freud no longer simply deals with primitive religion, as in *Totem and Taboo*. Now he explicitly confronts biblical religion, primarily Judaism, but also Christianity. I am not concerned here, as such, with either the personal (psychological) or the socio-political dimensions of the writing of *Moses and Monotheism*, fascinating though they are. I shall not enter into the debate over Freud's own self-analysis in terms of his relation to his Jewish heritage (including his parents). Nor shall I take up the context of the growing Nazi threat in Europe in the 1930s and the reluctance that Freud expresses in publishing his work out of fear of jeopardizing the support of the Roman Catholic Church in constituting a common front against Nazism. The critical essay III of *Moses and Monotheism* is published only once Freud has taken up residence in London (he does not countenance leaving Vienna until after the Germans invade Austria and his daughter Anna is interrogated by the Gestapo).

My interest, rather, is ontological. Freud is a wonderful test case of the sense in which the Bible and biblical religion – Judaism and Christianity – can be made the subject of a universally critical discourse. Freud claims that Judaism (together with Christianity), because it is simply a religion like any religion, is but one more primitive, illusory wish fulfilment that, like infantile neurosis, needs to be surmounted. Freud typically introduces an analogy (this time called "*Die Analogie*"!) to explain how Jewish monotheism repeats the primitive return of the repressed religious. At the same time, however, he also discovers elements – both intellectual and ethical – within Jewish monotheism that he acknowledges are not primitive but rather central to his own Jewish heritage, to the very tradition of modernity. Indeed, what we shall find – and, although Freud, in his own way, sees this, he also evades (denies) it – is that the principles of interpretation that are central to Freud's phenomenological insight are precisely those that characterize biblical religion. Thus Freud's claim to explain biblical religion as the illusory product of the father complex, whose foundation is the myth of the primal father and the castration complex, encounters two formidable obstacles. The first, as I have pointed out, is that, in viewing science (reason) as the secondary product of what is primarily religious (illusory), it is not the son (science) who is the father of man. Rather it is the patriarch (religion) who imposes the castration complex in the name of the father (complex) on his sons (and daughters).

The second obstacle, while not new to Freud, is now even more formidable. He acknowledges that the phenomenological practice of the ancient Israelites, as depicted in the Bible, is consistent with the intellectual and ethical heritage of Judaism and thus with the modern values of science and reason. But then he is faced with the problem of explaining how the principles of intellect and ethics, which characterize not only biblical religion but also both modern science and ethics, are utterly different from those generated by the murder of the primal father. For the whole purpose of *Moses and Monotheism* is to test and to validate the hypothesis that Moses is an Egyptian whose murder by the ancient Israelites repeats the murder of the primal father. Freud's aim is to show that biblical myth is but an instance of the universal

236 Depth Psychology, Interpretation, and the Bible

myth of the primal father. It is poignantly ironic that Freud, in undertaking to demonstrate that Judaism, together with Christianity, is reducible to the father complex, whose foundation is the myth of the primal father and the castration complex, shows, unbeknownst to himself, just the opposite. He claims to explain biblical phenomenology in the terms of scientific metapsychology. But what the brilliant contradictions that emerge in his metapsychology show us is the very opposite. Only biblical phenomenology, in stripping the pseudo-scientific mask from his metapsychology, can keep it from collapsing into the very religious illusion it pretends to explain. It is truly ironic that, in undertaking to reduce biblical phenomenology to scientific metapsychology, Freud falsifies both.

The paradox that emerges, then, is that Freud's metapsychology is only as true as the biblical phenomenology of which it claims to be the interpretation. The consequences of this position are enormous. I shall briefly outline them here in four points before proceeding to examine them in detail in the context of Freud's encounter with biblical religion. I shall then reflect in chapter 6 upon the more general implications of this paradox for a comprehensive theory of hermeneutics. In showing that it is not scientific metapsychology that explains biblical religion but rather biblical religion that explains metapsychology, four reversals in Freud's position result. First, the principles of his metapsychology are pseudo-scientific. Second, the real explanatory (hermeneutical) principles of psychoanalysis are not scientific (when science is understood on the model of Copernicus and Darwin). Third, these principles of interpretation are biblical. Fourth, it is the principles of biblical interpretation that are true to the depth of his insight into human psychology, consistent with the biblical principle of reciprocity. According to the golden rule, you get out of something precisely what you will to put into it. Is it not extraordinary that Freud explicitly acknowledges in *Moses and Monotheism*, as we shall see, that, in order to defend the metapsychology of the father complex, together with the myth of the primal father, he has to base it not on the science of Darwin but on the pseudo-science of Lamarck?

We shall additionally see that Freud is faced with the issue of explaining how biblical (Israelite) religion is not only the son of primitive religion, whose paternity it resolutely denies, but also the father of Christianity, the son whose legitimacy is profoundly problematic. He views Christian faith – *credo quia absurdum* – as the very antithesis of reason (and Judaism) and thus as the revenge of Egyptian polytheism on Mosaic (Egypto-Judaic) religion. At the same time, however, he claims that the religion of the son (Christ), in acknowledging the murder of the father, atones for its guilt, unlike Judaism, the religion of the father. The point is not to treat Freud as a theologian, although it is he who raises these issues. The point is to see that the relationship of biblical religion to both the primitive and the modern, and the relationship between Judaism and Christianity, can be determined solely when it is understood that biblical religion cannot be located as a stage or transition between primitive animism and modern science. Only then can a comprehensive concept of religion, of civilization, and, ultimately, of interpretation – as both the subject and the object of research – be rendered articulate in terms that are truly *wissenschaftlich*, at one and the same time rational and faithful.

II THE FUTURE OF ORIGINARY ILLUSION AS SCIENCE

Before taking up, within the context of biblical religion, the question of whether the psychology of religion is not, reciprocally, the religion of psychology – for is not the child (religion) the father (psychology) of man? – I shall broach the analysis of religion in Freud by way of discussing two works that he wrote in the decade prior to *Moses and Monotheism*.[3] In both *The Future of an Illusion* and "The Question of a Weltanschauung," the second being the last of the (fictional) *New Introductory Lectures*, he draws a sharp line between religion as illusory wish fulfilment and science (including psychoanalysis) as objective correspondence to the nature of external reality (to the reality of external nature). The distinction between correspondence to externality (nature) and internal coherence (psyche) simply repeats, however, the dualism of the two principles of mental functioning between the reality principle and the pleasure principle. Further, it also raises the question about the relationship between *Weltanschauung* (or worldview) and its future and thus its past, too. If in the beginning is illusion, as found in religion and its illusory commitment to the pleasure principle of wish fulfilment, how can the future of illusion not be the end of religion? How can the future not be illusory and illusion not be our future? Does not Freud repeatedly claim that, in the beginning, from the beginning, the psychical apparatus is governed by the pleasure principle? Are we not also led to suspect that the fact that the pleasure principle reveals itself as the death instinct – the inherent tendency of instinct to restore an earlier state of things – is connected with the initial illusion of the primal father? Is it not the illusory monopoly of patriarchal power as sexuality that is slain by the primal sons? Is it not the *Weltanschauung* of the primal father that the sons perpetuate in the ambivalence of their identification with the paternal penis? Once again, then, we arrive at the same question. Is the father complex the *Weltanschauung* of religion or of science?

From the beginning of his lecture on *Weltanschauung* Freud assures his (fictional) audience that for psychoanalysis, which, he claims, adheres to the general *Weltanschauung* of science, "the intellect and the mind are objects for scientific research in exactly the same way as any nonhuman things ... Its contribution to science lies precisely in having extended research to the mental field" (194). Still, since Freud also points out that the modern "distinction between animate creatures with a mind and an inanimate Nature" has replaced the cosmogonies of primitive animism in which there is no distinction between mind and nature, it is not obvious how the mind of your analysand, whom you (are to) treat as an end in himself, not as a means, is a scientific object (202). Nevertheless, Freud insists that, unlike art, religion, and philosophy, which, to the degree they are not scientific, are all illusory fulfilments of wishful impulses, science is concerned with objective knowledge. He absolutely rejects the suggestion that the field of mental activity can be divided up by making philosophy and religion the intellectual equal, at least, of science and by claiming, on that basis, that they are exempt from scientific investigation. "It is simply a fact," he writes, "that the truth cannot be tolerant, that it admits of no compromises or limitations, that research regards every sphere of human activity as belonging to it and that it must be relentlessly critical if any other power tries to take over any part of it" (195).[4] No holds barred – so long as one gets hold of the truth. "What is truth?" Pilate asks Jesus. Surely, Jesus answers, the golden rule. Does the primal father get (and bestow) a hold on the truth when he is intolerant of anyone holding on to his truth but when he is then the one whom the primal sons murder in order to get hold of it: the penis?

In his radical concept of truth as acknowledging no exceptions to its imperious sovereignty, Freud agrees with Spinoza who writes in the *Ethics* that, because truth is its own standard, the *index* of both itself and its errors, it is intolerant of any other standard. This leads Spinoza to argue that the more you know God the more you know individuals and that the more you know individuals (the more individuals you know) the more you know God (the more God you know, the more God there is to know). Spinoza is ruthlessly critical of any concept of God as father, generator, creator, lord, commander, ruler, precisely because his concept of God (truth) is utterly consistent with the biblical concept of creation from nothing. There is nothing (in finite nature) that provides the standard of God (as infinitely one, free, *causa sui*, the *index* of truth). God is the standard of all creation. There is nothing that cannot be rendered creative. Creation, we would say, is its own standard. Freud sets a high standard of analysis, indeed. He is absolutely right that there is nothing that is beyond criticism, including his concept of science as correspondence with the primal father, who, the standard of intolerant truth, brooks no opposition. Psychology is a knife that cuts both ways we read in the most psychological and the most religious of our great novels, *The Brothers Karamazov.*[5]

Of the three powers of art, philosophy, and religion, it is solely religion, Freud continues in his *Weltanschauung* lecture, that today constitutes a threat to the objective sovereignty of science, although all three involve illusion. Art is harmless in that it "makes no attempt at invading the realm of reality" with its illusions. Philosophy is also harmless, for it is either scientific in methodology, and so an ally of science, or it is illusory in content insofar as it claims to possess a complete picture of the universe that is "without gaps and is coherent, though one which is bound to collapse with every fresh advance in our knowledge" (196). To the degree, then, that philosophy pretends to know the whole, it is illusory yet also harmless; for it remains incomprehensible to the masses. But Freud holds that religion, unlike art and philosophy, "is to be taken seriously as an enemy" because it "is an immense power which has the strongest emotions of human beings at its service" (195–6).

Although the traditional claim of religion to possess a total, unchallengeable *Weltanschauung* has been severely shaken in modern times, Freud finds that it remains even today a formidable threat to the hegemony of science because of the strong, illusory appeal of its three basic functions. In its first or cosmological function, religion "satisfies the human thirst for knowledge" by providing answers to questions about the origin of the universe. In its second or providential function, religion exercises great influence over human beings by bringing them consolation: "it assures them of a happy ending and offers them comfort in unhappiness." Freud points out that science also has a similar function in that it can help human beings avoid dangers and alleviate suffering. He adds, however, that "there are many situations in which it must leave a man to his suffering and can only advise him to submit to it." The fact that Freud's prudential, scientific advice sounds remarkably similar to that provided by the religious authority that figures as diverse as Clarissa Harlowe and Ivan Karamazov reject as masking paternal autocracy suggests how inadequate Freud's conception of religion is. In its third or ethical function, religion lays down the moral precepts of life. Freud comments that in its third function "religion is furthest away from science. For science is content to investigate and to establish facts, though it is true that *from its applications rules and advice are derived on the conduct of life. In some circumstances these are the same as those offered by religion, but, when this is so, the reasons for them are different."* As regards the consolations "of protection and happiness," he observes further that they "are the reward for fulfilling these commands; only those who obey them may count upon these benefits, [while] punishment awaits the disobedient. Incidentally, *something similar is true of science.* Those who disregard its lessons, so it tells us, expose themselves to injury" (197ᵉ).

Freud then proceeds to summarize his doctrine that religious cosmology is a projection of how the small, weak, and helpless child, exposed to the dangers of the external world, looks upon its all-powerful father. "A religious man," he writes, "pictures the creation of the universe just as he pictures his own origin" (198). Because ethics develops as the rewards and punishments that a child learns from its parents, Freud concludes, "the religious *Weltanschauung* is determined by the situation of our childhood" (200).⁶ Finally, in connecting the childish origin of religion and belief in God as the paternal protector and benefactor with the origins of primitive religion, he arrives at what he calls "the judgment of science on the religious *Weltanschauung*":

Religion is an attempt to master the sensory world in which we are situated by means of the wishful world which we have developed within us as a result of biological and psychological necessities.⁷ But religion cannot achieve this. Its doctrines bear the imprint of the times in which they arose, the ignorant times of the childhood of humanity. Its consolations deserve no trust. Experience teaches us that the world is no nursery. *The ethical demands on which religion seeks to lay stress need, rather, to be given another basis; for they are indispensable to human society* and it is dangerous to link obedience to them with religious faith. If we attempt to assign the place of religion in the evolution of mankind, it appears *not as a permanent acquisition* but as a counterpart to the neurosis which individual civilized men have to go through in their passage from childhood to maturity. (203–4ᵉ)⁸

But is it so obvious that the basis of ethics is not religion when, as we have already noted, the science of psychoanalysis is the science of the father complex and the father complex constitutes the nature of religion? Or is science the basis of ethics? We have seen Freud indicate, however, that science, unlike religion, only investigates and establishes facts, although he does add that rules and advice are derived from its applications for the conduct of life. But he does not tell us how the moral *ought* can be extracted from the empirical *is*. With regard to Freud's conventional image of the religious child growing up to become the scientific adult, our foregoing analysis of Freud's analogy between taboo and neurosis in *Totem and Taboo* should make us suspicious of the analogy between humankind outgrowing the primitive childhood of religious neurosis and (some) modern individuals having to encounter neurosis in their passage from childhood to maturity. We may also recall that it is by no means obvious how civilization would outgrow its burden of guilt that descends phylogenetically from the murder of the primal father through the id to identification with the patriarchal penis, the castration complex, and the superego. We may also wonder how we can outgrow the illusions of the pleasure principle whose origin, Freud says, is to be found in "biological and psychological necessities."

Freud elaborates on what he calls "the psychical origin of religious ideas" in *The Future of an Illusion*. Religious teachings, he holds, are not the result of experience or thinking. They are, rather, "illusions, fulfillments of the oldest, strongest and most urgent wishes of mankind. The secret of their strength lies in the strength of those wishes." He argues that the three basic ideas of religion, those involving providence, a moral world-order, and immortality – which would broadly coincide, we may note, with Kant's three postulates of practical reason: God, freedom, and immortality – reflect belief in an all-powerful father who answers to the needs of what Freud calls "the terrifying impression of helplessness in childhood" that lasts throughout life. "It is an enormous relief to the individual psyche," he observes, "if the conflicts of its childhood arising from the father complex – conflicts which it has never wholly overcome – are removed from it and brought to a solution which is universally accepted" (212). Freud notes further that religious illusions are not the same as errors of fact and, although similar to psychiatric delusions, need not necessarily be false, although some of them are "so improbable, so incompatible with everything we have laboriously discovered about the reality of the world" that they are comparable to delusions (213). What is essential to understand about religious illusions, he concludes, is that wish fulfilment is central to them and that they disregard reality and are not susceptible of proof.[9]

In his *Weltanschauung* lecture Freud proceeds to argue that science, in contrast to the illusionary wish fulfilment of religion, "does not differ in its nature from *the normal activity of thought*, which all of us, believers and unbelievers, employ in looking after *our affairs in ordinary life*" – except for the special methods it has developed for eliminating factors of subjectivity, testing sense-data, and obtaining new experimental evidence (206e).[10] But Freud's claim that science is not fundamentally different from practical reason raises a number of unanswered, because unasked, questions. What happens, we wonder, to "the oldest, strongest, and most urgent wishes of mankind"? Are these not found in "the normal activity of thought" that we employ in look-ing after life's ordinary affairs? What are we to make of the fact that Kant bases thinking and practice, which he sharply distinguishes from scientific knowledge and theory, upon postulates whose origin is clear-ly religious and not "scientific" and which, as we have seen, are com-mensurate, broadly, with what Freud views as the utterly illusory doc-trines of religion: freedom, immortality, and God? In what sense are the ordinary affairs of life – making love, experiencing "psychical impotence"; raising children, being supported by one's children in old age; getting, holding, and losing a job; making money, losing money; paying taxes, cheating on taxes; walking the dog, cleaning up after the dog; getting sick, getting well, dying ... – scientific? Is science a subset or a special (limited) feature of our ordinary "activity of thought," or is the relationship between science and thinking the other way round?

Freud's answer is that it is the aim of science "to arrive at corre-spondence with reality – that is to say, with what exists outside us and independently of us and, as experience has taught us, is decisive for the fulfillment or disappointment of our wishes. This correspondence with the real external world we call 'truth'" (206–7).[11] Outside of the fact that Kant demonstrates, surely for all time, that we have no knowledge of the real, external (or internal) thing in itself except insofar as it appears to us, that is, that all knowledge involves synthetic *a priori* judgments – what we put into nature is precisely what we get out of nature – one wonders what Freud expects his audience to think about psychoanalysis and its constructions. What is the external reality that exists outside and independently of us, when both you and I, all of us, are subject to the father complex, which is at once external and inter-nal to us? In what sense do you – reader, friend, lover, parent, child, employer, colleague – exist outside of me? In what sense do I exist inside myself? The issue is not epistemological relativism, which Kant also deconstructs for all time, so long as one does not wish to remain suspended, like Hume, within the dualism between matters of fact and relationships of ideas, the result of which is to make blind custom – whatever is *must be*[12] – the mediator of self and desire. The issue is, rather, the ontology of relationship, where reality is neither internal (coherence) nor external (correspondence) but the in-between: our mutual construction of the future as the "complete result."

However, Freud, in not seeing (by evading) the uncanny parallel between the myth of the primal father and his correspondence model of scientific truth, continues to argue in his *Weltanschauung* lecture for the separation of science from religion. He holds that, whereas the illu-sions of religious wish fulfilment divide people, reason is a unifying influence among them. "Our best hope for the future," Freud writes,

243 Moses and Monotheism

"is that intellect – the scientific spirit, reason – may in process of time
establish a dictatorship in the mental life of man. The nature of reason
is a guarantee that *afterwards it will not fail to give man's emotional
impulses and what is determined by them the position they deserve.*
But the common compulsion exercised by such a dominance of reason
will prove to be the strongest uniting bond among men and lead the
way to further unions" (208ᵉ). Consistent with his hope that reason
will establish a dictatorship in the future psyche of humanity, Freud
concludes *The Future of an Illusion* with a paean to "our God, *Logos*,
[who] will fulfill whichever of these wishes nature outside us allows,
but he will do it very gradually, only in the unforeseeable future, and
for a new generation of men" (238). Belief in the modest work that science can presently accomplish, compared with an unforeseeable future,
means giving up the consolations of religious illusions and resigning
oneself to reality. "We believe that it is possible," Freud declares, "for
scientific work to gain some knowledge about the reality of the world,
by means of which we can increase our power and in accordance with
which we can arrange our life. If this belief is an illusion, then we are
in the same position as you. [Freud addresses here the "opponent" of
his critique of religion whom he conjures up from section iv on and
whose criticisms provide him with the opportunity of rebuttal.] But science has given us evidence by its numerous and important successes
that it is no illusion" (239).

Science is no illusion! But what does that claim mean? Is it true? Science begins in primary illusion, the pleasure principle of the primal
father. How does or how can science arrive at an end separate from its
beginning? The first principle of science is illusion. Science is knowledge of illusion. How, then, can knowledge of illusion not be the illusion of knowledge? How can we distinguish science from religion? Is
not religion, as illusory, the first principle of science? Do we not have
here another one of those unaccountable Freudian reversals? Although
the demonstration that the ego is not master in its own house indicates
that the conscious (rational) ego is absolutely subject to unconscious
illusion – to the illusions of religion – now it is reason that is made a
god by Freud. Is this a scientific or a religious argument?

Notwithstanding his claim that the god *Logos* can replace the future
of religious illusion with the present of scientific reality, Freud
acknowledges that his concept of scientific objectivity – the correspondence theory – is vulnerable to the criticism that it is itself indistinguishable from subjectivity or illusion. But, instead of seeing that his
god Logos shares with the God of religion a common origin in the
father complex, Freud responds to the critique of science as merely
subjective with all the characteristics of a massively (male) narcissistic

defense of the inviolability of the penis. Threatened with castration, the murder of the phallic god *Logos*, Freud does not undertake to rethink the metapsychological issues of the relationship between science and religion, between reality and illusion, between end and beginning from the ground up but simply reasserts the phallic pieties of his logic. Although, as we have seen, it is typical of Freud to raise questions about his beginning, about the metapsychological principles underlying his phenomenology, his response, inevitably, is to reaffirm his dualism without rethinking the opposition characterizing that dualism.

Before examining Freud's response to the attack on science as merely subjective, it is important to recall the split between mind and nature (consciousness and reality) that Freud blithely (but truly) accepts as characteristic of the modern, as distinct from the primitive, psyche. Is this split – the acknowledgment of this split – mindful or natural, religious or scientific? It is on the basis of this split that Freud truly founds psychoanalysis. For psychoanalysis is concerned with psychical, not somatic ("natural") phenomena. But it is precisely the split between mind and nature that makes the articulation of an adequate metapsychology so very difficult. In most cases (with a handful of thinkers like Kant excepted), the critique of the opponent (the dualistic other) simply results in a blind repetition of that position: the return of the repressed. (This is what distinguishes dualism from dialectical critique.) Given that the modern psyche is divided from (and opposed to) nature – the psychical is not natural or somatic – it is not surprising that Freud finds himself compelled, in both *The Future of an Illusion* and the *Weltanschauung* lecture, to defend his conception of scientific objectivity from the criticism that it is ultimately indistinguishable from subjectivity.

At the end of *The Future of an Illusion* Freud considers the argument that, because science is bound to the subjective organization of the mind, it yields not objective knowledge of external nature (which remains inaccessible to it) but only subjective knowledge of itself. The defense of scientific objectivity, of the correspondence theory of truth, that Freud then presents, in one, long sentence, is surprising. Of the five reasons that he gives in support of scientific objectivity, three (2, 3, and 5) simply support the subjectivist argument. Mind "is itself a constituent part of the world." The world appears "to us in consequence of the particular character of our [mental] organization." The world would be "devoid of practical interest" if it were "without regard to our percipient mental apparatus." The other two reasons (1 and 4) do not advance significantly beyond the subjectivist perspective. Since the mind was developed to explore the external world, "it must therefore have realized in its structure some degree of expediency." The findings of science are determined "not only by our [mental] organization but by the things which have affected that organization" (240). The point is not that Freud's reasons lack interest or value. Rather, what is important to see is that the claim that mind is itself a constituent part of the world (yet Freud insists that mind is split off from nature) and provides the practical interest (motive) for scientific investigation of nature neither supports nor is supported by the correspondence theory of truth. Nevertheless, Freud then proceeds to the triumphant conclusion of *The Future of an Illusion*: "No, our science is no illusion. But an illusion it would be to suppose that what science cannot give us we can get elsewhere" (241). This conclusion, however, is neither scientific nor true. It is true that what science can give us we cannot get elsewhere. Science is irreplaceable and irreducible. But it is not true that what science cannot give us we cannot get elsewhere. There is infinitely much that science cannot give us and that we can (and must) get elsewhere.

In his *Weltanschauung* lecture Freud considers yet another radical critique of science. He conjures up "intellectual nihilists" who advocate, he says, the "anarchist theory" that truth does not exist, that we have no objective knowledge of the external world, and that all we possess is merely the illusory contents of our own mind (212).[13] Since these nihilists, Freud holds, deny correspondence with the external world as the criterion of truth, they view all opinions as equally true or false. The argument that no one can be accused of error, because no one can claim to possess the truth, reminds Freud of what he calls the sophistry of the well-known paradox of the Cretan liar. When the Cretan liar says that all Cretans are liars, does he lie or tell the truth? Either it is a lie that he tells the truth, or it is true that he lies. His lie is his truth, and his truth is his lie. Freud responds to the conundrum generated by the Cretan liar's version of the law of contradiction – that whatever I say (or do) contradicts me in that I remain ignorant of and blind to my contradiction – with the observation that "I have neither the desire nor the capacity for going into this more deeply." He simply proceeds to conclude that such abstract sophistries always break down in practice; for people, he says, are guided by what works in their practical life, whether they are speculating "about the structure of atoms or *the origin of man*" or building a bridge (213ᵉ). What counts is correspondence with practical, external reality.

Once again, there is nothing to take exception to in Freud's argument against the Cretan nihilists (his argument is unexceptional). There is truth in pragmatism. But the question is what the nature of that truth is. Pragmatism no more fits the correspondence (external) theory of truth than it does the coherence (internal) theory of truth. What works for one person does not work for another. Aesthetic interests, not to mention economic (class)[14] and other interests, have an enormous bearing on the weight we want our bridge, real or metaphorical, to support. Indeed, the argument that the (illusory) doctrines of religion have worked for millennia for millions of people is a hoary one.

It is also important to note that Freud's appeal to the "paradox" of the Cretan liar as an example of abstract and thus irrelevant, unpragmatic, and unworkable (inapplicable) sophistry misses the mark. The Cretan paradox, like the Socratic paradox, is no paradox at all, when paradox is understood in the Kierkegaardian sense – consistent with Hegelian dialectic (another paradox!) – of truth. Paradox is the modern (biblical) recognition that of two positions – yours and mine, two lovers', beginning and end, self and other, internal and external, id and ego, pleasure principle and reality principle – neither is true unless both are true from a point of view that is reducible to neither of them. Paradox is the recognition – Hegel calls it the process of recognition – that one cannot begin with either side (master or slave) without beginning with both sides simultaneously.[15] Paradox embodies the principle of the golden rule, the principle of reciprocity.

The Cretan liar knows *that* he lies – he knows that he cannot distinguish his denial of truth from the truth that he denies – just as Socrates, in his ignorance, knows that he is ignorant. But the Cretan liar does not know *what* his lie is, just as Socrates does not know what he is ignorant of. It is in the analytic situation – from the Bible to Freud – that one is confronted with the responsibility of knowing *what* one is ignorant of. It is noteworthy that the Cretan liar does not say that he tells the truth, that he knows the truth, that he wills the truth. It is similarly noteworthy that Socrates, in holding that it is better to suffer evil (done to him by others) than to do evil (to others), does not and cannot conceive that what would be better than either of these contradictory opposites would be to will the good true for all. Both the Cretan liar and Socrates abide, ignorantly and blindly, by the law of contradiction, which (together with its sister laws of identity and the excluded middle) always opposes the one and the many, self and other, reality and appearance, mortal and immortal, such that, for one side of the opposition (or party to the dispute) to be true, the other side must be false (apparent).

In more psychological terms, paradox depends upon will, desire, love – action (and thus Freud rightly holds that working through contradictions means to overcome and not merely to repeat the dualisms of the past). It is precisely desire, will, love – action – that are absent from the primitive world of Socrates, the Cretan liar, Oedipus, and the Trobrianders. It is desire as the reciprocation of self and other (and self and other as shared desire) that can, at one and the same time, expose contradiction as ignorance – as denial, resistance, evasion, hypocrisy, and sin – and appropriate it as knowledge. Sin is not ignorance, for that is the Greek contradiction that blindly suspends the Cretan liar on the two horns of his dilemma. Sin is knowledge, knowledge of good and evil. In the modern world (of the Bible) there is freedom, choice, decision. It is not the difference between telling the truth and lying, between good and evil that is undecidable but rather the fact that one cannot choose not to choose between good and evil. For even the refusal to choose (the denial, the evasion of choice) is undecidably a choice. What is undecidable, then, is that there is a difference, a choice, between good and evil, not that we cannot decide between good and evil, but that it is undecidable that we must decide between them. What is undecidable is that the choice of the good – choose life, not death! – has been decided for all time. For, in the beginning, creation is from nothing, from nothing that has not, always already, been decided. It is the undecidable choice, the choice of undecidability, of which the Cretan liar, like Socrates, is ignorant. It is the undecidability of choice that Freud evades metapsychologically, as he embodies it in his phenomenology.

The statement on the part of Freud that he has neither the desire nor the capacity to analyze more deeply the difference between the Cretan liar and the modern analysand is typical of his disclaimers of modesty, as we have seen. We may recall his statement at the end of *Civilization and its Discontents* that he knows not whereof he writes. But such disclaimers are clearly inconsistent with the ruthless honesty that he demands of the analysand, who is commanded (quite rightly) to tell the analyst everything, including even what he does not (will to) know. Freud, the metapsychologist, in contrast, avoids analytic honesty by positivistically dividing knowledge between what he knows and what he does not know so that he can hide behind the pretence of scientific modesty. But the analyst, as we learn from Freud himself, is always more interested in what the patient does not (will to) know than in what he knows (all too easily)!

In *The Future of an Illusion* Freud gives momentary promise of analyzing, for once, what he does not (will to) know. Having claimed that the doctrines of religion are illusions, he acknowledges that he is then faced with the further question whether other aspects of culture that are central to our lives are also not illusory – our political and erotic relations, indeed, science itself. Actually, the formulation of the issue regarding science that Freud gives is yet more auspicious, for he asks whether belief in the correspondence theory of truth "has any better foundation." What he has in mind, he says, is that nothing ought to keep us from *directing our observation to our own selves* or from *applying our thought to criticism of itself*. In this field a number of investigations open out before us, whose results could not but be decisive for the construction of a "Weltanschauung." We surmise, moreover, that such an effort would not be wasted and that it would at least, in part, justify our suspicion. *But the author does not dispose of the means for undertaking so comprehensive a task*; he needs must confine his work to following out one only of these illusions – that, namely, of religion. (216ᵉ)¹⁶

Surely, however, it would be the case that, if an analysand told (or otherwise showed to) his analyst that he (the analysand) was incapable of directing his observation to his own self or of applying his thought to criticism of itself, the analyst would not consider him a competent (or honest) subject. But would it not also be the case that, if the analyst told (or otherwise showed to) an analysand that he (the analyst) was incapable of directing his observation to his own self or of applying his thought to criticism of itself, the analysand would not consider him a competent (or honest) analyst? I have no judgment on Freud's analytic practice. Dora is displeased with and breaks off her analysis. Little Hans has no memory of his analysis when, "a strapping youth of nineteen," he is "perfectly well" (304). Dr Schreber is known to Freud only from the autobiographical account of his interminable psychosis. The Rat Man, cured, dies in World War I. The Wolf Man, still subject to psychotic disorder, is pleased with Freud. The gay, young woman ("The Psychogenesis of a Case of Homosexuality in a Woman"), Freud is careful to point out, does not satisfy the criterion required for success in psychoanalysis. "As is well known," he writes, "the ideal situation for analysis is when someone who is otherwise his own master is suffering from an inner conflict which he is unable to resolve alone, so that he brings his trouble to the analyst and begs for his help." Since the young woman "did not suffer from anything in herself, nor did she complain of her condition," she entered analysis not because she wanted to change but rather because her family wanted her to change (374–5). I am only an ontologist. Disparity between metapsychology and phenomenology is unanalytic and deeply disturbing and needs, always, to be exposed. Freud's incapacity for self-reflection is astonishing. His lack of insight into the paradox of self-referentiality – whose contradictory consequences are then crippling – is massive.

Now that we have seen that in his defense of science Freud has not succeeded in showing how science is truly distinguishable from religious illusion, we shall not be surprised to discover that more reversals lie ahead. Freud repeats his modest claim in *The Future of an Illusion* that everything that he has written against the truth-value of religion had all been said long ago. Should it, however, turn out, he adds, that, although the critique of religion does not need the support of psychoanalysis, psychoanalysis has provided a new argument against religious truth, so much the worse for religion. But then Freud notes much more ominously that "defenders of religion will by the same right make use of psychoanalysis in order to give full value to the *affective* significance of religious doctrines." Nevertheless, Freud does not pursue the troubling paradox – or is it a contradiction? – that, because the first principle of psychoanalysis is illusion, religion is the truth of psychoanalysis. Instead, he veers away from discussing the fact that psychoanalytic demonstration of "the affective significance of religious doctrines" can be used just as effectively (affectively) by religion against science as by science against religion. He initiates, instead, a rambling discussion of how "religion has clearly performed great services for human civilization. It has contributed much towards the taming of the asocial instincts" (219ᵉ). Freud is quick to add, however, that there has not been much to show for this effort. Today, people are so dissatisfied with and unhappy in civilization that they want to change it or they show so much hostility to it that "they will have nothing to do with civilization or with a restriction of instinct." Although it would appear that religion, with its base in affective wish fulfilment, would be the opponent of civilization and its renunciation of instinct, the only thing that Freud remarks on is that it is doubtful whether people, when they lived under the sway of religion, were happier then than they are today. People were certainly not more moral, he observes, for "they have always known how to externalize the precepts of religion and thus to nullify their intentions." When supported by priests, people – as is seen in Russian introspectiveness! – even make sin indispensable for the enjoyment of divine grace. "It is no secret," Freud writes, "that the priests could only keep the masses submissive to religion by making such large concessions as these to the instinctual nature of man. Thus it was agreed: God alone is strong and good, man is weak and sinful. In every age immorality has found no less support in religion than morality has" (220).

Then Freud repeats the conventional wisdom that science has contributed to the decline of religion and notes further that "comparative research has been struck by the fatal resemblance between the religious ideas which we revere and the mental products of primitive peoples and times." What this means, he points out, is that, while civilization has little to fear from educated people and researchers, there is reason to fear "the great mass of the uneducated and oppressed, who have every reason for being enemies of civilization" (221). If, then, people were ever to wake up to the fact that God was dead – given that the sole reason not to kill their neighbour was because God prohibited it and punished sin in the next life – they would conclude that they could kill their neighbour with impunity, except insofar as they were restrained by force. "Thus either these dangerous masses must be held down most severely and kept most carefully away from any chance of intellectual awakening," Freud declares, "or else the relationship between civilization and religion must undergo a fundamental revision" (222).

Although it is clear that, in distinguishing between religious morality and religious hypocrisy, Freud has a much richer conception of religious phenomenology than merely illusory wish fulfilment, as dictated by his metapsychology, he does not reflect upon this disparity in his approach. He is concerned, rather, to advance the argument that ethics should be based on rational or secular and not on religious grounds. It's as if, because belief in God (the primal father) led to the primal murder, so ethics (law) as the prohibition of murder should be separated from belief in God (the primal father). Consequently, Freud proceeds to argue that the commandment that you shall not kill your neighbour is laid down not by religion but by civilization "in the interest of man's communal existence" (223). He holds that people can be properly united in security and justice under the authority of the golden rule (he does not use that term) only if they relinquish making its observance dependent upon belief in God and are content with its "social reason." All the problems of having to decide what is divine and what is human would be eliminated, he observes, "if we were to leave God out altogether and honestly admit the purely human origin of all the regulations and precepts of civilization" (224). Because laws would then lose their rigid inflexibility, people would come to view them as serving and not opposing their interests and would be prepared to work for their improvement, instead of their abolition. "This would be an important advance along the road which leads to becoming reconciled to the burden of civilization," Freud opines (225).

But it is hardly surprising that, in light of the duality that Freud assumes between wish fulfilment and reality, between religion and civilization, between illusion and morality, he suddenly calls a halt to his rational account of the origin of civilization. For, although it is true that civilization, as the renunciation of instinct, is opposed to religion as the fulfilment of humankind's primordial instincts, it is also true that civilization has its beginning in religion, in the father complex as the very origin of law and morality. Thus, it is at this point in his argument that Freud recalls that his rational account of the origin of civilized laws and morality, his derivation of, for example, the prohibition against murder from what he calls "social necessity," does not tally with his psychoanalytic account of historical truth: "in reality things happened otherwise," he declares. Since people today still act largely on the basis of affect, he remarks, we have to think of how the primeval human animal must have acted! Perhaps even today, Freud continues, people would kill each other without inhibition,

if it were not that among those murderous acts there was one – the killing of the primitive father – which evoked an irresistible emotional reaction with momentous consequences. From it arose the commandment: Thou shalt not kill ... The primal father was the original image of God, the model on which later generations have shaped the figure of God. *Hence the religious explanation is right.* God actually played a part in the genesis of that prohibition; it was His influence, not any insight into social necessity, which created it. And *the displacement of man's will on to God is fully justified.* For men knew that they had disposed of their father by violence, and in their reactions to that impious deed, they determined to respect his will thenceforward. Thus *religious doctrine tells us the historical truth* – though subject, it is true, to some modification and disguise – whereas our rational account disavows it. We now observe that *the store of religious ideas includes not only wish fulfillments but important historical recollections.* (225–6ᵉ)

The religious explanation is right! God is the origin of history. Religion has on its side what is primary: the originary wishes of humankind, (distorted) history, the murder of the primal father, the origin of the golden rule, God himself, and illusion. Science has on its side merely what is secondary: reason, the golden rule as social necessity, and truth – but neither affect (desire) nor history, and certainly not God. Can one imagine anything crazier? Is the correct religious explanation the basis of science? Or is the correct religious explanation actually scientific? But how can religion be the science of humankind if religion and science are divided as beginning and end, illusion and truth, affect and reason, murder and the golden rule? What is so extraordinary here is that it is actually Freud's "rational" explanation of the golden rule as social necessity that is accurate. What he does not see, however, is that, because the "rational" explanation of the golden rule as social necessity is compatible solely with biblical religion, it is not only the rational explanation but also the religious (biblical) explanation that is not compatible with the originary violence of primitive religion. In leading him to falsify his account of reason, the metapsychological commitment to the father complex blinds Freud to both the utter difference between the Bible and primitive religion and the utter identity between religion and reason as centred in the golden rule of "social necessity."

Freud's defense of religion as illusory, violent, and murderous is absolutely reactionary, commensurate with the Grand Inquisitor's defense of religion as the power of illusion (the illusion of power) in *The Brothers Karamazov*. Freud's defense of religion also leaves his concept of reason, having been stripped of both affect (desire) and history, totally vulnerable to being reduced to the religion of irrationality. This is precisely the position opposed by the lawyer Fetyukovich, who defends Mitya Karamazov against the murder of his father in light of the rationality of the biblical doctrine of the golden rule. Further, to oppose reason and history to each other, to be forced to renounce history in the name of reason, is absolutely unanalytic. It is contradictory, for reason is unable to explain its beginning in illusion, and can one imagine an analysand renouncing his history in the name of reason? Surely, he would then invite the most massive return of the repressed that is imaginable. Yet, it is precisely the return of the repressed to which scientific belief in the correspondence theory of truth leads as it regresses to its origin involving dependence on God as the primal father and the authority of external reality (identification with the penis).

Once Freud argues that it is the religious and not the rational explanation of the origin of civilization that is right, he is faced with the dilemma that characteristically emerges throughout the forty-year span of his work: either recognize that it is his metapsychology, not (biblical) religion, which is illusory, or maintain his illusory metapsychology by arguing that, although human beings begin in religious illusion, they end in secular rationality. Since he is never prepared to rethink the dualistic structure of his metapsychology, Freud has no option but to fall back on his pseudo-historical argument that religious illusion or primitivity is the childhood neurosis that civilization outgrows. But then, as always, he has no explanation of how the primitive becomes modern, of how the weak, dependent, childish ego becomes the strong, independent, adult ego.

Still, Freud is uncanny – or is he canny? – in his ability to let his analysis of reality carry him away into (by exposing) the metapsychological impasse, but (for) he consistently reimposes the inconsistency of his metapsychology on his phenomenological insight. We have already seen Freud consider at the end of *The Future of an Illusion* the radical critique that science is itself subjective (illusory). More significantly, he conjures up a putative opponent, a champion of religion who challenges the account that Freud provides of both religion and science. The interlocutor points out to Freud that the two of them, in their mutual opposition, appear to exchange places in their respective views on science and religion. This is doubly ironic. We have just seen

Freud advance a rational account of the origin of civilization (of justice and morality as based on the golden rule), only to renounce it as completely illusory. What psychoanalysis demonstrates, he reminds the reader, is that it is not rational science but illusory religion whose account of civilization is true! But, once he has reasserted the religious right of the primal father over reason, Freud again reverses course to argue that, although the past was dominated by religious illusion, the future will belong, he hopes, to scientific rationality. It is here, however, that the religious opponent intervenes to support, against Freud, the psychoanalytic insight that human beings are dominated by religious illusion, not by scientific reason. It is Freud, the opponent argues, who is subject to illusion, while it is he (the opponent) who argues rationally (psychoanalytically) – as Freud himself had forecast, as we saw! – in support of the role that religion as illusory wish fulfilment plays in the lives of human beings. The result of the dialogue between Freud and his opponent is then this. Freud supports reason (science) over illusion (religion); but we have already asked whether – given the fact that illusion is the first principle of science, in other words, given that science, like religion, is based on the father complex – the father complex is scientific or religious. The religious opponent supports religion (illusion) over science (reason). But does this mean that it is he who champions Freudian metapsychology against Freud? Is religion the truth of life? Is science the illusion of life? What is religion? What is science?

When the opponent intervenes in the discussion of the relationship between reason (science) and illusion (religion), he points out to Freud that his (Freud's) account is full of contradictions. You argue, he tells him, that people are ruled by affective, instinctual forces. "'But on the other hand you propose to replace the affective basis of their obedience to civilization by a rational one. Let who can understand this. To me it seems that it must be either one thing or the other'" (229).[17] Freud responds to the opponent by saying that surely he (Freud) is justified in having hope for the future, hope that people will finally give up believing in the absurd illusions of religious doctrines and, by redirecting their energies to this life, will make civilization tolerable for all. He assures the opponent that people can be counted on to leave behind religion as children leave behind their warm, comfortable, parental home (although we remember that the ego [of children] is not the master in its own house and that the parental home is occupied by helpless, fearful children whose weak, incompetent, and neurotic egos make them dependent on the ambivalent penis of the dominating patriarch). "But surely infantilism is destined to be surmounted," Freud declares. "Men cannot remain children for ever; they must in the end go out into 'hostile life.' We may call this *education to reality.*' Need I confess to you that the sole purpose of my book is to point out the necessity for this forward step? You are afraid, probably, that they will not stand up to the hard test? Well, let us at least hope they will" (233).

The opponent's riposte is swift. You believe, he tells Freud, that human beings will be able to overcome all their illusions and to create a tolerable life on earth. I do not share your expectations. "'We seem now to have exchanged roles'" (235). You have been carried away by your illusory wish fulfilments, the opponent continues, while it is I who adhere to the skeptical claims of reason, I who recognize that "human needs, too, are a piece of reality" and must be accepted (236). Freud responds by acknowledging the cogency of his opponent's argument, yet he still contends that scientific illusions, unlike religious illusions, are capable of correction. He reiterates his hope that religion, like childhood neurosis, will be outgrown, left behind, and discarded. However much one may insist upon the weakness of intellect, compared with instinctual life, he remarks, the voice of intellect, although soft, is persistent and will win out in the end. The primacy of intellect, he declares, "lies, it is true, in a distant, distant future, but probably not in an *infinitely* distant one" (238). Intellect has the same goals as does your God, within the limits of external reality prescribed by *Ananke*:

the love of man and the decrease of suffering ... Our antagonism is only a temporary one and not irreconcilable. We desire the same things, but you are more impatient, more exacting, and ... more self-seeking ... Our god, *Logos*, will fulfill whichever of these wishes nature outside us allows, but he will do it very gradually, only in the unforeseeable future, and for a new generation of men. He promises no compensation for us, who suffer grievously from life. On the way to this distant goal your religious doctrines will have to be discarded ... In the long run nothing can withstand reason and experience, and the contradiction which religion offers to both is all too palpable ... Since we are prepared to renounce a good part of our infantile wishes, we can bear it if a few of our expectations turn out to be illusions. Education freed from the burden of religious doctrines will not, it may be, effect much change in men's psychological nature. Our god *Logos* is perhaps not a very almighty one, and he may only be able to fulfill a small part of what his predecessors have promised ... We shall accept it with resignation. We shall not on that account lose our interest in the world and in life, for we have one sure support which you lack. We believe that it is possible for scientific work to gain some knowledge about the reality of the world, by means of which we can increase our power and in accordance with which we can arrange our life ... Science ... is no illusion. (238–9)

Thus we have rejoined our earlier discussion. Our god Logos, Freud tells his opponent, has the same goal as yours – the golden rule – but more realistically envisaged. Its future realization, while extremely distant, is probably not infinitely distant, and it involves earthly progress. Science is not illusory. But the rebuttal of the radical critique of science – the claim that, because reason is bound to the subjective organization of the mind, it yields only subjective or illusory results – that Freud then launches in the final paragraph of *The Future of an Illusion* only confirms that critique, as we have seen.

Once again, the defense that Freud mounts, in this case, in support of reason as the god of modernity, is unexceptional, except for the fact that he cannot account for the exceptional position of reason, which is precisely the point that Freud allows his opponent to make against him. Not only can Freud not explain how reason replaces affect as the basis of civilization – save as a creed expressing faith, hope, and love – but he also cannot explain how science has the same goals as religion, when religion begins in illusion and science ends with reason. The analogy between religion and childhood neurosis is absurd, purely illusionary. Childhood is not to be equated with neurosis; for the conflicts of childhood, when appropriated, are precisely the conflicts of adulthood – both personal and social – that must be constantly confronted and overcome. Freud is forced by the metapsychology of the castration complex, as we have seen, to view the child and its ego as helpless, dependent, weak, immature, and incompetent; but then he is never in a position to explain how the child and the ego grow up, except on the basis of education in reality. The idea of education as external imposition simply reinforces, however, the dependence of the childish ego on the father complex (and thus ultimately reflects the metapsychology of identification with the patriarchal penis, the castration complex, and the superego: the phylogenetic heritage stemming from the murder of the primal father). The analogy between religion and childhood neurosis also fails because religious illusion, as originary and primitive, would have had to have been normal and institutional – as taboo – which leaves Freud, as ever, unable to explain the transition from primitive humanity to modern civilization. There is absolutely no analogy between (primitive) taboo and (modern) neurosis. There is equally no transition from primitive illusion to modern reason, from religion to science.

What is so extraordinary about *The Future of an Illusion*, together with the lecture on *Weltanschauung*, yet so characteristic of Freud, as we continue to see, is that he sees what he sees; that he then sees that what he sees is problematic; and that, finally, he does not see what the problem is with what he sees. He ultimately fails his own analytic test.

But is this surprising when, given his conception of both religion and science, of both illusion and reason, he is compelled to renounce not only desire (the primordial wishes of humankind, human affectivity) but also history as rational? *The Future of an Illusion* is a particularly interesting work in that Freud builds into its structure, at least in part, his own opposition. But the dialogue between Freud and the opponent embodying the conflict between science and religion, between reason and illusion is ultimately not successful: it is not psychoanalytic. Freud, through his opponent, does raise the problem of how affectivity (illusion), religion, history, reason (external reality), and science are to be related. But he never gives up his metapsychological commitment to the priority of the pleasure principle – of affectivity, illusion, primordial wish fulfilment – and of the primal father and his murder. This means that Freud is then unable to explain how his own rational creed, belief in the god *Logos*, involves the same content as religion: the faith, hope, and love of the golden rule.

The most extraordinary element in the argumentation that Freud develops in *The Future of an Illusion* and that then results in his spectacular reversals is his acknowledgement that the rational account of civilization is false. The social necessity of the command not to kill your neighbour – the golden rule – is not rational but religious. "The religious explanation is right." The religious opponent is right. Freud is wrong. But Freud can explain neither why the opponent is right nor why he (Freud) is wrong, which naturally means that Freud, in a reprise of the Cretan liar's position, is right in being wrong! He does not see that the golden rule – the command not to kill your neighbour – cannot be founded on the trauma of the murder of the primal father.[18] It is true that Freud does not openly acknowledge that the command not to murder your neighbour embodies the golden rule; but, in recognizing that the only basis of society is reciprocity – the elimination of vengeance: "love of mankind" – it is patently the golden rule that he envisages (even as he represses acknowledgment of this fact). Freud does not see that the golden rule is not found in primitive (extra-biblical) society. It is absent from the world of Socrates, Oedipus, and the Trobrianders. The golden rule is unthinkable to the Cretan liar who cannot imagine loving the other as he would wish the other to love him. The ambivalence of taboo – the blind, ignorant opposition of love and fear (hate), of truth and lying – does not involve or express the golden rule.

It is astonishing that Freud, notwithstanding the fact that he advances an accurate (a "rational") conception of the golden rule, repudiates it on behalf of a concept of religion that embodies the very illusion and violence that he claims to oppose: the notion that the origin of religion is violence and that the repression of violence represents what is most ugly and tyrannical in Christianity. It is this image of Christianity that Ivan Karamazov conjures up in his parable of the Grand Inquisitor but whose sophistry is seen through by his brother Alyosha when he kisses Ivan on the lips, just as Jesus, in Ivan's parable, kisses the Grand Inquisitor on the lips. Ivan is delighted and moved that his (in his eyes) naïve but fresh and charming younger brother loves him. He wants the love of his brother, and he wants to love his brother. But this does not mean for a moment that Ivan will be able to overcome the delusion that ultimately leads to his madness at the end of the novel: that it is he who is guilty of his father's death and so of his brother Mitya's conviction for the murder of their father. Phenomenology is dominated by metapsychology, reality by illusion. Ivan, the man who lives by reason alone, is, finally, beyond analysis. The analytic center of the novel is constituted, on the one hand, by Alyosha and Zosima and their commitment to active love and, on the other hand, by Fetyukovich who, in recognizing that psychology is a stick with two ends, defends the rationality of love on the basis of the Bible. Freud fails to see, however, that, if he is to join the two opposites of the stick – beginning and end, religion and science, illusion and reason, violence and the golden rule – he must be able to find rationality within affect and the history of religion, on the one hand, and affect and the history of religion within rationality, on the other. He recognizes that religion embodies not only the primordial wishes of humankind but also the primordial recollections of history – with the wishes fulfilled as illusion and the history recollected as distortion. But if it is true that, in the beginning, the fulfilment of desire is historical reality and that history is initiated by the violent act of murdering the primal father, then Freud will have no way of accounting for the true nature of either this illusion or this distortion.

When Freud undertakes, in *The Future of an Illusion* and the *Weltanschauung* lecture, to argue for the rationality of viewing religion as illusory, we find that he is constantly reversed. The rationality of science turns out to begin with the truth of religious illusion, and religious illusion turns out to end with the truth of rational science. But Freud can explain neither how religion is true in the beginning and illusory in the end nor how science is illusory in the beginning and true in the end. Is it not, consequently, reason, with its opposition, in the beginning, to originary wish fulfilment and to the historical truth of religion, that, in the end, represents the return of the repressed religious? Is it not psychoanalysis that, in the end, proves that, in the beginning, the religious explanation that human beings are dominated by instinctual affect is right? Does it not begin to dawn upon us – readers of Freud – that if, in the beginning, we do not conceive of reason as united with religion, with desire and history, then, in the end, we shall be compelled to adopt a concept of reason according to which desire and history can represent nothing other than the return of the repressed religious? Does not the reversal of reason, in embodying the return of religion as the repressed, suggest that the stick representing psychology can be picked up at both extremes only when beginning and end, illusion and truth, religion and reason are made the paradox such that neither is true in the beginning unless both are true in the end? Is this not the truth of the Bible that Alyosha demonstrates to Ivan and that Fetyukovich demonstrates to the court trying their brother Mitya? (It is this biblical truth that Ivan and the court, like Freud, deny.) Is it not in and through the Bible that beginning and end, religion and reason, illusion (fiction) and truth can be united such that both are distinguished from the primal myth of the father complex? We shall now see that the fundamental issue at stake in *Moses and Monotheism*, when Freud confronts the founding fathers of the Bible – "the man Moses" and his monotheistic God – is that already broached in *The Future of an Illusion* and the *Weltanschauung* lecture. Will biblical phenomenology support the contradictory demonstration of his metapsychology that, in the beginning, religion is the repression of reason and, in the end, reason is the repression of religion?

III *MOSES AND MONOTHEISM*: THE CONFLICT BETWEEN METAPSYCHOLOGY AND PHENOMENOLOGY

a Introduction: If Moses Was an Egyptian

In seeking, in *Moses and Monotheism*, to explain the origin of Jewish monotheism, Freud acknowledges that "one must reflect that what is probable is not necessarily the truth and that the truth is not always probable" (254). He observes that it is no light undertaking for a Jew to deprive his fellow Jews of their hero Moses by making him a highborn Egyptian. It is even more extraordinary to locate the origin of Jewish monotheism in Egypt, to base Yahweh on Pharaoh, from whose enslavement Moses liberates his fellow Israelites on behalf of the One I AM, according to the biblical account that Freud reads as covering up the murder of Moses by his fellow Israelites.[19] As I have already explained in my introductory remarks, I am not directly concerned either with Freud's personal (psychological) motives for writing *Moses and Monotheism* (including the diffuse form of the work, together with its compulsive repetitions) or with its social setting (the rise of Nazism). I shall focus on the ontological question of origins.

In undertaking to account for the origin of biblical monotheism in Egyptian religion, Freud finds himself confronting a problem that is new for him. In his earlier accounts of religion he avoids the question of whether there are significant differences between primitive religion and biblical religion. When he takes up what he considers to be the basic doctrines of Christianity in *The Future of an Illusion* and in his lecture on *Weltanschauung*, he deals with "what the common man understands by his religion," as he points out in *Civilization and its Discontents* (261). [20] Freud acknowledges in *The Future of an Illusion* that he belongs to a long and distinguished tradition of (presumably) modern critics of religion, but it is regrettable that he declines to name and to discuss those whom he considers to be his most important predecessors. [21] He shows no evidence of having pondered deeply the issues that Descartes, Spinoza, Vico, Kant, Hegel, Kierkegaard, and Nietzsche make central to their ontological engagement with biblical religion. Had he done so he would have been confronted with the argument that thinking (existence) is profoundly bound up with the God of the Bible, with the biblical ideas of creation, sin, covenant (the golden rule), idolatry, and salvation (liberation). Freud is vividly aware and clearly proud of (if also perplexed by) the fact that the children of Abraham have an unbroken continuity of existence, notwithstanding their rich, complex, and dazzling diversity and the history of their persecution (and even the unthinkably worse history that they were facing in his time). He is equally aware of the fact that the grandchildren of Abraham are one of the two great groups he considers to be the dominant forces in modernity: Christianity. He is proud to belong to the other dominant force in modernity, what he views as scientific, intellectual, and artistic secularism, whose identity is profoundly shaped by its opposition to – and its persecution by – religion, above all, Christianity. Consequently, Freud finds himself confronted with issues that he had not faced in his earlier critique of religion. There is nothing new as such in his metapsychological claim that Jewish monotheism, like all religions, is to be understood in terms of the father complex. But he also finds in Jewish monotheism a phenomenology that openly contradicts his metapsychology. He sees in ancient Judaism a characterology, an advance in intellectuality, and a commitment to ethical life that not only are absent from primitive religion but, more significantly, are coextensive with modernity, with his own very thinking and existence. The ontological question, then, is this: is it the murder of the primal father or the divine father's creation of life from nothing – from nothing that is dead and buried – that constitutes the origin of character, thinking, and ethics?

I shall not consider the arguments that Freud uses to "construct" his version of ancient Israelite history. But it is important to know the basic details of that construction in order to see that it is determined by Freud's need to salvage his myth of the primal father. Freud argues that Pharaoh Akhenaten radically reformed traditional Egyptian (poly-theistic) religion by transforming it into monotheism. But at his death there was a deeply furious reaction on the part of the Egyptians against his reforms. Shocked by the overturn of enlightened monotheism and the return to superstitious polytheism, the fervent follower of Akhen-aten, Moses, saved his reformed religion by imposing it on the Israelite slaves. At the end of essay II, entitled "If Moses was an Egyptian," Freud summarizes his construction of Israelite history in a suite of dualities: *two groups of people* (the Israelites who depart from Egypt under the leadership of Moses, whom they subsequently murder,[22] but whose religion and the memory of whose murder return when this group fuses with a second group at Kadesh, who worship the primitive, volcanic god Yahweh[23] – with the result that the Jewish God is Egypt-ian in all but name); *two gods' names*; *two religions* – "the first [that of the Egyptian Moses] repressed by the second but nevertheless later emerging victoriously behind it"; and *two religious founders* (the Egyptian Moses and the Kadesh Moses) (293).

The displacement of the origin of biblical monotheism onto its Egyptian forebear allows Freud to appear to solve the problem of orig-inality. "Every novelty," he writes, "must have its preliminaries and preconditions in something earlier" (258). But Freud fails to make the elemental observation that everything earlier is also later than what is still earlier than it. His real aim, however, is to argue that what he views as the parochial religion of the lowly Jews could only have its origin in the universalism of Egyptian imperialism.

In Egypt, so far as we can understand [he writes], monotheism grew up as a by-product of imperialism: God was a reflection of the Pharaoh who was the absolute ruler of a great world-empire. With the Jews, political conditions were highly unfavorable for the development from the idea of an exclusive national god to that of a universal ruler of the world. And where did this tiny and pow-erless nation find the arrogance to declare itself the favorite child of the great Lord? The problem of the origin of monotheism among the Jews would thus remain unsolved, or we should have to be content with the common answer that it is the expression of the peculiar religious genius of that people. (306–7)[24]

I cite this unexceptional passage in order to show that Freud, like so many moderns, fails to see that it is biblical monotheism (with its attendant concepts of creation, sin, covenant, golden rule, and salvation) that eschews all notions of history as the explanation of posterior effects by prior or first causes. It is precisely the view of himself as the product (or victim) of past relationships that the analysand has to relinquish if, with Zarathustra, he is to transform "it was" into "thus I willed it" – as *my* history. It is biblical ontology that lies behind Hegel and Kierkegaard's concept of history as the story of coming freely – thoughtfully – into existence. History is the account of the one thing that cannot be thought without existing (and cannot exist without being thought) – the history of the biblical God and his people, which remains our history today. History as the search for prior (first) causes always begs (presupposes) the question of the first cause and *its* history. There is no first cause that is not itself also the effect of yet another prior cause. Thus history, in the mode envisaged by Freud, but not by Hegel, Kierkegaard, or Nietzsche, necessitates explanation by miracles, by unknown and unknowable causes that are either external (cosmic) or internal (psychical). Freud claims to explain Jewish monotheism on the basis of Egyptian imperialism (while begging the question of how Akhenaten's empire differs from that of his predecessors and successors). But what is the origin of Egyptian monotheism? The myth of the primal father, clearly.

When Freud, however, comes to ponder the peculiar character of the Jews, he will find, as we shall see, that it has nothing to do with either imperialism or genius. Indeed, notwithstanding his claim that monotheism is originally Egyptian, he points out that what we find in Judaism is "the notion of a god's all at once 'choosing' a people, declaring them to be his people and himself to be their god ... This is the only instance of its sort in the history of human religions" (285).[25] Later, Freud himself acknowledges that, in constructing ancient Israelite history, his procedure is one "of accepting what seems to us serviceable in the material presented to us and of rejecting what does not suit us and of putting the different pieces together in accordance with *psychological probability*." The only appeal he can make, he says, is "to the work's outcome" (351e). But we have already seen Freud write that what is probable is not necessarily true and that the truth is not always probable. What, however, is psychologically true but improbable? Are we going to find that Freud's improbable metapsychology is the truth of biblical religion? Or are we going to find, rather, that biblical religion is the improbable truth of Freudian psychology? Is the latter improbability the truthful outcome of *Moses and Monotheism*?

After Freud argues for an Egyptian Moses and for an Egyptian origin of monotheism in parts I and II of *Moses and Monotheism*, on the apparently restricted grounds of historical construction, he vastly expands the scope of his inquiry into the origin of Jewish monotheism in part III (in two repetitive sections). This greatly enlarged inquiry is composed of two very different approaches. The first I shall call metapsychological, the second phenomenological. Freud in no sense divides part III into discrete sections of metapsychology and phenomenology, which are then clearly demarcated from each other. Nevertheless, although metapsychology and phenomenology are found interspersed and intermixed, cheek by jowl – in individual sections, paragraphs, and even sentences – his argumentation clearly divides into these two distinct approaches. Metapsychology is constituted by his concept of the father complex, while phenomenology is constituted by what he finds to be the Jewish qualities of character and mind. In the analysis of *Moses and Monotheism* that follows, I shall first discuss Freud's metapsychological approach and then his phenomenological approach. Finally, I shall show in a coda that the interaction between these two approaches reaches its denouement when Freud concludes *Moses and Monotheism* by arguing that the metapsychological explanation of the return of the repressed father complex in the phenomenology of Judaism is provided by Christianity.

b Metapsychology: The Father Complex

In determining the origin of monotheism in accord with what he calls psychological probability, Freud makes it clear that he is even more convinced now than when he wrote *Totem and Taboo* that "religious phenomena are only to be understood on the pattern of the individual neurotic symptoms familiar to us – as the return of long since forgotten, important events in the primeval history of the human family – and that they have to thank precisely this origin for their compulsive character and that, accordingly, they are effective on human beings by force of the historical truth of their content." But he then goes on to remark that uncertainty arises "when I ask myself whether I have succeeded in proving these theses in the example which I have chosen here of Jewish monotheism" (299).[26] In any case, Freud proceeds to argue that the Jews abandoned the religion that Moses had brought to them – with its emphasis on monotheism, the rejection of magic, and the stress upon ethical demands – and turned to a local volcanic god, Yahweh. But the Mosaic (Egyptian) tradition was kept alive, latent and distorted, on analogy with the formation of neurosis, composed of five factors: early trauma, defense, latency, outbreak of the neurosis, and return of the repressed. It is precisely the event of the murder of the primal father and the consequent establishment of religion as the ambivalence of guilt and love that shows that religion is to be understood in terms of *die Analogie* (the title of one of the sections of essay III). Freud notes that he has been strongly attacked for his "construction," especially since ethnologists have unanimously rejected Robertson Smith's hypothesis of the sacrificial meal as being central to totemism and have replaced it with new arguments. But he observes that he is convinced neither by the new arguments nor by Smith's errors. "A denial is not a refutation," he declares, and "an innovation is not necessarily an advance ... I had a right to take out of ethnological literature what I might need for the work of analysis" (380).[27]

Freud acknowledges that the analogy between individual psychology and group psychology raises two problems. First, he has only one example in the history of religion of originary trauma leading first to repression and finally to the return of the repressed – that of the ancient Israelites. (I would add, however, that his model of the primal father presupposes that the sequence of trauma-repression-return of the repressed religious must be true for all religious traditions.) Second, and much more important, Freud has to explain the nature of tradition, of how the original murder is transmitted in repressed form (but ultimately becomes unrepressed in and as scientific knowledge of religion!). He recognizes that he needs to show what it is in group psychology that would be the equivalent of "the existence in the [individual] unconscious of memory-traces of the past" (338). Freud then summarizes his concept of the id as involving unconscious processes, including the repressed, which, he holds, are governed by laws different from those found in the ego. But he acknowledges that this topographical model is unsatisfactory because of what he calls "our complete ignorance of the *dynamic* nature of the mental processes" (342). What Freud is primarily concerned to show is that, in individual cases, reactions to early traumas

are not strictly limited to what the subject himself has really experienced but diverge from it in a way which fits in much better with the model of a phylogenetic event and, in general, can only be explained by such an influence. The behavior of neurotic children towards their parents in the Oedipus and castration complex abounds in such reactions, which seem unjustified in the individual case and only become intelligible phylogenetically – by their connection with the experience of earlier generations ... The archaic heritage of human beings comprises not only dispositions but *also subject-matter* – memory-traces of the experience of earlier generations. (344–5[e])[28]

Freud points out that he has actually been operating for a long time "as though the inheritance of memory-traces of the experience of our ancestors, independently of direct communication and of the influence of education ... were established beyond question." He acknowledges that he is thus forced to oppose contemporary biology, which rejects any notion of "the inheritance of acquired characters by succeeding generations." Then Freud adds:

I must, however, in all modesty confess that nevertheless I cannot do without this factor in biological evolution ... If we assume the survival of these memory-traces in the archaic heritage, we have bridged the gulf between individual and group psychology: we can deal with peoples as we do with an individual neurotic. Granted that at the time we have no stronger evidence for the presence of memory-traces in the archaic heritage than the residual phenomena of the work of analysis which call for a phylogenetic derivation, yet this evidence seems to us strong enough to postulate that such is the fact. *If it is not so, we shall not advance a step further along the path we entered on, either in [individual] analysis or in group psychology.* The audacity cannot be avoided. (345–6ᵉ)

Not only does Freud connect human beings to their primitive past by means of the phylogenetic inheritance of memory-traces, but he also proceeds to link them with their animal past. Just as the only explanation of behaviour in animals that is not learned is that they instinctively repeat the memories of their ancestors, he remarks, so "the position in the human animal would not at bottom be different. His own archaic heritage corresponds to the instincts [*Instinkte*] of animals even though it is different in its compass and contents." What this means, Freud declares, is that "men have always known (in this special way) that they once possessed a primal father and killed him." The only thing, then, that he has left to explain, he points out, is the circumstances under which a memory both originally enters into the archaic, unconscious heritage (of the id) in human beings and subsequently is remembered by advancing into consciousness, although in distorted and repressed form. Something becomes a part of our unconscious archaic heritage, he remarks, "if the event was important enough, or repeated often enough, or both. In the case of parricide both conditions are fulfilled" (346). With regard to the factors that activate the repressed memory-trace, what is most important is the repetition of the original event, in the case at hand, the murders of Moses and also Jesus. "It seems as though the genesis of monotheism could not do without these occurrences," Freud observes. But, since religious phenomena are compulsive and thus "liberated from the constraint of logical thought," he continues, the archaic tradition that is revived would also have had to have been repressed. For this alone explains how "it is able to display such powerful effects on its return, to bring the masses under its spell, as we have seen with astonishment and hitherto without comprehension in the case of religious tradition" (347).

In the final three sections of *Moses and Monotheism* – entitled "The Return of the Repressed," "Historical Truth," and "The Historical Development" – Freud repeats the gist of his explanation of Mosaic religion by analogy. Its key elements are the centrality of trauma in neurosis, phylogenesis, the murder of the primal father, and the return of the repressed. He acknowledges again the difficulty of bridging the gap between individual and group psychology and, while dismissing the concept of the "collective unconscious" as useless, he adds that "the *content* of the unconscious, indeed, is in any case a collective, universal property of mankind." Then, after reiterating that he has no choice but to make use of analogies, Freud declares that "the processes in the life of peoples which we are studying here are very similar to those familiar to us in psychopathology, *but nevertheless not quite the same*. We must finally make up our minds to adopt the hypothesis that the psychical precipitates of the primeval period became inherited property which, in each fresh generation, called not for acquisition but only for awakening" (381^e). Freud then appeals to what he calls the "innate symbolism" that, he says, is the same in all children, prior to education, and found in all peoples, despite their different languages.[29] He also adds that children, in important circumstances, "react, not in a manner corresponding to their own experience, but instinctively [*instinktmässig*], like the animals, in a manner that is only explicable as phylogenetic acquisition" (381–2).

From what we have now seen, it is clear that, when Freud says that he intends to proceed in *Moses and Monotheism* "in accordance with psychological probability," what he means is that metapsychology will reign supreme in the name of *die Analogie*. Freud claims that the Mosaic religion of the Jews, in compulsively repeating the myth of the murder of the primal father, represents the return of the repressed. Although Freud's key facts – Egyptian "monotheism," the Egyptian Moses, his murder by the Israelites, their repression of the Mosaic religion, and then its return, as repressed, above all, in the prophets – have no solid documentary basis and are as tendentiously asserted as he holds the claims of the biblical text itself to be, Freud cannot be refuted by facts alone. It is important to know or, indeed, as Freud would put it, to construct the facts as accurately as possible. But we never know the facts separate from our perspective on them. There are no facts knowable in themselves. Indeed, although Freud's key "facts" are largely a product of his metapsychology, his analytical strength is that he knows that facts are indeed the product of wish fulfilment. But there is wish and wish, and there is fulfilment and fulfilment, as Freud would say. His weakness is that he never integrates his two conflicting, metapsychological impulses: the role of construction (theory) in determining the reality of facts and his positivistic claim that truth is correspondence with the facts of external reality.[30]

Freud holds to both of the standard, traditional, and dualistically opposed positions in epistemology: coherence (adherence to internal criteria) and correspondence (adherence to external criteria). He does not recognize, however, that these two positions are inherently contradictory when opposed to each other. (He does not grasp the paradox that for one to be true both must be true.) He also does not see that they reflect the contradiction inherent in his conception of wish fulfilment. For, while wish fulfilment, on the one hand, adheres to the notion of internal coherence – according to the pleasure principle – it clearly becomes, on the other hand, a criterion of external correspondence when it is subject to the castration complex (the renunciation demanded by external authority). Implicit, phenomenologically, in the psychotherapeutic context, but never thematized, indeed it is contradicted metapsychologically, is the concept of wish as desire or will, the dialectic of self and other, the interpretive imperative of the golden rule to do unto others as I would desire others to do unto me. The concept of desire cannot be understood on the basis of either coherence (internality) or correspondence (externality), of either construction or fact. Desire (will) is at once construction and fact, the paradox of self-referentiality, where self involves and expresses, constructs, both your (God's) and my desire.

Freud is quite right to be suspicious of the tendentiousness of both dogmatic explanation and historical scholarship. He is, however, no more successful that the most dogmatic apologist or the most skeptical historian in dealing with the strange and estranging text of the Bible. The Bible cannot be understood internal to itself, for it is not mere wish fulfilment (the pleasure principle). Nor can it be understood comparatively – compared with external reality, in the case at hand, with the so-called Egyptian monotheism of Akhenaten. What Freud, like so many readers of the Bible – whether believing or unbelieving, pious or scholarly, simple or learned – cannot grasp is that the Bible is its own absolute standard, the standard both of its truth and of its idols. The Bible contains its absolute standard, however, in plural forms: God; the human person; the human community; the covenant (between human being and God, between community and God, between human individuals, both personally and communally); the golden rule. It is the

golden rule that I find to be the most succinct and also the most powerful expression of biblical reality as its own standard, at once internal
and external but never the one in opposition to the other. It is the concept of truth as its own standard, articulated in the *Ethics*, that Spinoza works out hermeneutically in the *Theological-Political Treatise*.
The Bible, Spinoza shows, is constituted by the double, the dialectical
truth that it can be interpreted from (by) itself alone only insofar as it
can be interpreted by (from) the reader alone. The truth that the Bible
can be interpreted from itself alone is directed against Maimonides
(whose position Spinoza equates with dogmatism). The truth that the
Bible can be interpreted by the reader alone is directed against Maimonides' opponents (whose position Spinoza equates with skepticism).
The paradox is that the Bible is the (de)construction of both itself and
the reader simultaneously – with each external and internal to the
other at one and the same time. The reader of the Bible finds that, as
he brings the Bible into his life, it is his life that is portrayed in the
Bible. The reading, the interpretation of the Bible, thus duplicates the
relationship of the individual (and the community) to God. To bring
God into your life is to find God bringing your life into his. This is also
what we experience in our personal and communal relations. As I
bring the life of the other into my life, so the other brings my life into
his. It is no accident that it is precisely the golden rule – love (*caritas*)
– that Spinoza makes the touchstone of biblical truth and interpretation, of ethics, of life: the more you know (love) individuals, he holds,
the more you know (love) God; and the more you know (love) God,
the more you know (love) individuals. The relationship of reader and
Bible, of individual and God, of self and other is not that of either
coherence or correspondence, of either internality or externality. That
way is always idolatry: the reduction of God to the reader (in the dogmatic tradition of Maimonides) or the reduction of the reader to God
(in the skeptical tradition of Maimonides' opponents).

Freud's relentlessly brilliant – compulsive! – metapsychological
reduction of biblical monotheism, of the Bible itself, to what is external to itself, to the suppressed facts of Egyptian monotheism and its
fervent, Egyptian adherent, Moses, and to the explanatory mythology
of the primal father and his murder and its delayed (repressed) and
compulsive return in and as the history of ancient Judaism (and Christianity), is fruitful for two closely intertwined reasons. In the first
place, Freud compels the reader – the reader who is free to learn from,
and through, the analytic demands of the other – to meditate deeply on
what it means to consider beginnings, origins, principles. If the reader
accepts Freud's approach, he will be compelled to embrace the consequences that follow from it. If the reader rejects the model that Freud

provides, he will have to ask himself, at the least, what model he would put in its place. What is the relationship between ancient Judaism – the Bible – and civilization? Freud, interestingly, accepts the idea that monotheism is universal. But he argues for a concept of universality that is not biblical but Egyptian or primitive, as found in the murder of the primal father and repeated in the murderous impulses of the Oedipal child whose end, castration, symbolizes the beginning of patriarchal identification with the ambivalent penis: murder. (It hardly needs to be pointed out yet again that in all this discussion it is the father complex, not the horror of incest, that occupies Freud.)

In the second place, the attempt on the part of Freud to read Jewish monotheism in terms of the father complex is fruitful because he is compelled to expose his metapsychology to the one text that not only proclaims the creation of beginning, the beginning of creation, but also contains the beginning of creation as the creation of beginning. Freud claims to contain the Bible within *his* construction, but who, here, is the true master (the servant) of analysis, of (de)construction? He claims to proceed in accordance with psychological probability, but is not that psychology more probable that goes beyond the dualisms of primitive and modern, of beginning and end, of internal and external, of coherence and correspondence, of desire and self? Is it not this psychology that shows us how improbable the truth of Freud's metapsychology is?

Freud's metapsychological commitments are brought to their extreme exposure in *Moses and Monotheism*. He admits openly that if he is to be able to explain Mosaic religion by analogy with Egyptian monotheism, behind which stands the ultimate analogy, the father complex, whose origin is the murder of the primal father, he must accept two claims that have no basis in science. First, human, like animal, behaviour is based on instinct. Second, the memory traces, the actual content of our archaic inheritance, are transmitted phylogenetically from one generation to the next. But it is precisely the inheritance of acquired characteristics, in the tradition of Lamarck, that the science of modern biology, following Darwin, as Freud explicitly acknowledges, resolutely rejects. Although Freud claims that the archaic inheritance of humanity would thus correspond to the instinctual inheritance of animals, his concept of instinct would then be utterly unbiological. Either he adheres to biological science, or he does not. If he adheres to biology, then he will have to give up his metapsychology and thus not only his construction of Israelite history but also his concept of modern neurosis, based on the castration complex, as we have seen him indicate. If he does not adhere to biological science – as he admits he does not, cannot, will not – then his appeal to the analogy between phylogenesis in human inheritance and instinctual inheritance in animals will be empty.

Further, if Freud's concept of the instincts (*Triebe*) has no basis in the instincts (*Instinkte*) of biology, what shall we make of his claim that "the *content* of the unconscious is a collective, universal property of mankind"? That claim has no biological basis. Does it have any historical basis? I mean, what is the relationship between history and the unconscious? As I showed earlier, the dualism between internal (id) and external (ego), which dominates the metapsychology of Freud, leaves him with no explanation of how what is externally experienced – because it is important and repeated! – becomes historically (internally) imprinted on the unconscious. Nor can he explain how what is internally unconscious then re-emerges historically (externally), repressed, in the individual ego. He recognizes, phenomenologically, the difference between compulsive repetition and working through. But he fails to see that his metapsychological concept of repetition remains compulsive precisely because he has no theoretical concept of working through or, in other words, no concept of desire or will, no concept of historical dialectic connecting self, both your self and my self, with desire, equally yours and mine. What Freud exposes in *Moses and Monotheism*, what he sees exposed by his confrontation with the biblical concept of beginning, is his metapsychology of the unconscious. If, in the beginning, the unconscious is unconscious of being unconscious, then, in the end, the unconscious will remain utterly unconscious of its beginning, that is, the beginning will return as the repressed end. But the solution to the contradiction of the unconscious being unconscious that it is unconscious in the beginning is not to posit a conscious beginning prior to the unconscious – in the guise of the primal father. In the beginning, (external) consciousness can no more precede the (internal) unconscious than the unconscious (or id) can precede consciousness (or ego). What we see exposed by the confrontation between the Freudian and the biblical concepts of beginning is the difference between phylogenesis and history. Phylogenesis is not only pseudo-biology but also pseudo-history. History, in contrast, has no pretenses of being "scientific." It wills only to be truthful. History is the beginning in freedom that presupposes (wills) a concept of the unconscious as that for which we humans, in the end, bear conscious responsibility. History, in appropriating the dualistic opposites central to Freud's metapsychology, reveals them to be true no less to his phenomenology than to the Bible.

c The Phenomenology of Judaism

We have now seen that the metapsychology of the father complex, as found in both the myth of the primal father and the castration complex of the Oedipal father, involves a concept of biological inheritance – of the content of memory traces – that is utterly unscientific and a concept of the unconscious that is utterly unhistorical. We shall now examine what I am calling the second approach that Freud takes to the question of the origin of monotheism in *Moses and Monotheism*, the phenomenological. Where in Freud there is strongly asserted metapsychology, there, always, are to be found strongly meditated phenomenological data that utterly refuse to accommodate themselves to his psychological probability. Closely connected with Freud's research into the origin of monotheism is his fascination with Jewish history, with the question of how the people chosen by God have survived, while subject to endless persecution, down to his own day. Here is Freud, one of Judaism's proudest sons, the creation of that God and that history, engaged in the most fundamental struggle of his life, that between his metapsychology and the phenomenology of the Bible. He knows, if only intuitively (and this is why there is so much interest in Freud's conception of his own Jewish identity), that the biblical concept of psyche is the great challenge – the only real challenge there is – to his metapsychology. He also knows that his metapsychology is as great a challenge as there is to the Bible as the cause of itself, as the standard of its own truth. The ultimate irony of *Moses and Monotheism* is that Freud, in attempting to assimilate the Bible to his metapsychology, ends up being untrue to both the psychology of the Bible and to his own phenomenology. It remains utterly improbable to Freud that the sole metapsychology that is true to his phenomenology is the ontology embodied in biblical psychology.

Freud's opening claim is that "the special peculiarities of the monotheist religion borrowed from Egypt ... [were] bound to leave a permanent imprint" on the character of the Jewish people "through its rejection of magic and mysticism [*sic*], its invitation to advances in intellectuality [*Geistigkeit*: spirituality] and its encouragement of sublimations." The Jewish people, having been "enraptured by the possession of the truth" and "overwhelmed by the consciousness of being chosen, came," Freud holds, "to have a high opinion of what is intellectual [spiritual] and to lay stress on what is moral" (329–30). In the section entitled "The People of Israel," he points out that the Jews are almost the only people from the ancient Mediterranean world to survive today in both name and substance and that what shapes their relations to other peoples has been their sense of being distinct and superior.

At the same time [he continues] they are inspired by a peculiar confidence in life, such as is derived from the secret ownership of some precious possession, a kind of optimism: pious people would call it trust in God. We know the reason for this behavior and what their secret treasure is. They really regard themselves as God's chosen people, they believe that they stand especially close to him; and this makes them proud and confident. Trustworthy reports tell us that they behaved in Hellenistic times just as they do today, so that the complete Jew was already there ... It was the man Moses who imprinted this trait – significant for all time – upon the Jewish people. He raised their self-esteem by assuring them that they were God's chosen people, he enjoined them to holiness and pledged them to be apart from others. Not that other peoples were lacking in self-esteem. Just as today, so in those days each nation thought itself better than any other. But *the self-esteem of the Jews was given a religious anchorage by Moses: it became a part of their religious faith. Owing to their especially intimate relation to their God they acquired a share in his grandeur.* (351-3^e)

In the next section, entitled "The Great Man," Freud goes on to argue that behind God stands *der Grosse Mann*, the father figure Moses. It is Moses who creates the Jews. But Freud also recognizes that "the great man" conception of history begs the question of how the character of a people could be molded for millennia by just one genius. The solution to the origin of the character of the Jews, as shaped by their intimate relation to their God, behind whom stands Moses, is, Freud holds, the father complex: "We know that in the mass of mankind there is a powerful need for an authority who can be admired, before whom one bows down, by whom one is ruled and perhaps even ill-treated. We have learnt from the psychology of individual men what the origin is of this need of the masses. It is a longing for the father felt by everyone from his childhood onwards." The "paternal characteristics" of the father figure for whom all people long, he remarks, are decisiveness of thought, strength of will, energy of action, autonomy, independence, and, finally, divine unconcern, which may grow into ruthlessness. "One must admire him, one may trust him, but one cannot avoid being afraid of him, too ... Who but the father can have been *der 'grosse Mann'* in childhood?" Freud asks. The Jews, he holds, were thus doubly overwhelmed by the father complex: by the prototypical father figure Moses, who "stooped to the poor Jewish bondsmen to assure them that they were his dear children"; and by "the idea of an only, eternal, almighty God, to whom they were not too mean for him to make a covenant with them and who promised to care for them if they remained loyal to his worship" (356). Because the lowly Jews, Freud continues, doubtlessly confused the image of Moses with the image of God, when, one fine day, they killed their great man, they only repeated a misdeed that goes back to the murder of the primal father.

But then Freud recalls that Moses is not only a father whose image grows to divine proportions in Judaism but also a son who takes over what becomes Jewish monotheism from the God-father Akhenaten.[31] Further, the pharaoh, who would himself have had to have been the son of a murdered primal father, may have absorbed patriarchal (that is, childish) hints about monotheism coming from Asia. The point Freud is driving at is that, although the chain of events *status quo ante* cannot be pursued further, "these first" (that is, these last!) links in the unbroken chain of cause and effect show that "the monotheist idea returned like a boomerang to the land of its origin. Thus it seems unfruitful to try to fix the credit due to an individual in connection with a new idea. It is clear that many have shared in its development and made contributions to it." Not only, then, is *der grosse Mann*, Moses, not the founder of ancient Judaism; but when, after his murder and the repression of that event and his religion, his religion returns, like a boomerang to (from) its Egyptian origin, it is consequently carried on by the prophets, while "the seed of monotheism failed to ripen in Egypt" (357).[32] Indeed, Freud adds, "evidence of the presence of *a peculiar psychical aptitude in the masses* who had become the Jewish people is revealed by the fact that they were able to produce so many [prophetic] individuals prepared to take on the burdens of the religion of Moses in return for the reward of being the chosen people" (358e).[33]

The suite of ideas by which Freud initiates his inquiry into what he acknowledges to be the peculiar character of the Jews – both ancient and modern, which, in their case, it turns out, are one and the same without analogy! – is characteristic of his approach, as we have learned to see. He is sensitive to what I am calling in this study phenomenological difference; yet, while he properly wants to avoid the apologetic stance of the opponents of Maimonides in locating that difference internal to itself, he can find no alternative to locating it metapsychologically external to itself, consistent with the hermeneutics of Maimonides. He recognizes that what he views as the Jewish sense of self-esteem, the Jews' sense of being distinct, different, and superior, is closely connected with their view of themselves as God's chosen people. Anchored in an intimate relationship with God, they share in his grandeur. It is clear that Jewish humanism is inseparable from Jewish theology (and vice versa). But then Freud proceeds to say that it is Moses who creates the Jews. No, it is not Moses who explains the particular character of the Jews but the fact that all people have a father complex. The Jews are weak and want to be dominated by the father (although what Freud has shown is precisely the opposite), whose role Moses fulfils, like all great men. The Jews kill Moses, compulsively and instinctively, repeating the phylogenetic inheritance of the primal sons

who transmit the unconscious guilt (the original sin) of killing the primal father. No, Moses is not simply the founding father of the Jews but
also a foundling himself who has a spiritual father, Pharaoh Akhenat-
en, whose paternal (childish) inheritance cannot be further pursued.
But what this means is that Moses is not the creator of the Jews, for
their creators are many. Indeed, the fact that the Jewish people produce
so many individuals who "take on the burdens of the religion of
Moses" (including Freud?) "is proof of a *peculiar psychical aptitude* in
the masses who became the Jewish people."

Freud adheres doggedly both to the two key facts that Moses is an
Egyptian and that monotheism is an Egyptian boomerang and to the
phylogenetic hypothesis that the masses' dependent longing for a
strong father figure – at once Moses and God – repeats the ambivalence of the murder of the primal father. The phenomenological por-
trait that he gives of the Jews is, however, completely other. He shows
that it is the Jewish people (and not simply Moses) who share in the
grandeur of God and that it is because of their "peculiar psychical aptitude" that they are clearly distinguished from "the mass of mankind,"
that they produce leaders who possess the very characteristics that
Freud imputes to patriarchal Moses (and to God the father) but that
are clearly those of the Jews themselves: decisiveness of thought,
strength of will, energetic action, autonomy, independence, and divine
unconcern (which can become ruthless). Freud acknowledges – evasively, as always – that he cannot pursue the origin of monotheism
beyond Moses and Akhenaten. When, then, he summarizes the history
of the Jews from Moses on (following the biblical story), he shows that
it has nothing to do with either the Egyptian or the primal father. But,
as always, he lets stand, without acknowledgment, the flagrant contradiction between his phenomenological and his metapsychological
accounts. Although he criticizes those who claim to explain the uniqueness of the Jews in terms of genius, he himself appeals to their "peculiar psychical aptitude," which is neither Egyptian nor primitive. It is
precisely the uniqueness of the Jewish psyche that Freud describes
without being able to account for it.

Freud pushes his investigation into Jewish character yet further. Not
only is the self-esteem of the Jews enhanced by their consciousness of
having been chosen by God, but it is also the case, he argues, that they
had "a far grander conception of God, ... the conception of a grander
God. Anyone who believed in this God had some kind of share in his
greatness, might feel exalted himself."[34] Especially important in this
context, Freud points out, is "the prohibition against making an image
of God – the compulsion to worship a God whom one cannot see. In
this, I suspect, Moses was outdoing the strictness of the A[khena]ten

religion" (359). What the ban on idolatry signifies, he argues, is the triumph of an abstract idea over sensory perception, of intellectuality over sensuality, "or, strictly speaking, an instinctual renunciation,[35] with all its necessary psychological consequences" (360). Freud repeats a few paragraphs later that

> the Mosaic prohibition [against images] elevated God to a higher degree of intellectuality ... All such advances in intellectuality have as their consequence that the individual's self-esteem is increased, that he is made proud – so that he feels superior to other people who have remained under the spell of sensuality. Moses, as we know, conveyed to the Jews an exalted sense of being a chosen people. The dematerialization of God brought a fresh and valuable contribution to *their secret treasure*. The Jews retained their inclination to intellectual interests. The nation's political misfortune taught it to value at its true worth the one possession that remained to it – its literature[36] ... The Holy Writ and intellectual concern with it were what held the scattered people together. This much is generally known and accepted. All I have wanted to do is to add that this characteristic development of the Jewish nature was introduced by the Mosaic prohibition against worshipping God in a visible form. (362[e])[37]

Freud suggests that there are three "other processes of the same character in the development of human civilization" that may help the reader to understand the Jewish "triumph of *Geistigkeit*": (1) the omnipotence of thoughts or magic (as found in children, neurotics, and primitive peoples); (2) the replacement of matriarchy (reliance on the senses) by patriarchy (reliance on scientific hypothesis involving inference and premise);[38] and (3) the human obligation to recognize *geistige* forces – on analogy with air (*animus, spiritus*) – involving the discovery of both the soul and the *geistige* principle in individual human beings: in attributing to Nature the *Seele* that they discovered in themselves, people animated (*beseelt*) the whole world, which then later science had to disenchant (360–2). The introduction by Freud of these three analogies with what he calls the Jewish "advance in *Geistigkeit*" is strange. He does not discuss them further. In other words, he does not show how or in what sense they are of "the same character" as the Jewish "triumph of *Geistigkeit*." We can also note, additionally, that the first and the third processes only serve to emphasize, by contrast, the "peculiar psychical aptitude" of the Jewish people, while the second raises new questions. The first and third processes are clearly "primitive," which, as we shall increasingly see, is not how Freud understands Jewish phenomenology (and we may recall that he emphasizes that Jewish character remains the same today as it was two thousand years ago). As for the second process, involving the patriarchal principle of scientific thinking, which is far more interesting (and which we discussed in chapter 3), it waits to be seen if (and if so, how) Freud will connect Jewish psyche and *Geist* with patriarchy and science.

We have now seen Freud directly connect the Jews' "triumph of *Geistigkeit*" with both the self-esteem arising from being chosen by a God whose greatness constitutes their own self-identify and the "dematerialization of God" (the ban on divine images) and the resultant commitment to Torah study and intellectuality. We have also seen that he does not indicate how "other processes of the same character" help to understand the Jewish advance in intellectuality. Now Freud introduces yet another "analogous case" in his attempt to explain Jewish character and intellect. In the section entitled "Renunciation of Instinct," he indicates that it is not self-evident or clear without further explication "why an advance in intellectuality, a set-back to sensuality, should raise the self-regard both of an individual and of a people. It *seems* to presuppose a definite standard of value and some other person or agency which maintains it." He proposes to clarify the issue of the Jewish "advance in intellectuality" by what he calls "an analogous case in the psychology of the individual" (363^e). Since his exposition involves a series of unexpected reversals, we must attend to its twists and turns with care.

The analogy with the Jewish advance in intellectuality that Freud introduces here involves the renunciation of instinct that arises when the ego refuses, in obedience, either externally, to the reality principle, or internally, to the superego, to satisfy an instinctual demand arising from the id. He holds that, while instinctual renunciation for external reasons is only unpleasurable,[39] when it is for internal reasons, not only is it unpleasurable but "it also brings the ego a yield of pleasure – a substitutive satisfaction, as it were. The ego feels elevated; it is proud of the instinctual renunciation, as though it were a valuable achievement." The reason for this sense of satisfaction on the part of the ego, Freud explains, is that the superego, as the heir to the individual's parents (educators), "keeps the ego in a permanent state of dependence and exercises a constant pressure on it." Just as the child fears losing the love of its parents and experiences their approval as pleasure, so, analogously, when the ego renounces instinctual satisfaction, it anticipates the pleasure of receiving approval from the superego. How, then, Freud asks, does the pleasure arising from internal, instinctual renunciation help us to understand "the elevation of self-regard when there are advances in intellectuality? Very little, it seems. The circumstances are wholly (*ganz*) different" (364–5).[40]

Having, typically, developed an analogy only to reject it – but in this case the analogy that he dismisses involves the very heart of his psychical theory, the (unnamed) Oedipus complex – Freud then introduces a distinction, by which he, in part, reintroduces the analogy, only to reject it yet once again. When he writes that the circumstances involving the advance in intellectuality "are wholly different" from those found in instinctual renunciation as understood on the model of the relationship between child-ego and father-superego, what he means, he points out, is that "there is no question of any instinctual renunciation and there is no second person or agency for whose sake the sacrifice is made." Yet he immediately qualifies the second circumstance by noting that it can be said that, as sacrifice is made to the authoritative father-figure whose role in group-psychology is that of the superego, so the Jewish people are dependent on Moses. (It will be noted that Freud hereby reinstates the analogy of "instinctual renunciation" that he had just dismissed.) "As regards the other [first] point, however," he observes, "no proper analogy can be established. An advance in intellectuality consists in *deciding* against direct sense-perception in favor of what are known as the higher intellectual processes" (365ᵉ). It consists in deciding, for example, that paternity is superior to maternity or sensuality (the reader will recall the second of the three "other processes of the same character" outlined above) or that our God, although invisible, is the greatest and the mightiest of all.

Once he has shown that the analogy with the renunciation of instinct (involving the parent-superego model) does not help in understanding the Jewish advance in intellectuality, notwithstanding the fact that he appears to reintroduce it, in part, by suggesting that the relationship of the Jews to Moses is that of child to father, ego to superego, and group to leader (although he has now stripped the father-superego-leader analogy of its role in renouncing instinct), Freud is ready to conclude his inquiry into the origin of the Jewish advance in intellectuality. Before considering his conclusion, however, it is important to recall, first, that, as we have seen, he introduces his analogy with instinctual renunciation (that he subsequently dismisses and then, in part, reinstates) because, he says, the fact that the advance in intellectuality over sensuality raises both individual and community self-regard "*seems* to presuppose a definite standard of value and some other person or agency which maintains it." Now that he is ready to draw his discussion of the origin of the Jewish advance in intellectuality to a close, the model of the father-superego-leader would appear to fit the required person or agency. But what would be the definite standard of value, the *Wertmaßstab*, that the person or agency is to maintain?

What Freud concludes is that the "the rejection of a sexual or aggressive instinctual demand" – on analogy with the dependence of the child-ego-group on the father-superego-leader – appears to be "altogether different" from the advance in intellectuality that decides against direct sense-perception in favour of the higher intellectual processes, as are seen in the examples, which we have already mentioned, of deciding that paternity is superior to maternity and that our invisible God is the greatest and the mightiest.

Moreover [he continues], in the case of some advances in intellectuality – for instance, in the case of the victory of patriarchy [now for the third time invoked!] – *we cannot point to the authority which lays down the standard which is to be regarded as higher. It cannot in this case be the father*, since he is only elevated into being an authority by *the advance* itself. Thus we are faced by *the phenomenon* that *in the course of the development of humanity* sensuality is gradually overpowered by intellectuality and that men feel proud and exalted by every such advance. *But we are unable to say why this should be so.* (365ᵉ)⁴¹

This is another of those extraordinary passages in which Freud lays bare his soul. He sees clearly. He clearly sees that he does not clearly see what he sees. But he is clearly unable to account for what he so clearly sees. Once again, there is a complete impasse between phenomenological insight and metapsychological principle. The metapsychology of instinctual renunciation does not account for the phenomenon of the Jewish advance in intellectuality.

What is so characteristic of this passage – and of the argumentation and documentation of which it is the conclusion – is the consistency with which Freud pursues the inconsistency of adhering to metapsychological principles that are utterly inconsistent with his phenomenological insight. Freud rightfully sees that what he calls the Jewish advance in intellectuality cannot be understood in terms of his father-superego-leader analogy of instinctual renunciation. Even when he appears to retain that part of the analogy that involves dependence on the leader – which he has already undercut by showing that it is the Jewish people themselves who identify with the greatness of God, as his chosen people, and who are creative in producing leaders in the mold of Moses – he recognizes that the authority of the father (superego, leader, God) presupposes a standard of which it is not itself the origin. Patriarchal authority cannot be understood apart from the advance to patriarchal authority. (Freud could not be more Hegelian!) The authority of the father cannot itself be due to the authority of the father. Authority, we thus see, is as much end as beginning, as much effect as cause, as much consequence as antecedent. But, because he is not prepared to rethink his metapsychological principles, Freud falls back on the jejune rhetoric that things simply develop and advance – from sensuality to intellectuality – although he has just indicated that such development and advance are impossible outside of a *Wertmaßstab*: God, the covenant, the chosen people, revelation, the golden rule, Spinoza's concept of truth as its own standard. There can be no advance, no development – no history – unless there are advance and development both from and to a *Wertmaßstab*, both from freedom and to freedom, say. One cannot advance from slavery to freedom (and thus the Israelite slaves freed by Moses are, like him, the children of Abraham), for that begs the question of how slaves begin, unconscious of their freedom (slavery). The only advance and development – history – are from freedom (creation) through slavery (fall) to freedom (salvation). There can be no historical advance and development from the unconscious to consciousness, from internal (pleasure principle) to external (reality principle). What Kierkegaard calls the historical "moment" of coming into existence is the paradox whose priority is at one and the same time synthesis, both internal and external. The only advance and development – history – are from the unconscious through consciousness to the unconscious.

Let me then summarize, briefly and tentatively, in the following four points what it is that we find in Freud's baffled attempt to account metapsychologically for the phenomenological advance of what he calls Jewish intellectuality. First, there is utter conflict between phenomenology and metapsychology. Freud makes it clear that he has no (metapsychological) understanding of the phenomenology that he examines, but the resultant impasse does not lead him to rethink his metapsychology at base. Second, Freud's account of the Jewish advance in intellectuality involves a rejection of his account of the renunciation of instinct. This means that he is unable to account for the Jewish advance in intellectuality in terms of the father complex, with its attendant notions of the Oedipus complex (the castration complex) and the myth of the primal father and his murder. In other words, Freud's account of the Jewish advance in intellectuality does *not* fit his model of the origin of religion that he presents in terms of the *Analogie* with neurosis and the murder of the primal father, not to mention his claims about the Egyptian origin of both monotheism and its fervent expositor (if not founder) Moses. What is clear, then, is that the father complex does not account for the ancient Israelites and their Bible. Third, Freud has no way of accounting for history, for development and advance, except to say that things just develop and advance. Fourth, and last, what he calls "the advance in intellectuality"

(*Geistigkeit*) over sensuality is not an adequate categorization of the phenomenology that he describes. On the one hand, the dualism between intellectual (spiritual) and sensuous is not sufficient to capture the rich content of not only intellect (spirit) but also the characteristics which he ascribes, as we saw, to "great men" – decisiveness of thought, strength of will, energy of action, autonomy, independence, divine unconcern (which risks becoming ruthlessness). These are the qualities, surely, that describe the psyche of biblical men and women. On the other hand, the advance is not from sensuality to intellectuality but from their *a priori* synthesis to their *a priori* synthesis. (Kant and Hegel show that one does not advance from sensibility to understanding or from understanding to sensibility. Advance is made rationally, in good faith, when, and only when, sensibility and understanding are each willed as the prior synthesis of the other.)

Having shown that the Jewish advance in intellectuality cannot be understood in terms of the renunciation of instinct, Freud then goes on to recall that totemism, the originary religion, is constituted by three fundamental regulations involving instinctual renunciations. He divides the regulations into two prohibitions and one command: (1) the prohibition against harming or killing the totem (father); (2) the prohibition against incest, that is, exogamy ("renunciation of the passionately desired mothers and sisters in the horde"); and (3) "the granting of equal rights to all the members of the fraternal alliance – that is, restricting the inclination to violent rivalry among them." Although Freud notes that "in these regulations are to be seen the first beginnings of a moral and social order," he is careful to add that "it does not escape us that *two different motives are at work here*" (366–7ᵉ). The first two regulations – the taboos against parricide and incest – are prohibitions that, he says, "operate on the side of the father" by carrying out his will.[42] Freud observes that the third regulation, the command granting "equal rights to the allied brothers,"

disregards the father's will; it is justified by an appeal to the necessity for permanently maintaining *the new order* which succeeded the father's removal. Otherwise a relapse into the earlier state would have become inevitable. It is here that *social commands diverge from the others* [i.e., the prohibitions dependent upon the father's will] which, as we might say, are derived directly from religious connections. The essential part of this course of events is repeated in the abbreviated development of the human individual. Here, too, it is the authority of the child's parents – essentially, that of *his autocratic father*, threatening him with his power to punish [the castration complex] – which calls on him for a renunciation of instinct and which decides for him what is to be allowed and what forbidden ... [Society and superego, Freud continues, succeed parental authority.] It is still always the same thing – *instinctual renunciation under the pressure of the authority which replaces and prolongs the father.* (367ᵉ)

   This is yet another of those astonishing passages that reveals, once again, a fundamental contradiction in Freud's compulsive attempt to account for the Jewish advance in intellectuality. But here the split is not between phenomenology and metapsychology but within metapsychology itself and is due, I think, to the phenomenological pressure on his thought that Freud thus acknowledges, if only evasively. One notes with immediate suspicion a distinction between old prohibitions (the old religious order of the father) and the new command (the new social order of the brothers). But before pursuing that suspicion, it is important to remark on the presence of another jarring element in the passage under discussion. Here Freud asserts that it is the primal father who imposes the prohibitions against not only murder but also incest, while in *Totem and Taboo*, as we saw, he makes a point of explicitly indicating that it is the primal sons (as brothers), not the father, who impose the ban on incest on themselves. We may also note that the two passages[43] in *Moses and Monotheism* in which Freud summarizes the myth of the primal father are consistent with the version found in *Totem and Taboo*. It is not so much the disparate or contradictory content of Freud's metapsychology that counts here, as it is the fact that his metapsychology – the ultimate analogy for understanding the origin of monotheism – is inherently unstable (contradictory).
   What is most striking in the above passage is the clarity with which Freud carefully distinguishes between the "two different motives" separating the old (religious) prohibitions from the new (social) command, sons from brothers. As always, Freud is compelled to distinguish sharply between the relationship of fathers and sons and the relationship of brothers. In the passage before us he acknowledges a dramatic distinction between autocratic (patriarchal) "prohibition" – reflecting the idea in *Totem and Taboo* that prohibition is coextensive with desire – and fraternal "command" involving equal rights (desires) for all. He points out that the (old) revenge cycle of murder, initiated by the old order of the father's will, would simply repeat itself (compulsively) if it were not replaced by a different motive, that of a new order guaranteeing the equal rights of fraternity (solidarity). It is in the new order of command that one is, and I interpolate, first and last, (freely) brother or sister – a citizen of the democratic, general will – both before and after one is (necessarily) a child and (commonly) a parent. The origin, the beginning, the principle of the new order of society, of the new motive recognizing the equal rights of all brothers (and sisters), is not

281 Moses and Monotheism

patriarchal (or matriarchal) will but the general will (command) of all brothers (and sisters).

As Freud, typically, makes no attempt to account for the conflict that emerges between his phenomenology and his metapsychology, so here he simply allows the two versions of his metapsychology to stand. He does not (want to) see that it is not the old order of patriarchal autocracy but the new order – the new motive – of the brothers (and sisters) that is consistent with the origin of Jewish monotheism and the Jewish advance in intellectuality. The inconsistent elements that are central to the consistency with which Freud remains blind to his metapsychological inconsistency are stunning. I shall outline four of them. First, he provides no account of how the second, the new, social order (motive) – the command to be free! – would (or could) emerge from the old, religious order or prohibition. The new fraternal order simply "disregards the father's will." Second, Freud provides no account of how the old order, consisting of the two totemic taboos, would (or could) continue in light of the new order. Third, in claiming that this course of events is epitomized in the development of the (modern) individual child, what Freud, in fact, shows is that the child repeats the autocratic order of the father – consistent with the Oedipus complex (ultimately, the castration complex and its repetition of identification with the father['s penis]). The son becomes a man on the model of the father (and the daughter becomes a woman on the model of the father): identification with the father complex is given in the beginning. But Freud provides utterly no idea of how the son becomes a brother (or the daughter a sister). Where in the patriarchal order of the castration complex is to be found the new order, the new motive, the new beginning, the new principle? Where does it contain the new order commanding brothers and sisters to equal rights (desires)? Because castration is given complete in the metapsychology of both the primal father and the Oedipal father – the two basic versions of the father complex – there is no history, no development possible in Freud's metapsychology but only repetition compulsion, consistent with the pleasure pleasure, when revealed as the death instinct. Fourth, and last, Freud insists upon the centrality of the renunciation of instinct in the metapsychology of the father complex. Yet, what Freud shows us is that the Jewish advance in intellectuality cannot be accounted for in terms of the renunciation of instinct. Once again it is clear that the origin of Jewish monotheism cannot be understood on analogy with the father complex.

In summary, then, when Freud briefly takes up his old theme of totemism, he does not directly relate it to his discussion of the origin of the Jewish advance in intellectuality. Indeed, it unaccountably leads him to distinguish between the old, patriarchal order of prohibitions

282 Depth Psychology, Interpretation, and the Bible

(the totemic taboos) and the new, fraternal order commanding equal rights for all. But this distinction, while supporting his phenomenology, contradicts his metapsychology. Is this distinction the same as that between renunciation of instinct and the advance in intellectuality, between the castration complex involving the identification of children with the father and the free and equal rights of brothers and sisters? Can the new order motivating the sons and daughters as brothers and sisters – whose identification is not constituted in and through the father complex – be linked with the Jewish advance in intellectuality? The essential distinction that Freud makes between instinctual renunciation and the advance in intellectuality and between the old patriarchal order and the new fraternal order suggests that it can. We have also seen that he greatly qualifies Judaism as a father religion when he argues that it is not the creation of *der grosse Mann* (Moses), since many (brothers and sisters!) contribute to it, both in its beginning and in its development and advance. Freud is especially laudatory of the prophets who, in restoring and developing the heritage of Mosaic monotheism, denounce not only, however, ceremonial idolaters, to Freud's delight, but also, which he fails to mention, the Jewish father-kings, in the name of the lord and king of all, God the father. Indeed, in emphasizing the role that the ban on divine images plays in Judaism – and that he recognizes is patently more stringent in the Jewish than in the Egyptian tradition – Freud acknowledges that the great and mighty Jewish God has no analogy in individual father (or mother) figures. Freud knows that the commandment banning idols constitutes a revolution in the ancient Near East. But he does not acknowledge that the ban on idols, on any finite analogies, presupposes the equally revolutionary idea of Genesis. It is not God who is made in the (finite) image of fathers and mothers. Rather, it is men and women who are created in the (infinite) image of God. This is the alternative metaphor to which there is no alternative, the metaphor than which no greater or other can be ontologically imagined or thought. It is also the case, as we saw, that it is the Jewish people, not any particular father-figure (including Moses), to whom Freud imputes "a peculiar psychical aptitude."

Overall, Freud makes two things clear, I think. First, it is the close relationship that the Jews have with their great and mighty God that makes them feel exalted, superior, self-confident, chosen for a special destiny, and involved in the advance in intellectuality, for which there is no analogy in the father complex. Second, the Jews' relationship to God (the father who creates from nothing, from nothing that is naturally patriarchal or matriarchal) is not one that makes them slavishly and helplessly dependent on the father complex. (The father complex involves both the prohibition of tabooed, ambivalent desires in primitive religion and the renunciation of instinct in the modern castration complex.) Rather, it is precisely their relation to God that liberates the Jews from the father complex.

Freud is still not through with providing evidence that supports the idea that the Jewish advance in intellectuality involves the new order of brothers (and sisters) and not the old patriarchal order of the father complex. This further evidence involves the place of ethics within Judaism. Freud notes that

the religion which began with the prohibition against making an image of God develops more and more in the course of centuries into a religion of instinctual renunciations. [*sic*!] It is not that it would demand sexual *abstinence*; it is content with a marked restriction of sexual freedom. GOD, HOWEVER, BECOMES ENTIRELY REMOVED FROM SEXUALITY and elevated into the ideal of ethical perfection. But ethics is a limitation of instinct. The Prophets are never tired of asseverating that God requires nothing other from his people than a just and virtuous conduct of life – that is, ABSTENTION FROM EVERY INSTINCTUAL SATISFACTION WHICH IS STILL CONDEMNED AS VICIOUS BY OUR MORALITY TODAY AS WELL. And even the demand for belief in him seems to take a second place in comparison with the seriousness of these ethical requirements. (366ᵉ)

What Freud means when he states that "ethics is a limitation of instinct," given that God becomes the non-sexual (non-incestuous!) ideal of perfection, is not evident. For surely all instinct is limited: it depends how and why. Freud clarifies his meaning a little later on, however, when he observes that "a part of its [ethics'] precepts is justified rationally by the necessity for delimiting the rights of society as against the individual, the rights of the individual as against society and those of individuals as against one another." But he then remarks that what we may here call the other part of ethics possesses grandiose, mysterious, and mystical qualities owing "to its connection with religion, *its origin from the will of the father*" (370ᵉ).

These two passages, when taken together, are striking. The part of ethics that Freud considers rational (and modern) is clearly that which is consistent with prophetic Judaism, which is itself the heir of Mosaic religion, whose God is the source of all that truly characterizes the Jewish people. The part of ethics that is "religious" and has its origin in the will of the father is clearly that which is consistent with the primitive religion of the primal father. Judaism, with its God, is ethical and rational (modern) and patently not primitive, religious, or patriarchal. It is equally the case, I think, that the distinction that we saw Freud make between the old patriarchal order of totemic prohibition and the new fraternal order commanding equal rights is precisely that between "religious" ethics, stemming from the will of the father, and "rational" ethics, embodying Mosaic and prophetic Judaism. The advance in intellectuality cannot be understood on analogy with the renunciation of instinct as demanded by the patriarchal autocracy of either the primal father or the Oedipal father, identification with whom always involves the sons' (and the daughters') castration. What Freud clearly demonstrates, although the rhetoric of his metapsychology constantly belies it, is that Judaism is a religion not of the father but of "brothers" (and "sisters") who together share, as the chosen people, an intimate relationship with God whose grandeur they embody. The fact that Judaism cannot be understood on analogy with prior or primitive (including Egyptian) religion Freud indeed acknowledges when he writes that Judaism "reached – in doctrine and precept, at least – *ethical heights which had remained inaccessible to the other peoples of antiquity*. Many Jews regard this attainment of ethical heights as the second main characteristic and the second great achievement of their religion. The way in which it was *connected with the first one – the idea of a single god* – should be plain from our remarks" (383–4ᵉ).

It is important to note, however, that this passage on the unique phenomenology of the Jewish religion – both its God and its ethics – is embedded, typically, in a complex metapsychological context. Here Freud views Judaism both as the consequence of the primitive religion of patriarchy and as that whose consequence is Christianity, the religion of the son. Freud continues to argue that Judaism, as a father religion, is heir to the myth of the primal father; but he also advances the argument that Judaism gives birth to and is in some sense superseded by Christianity, whose son replaces the father. Yet Christian faith, since it reverts to the polytheism of traditional Egyptian religion, which, in its violent reaction against the monotheism of Akhenaten, had overturned it, truly embodies the return of religion as the repressed. Christianity, he says, is historically but not materially true. Do we not begin to suspect, however, that the tortured argumentation that Freud uses in order, first, to make Judaism independent of but dependent on primitive religion and, second, to make Christianity dependent on but independent of Judaism, yet also dependent on primitive religion, reflects his metapsychology? This argumentation is not consistent with his rich insight into Jewish character, the Jewish advance in intellectuality, and Jewish ethical life that results from his investigation into the origin of Jewish monotheism. Is it possible that what we shall find is that, just as Judaism is not the religion of the father, so Christianity is not the religion of the son and that, therefore, both express the golden rule of the covenant commanding the equal rights of all brothers and sisters?

Once again, the issues are intricate and fraught with complexity (controversy). They need to be carefully distinguished in order to be truly comprehended.

d Coda: The Religions of Father and Son

Freud claims that the ethical heights uniquely attained by the Jews in antiquity emerge out of a common background of ambivalence that, he writes, "is a part of the essence of the relation to the father: in the course of time the hostility which had once driven the sons into killing their admired and dreaded father could not fail to stir, too." Since the Jews have no way of atoning for murdering the father, for sinning against God, he continues, they possess a massive sense of guilt; and their bad conscience is kept alive by the prophets. Freud also remarks that the sense of guilt on the part of the Jews increases consistent with their bad fortune. However, instead of blaming God for what happens to them, they accept their guilt as punishment for not obeying his commandments.[44] Freud argues that, as the need on the part of the Jews to satisfy their sense of guilt constantly intensifies, they increasingly impose upon themselves ever stricter commandments. It is, however, the resultant increase in "moral asceticism" and in "instinctual renunciations" (*sic*!) that leads the Jews to embrace ethical ideas that, commensurate with the uniqueness of their God, are without parallel in antiquity, as we have already seen Freud indicate. But what interests us here is the fact that he then goes on to state that "these ethical ideas cannot, however, disavow their origin from the sense of guilt felt on account of a suppressed hostility to God. They possess the characteristic – uncompleted and incapable of completion – of obsessional neurotic reaction-formations; we can guess, too, that they serve the secret purposes of punishment" (383–4).

The confusion (elision) of ideas in this passage and thus the resultant evasion of seeing and making critical distinctions are massive. The confusion and the evasion stem, as always, from the conflation of metapsychology with phenomenology. The critical concepts under discussion here are guilt, ethics, and neurosis – all three, in my judgment, the creation of the Bible (of Judaism and thus also Christianity). But Freud fails to explain how guilt – responsibility before God and neighbour – leads not only to ethics, which, as we have seen, he calls rational, as distinct from the prohibitions imposed by the father's will, but also to neurosis. Further, he fails to explain how the fact that ethics is "uncompleted and incapable of completion" can provide the Jews with their exalted sense of self-regard, self-confidence, and superiority, with their sense of having taken on themselves the very grandeur of God.

Most blatant, however, is Freud's failure to explain how guilt, repeating the common ambivalence stemming from the murder of the primal father, can lead to ethical ideas that are without precedent in antiquity and that are also, as he himself points out, precisely those of modernity. As always, Freud tries to place the unique phenomenology of the Jews – their monotheism, intellectual advance, and ethics – within the metapsychology of the primal and Oedipal fathers. The ambiguous, often contradictory result constantly distorts his phenomenological insight. Nowhere is this more startlingly evident than in Freud's estimation (briefly tendered, it is true) of the relationship between Judaism and Christianity, always a difficult relationship to comprehend in the most favourable of circumstances and one that is further complicated and, indeed, severely distorted by Freud's metapsychology. Freud claims to find in the relationship between Judaism and Christianity the ultimate demonstration of the father complex. I call this demonstration the coda to *Moses and Monotheism* because it reveals the ultimate gap between the metapsychological and the phenomenological approaches that he takes to the origin of Jewish monotheism.

Up to now we have seen how unsuccessful Freud has been in his attempt to show that Judaism is both unique in the ancient world – while its ethical ideas underlie the rationality of modern social relations – yet the product of not only Egyptian monotheism but also the myth of the primal father. Now he proceeds to raise the question of how Christianity is related not only to its Jewish and its primitive backgrounds, on the one hand, but also to modernity, on the other. The results are profoundly disturbing. He suggests that Christianity, as the religion of the son, replaces Judaism as the religion of the father. He views Christian faith as the revenge of Akhenaten's successors against monotheism (and thus against Moses). It is salutary, indeed, that Freud raises the issue of Christian anti-Semitism.[45] But, although his discussion of the sources of anti-Semitism is suggestive, he fails to develop systematically the implications of the fact that anti-Semitism is unthinkable outside of the context of the Bible's revolutionary ideas: one God, one creation, one fall, one (chosen) people, one book, one truth, one ethical standard, one covenant. Freud knows that there is an unholy alliance between truth, moral (sexual?) fervour, and intolerance. But the fact that he is not able, in my judgment, to formulate adequately the relationship between Judaism and Christianity directly reflects the enormous pressure that his metapsychology exerts on his phenomenological insight.

Having argued that it is guilt, stemming from the murder of the primal father, that explains Jewish ethics, Freud now proceeds to discuss the further development of that guilty inheritance in Christianity.[46]

"The remainder of what returned from the tragic drama of the primal father was no longer reconcilable in any way with the religion of Moses," he writes. Freud claims that it was the general sense of guilt and depression, springing from the Jews and infecting the ancient world, that the Jew Saul of Tarsus – Paul – was able to capture, thanks to his religious genius.[47] It was Paul who realized the magnitude of the fact that the unhappiness of human beings results from their recognition that they have killed God, the father. "And it is entirely understandable," Freud observes, "that he could only grasp this piece of truth in the delusional disguise of the glad tidings: 'we are freed from all guilt since one of us has sacrificed his life to absolve us.'" Although Freud claims that this formula hides the fact that it is God who is killed, he adds that "a crime that had to be atoned by the sacrifice of a victim could only have been a murder. And the intermediate step between the delusion and the historical truth was provided by the assurance that the victim of the sacrifice had been God's son" (384). The result of Christ's sacrifice for the murder of the primal father is that the (Christian) liberating sense of redemption replaces the (Jewish) blissful sense of being chosen and that the unnameable crime is replaced by "original sin." Because the crime against God the father can only be atoned by the sacrifice of his son, who, guiltless, takes on the guilt of all people, Freud remarks, "it had to be a son, since it had been the murder of a father ... Judaism had been a religion of the father; Christianity became a religion of the son. The old God the Father fell back behind Christ; Christ, the Son, took his place, just as every son had hoped to do in primeval times" (330–2).[48]

But Freud is perplexed how it is that Christianity, while exposing, through the sacrifice of the son, the Jewish guilt lurking within the murder of the father, can be, at the same time, the heir to Judaism's advance in intellectuality. Immediately following the passage in which Freud says that he cannot explain why the Jewish people feel proud and exalted by their advance in intellectuality over sensuality – since the analogy with the renunciation of instinct is not applicable in this case – he adds: "It further happens later on that intellectuality itself is overpowered by the very puzzling emotional phenomenon of faith. Here we have the celebrated '*credo quia absurdum*,' and, once more, anyone who has succeeded in this regards it as a supreme achievement" (365).[49] The fact that Freud considers religious faith in the absurd to constitute the very basis of religion as illusory wish fulfilment is consistent with his contention that Christianity "did not maintain the high level in things of the mind to which Judaism had soared" (332). No longer strictly monotheist, Christianity takes over rituals and divine figures (idols) from polytheism. "It was as though Egypt was taking vengeance once more on the heirs of Akhenaten," Freud comments (385). His apparently final judgment on the religion of the son, which replaces the religion of the father, is harsh and unqualified. Because of the "superstitious, magical and mystical elements" that Christianity absorbs from primitive polytheism, it will "prove [to be] a severe inhibition upon the intellectual development of the next two thousand years" (333).[50]

According to Freud, then, Christianity advances (beyond) Jewish guilt with the revelation that only the innocent son can atone, by the sacrifice of his life, for the murder of the father, although it is by no means clear how the son can be innocent when all sons have inherited the wish to kill the father, even if they do not perform the deed.[51] Christian faith also regresses to the superstition of polytheism that Judaism had abandoned in its commitment to monotheism and its consequent advance in intellectuality. Although "the triumph of Christianity" over Judaism represents a new victory of the Egyptian priesthood "over Akhenaten's god," who is the Mosaic God, nevertheless, Freud adds, "in the history of religion – that is, as regards the return of the repressed – Christianity was an advance and from that time on the Jewish religion was to some extent a fossil" (333). In thus producing the most spectacular reversal in the whole of *Moses and Monotheism*, does Freud mean that Christianity, as the religion of the son, reveals the truth of the religion of the father (the father religion)? Does he mean to suggest that Christianity, as an advance in the return of repression, is truer to his metapsychology than (it is to) Judaism? Is Christianity the metapsychological truth of Jewish phenomenology? Is Christianity the truth of the father complex? If so, what a supreme irony that would be!

Freud initiates his discussion of how Christianity advances beyond Judaism "as regards the return of the repressed" by giving yet another version of why monotheism has such a deep and abiding impact on Judaism. Instead of "remembering" the murder of the primal father, for the Jews, he says, it was a case of "acting out" by repeating it in their murder of Moses, "as happens so often with neurotics during the work of analysis." (333) Assuming, as always, an analogy between primitive deed and modern wish (intention), Freud observes that the Jews, in disavowing their murderous action,

remained halted at the recognition of the great father and thus blocked their access to the point from which Paul was later to start his continuation of the primal history. It is scarcely a matter of indifference or of chance that the violent killing of another great man became the starting-point of Paul's new religious creation as well ... The killing of Moses by his Jewish people ... thus

becomes an indispensable part of our construction, an important link between
the forgotten event of primeval times and its later emergence in the form of the
monotheist religions ... Remorse for the murder of Moses provided the stimulus for the wishful fantasy of the Messiah, who was to return and lead his people to redemption and the promised world-dominion. If Moses was this first
Messiah, Christ became his substitute and successor, and Paul could exclaim to
the peoples with some historical justification: 'Look! The Messiah has really
come: he has been murdered before your eyes!' Then, too, there is a piece of
historical truth in Christ's resurrection, for he was the resurrected Moses and
behind him the returned primal father of the primitive horde, transfigured and,
as the son, put in the place of the father. (333–4)

It is no wonder, Freud observes further, that the Jews, in stubbornly
refusing to acknowledge the murder of the father, had to atone for it
heavily. The Christian reproach against the Jews that "You killed our
God" is, therefore, "true, if it is correctly translated. If it is brought
into relation with the history of religions, it runs: 'You will not *admit*
that you murdered God (the primal picture of God, the primal father,
and his later reincarnations).' There should be an addition declaring:
'We [Christians] did the same thing, to be sure, but we have *admitted*
it and since then we have been absolved.' Not all the reproaches with
which anti-Semitism persecutes the descendants of the Jewish people
can appeal to a similar justification" (334).

In the second to last paragraph of *Moses and Monotheism* Freud
reformulates what he understands to be the correct translation of the
reproach of Christians against the Jews for murdering their God as follows: "'They [the Jews] will not accept it as true that they murdered
God, whereas we [Christians] admit it and have been cleansed of that
guilt.' It is easy therefore to see how much truth lies behind this
reproach. A special inquiry would be called for to discover why it has
been impossible for the Jews to join in this foreword step which was
implied, in spite of all its distortions, by the admission of having murdered God. In a certain sense they have in that way taken a tragic load
of guilt on themselves; they have been made to pay heavy penance for
it" (386).

There is no alternative, I believe, to quoting Freud at length, for only
then are we in a position to appreciate fully the pressure that the
metapsychology of the father complex – here in the guise of the murder of the primal father – exerts on his thinking. It is simply astounding that he accounts for Christian anti-Semitism – Christians reproach
Jews for murdering God the father, and, although they also murdered
him, at least they admit it and so, unlike the Jews, are absolved of their
crime – on the basis that it correctly translates the history of religion

as the return of the repressed. One might wish to think that Freud in this way brilliantly achieves a double coup, eliminating Judaism along with Christianity. Such a wish (fulfilment) would proceed as follows. Freud eliminates the religion of Moses in the name of Christianity – for Christ is the messianic successor of Moses – and he eliminates the religion of Christ in the name of the myth of the primal father. While the Jews disavow the murder of the father and so remain "halted at the recognition of the great father," Christianity, in accepting the guilt for killing the father, fully represents the return of the repressed religious, whose essence is illusory wish fulfilment. Christianity is superior to Judaism precisely because it is more, that is, it is fully primitive, the true heir of the myth of the primal father. With such a wished-for coup, Freud would simply dispose of biblical religion altogether as illusory wish fulfilment.

But there are two reasons why such a renunciatory coup cannot represent Freud's intention or, at the least, the realization of that intention. First, it accounts neither for the high regard in which Freud holds his ancient Jewish forebears for their commitment to intellectual and ethical principles nor for his acknowledgment that the principles of prophetic ethics, as the very heart of Mosaic religion, are commensurate with modern social ethics. It also does not account for the fact that Freud is compelled to swerve from the metapsychology of the father complex when he acknowledges that what he calls the Jewish advance in intellectuality cannot be comprehended on the basis of the renunciation of instinct (as imposed by the father). Second, even if, in claiming to show that Christianity fulfils Judaism by explicitly acknowledging the return of the repressed murder of the primal father, Freud's intention were to dismiss both biblical religions as illusory wish fulfilment, his metapsychology would still remain at (as) the very heart of his thinking. He would still have to explain how the historical truth of religion – the return of the repressed religious as illusory wish fulfilment – could be revealed as material truth by psychoanalytic science, when the first principle of that science is itself illusory wish fulfilment.

The contradiction in which Freud finds himself – a contradiction that is fully revealed in his justification of Christian anti-Semitism as demonstrating the father complex to be the illusory truth of religion – is as follows. If biblical religion is true, then his metapsychology will be false. If his metapsychology is true, then biblical religion will be false. While it is the first formulation that accurately represents the situation, in my judgment, it will doubtless appear that it is the second formulation that is consistent with the position not only of Freud but also of all those who, like Freud, believe that modern science succeeds (replaces) primitive religion. But the problem that has to be faced is that adherence to the first formulation – biblical religion (as exposed by Freud) is true, while Freudian metapsychology is false – entails holding the position that biblical religion is true both metapsychologically (ontologically) and phenomenologically (psychologically). Adherence to the second formulation, however, involves maintaining a dualism between metapsychology and phenomenology, between truth and history, between the primitive and the modern, between desire (the pleasure principle) and reality (science). In other words, the truth of Freud's metapsychology depends on religion's being both true and false – historically true but materially false – simultaneously. But it is precisely the relationship between truth and falsehood that his metapsychology itself can never sort out, given that its first principle is that of illusion (whose origin is the primal violence of murder). The problem that Freud never faces, as we saw in the previous section, is that, once science surrenders both the primordial wishes of humanity and historical recollection to religious illusion, then science (as metapsychology) has no alternative to founding itself on the illusion of history as its first principle. It is the religious explanation – the father complex – that is true precisely because it is historically illusory (true yet false). The fact that the religious explanation is scientific and that the scientific explanation is religious – each at once indistinguishably (contradictorily) true and false – represents the ultimate *cul de sac* of the father complex as Freud's metapsychological beginning.

Freud's defense of Christian anti-Semitism is a defense of the father complex; and his defense of the father complex results in his defense of anti-Semitism. In the end, metapsychology triumphs over phenomenology, although Freud shows that, in the beginning, Jewish character and the Jewish advance in intellectuality involve the ethical command granting equal rights to brothers (and sisters) over fathers and sons. The only way to overcome – to resist, absolutely, without denial or repression – the metapsychology of the father complex and its denouement in Christian anti-Semitism is to see that Judaism is not the religion of the father and that Christianity is not the religion of the son. The first is not patriarchal, and the second is not filial; the first is not old, and the second is not new; the first is not first, and the second is not second. Both are old and new. Both are first and last. Both represent the "new" motive and the "new" order of equal rights, at once divine and ethical, compared to the "old" patriarchal order of totemic primitivism, in which desire on the part of the sons is prohibition. Judaism and Christianity are each – distinctively, differently, paradoxically, undecidably, uniquely, and universally – the religion of the covenant whose golden rule expresses the dialectic of self and desire.

e Conclusion: The Phenomenological Truth of Metapsychology

It is now time to turn back from the extraordinary denouement of *Moses and Monotheism* in the metapsychological triumph of the father complex as the justification of Christian anti-Semitism to consider the work as a whole. We see that it is shaped, as are all of Freud's works, by the enormous tension between metapsychological contradiction and phenomenological insight. But here the tension reaches new heights. Although Freud had reflected on primitive religion and had attacked popular Christianity in earlier works, now, by going to the foundation of his own Jewish heritage in *Moses and Monotheism*, he probes the foundational experience of the whole of modern (world) civilization. Not only does he bring to bear upon Judaism the full play of his metapsychological doctrine – both the myth of the primal father and the traumatic theory of neurosis (the castration complex), including the return of the repressed. But, at the same time, he also exposes the fundamental principles of his metapsychology to what I call the dialectic of biblical critique. As I emphasize in this study, what Freud never sees – following the dialectic of the golden rule and its principle of reciprocity – is that that which explains is subject to that which it explains. That by which we explain is itself the subject of explanation. But it is precisely this test, the test conducted daily in the analytic situation, that the father complex fails. The father complex claims to explain all without itself being subject to the explanation of all. It is precisely this autocracy that explains why the father, erstwhile son, is no less subject to murder (symbolic castration) at the hands of the sons than the sons, putative fathers, are subject to castration (symbolic murder) at the hands of the father. The explanatory principle of reciprocity is embodied not in the mythology of the father-son complex but in the historical relationship of brothers and sisters, what the Bible views as the covenant and Rousseau as the general will.

Moses and Monotheism thus divides into two structural parts – not that they are easy to discern, given the fitful construction of the whole – metapsychology and phenomenology, with a coda (repeated) on the metapsychological superiority of Christianity to the phenomenological repression of the father complex in Judaism. With regard to his claim that Judaism (together with Christianity) compulsively repeats the murder of the primal father, Freud openly acknowledges that for a long time he has accepted, as a consequence of his metapsychology of the father complex, the inheritance of acquired characteristics. Thus he has been compelled to abandon Darwinian biology, even as he appeals to animal instinct in support of his idea of the archaic heritage of phylogenesis. The fact that Freud has no alternative to the inheritance of acquired characteristics to explain the transmission of cultural values from father to son, from past to present is also reflected in his view of the unconscious as "a collective, universal property of mankind," even as he claims to dismiss the (Jungian) idea of the collective unconscious.

Phylogenesis, together with the concept of the unconscious as unaware of itself in the beginning as unconscious, can explain the contradictory ambivalence of totemic prohibition. But, because it cannot explain the historical difference between primitive prohibition and modern (or biblical) desire commanding equal rights between brothers (and sisters), Freud finds himself compelled to shore up phylogenesis with *die Analogie*. He attempts to establish an analogy between the return of the repressed as typical of religious phenomena – both primitive and modern – and the return of the repressed in the modern Oedipal child. We had already seen the analogy between primitive and modern in *Totem and Taboo* founder on the "psychological difference" between (primitive) taboo as uninhibited and (modern) neurosis as inhibited, even as Freud indulges in incredibly loose (evasive) distinctions between fact (action) and wish or intention (thought). Now we see the revenge that (Egyptian) phylogenesis exacts on (biblical) phenomenology! Freud cannot explain how what is originally acquired, or external, becomes inherited, or internal, how repeated egos turn into the id. Equally, he cannot explain how, in the Oedipal model centred on the castration complex, itself the repetition of identification with the father('s penis), the son, who is subject to the father complex (autocracy), is anything but a repetition of the father complex. In other words, in attempting to force biblical religion into the mythical mold of the primal father, Freud finds himself compelled to embrace the most extreme theory of phylogenesis – the inheritance of acquired characteristics – without the support of either biology or history. Further, the need to maintain "the Analogy" between primitive, infantile, and neurotic also compels him to defend the hardened doctrine of the Oedipus complex as the castration complex. The ambivalent relation on the part of the son to the father – both identification with and opposition to the father('s penis) – eliminates any concept of history as the dialectic of self and desire when founded on the reciprocal relations of the golden rule.

What is so deeply ironic about Freud's attempt to explain biblical phenomenology on the basis of his patriarchal metapsychology is that it is precisely the ontological values implied by and presupposed in biblical values that underlie and support his insight into the dynamics of the modern (because biblical) Oedipal family. But, typically modern, Freud refuses to see what he sees, to *believe* what he sees. Instead of

allowing the confrontation with the Bible to liberate him from a pseudo-biology and a pseudo-history, he reconfirms his metapsychological
commitment to the father complex. The deepest root of the father complex is doubtless the pleasure principle that Freud himself reveals to be
the inherent tendency to restore an earlier state of things, the death
instinct of originary violence: the murder of the primal father. The ultimate result of Freud's refusal to see that it is biblical ontology that
"explains" modern phenomenology is his defense of the father complex in the name of Christian anti-Semitism. This represents the ultimate refusal on Freud's part to see the phenomenology of biblical
Judaism as the deconstruction, for all time, of the father complex and
of its metapsychological beginning in the autocracy of the death
instinct.

What is always so extraordinary about Freud is that, in developing
a rich phenomenology, he openly acknowledges that it contradicts, that
it cannot be explained by, the metapsychology of the father complex.
But he lets the contradiction stand without raising the question of
whether his phenomenological data do not compel him to reformulate
his metapsychological principles. He argues that the origin of Jewish
monotheism is to be explained on the basis of its background in Egyptian imperialism and the murder of the primal father. But what he
demonstrates is that the founding elements of Jewish character and of
the Jewish advance in intellectuality cannot be accounted for on the
basis of the father complex with its imposition of the renunciation of
instinct. Not only is his construction of ancient Israelite history no less
vulnerable to the charge of tendentiousness than is the biblical account
against which he makes the same charge, but he explicitly shows that
Jewish character embodies Jewish theology. He indicates that the self-
confidence, the self-regard, and the sense of superiority that characterize the ancient Israelites stem from their self-conception as the chosen
people who enjoy an intimate relationship with their great and mighty
God. This God they (like Job) do not abandon even when he does not
appear to bring them good fortune.

Freud subscribes to the common view that it is historically incongruous and consequently not psychologically probable that a great and
universal God would be born into the humble presence of a lowly and
insignificant people like the Jews. Although this view is consistent with
the metapsychology of the father complex, according to which all people, like the Oedipal child, are helpless, weak, dependent, and long for
a strong, autocratic father figure, what he shows us, rather, is a people
who are strong, proud, and independent. The relationship that the
ancient Israelites enjoy with the God who liberates them from slavery
(God could be called the narrative principle of the Jews) is covenantal.

This is in stark contrast with the hierarchical, master-slave relationships that characterize both the theology and the politics of all other peoples in the ancient world (including the Greeks). Notwithstanding a rhetoric and a metapsychology that are patriarchal, Freud's description of the Jews results in a characterology that utterly contradicts the father complex. Ultimately, he even downplays the role of (the Egyptian) Moses in the historical formation of the Jews, as he imputes their success in bearing the great burdens of Mosaic religion to their "peculiar psychical attitude," that is, to their capacity to create their own prophetic leaders.

When Freud, in attempting to account for what he calls the Jewish advance in intellectuality, eschews all analogy with the renunciation of instinct, he throws into grave doubt the efficacy, indeed, the validity of the Oedipus or the castration complex. He states expressly that he cannot explain – on the basis of the father complex – why the Jews feel proud and exalted by every intellectual advance. None of the analogies (or processes) suggesting similar intellectual or spiritual achievement fits the Jewish case, not even the so-called advance of paternity (scientific reasoning) over maternity (sensuality). Freud indicates that the advance in intellectuality appears to presuppose both "a definite standard of value" and "some other person or agency which maintains it." He never says directly what he thinks this standard of value or who he thinks this person or agency is, although it is clear, I think, that they cannot be paternal. For, as he himself correctly points out, the advance of patriarchy (understanding) over matriarchy (sensibility) – that is, the relationship (as distinct from the opposition) between understanding and sensibility – presupposes a standard of value and some "other" person or agency who maintains it. Patriarchy is thus dependent on a standard of value and on some other person or agency that maintains that standard for its own advance. Because patriarchy is not the source of that advance, it is not the source of either the standard of value or the person or agency that maintains the standard. Although, to repeat, Freud does not name the standard of value and its authority (the person or agency) that the advance in intellectuality presupposes, surely they can be none other than God and the Jewish people. The standard of value and the person or agency that maintains it are identical. They constitute (and are constituted by) the covenant, truth as its own *index* (authority). Indeed, it is precisely the covenantal relationship that Freud discovers when he returns, yet again, to totemic religion only to distinguish sharply between the old totemic prohibitions of patriarchal will and the new order and the new motive commanding the equal rights of brothers (and sisters).

The fact that Jewish character and the Jewish advance in intellectuality are fraternal (and sororal) and not patriarchal is finally confirmed in the ethical commitment to the reciprocal relationship between individual(s) and community, which, as Freud indicates, is no less modern than it is biblical. When he says, rather tendentiously, that this part of ethics is rational and not religious, we can interpret his statement to mean that it is biblical (both rational and religious) and not primitive (neither rational nor religious).

Although Freud recognizes that what he calls the Jewish advance in intellectuality and the Jewish commitment to rational ethics together presuppose biblical theology, he is still not prepared to reconsider the metapsychology of the father complex. It is yet more striking that he is even willing to sacrifice the profundity of his insight into Jewish phenomenology to that metapsychology. He refuses to allow the perplexing relationship between Judaism and Christianity to unsettle him sufficiently to ask if these great biblical religions cannot be more properly comprehended on the terms of the new fraternal (and sororal) order of rational ethics and equal rights that he envisages. Instead, he simply invokes the father complex in order to reimpose the conventional misconceptions of father religion on Judaism and of son religion on Christianity. He fails to see, therefore, that fundamental concepts of the Bible like covenant and golden rule are not constituted by the natural relationship of father and son, except when that relationship, like that of shepherd and sheep, is understood metaphorically. But covenant and golden rule are expressed in and through the relational images of husband and wife, bride and groom, two lovers – all wonderful biblical images. Here I stress brothers (and sisters), for such is the image profoundly conjured up by Freud, having been made famous not only by Paul but also by French and socialist revolutionaries. The fraternal (and sororal) relationship bears the meaning of solidarity that is radically subversive of all hierarchical relationships that are rationalized in terms of nature, the natural family, or pseudo-biology.

It is, therefore, fascinating to see what happens when Freud conjures up the "paternal characteristics" of "the great man," the father figure for whom, he says, the masses long, before whom they bow down, and by whom they are ruled. What he actually depicts, however, fits not his metapsychological description of patriarchy but his phenomenological description of biblical character (male and female): decisiveness of thought, strength of will, energy of action, autonomy, independence, and divine unconcern (which threatens to grow into ruthlessness). None of these characteristics is, in my judgment, to be found outside the biblical, that is, the modern, world. While, on the one hand, they are certainly not found in the Socratic dialogues of Plato, the Oedipus plays of Sophocles, or the Trobrianders as described by Malinowski and Spiro, on the other hand, they typify with equal certainly the figures who both constitute the world of Shakespeare, *Paradise Lost* (Adam and Eve but also, above all, the fallen reader), and Dostoevsky and are presupposed by the worlds of Spinoza, Kant, Hegel, Kierkegaard, and Nietzsche. The characteristics that Freud ascribes to the father figure are not the product of helpless, slavish, fearful dependence on the father complex, which they would have to be, since all fathers are sons of autocratic fathers (except for the contradictory primal father). The characteristics that Freud ascribes to the father figure belong, rather, to the new order of brothers (and sisters). The fact that all fathers are, first, slavish sons and all sons are, at last, enslaving fathers is consistent with the castration complex. In contrast, brothers and sisters are, like God, in whose image they are created, decisive in thought, strong of will, actively energetic, autonomous, independent, and divinely unconcerned (as this last quality constantly threatens to grow into ruthless, human unconcern). We may also recall that Freud writes (and repeats) that Moses stoops from the heights of Egyptian imperialism to the lowly world of the poor Jewish slaves. But what he in fact shows, as he deconstructs the myth of *der grosse Mann*, is that Judaism is the creation of not one but many contributions, above all, of the "peculiar psychical aptitude" of the people of Israel. What is peculiarly apt about the psychology of the ancient Jews, as Freud describes them, is that it is the creation precisely of those characteristics that he imputes to "the big man."

In ascribing a psychology to the patriarchal figure that characterizes not primitive paternalism but the biblical world of fraternal (and sororal) relations, Freud shows that it is impossible to grasp the double-edged knife of psychology without yourself being wounded by it. He claims that his technique of using only the material that suits him and "of putting the different pieces together *in accordance with psychological probability*" can be justified, not by the certainty that he will arrive at the truth, but by "*an appeal to the work's outcome*" (351e). But what is the work's outcome, when the conscious ego is not the master of its own unconscious, overdetermined, *unheimlich* labour?[52] The outcome of a work is not (to be found in) its final sentence, paragraph, or chapter but rather (in) the whole of its cumulative impact, from beginning to end. Indeed, the beginning of a work's outcome is found in its historical relationships, both past and present; and the end of a work's outcome is found in its historical relationships, both future and present. Freud points out about construction in the analytic situation, as we saw, that the past is rendered eternally uncertain by the complete result that the analysand constructs in and through the future. One supposes that he would hold that the "outcome" of *Moses and Monotheism* is the demonstration that the origin of Jewish monotheism is explained by the metapsychology of the father complex in both its mythical and its Oedipal versions. But such an outcome would mean that the religious explanation of the father complex was true, which is a conclusion consistent with his justification of Christian anti-Semitism but hardly the outcome, it seems, that Freud had in mind!

When Freud appeals to the work's outcome as according with "psychological probability," the same problem emerges. The psychological probability that the origin of biblical monotheism can be understood on the basis of an Egyptian forebear and of the originary myth of the primal father turns out to be so contradictory that it is simply false. Indeed, the high degree of "psychological probability" (truth) with which Freud describes the character of the ancient Israelites and their advance in intellectuality (spirituality) is a direct reflection of the God by whom they are chosen and with whose grandeur they identify. When I wrote earlier how important it is to see that the argument advanced by Freud in *Moses and Monotheism* cannot be refuted by facts alone, I wanted to indicate my agreement with him that what counts is the construction and its outcome. His procedure (the construction) and his criterion (the outcome) are profoundly psychological. What is so astounding, consequently, is that, although his procedure and his criterion reveal his metapsychology to be false psychologically, he continuously subverts his psychological insight in the name of his metapsychology. When, however, we agree with Freud's procedure and criterion and appeal to the work's outcome, to its construction "in accordance with psychological probability," we discover the following: (1) his phenomenological description of the ancient Israelites is psychologically probable (true); (2) this psychology shows his metapsychology to be psychologically improbable (false); and (3) the only metapsychology that is true to that psychology is one that is consistent with biblical ontology and thus creative of the rational ethics whose command of equal rights, fraternal and sororal, is the golden rule. Otherwise, the outcome is the religious truth of the father complex justified as Christian anti-Semitism.

In our final chapter we shall examine the implications of the ontology of reciprocal explanation for biblical religion, the improbable truth that biblical religion is no less subject to psychoanalytic explanation than psychoanalysis is subject to religious explanation. For surely Freud is right when he observes in his lecture on *Weltanschauung* that *truth* tolerates no exceptions, "that it admits of no compromises or limitations, that research regards every sphere of human activity as belonging to it, and that it must be relentlessly critical if any other power tries to take over any part of it" (195). What, however, is truth? What is research (*Forschung*)? Truth is research whose ontological demonstration reveals the explanatory reciprocity of phenomenology and metapsychology. When phenomenology does not demonstrate itself to be its own metapsychology and when metapsychology does not demonstrate itself to be its own phenomenology, then truth is not shown to be ruthlessly – lovingly – analytic. What Freud demonstrates in and through *Moses and Monotheism* is that it is only insofar as truth accords with Jewish monotheism that research in depth psychology has any probability. But it is equally the case that it is only insofar as truth accords with depth psychology that research in Jewish monotheism has any probability. The ontological principle that truth is its own reciprocal standard and agency holds that neither theological explanation nor psychological explanation can be true except insofar as both are true.

IV CONCLUSION

Moses and Monotheism provides a dramatic conclusion not only to Freud's writings on religion, including *The Future of an Illusion* and the lecture on *Weltanschauung*, not to mention *Totem and Taboo*, but also to his career, as a whole. It is fitting that, in making religion the illusory fulfilment of "the oldest, strongest, and most urgent wishes" of humankind, Freud returns in the end to his beginning in religion, to the very beginning of civilization. In the beginning is the father, both primal and Oedipal, whose rule over the helpless, dependent, and fearful sons, primal and modern, fulfils the illusory wish of religion for providential consolation. The father complex, as the very essence of religious illusion, constitutes the center of Freud's metapsychology, of, that is, his explanatory principles of psychoanalysis as a depth psychology. The myth of the primal father supplies the basis of his phylogenetic model of the archaic heritage of humankind, the inheritance of acquired characteristics. The castration complex, centred in identification with the father('s penis) and leading to the superego, constitutes the core of the Oedipus complex and thus of Freud's psychical model of ego, id, and superego (succeeding his earlier model of consciousness, the preconscious, and the unconscious). Where the primal father, whose heir is the Oedipal father, was, there the primal son, whose heir is the modern son, shall be.

But it is precisely how the father becomes the son and how the son becomes the father that Freud never explains and is never able to explain, given the metapsychology of the father complex. The choices are comparison with external reality, that is, murder (of the father), and the coherence of internal reality, that is, identification (with the father['s penis]). Why the late works that Freud devotes to religion, above all, *Moses and Monotheism*, are so fascinating is that they bring out – compulsively and repetitively – the contradictions that are inherent in his metapsychology. It's as if Freud, like the guilty murderer, cannot help returning to the primal scene and repeating it yet once again. It's as if Freud, like Lady Macbeth, obsessively washes his sinful hands as he remains fixated on and unable to escape from the contradictions of the primal crime.

Although Shakespeare's plays, in plumbing the depths of the family romance – the Oedipal drama – make the relations of parents and children central to dramatic revelation, what they envision as their interpretive centre is not the father complex but the relationships of love and justice, to whose demands father and mother figures must accede, as Claudius, Gertrude, Lear, Angelo (and even his Duke), not to mention Prospero, find. The paradox of *Hamlet* is that the oath of revenge that the prince swears – "adieu, adieu, remember me" – contains his self-conscious recognition that his model of thought and action is not the heroic father complex. He conjures up ancient heroes only to distinguish himself from them: Pyrrhus (over whose slaughter of father Priam the player openly weeps, while Hamlet finds that he must ironically contain, without outward show, his profound distress over the reality of the Danish court as revealed to him by his ghostly father) and Alexander and Caesar (whom Hamlet, in the Graveyard scene, reduces to the common dust of humanity, to the scandal of Horatio). Hamlet also finds that his contemporaries do not provide him with a heroic model of thoughtful, active revenge: Laertes, Fortinbras, and finally also Horatio (his devoted friend, whose heroic gesture at the end of the play, to die like an antique Roman, Hamlet, dying, rejects with the demand that he live "like a man"). Even Ophelia, although she sees through her brother's patronizing advice to resist the blandishments of Hamlet, is unable to escape the seductive power of the father complex embodied in her father and the king and queen. But Hamlet resists, resolutely (as he mocks himself over how conscience, indeed, makes one appear cowardly before oneself, let alone, before others), the compulsion and the rhetoric of the father complex. It is truth and justice, not the honour of fathers (and sons), that move Hamlet. It is Laertes, rather, who is moved to revenge by the father complex ("to thine own self be true," his father instructs him), the son whose father is also killed and the foil by whom and from whom Hamlet is altogether distinguished. (We find the same distinction between the two sons in *Henry IV*, Part I – Prince Hal and Hotspur – and in *King Lear* – Edgar and Edmond, not to mention between Cordelia and her two sisters.)

Shakespeare remains the great playwright he is among the public, both popular and learned, because his plays represent a massive, penetrating, and relentless deconstruction of the father complex, from beginning to end.[53] He conjures up the father complex, with all its powers of seduction, fascination, and compulsion, both sexual and political, and thus embodying our most primitive, selfish, and unselfreflexive feelings, only to subject it to the most sustained, penetrating critique. Like all of our great artists and thinkers, Shakespeare knows that the father complex is the most powerful source of idolatry in the (biblical) tradition of modernity. The father (together with the mother) touches upon chords that resonate so deeply within us – as children, parents, subjects, lovers – involving hate, love, revenge, anger, frustration, dependence, freedom, rivalry, sexual desire, the impulse to dominate and to be dominated by others. But Shakespeare's vision is that of *caritas* – love that is sexual, social, personal, familial, parental, human, divine, fraternal, sororal – as it involves and expresses forgiveness, reconciliation, and reciprocity: grace – graciousness, gratification, gratitude, gratuity, gratulation. Shakespeare knows that it is *caritas*, insofar as it is at once unique and universal, that provides the eternal critique of the father complex, together with its sexual and social autocracies. Love constitutes the beginning and end, the subject and object, the content and form of his plays, even in his extraordinary Roman and Greek plays, above all, *Troilus and Cressida*, from which *caritas* is absent, because resisted, denied, repressed, and expelled.

Unlike Shakespeare, Freud fails to see that it is not the father complex that constitutes the structure of modern society. Indeed, what he does not see is that it is precisely the father complex, together with the interminable legions (all hydra-headed) of its attendant dualisms, that, from beginning to end, is the common object of the modern critique of pure reason, regardless of whether reason is comprehended as artistic, sexual, political, philosophical, scientific, religious, social, or the like. In particular, Freud does not see that the Bible (both Jewish and Christian), as the font of modernity, embodies the deconstruction of the father complex, from the story of creation *ex nihilo* (creation is from nothing that is naturally patriarchal or matriarchal) through the story of the "fall" (the fall from the paradise of natural hierarchies) to the golden rule, whose fundamental relationships are those of self and others – brothers and sisters, lovers, friends, the general will of Rousseau, but not of natural fathers and sons (parents and children). The Bible, with its ontology of creation *ex nihilo*, is, so far as I can figure it out, the unique story that universally holds that history does not constitute and is not constituted by the father complex, the natural relations of fathers and sons (parents and children). Indeed, precisely because the

Bible views the father complex as the very substance of idolatry, the Bible and its traditions constantly fall into the idolatry of reading the relationships of the golden rule as those of fathers and sons (mothers and daughters). The father complex is so potent a source of idolatry precisely because it touches all of us so deeply. We are all children, most of us are natural parents, and all of us are putative parents (authorities) vis-à-vis others in our myriad relationships.

From the beginning of this study I have emphasized the acute tension in Freud between his phenomenological insight and his metapsychology that falsifies that insight. In *Moses and Monotheism* the conflict between the phenomenological concept that the ancient Israelites, as depicted in the Bible, have of themselves, thanks to the unique relationship that they enjoy with their God, and the metapsychology of the father complex is brought to a new height. What Freud fails to see is that, in analyzing the roots of his own critical (interpretive) principles, it is the father complex that is deconstructed by the biblical concept of reality – the golden rule – and not the Bible that is deconstructed in the name of the father complex. The evidence that Freudian metapsychology, centred on the father complex, is exposed as utterly contradictory is of two general kinds. The first is the phenomenology of the ancient Jews that Freud so intelligently depicts. The second is the spectacular reversals that Freudian metapsychology is compelled to undergo as it attempts to explain how we begin in the illusory wish fulfilments of religion and how in the end the return of the repressed religious has become the scientific explanation of psychoanalysis. The impasse that Freud encounters is that he cannot explain how science, when its first principle is illusory, is distinguishable from that illusion in the end. He comes close to acknowledging in *The Future of an Illusion* but ultimately does not comprehend that the demonstration by psychoanalysis that human beings, in the beginning, are subject to illusory wish fulfilments can just as easily be used against psychoanalysis by the religious opponent as by the psychoanalyst against religion. Indeed, what he actually shows is that the psychoanalytic defender of the father complex demonstrates, in the end, that it is the religious explanation of the father complex that, in the beginning, is true.

There is nothing in Freud's cogent and intelligent description of Jewish character, the Jewish advance in intellectuality, and the Jewish commitment to ethics that can be explained on the basis of the father complex, as he systematically demonstrates. But it is also the case that the rich phenomenology of Jewish attitudes that Freud depicts shows the entire basis of patriarchal metapsychology to be utterly false, as Freud consistently evades acknowledging, even though this is the precise result of his demonstration. It cannot be repeated too often that Freud is uncanny in his willingness, in his ability, to see clearly, without immediately subjecting his insight to the distortions of his metapsychology. He makes patent that the content of Jewish character, mind, and ethics – all intimately related, he knows, to the Jews' identification with their God – is not explicable, notwithstanding his rhetoric, on the basis of the father complex: helpless longing for and dependence on the father figure (God).

What Freud, like most of his predecessors and successors, does not see, however, is that the Bible demands that we reconfigure, reimagine, and reconstitute our fundamental relationships on the basis of the covenant and the golden rule. The Bible rejects the father complex with its attendant notions of phylogenetic heritage and identification with the father leading to the castration complex and the repudiation of femininity – the split between man and woman, between possession of the penis (lack of desire) and desire of the penis (lack of possession). In a radical articulation of the biblical critique of the father complex, Jesus says that one has to hate one's father and mother, one's natural relations, one's own friends and even one's natural self and follow him into the covenantal relationship of the golden rule. The Bible shows – indeed, this is precisely what Freud reveals in his reading of biblical history – that it recognizes no paternal antecedents: it is not the natural son of an interminable natural chain. Rather, the Bible begins, *ex nihilo*, with Abraham, who renounces his natural parents in the name of his new God, who is unlike all other gods in having neither parents nor children but only a chosen people. The brothers and sisters of the covenant are created in the infinite (non-natural) image of God as human beings, as men and women, not as primal fathers and mothers. God is not created in the natural image of fathers and mothers, nor is his image to be engraved in the tradition of the gentile idols, imitating natural fathers and mothers. It is also the case that, in renouncing all fathers (parents), the Bible renounces all sons (children), except in the metaphoric sense that God is the father of all and that the Israelite people are his children. But these are children, as Freud knows, like no other children; for, above all, they are called the children of promise, the chosen people who are commanded to choose life – the life of spirit – and not death (the death of nature). This does not mean that men and women do not naturally die, for the Bible is without a concept of (natural) immortality (of the soul); but it is precisely the acknowledgment of (natural) death that means that men and women do not live by bread alone but, rather, by the eternal spirit of their creative God, by the covenant, whose golden rule of relationship involves a communal life of love, justice, freedom, sacrifice, and forgiveness.

The Bible demands that the natural relationships of father and son be transformed into, be reconfigured as, the covenantal relationship of the golden rule – what Freud calls the new order commanding equal rights between brothers (and sisters). It also demands that the honour due to father and mother, and to children, be subject to the commandment that there be no other gods before God, that God be the standard of justice and truth to which all fathers and mothers, together with their sons and daughters, are subject. What Freud, for all his phenomenological insight into Judaism, fails to recognize, then, is that the Bible itself cannot be placed within a natural chain of paternal transmission. There is nothing prior to the Bible, and there is nothing posterior to the Bible; for all (its) creation is from nothing. The Bible is not the heir of primitivism, and it is not primitive compared with modern developments. The Bible is not religious when compared with what is modern, scientific, philosophical, literary, or secular. It is true that the Bible is not modern as Rousseau is modern, or scientific as Darwin is scientific, or philosophic as Kant is philosophic, or literary as Shakespeare is literary, or secular as Freud is secular. But with its concept of the human and the divine, of their relationship, as covenantal, the Bible contains all that is rational and faithful, secular and religious, literary and philosophical. It deconstructs all the hierarchical (natural) dualisms of our life from the beginning unto the end.

Freud recognizes the intimate relationship between the Jewish God, on the one hand, and Jewish character, Jewish mind (the advance in intellectuality), and Jewish ethics, on the other. But he utterly refuses to see that it is precisely this relationship, the relationship between divine and the human, which demands that we reconfigure the relationship between internal and external, beginning and end, unconscious and consciousness, id and ego, and pleasure principle and reality principle. These dualisms are to be rendered dialectical – the relationship of self and desire as constituted in and through the golden rule.

We saw in earlier chapters that, with regard to the pleasure principle, the unconscious, the Oedipus complex, and the primal father, the phenomenological insight of Freud is severely compromised by his metapsychological commitments. But what I emphasize here is that the conflict between phenomenology and metapsychology becomes especially evident in the context of his analysis of religion. It is richly ironic that it is, above all, religion – biblical religion – that reveals Freud's metapsychology to be illusionary when it is the basic claim of his metapsychology that it is religion that represents the originary illusion of wish fulfilment. But, as I have shown, Freud fails to realize that no analysis can ever advance beyond its beginning – its origins, roots, principles, foundations, grounds – except in terms of that beginning.

He fails to recognize that how we conceive of our beginning is precisely the end that we are destined to attain. It is thus even more ironic that psychoanalysis, as the study of origins, as the study which shows that we are compelled, eternally – historically – to repeat our origins, thus repeats its own religious origins as repressed, obsessively and compulsively.

In positing the beginning in illusion Freud can never explain how the first principle of science is illusion, just as he cannot explain how the first principle of reality is the illusory pleasure principle. It is equally the case that he cannot explain how the command not to murder your neighbour – the golden rule – can be based on the principal murder of the primal father. It is little wonder, then, that Freud is constantly reversed by his beginning. Indeed, the wonder is that, ultimately, it is psychoanalysis itself, when understood metapsychologically (if not phenomenologically or therapeutically), that represents the return of the repressed religious. The explanation of religion is true, Freud is compelled to admit; but it is true only because it remains illusory, repressed, and distorted, the historical but not the material truth. But does not the metapsychological science of psychoanalysis itself duplicate the illusory beginning in reality when it claims that it possesses the criterion of truth in correspondence with external reality? What, however, is external reality? External reality is the father complex, the originary, primary father, the Oedipal father, whose phylogenetic inheritance of the primacy of illusionary wish fulfilment, in being transmitted from father to children, is renewed, in every generation, by the boy who identifies with the father('s penis) and by the girl who desires the father('s penis). The resultant repudiation of femininity is, as I have shown, no less the repudiation of masculinity; and the repudiation of both reflects the impasse of beginning with the illusion of the father complex.

If religion and reason are not shown to be identified, dialectically, differentially, undecidably, in the beginning, then, in the end, each will turn contradictorily into the other, just as Freud and his religious opponent exchange places in *The Future of an Illusion*. If, in the beginning, the Bible is not shown to be at once rational and faithful, conscious and unconscious, psychological (secular) and religious, philosophical and theological – undecidably human and divine – then, in the end, it will be impossible to configure a concept of modernity that is self-consciously, self-referentially, and self-reflexively historical. Just as the historical is not a movement from prehistory to what is historical, so modernity is not a movement from what is premodern to modern (and now postmodern). The child grows up and becomes an adult; but "infantile" or "immature" as judgments of unfitting behaviour – as distinct from Jesus' terrifying, because analytic, command to his disciples that they become *like* little children – describes what is inappropriate for a child or an adult, not the state of childhood or adulthood as such.

This seems elemental, but, given a metapsychology that is incapable of conceiving of change as historical, Freud is constantly forced into the contradictory position of confusing primitive with "primitive," infantile with "infantile," and thus, broadly, neurotic, infantile, and primitive. What is primitive, anthropologically, or infantile, psychologically, is not a "primitive" or an "infantile" state to be left behind by the rational individual. Historical development – whether cultural or individual – is not from primitive to modern, from illusory to rational, or from "infantile" to mature. Every individual, in his own particular, historical context, passes from childhood to adulthood. The changes involved are enormous and fascinating for all of us, both children and adults. The changes, while obvious to all of us, are so difficult to see precisely because of the inadequacy of our metapsychology (ontology) in accounting for them historically. The passage from childhood to adulthood is not from helplessness to autonomy, or from a weak ego to a strong ego, or from dependence on instincts to control of the instincts, or from id to ego. However we conceive of a loving life, that life is appropriate to every stage of our development. Lacan's mirror stage is an absurd denial of our phenomenology, although it is a perfect image of Freudian metapsychology based on the father complex.

Because Freud is unable to conceive of religion and reason as at once historical and original desire – although this is what he demonstrates phenomenologically with regard to the ancient Israelites – he is unable to work out a coherent conception of the Bible with regard to either primitivity or modernity. This also means that he is unable to think through the burdened relationship of Judaism and Christianity. It is shocking that the ultimate defense of the father complex is Christian anti-Semitism and that the ultimate defense of Christian anti-Semitism is the father complex. Freud knows that Judaism as depicted in the Bible is mature (modern) in character, mind, and ethics even while he vainly attempts to assimilate Jewish monotheism to Egyptian antecedents. The compulsive demands of the father complex also force him into the utterly contradictory position that Christianity, although primitive when compared to Judaism, is superior to Judaism because it is truly primitive in its embodiment of the return of the repressed religious, the father complex. Once again, the religious explanation of the father complex, of the origin of civilization, is true – although religion, as primordial wish fulfilment, as the repudiation of instinctual renunciation, is the very antithesis of civilization! – precisely because it is illusory. The fact that the religious explanation is true, although illusory, makes the psychoanalytic explanation false, although rational.

Freud fails to see that, however we construe the relationship between Judaism and Christianity, we can be historically and ontologically true to each, and thus true to both, only insofar as we do not view their relationship in terms of father and son, old and new, first and second. These dualisms are true only in the paradoxical sense that the end is in the beginning, the first will be last, and the child is the father of man. Both the child and the adult, both Judaism and Christianity, both the Hebrew Bible and the New Testament are each the standard of itself and of its distortions, as Spinoza demonstrates, both directly in the *Theological-Political Treatise* and indirectly in the *Ethics*. Christianity cannot be thought outside Judaism. Judaism cannot be thought inside Christianity. Judaism and Christianity together constitute the outside and the inside, the very dialectic of external and internal that Freudian metapsychology falsifies from beginning to end. Judaism is not the father religion. Christianity is not the son religion. Both begin and end, historically, with and as *caritas* – the dialectic of self and desire.

It begins to appear that, insofar as we can speak of a psychology of religion, we should also want to be able to speak of a religion of psychology. But the fact that the reversed phrase appears stilted shows us how far we remain from grasping, *geistig*, the two ends of the stick of psychology, which are also the two ends of the stick of religion, without being wounded, to shift images, from behind, as Kierkegaard says. Having to grasp the two-edged knife, without a hilt, to pick up the stick at both extremes, simultaneously, is not merely to balance on one tip of the toe, as Freud describes his own precarious stance in *Moses and Monotheism*. It is, rather, to land on both feet dialectically, without a fall into dualism, but not without having been *blessé*, it is true, although truly blessed. What Freud shows us – not having attained the serenity of Michelangelo's Moses, in whom, he says, we find the "concrete expression of the highest mental achievement that is possible in a man, that of struggling successfully against an inward passion for the sake of a cause to which he has devoted himself" ("The Moses of Michelangelo" 277) – is the intellectual debacle that results from failing to work through the metapsychology, the ontology, of origins, of beginnings.

This failure is particularly ironic, as I stress, since psychoanalysis is sensitive, above all, to the past as the return of the repressed and to the repressed as the return of the past. But psychoanalysis as method, as psychotherapy, is constantly compromised by a metapsychology whose content, the father complex, is compulsively repeated in the concept of the past as that which is, at one and the same time, external, and so unapproachable, and internal, and so inescapable. Freud never sees that his concept of origin, generally, and his concept of origin as the father complex, in particular – each the mirror image of the other – are precisely what the analysand must work through if he is to overcome the repetition compulsion of the father complex. The analysand must relinquish believing that, as internal, he is dependent on an external reality, the truth of the father as correspondence to external reality. The analysand must give up looking upon himself as mere son and must, instead, look upon himself as brother, colleague, lover, the other, as the one whose ontology, although profoundly shaped by the father-son relation, is not a creation of the father – except when "father" is understood metaphorically as the general will, the archetypal mother of us all. It is also true that the transference to the analyst will be successfully worked through – by both analysand and analyst – only insofar as it does not repeat the father complex but overcomes it as a relationship between equals, loving workers in the analysis of the psyche. It would also appear that, as soon as the father complex is deconstructed as the idol, and thus is no longer constructed as the truth, of modern (biblical) culture, then it will be equally recognized (as Freud implies by his virtual ignorance of it) that the incest motive, together with the concept of desire as prohibition, is not central to the origin of modernity.

It is thus the case that illusion is not the beginning from which we never escape in the end. Rather, illusion is the enemy against which we must constantly struggle as we grasp, comprehend, life at both extremes. It is equally the case that the murder of the father and the possession of the mother are not the beginning of life from which we never escape. This is not to deny but rather to acknowledge the reality of aggressive and libidinous desires and acts – involving parents, children, and others – in our lives, realities that are the very illusions, as Hamlet discovers, poisoning life with the reality of murder and deception. But they are not our beginning, and they are not our end, insofar as we work through the relationship of beginning and end and demonstrate it to be *caritas* and not the father complex.

We can work through the phenomenological insight and the metapsychological impasse of Freud – and thus learn to distinguish carefully his accomplishment from his failure – only insofar as we ourselves learn the truth of the ontological principle that where metapsychology was, there phenomenology shall be (and vice versa). It is precisely the father complex that is untrue to this ontological principle. In constituting beginning and end as the primal and Oedipal fathers, whose sons and daughters then split possession and desire of the penis,

309 Moses and Monotheism

the father complex leaves beginning and end opposed to each other. The result is the reversals to which Freudian metapsychology is constantly subject, those involving illusion and truth, religion and science, internality (the pleasure principle of coherence) and externality (the reality principle of correspondence), feminine desire as lack of possession and masculine possession as lack of desire. There is only one alternative to the father complex, one alternative to which there is no alternative, and that is the biblical concept of ontology whose phenomenology is at once, both in the beginning and in the end, metapsychology. It is the biblical concept of ontology that creates all alternatives from nothing, from nothing that does not admit all alternatives. The one alternative disallowed by biblical ontology is that which refuses to admit alternatives. Consequently, there is no alternative to the truth, to truth as its own undecidable standard. For it is solely truth to which, as Freud himself recognizes, as we saw, there is no alternative. Truth is its own standard, the standard of all alternatives that are truly alternatives, those embodying *caritas*, and of all alternatives that are no alternative at all, like that of the father complex.

The fact that alternatives can be true, without one alternative being forced by or forcing another alternative into the hierarchical (dominating) relationship of father and son, master and slave – that is the paradox, to which there is no alternative. There is no alternative to viewing the alternatives of reason and religion as each the truth of the other, in the beginning, as in the end. If, however, we choose Freud's alternative of the father complex, which is no alternative and choice but the denial of alternative and choice, then we shall find that the religious explanation of the father complex is true in the beginning, as illusory, and that the scientific explanation of the father complex is true in the end, as illusory. It is precisely the metapsychology of psychoanalysis that represents the return of the religious past as repressed so long as it cannot work through the alternative to beginning with the illusion of religion and thus to ending with the illusion of science, each of which is the illusory truth (the truthful illusion) of the other. The alternative to beginning with and thus to ending with illusion, that which the Bible calls idolatry, above all, the idolatry of the father complex, at once divine and human, is the biblical conception of character, mind, and ethics that is no less rational than it is faithful, both secular and religious, and consequently truly historical.

It is equally the case, as we shall see in our concluding chapter, that there is no alternative to a concept of interpretation that acknowledges the truth of the alternatives of reason and revelation. But the knife of interpretation cuts both ways. It shows (to depth psychology) that the concept of reason will be true in the end only insofar as it is truly religious (true to religion) in the beginning. It also shows (to religion) that the concept of religion will be true in the beginning only insofar as it is truly rational (true to reason) in the end. There is no concept of reason that is not religious in the beginning, and there is no concept of religion that is not rational in the end. When reason views religion as illusory in the beginning, reason returns as the repressed religious in the end. When religion views reason as illusory in the beginning, religion returns as the repressed rational in the end. What is so remarkable, then, is that Freud shows that ancient Israelite phenomenology presupposes the reciprocity of divine and human, religious and rational. But it is precisely this insight that he denies with his contradictory metapsychology of the father complex, whose religious truth is indistinguishable from rational illusion and whose religious illusion is indistinguishable from rational truth. To overcome the contradictions of Freudian metapsychology, as centred in the father complex, is to show that biblical phenomenology is its own metapsychological standard, at once rational and faithful, both psychoanalytic and religious.

6 Conclusion: Interpretation and the Ontology of Creation *ex nihilo*

My study has two main purposes. First, I want to show that the metapsychological principles that Freud formulates in order to explain the origin and the development of the human mind – the psychical apparatus – are contradictory and, in that precise sense, false. Not only is this metapsychology inherently contradictory but it also contradicts, it falsifies, the rich phenomenology that is the subject of Freud's analysis. In the previous chapters we have seen that the fundamental concepts of Freudian metapsychology – the pleasure principle, the unconscious, and the father complex – fail to account for human phenomenology. The father complex unites the Oedipus complex (the castration complex) with the myth of the primal father (the phylogenetic inheritance of acquired characteristics). Freud constantly finds himself compelled to confront questions that arise due either to the inherent contradictoriness of his metapsychological principles or to their incapacity to account for the phenomenological material that he brings forward.

In this regard the pleasure principle is exemplary. Freud insists that all psychical life, indeed, all organic life, is regulated by the pleasure principle. All forms of life strive to attain pleasure and to eliminate pain. But this claim results in the spectacular reversals that characterize the whole of his metapsychology. Let us recall the two most astonishing.

First, because Freud conceives of the mind or the organism as internally coherent and inherently constant – without tension, desire or wish, conflict, or even life – he then views all stimulus as having its origin in external reality and thus as painful. The mind (organism), in reaction to external stimulation that produces tension and conflict, responds with a wish (desire) whose function is to eliminate the painful stimulus and to reduce the resultant tensions and conflict, insofar as it can, back to constancy (to null). But Freud himself is compelled to recognize that such a mechanism as the pleasure principle cannot come into existence – for existence is defined in terms of external stimulus – without presupposing external reality, that is, the reality principle. Consequently, although the pleasure principle is said to be the primordial mechanism governing all life, it is blindly dependent on external reality for its existence. It cannot exist independently of external reality, yet it is external reality (as stimulus, pain, tension, or conflict) that it seeks to eliminate. Pleasure seeks to eliminate pain, yet it is dependent on the very pain that it must eliminate in order to attain pleasure. Does the pleasure principle, then, explain the phenomena of sadomasochism, or does it rather reveal itself to be the very mechanism underlying them? Is it not a terrible contradiction that to seek pleasure makes pleasure dependent on pain, on the death of pleasure?

Second, since it is part of the genius of Freud to press his metapsychological principles to their contradictory breaking-point, without ever being willing to account for their inherent contradictions, he comes to realize (although it takes him twenty years!) that the pleasure principle is essentially the death instinct. To seek pleasure means that it is the inherent tendency of instinct to eliminate external stimulus and to restore an earlier state of things: stasis, constancy, nirvana, the inorganic – death. The aim of life is pleasure. The aim of life is the avoidance of pain. The aim of life is death.

Freud vigorously protests the phenomenological absurdity of the conclusion to which he is led by the metapsychology of the pleasure principle by insisting upon the independence of Eros, the life or sexual instinct. But the same problems re-emerge. On the one hand, Freud shows (following Plato) that Eros represents the inherent tendency of instinct to restore an earlier state of things, consistent with the death instinct. On the other hand, in claiming that Eros represents the unifying, binding elements of civilization, Eros is distinguished not only from the hostile, disintegrating tendencies of the death instinct, and thus pleasure, but also from sexuality (libido), which Freud views as anti-social. It is also not clear how Eros, the representative of civilization, is to be distinguished from the superego, which is the source of civilization together with its laws, morality, social relations, and religion, and from the sense of guilt that increasingly burdens civilized men and women with unhappiness. As both the heir of the castration complex and the representative of the id, the superego embodies the father complex, by which civilization is generated. The castration complex is heir to identification with the father's penis, its presence (in the male child) and its absence (in the female child). The (unconscious) id, governed by the death instinct, constitutes the phylogenetic inheritance of the guilt of ambivalent love and hate for the father, for civilization, stemming from the murder of the primal father.

The only possible explanation of how (or why) at birth the male child identifies with the presence, and the female child identifies with the absence, of the patriarchal penis is metapsychological and not phenomenological: the phylogenetic inheritance of the id. Freud contends, without evidence, indeed, in the face of overwhelming evidence to the contrary, that the (unconscious) id is complete in the beginning, at birth, while the (conscious) ego, together with the secondary process of the reality principle, is, in the beginning, at birth, nonexistent. It thus follows that the inheritance of the ambivalent sense of guilt – one both loves and hates the father – is indistinguishable from the original identification with the father whether on the part of the primal sons (and the primal daughters in their absence) or on the part of the pre-Oedipal boy or girl, involving either the presence or the absence of the patriarchal penis.

The fact that identification with the penis – its presence or absence – reflects the originary ambivalence of love and hate means that Eros, no less than the death instinct, has its origin in the id and the castration complex, whose heir (representative) is the superego. Civilization as "the [metapsychological] struggle *between* Eros and death" is utterly different from "the [phenomenological] struggle *for life* of the human species" against death. The first formulation reveals the metapsychological dualism of Freud, in which Eros, with its origin in the ambivalence of identification with the patriarchal penis, is no less a representative of the father complex than is the death instinct and thus, like the superego, the representative of the (unconscious) sense of guilt with which modern men and women are so heavily burdened. The second formulation – life against death – is Freud's phenomenological protest against the death instinct on behalf of Eros. It is vigorous (manly), heart-felt, but also illusory insofar as Eros, or rather the ontology of existence, is not liberated from the metapsychological dualism of the father complex.

It is the emergence of the pleasure principle as the death instinct and its close alliance with the castration complex – itself the mirror of the father complex, whose origin is the murder of the primal father – that forces us to realize that, although Freud makes the phenomenology of libido, sexuality, and love central to his study, he has no concepts of them. The originary division between the ego instincts and the sexual instincts (libido) provides Freud with the metapsychological (biological) basis of his theory of neurosis, the opposition between ego and sexuality. But this division, while contradictory in itself, collapses with the discovery of the narcissistic ego as the origin of libido (and with the discovery of the ego as, in part, unconscious). Narcissism, however, is the logical heir of Freud's never-wavering belief in originary autoerotism (itself a version of the pleasure principle), one that is utterly inconsistent with the division between ego instincts and sexual instincts. It also leads to his final theory of the opposed instincts of death and life. The contradictory division between the death instincts and the life instincts eliminates the contradictory division between the ego and sexual instincts, which had served as the metapsychological basis of neurosis. Gone is the division between civilization (represented contradictorily by the ego, or the individual, self-preservative instincts) and sexuality (represented contradictorily by the sexual instincts, which oppose the interests of the individual in the name of the species, the group, or society). The division between the death instincts and the life instincts also means that Freud is unable to account for libido, sexuality, and love. While aggressivity (activity and its perversions) is reduced to the hostile and disintegrating impulses of defusion associated with the death instincts, sexuality (together with libido and love) is viewed, like neurosis, as anti-social, in opposition to the unifying impulses of fusion associated with Eros. (In the earlier model, the sexual instincts had been social, in opposition to the individualistic instincts of the ego.)

Freud undertakes to develop his depth psychology, whose subject is the meaningfulness of *all* psychical phenomena, independently of biology. It is then strangely ironic that it is only the biological distinction between hunger and love, between the ego instincts and the sexual instincts, which, he says, allows him to explain the rich phenomenology of psyche. The fact that his theory of psychoanalysis rests upon a concept of instincts that, he constantly acknowledges, remains completely unknown, never leads Freud to re-examine the inadequacy of his metapsychological beginning. He does not see that the idea that the instincts are somatic in origin but psychical in representation is as crude and unthinking as Descartes' concept of the brain-mind link in the pineal gland. Instead of rethinking his concept of instincts, which is at once biological and mythical – and it is this dualism that constitutes the very essence of his metapsychology – Freud increasingly hardens his metapsychological dualism into a dogmatism whose contradictions then return as the repressed. Indeed, he will even come to call the instincts his mythology and metapsychology the witch whose revelations are neither clear nor exact but whose single clue, "the antithesis between the primary and the secondary processes," is indispensable. But it is precisely the illusory dualism between primary and secondary, between beginning and end, that Freud is never able to dispel and by which he is hexed from the beginning to the end of his work.

The irony becomes stranger (more estranging) when Freud finally confesses that his attachment to the phylogenetic thesis of the inheritance of acquired characteristics means that he does not have a biological basis for his metapsychology and when the context in which he makes this confession is *Moses and Monotheism*. For it is here, in his last innovative work, that he attempts, for the first time, to account for the origin not generally of religion but, in particular, of Jewish monotheism, which, it turns out, to the utter astonishment of his metapsychological witch, is at once unique and universal. Not only is Freud right that his theory of the father complex – in both its mythical and its Oedipal versions – is not biological. But it is equally the case that it can never be biological. Freud's intuition to go outside (beyond) biology to find the explanatory (interpretive) principles of psychoanalysis is sound. But the problem is that he still believes that his *Wissenschaft* is scientific (in the sense of biology and physics – yet recall his statement to Einstein that all science is mythical!). Consequently, Freud never comprehends three simple but profound issues. First, the metapsychological – the interpretive – principles inherent in his phenomenology are not scientific. Second, they cannot be scientific. Third, they are, in fact, biblical. It is only on the basis of the biblical ontology of creation *ex nihilo*, as I have attempted to show throughout my study, that a comprehensive and systematic conception of desire can be developed that is true at once to history (to the concepts of both origin and development) and to the dialectic of self and desire, of individual and community (including the notions of family, society, and civilization). It is, therefore, the second purpose of my study to argue that it is only on the basis of biblical ontology that the dualism of Freud's metapsychology can be overcome and that his psychoanalytic insights, in their true depth, can be systematically comprehended. But I also expand this argument to hold that psychical life, when understood, consistent with Freud, as meaningful, can be comprehended solely on the basis of the principles of interpretation that are consonant with (as they originate in) the Bible.

Freud is an exemplary modern thinker in revealing (unconsciously) the impasse that results when rich phenomenological insight is severely compromised, indeed, fundamentally contradicted, by principles of

316 Depth Psychology, Interpretation, and the Bible

metapsychology that are not true to it. He cannot imagine that all that he holds dearest, the truth, above all, but equally ethics (right relations, both individual and social) and, finally, the secular values associated with science, research, and reason are consistent with – indeed, cannot be *thought* independently of – religious, that is, biblical, values. It is understandable, even meritorious, that Freud, together with his secular compeers, is deeply suspicious of the authoritarian attitudes and structures of religion, above all, Christianity. (He refers to, among other things, the contemporary repression of female sexuality and the historical suppression of intellectual innovations.) But the reason that Freud is so fascinating – and important – is that he pushes both his insight, phenomenologically, and his contradiction of that insight, metapsychologically, sufficiently far for the reversals that characterize his thought to come to the fore. He constantly acknowledges that his work, his approach, is replete with problems that reveal the inconsistency of his approach and his findings. He consistently sees the problems that emerge, but he is also consistent in failing to comprehend the inconsistencies that his metapsychology creates for his phenomenological insight from his beginning in *The Interpretation of Dreams* to his end in *Moses and Monotheism* and *An Outline of Psychoanalysis*. In undertaking to reformulate, instead of rethinking, his metapsychological dualism, Freud increasingly sacrifices his phenomenology to it. The result is the father complex composed of two basic elements. The first is the Oedipus complex, whose end in the male and whose beginning in the female as the castration complex involve the repudiation of femininity (and of masculinity) as the bedrock of biology. The second is the phylogenetic inheritance of acquired characteristics, whose bedrock is the repudiation of biology.

Still, Freud is particularly fascinating because he pushes his reversals far enough to demonstrate – to those who have the eyes to see that they are not themselves subject to the father complex – that his own metapsychology becomes in the end the return of the repressed religious. This is surely the ultimate irony of psychoanalysis, which is dedicated to revealing the return of the repressed past, the return of the past as repressed, in our lives. In Freud, repetition compulsion becomes the demonstration, on the one hand, that the pleasure principle is the death instinct, the fact that to seek pleasure is to reduce life with all its conflicts and tensions to pain, which is then to be eliminated in the name of the pleasure principle. On the other hand, Christian anti-Semitism (Christians correctly accuse Jews of refusing to acknowledge that they killed their God) is justified by and justifies the father complex. More generally, then, basic elements of Freud's metapsychology become grotesque parodies of Christian theology, his nemesis: the father complex itself and the inheritance of the original sin of the "biological" (instinctual) transmission of guilt on the part of the primal sons for their murder of the primal father. Still, more generally, Freud never sees that if he does not develop an ontology that dialectically overcomes the dualism – between internal and external, species and individual, sexual instincts and ego instincts, primary process and secondary process, coherence and correspondence, unconscious (id) and consciousness (ego), illusion (fiction) and fact, beginning and end, religion and science (*Wissenschaft*) – then psychoanalysis will in the end repeat the opposition that it precisely aims to overcome, both phenomenologically and metapsychologically.

I have appealed to two simple formulas to capture the spirit of the ontological argument for thought and existence (at once divine and human) that is presupposed by Freudian psychoanalysis, as by all interpretive procedures. (1) What you put into a system is what you will get out of it. (This is the informal understanding on the part of Kant of his elegant concept of the synthetic *a priori* judgment, the categorical imperative yoking individual and universal.) (2) To explain another is to make yourself no less subject to the explanation of the other. The notion that the beginning is in the end as the end is in the beginning I am calling here the law of reciprocation. This is but another name for the golden rule, the law of mutuality overcoming the dualism between personal and social, between individual and community. We saw Freud argue, in *The Future of an Illusion*, that the golden rule – the law commanding that you shall not murder your neighbour (who, patently, does *not* represent the father complex!) – is the rational basis of communal life. But he then repudiates the rationality of the golden rule, the golden rule of rationality, in the name of the metapsychological myth of the primal father. Freud does not see that he has thereby repudiated the sole basis of truth and ethics, values to which he is absolutely committed and which he shows, in *Moses and Monotheism*, to be consistent with the phenomenology of the Hebrew Bible. Freud does not see that, if the principle of civilization is violence (the murder of the primal father), then the end of civilization will be the blind repetition of that violence.

What is uncanny is that it is precisely the originary violence of the father complex that is compulsively repeated in the death instinct, the superego, and the irremediable guilt from which there is no exit in and through civilization. But it is also the case that the myth of the primal father and his murder is but another version of the primacy of the pleasure principle, according to whose governance all life is disturbance due to the external, painful, and violent imposition of the castration complex by the father. Not only, however, does the father castrate the sons' libido but the sons also kill the father as representative of narcissistic, autoerotic pleasure. The father must be killed by the sons, his nemesis, in order for the principle of narcissistic, autoerotic pleasure to be embodied, phylogenetically, in the id. Because the sons represent the id of the father as he does their ego, father and son, ego and id, external and internal are forever opposed to each other. The fact that, at the birth of the pre-Oedipal child, the id precedes the ego, although at the birth of civilization the ego precedes the id, explains, as we noted above, why, spontaneously, the pre-Oedipal son identifies with the presence, and the pre-Oedipal daughter with the absence, of the patriarchal penis. A consequence of the contradictory dualism of ego and id is that the pleasure principle, whose representative is the primal father, is originally external and can be rendered internal only because the sons, when subject to the ambivalence of the father complex (i.e., to ambivalent identification with the patriarchal penis), murder the father. In other words, the sons demonstrate, by killing him, that the father – the pleasure principle, narcissism, autoerotism – is castrated, always already, from the beginning. In the beginning the pleasure principle is both death instinct and castration complex.

Freud argues that it is not the rational but the religious explanation of communal life that is right. But the irony here is that, in utter confusion and incoherence, reason and religion reverse themselves as end and beginning. In the end reason is made to depend upon a religious beginning that is illusory but true. In the beginning religion is made to depend upon a rational end that is true but illusory. Reason is true only insofar as it is religious (illusion), and religion is true only insofar as it is rational (illusion). What is so peculiar about Freud is that he constantly arrives at the truth, but only in illusory fashion. The (religious) truth that he sees he can see only as illusory, and the (rational) illusion (the pleasure principle, the primal father) that he sees he can see only as true. What Freud fails to see is that the only alternative to the dualism between religion and reason, beginning and end, truth and illusion is a concept of reason that is truly religious in the beginning and a concept of religion that is truly rational in the end. Then illusion can be seen as the product not of either religion or reason but of their interminable opposition. Truth, consequently, is the product of the reciprocal relationship of religion and reason such that either can be true only insofar as both are true.

The fact that Freud's metapsychology is constantly subject to contradictory reversals is not accidental. Nor are its contradictory reversals remediable – thanks to constantly projected future research – on the basis of their own dualistic terms. Rather, his metapsychology is inherently dualistic, and all dualisms are intrinsically contradictory and, as such, subject to their own blindness. What characterizes dualism is that either side of the dualism is but a projection both of and onto its opposite: it repeats compulsively the return of the opposed other as repressed. This is why I say that Freud fails to meet his own analytic test than which there is none higher and to which there is no exception: truth as its own standard. His dualism is subject to the very projection that his analytic practice is committed to (de)constructing. Indeed, I have suggested that it is precisely the father complex, together with its whole metapsychological hex, that has to be dispelled in the analytic situation if the analyst can expect the analysand to commit himself to their mutually created construction as a complete result.

It is not only the case, however, that the dualistic principles that constitute Freudian metapsychology constantly suffer reversals into their opposite. Freud also acknowledges the complete inadequacy of his own metapsychological principles, without, it is true, the self-conscious conviction that is experienced by the analysand who accepts the construction of the analyst insofar as it allows him to overcome the contradictory return of the repressed father complex.

We noted the problem that emerges in *Beyond the Pleasure Principle* when Freud, holding that "an instinct is an urge inherent in organic life to restore an earlier state of things," argues that the goal of instincts cannot be "a state of things which has never yet been attained" but solely "an *old* state of things." This leads logically to the conclusion that the aim of life is death. But Freud is then forced to acknowledge, illogically, that "the attributes of life were at some time evoked in animate matter by the action of *a force* of whose nature we can form no conception" (perhaps on analogy with the subsequent emergence of consciousness, he adds) (308–10). This passage is similar to that in *Civilization and its Discontents* where, in the context of tergiversating between "the struggle between Eros and death" and the "struggle for life," Freud notes that he speaks of "a struggle for life in the shape it was bound to assume after *a certain event* which still remains to be discovered" (314). What is so deeply puzzling, indeed, disturbing about Freud is that, while introducing, almost as if by free association, the telltale signs of a mysterious force and an unknown event as the very basis of (his) life, he evades thinking about them further. He frequently denies understanding such deep matters, although the reason he gives for dismissing philosophers (the benighted Schopenhauer excepted and the exceptional Nietzsche largely occluded) is *their* failure to deal with the unconscious. But it is especially ideas (associations) whose undeveloped, that is, unconscious, appearance creates gaps in analysis that, above all, interest the analyst. (This has always been the case in social and textual analysis. In this sense psychoanalysis is the heir, not the origin, of analysis.) Can one imagine the analyst hearing the analysand speak of, but then say he has no understanding of, a critical force and a certain event in his life and not ask him further about them? It is precisely such a force and such an event that return in Freudian psychoanalysis as the repressed religious because they remain unanalyzed, un(de)constructed.

It is not so much that the force is, say, God, or that the event is, say, the covenant that God makes with the Israelites or the incarnation of God in Jesus as the Christ. For our purposes here, the force and the event represent the ontological argument connecting, dialectically, paradoxically, thought and existence and thus signal, in their absence, the psyche, the unconscious, history, and desire (love, action). The fact that Freud fails to account for the force or the event creating thought and existence from nothing means that he fails his own analytic test that truth knows no exceptions. In excepting from analysis the truth of the ontological argument – the creation of thought and existence from nothing – he is unable to explain the suffering of the analysand before him except on the basis of the father complex, the dualisms of whose metapsychology result in and are the result of the castration complex and the subsequent repudiation of femininity, as of masculinity.

Not only are there metapsychological reversals and ontological gaps that Freud sees yet avoids seeing at the same time. But additionally there is actual content whose explication represents an affirmation of his phenomenological insight and a deconstruction of his metapsychology. Yet, even in these cases Freud refuses to rethink the whole of his system in light of the glaring anomalies that emerge. Perhaps most astonishing is that, in a book on *Group Psychology and the Analysis of the Ego*, he fails to provide a systematic analysis of the relationship between his concept of the group and the only real groups that count, the family and society. He then finds himself reversed, typically, by his inability to distinguish in coherent terms between uninhibited and inhibited libidinal (sexual) instincts, although he claims that group libido rests on inhibited sexual instincts. Finally, in one paragraph, in the work's Appendix, Freud shows that the libidinal relations constituting Christianity (the Church) reveal that it is not a group. Not only does this conclusion compromise, in principle, his "group" (and thus his "individual") psychology and consequently the application of the myth of the primal horde and its dependence on the chief as its primal father to group (and individual) psychology. But it also undermines the whole of his theory of the Oedipus complex, beginning in identification with the father('s penis) and ending in the castration complex, whose heir (for men), the superego, burdens individuals with the guilt destructive of their happiness. Freud shows that, whatever the actual relations that the individual Christian has to his chief (Christ: God) and to his fellow Christians, Christianity demands that he relate to Christ as he relates to his fellow Christians and that he relate to his fellow Christians as he relates to Christ. In this manner Freud invokes, in precise and succinct terms, the golden rule, without naming it.

We may recall that when, in the Gospels, Jesus is asked what the law is, he responds that you are to love God above all others and your neighbour as yourself. You are to do unto others as you would have them do unto you. However, instead of acknowledging the biblical origins of desire, Freud simply points out that, in Christianity, libido (uninhibited or inhibited?) is to be "supplemented" by adding identification[1] (with fellow Christians) to object choice (that is, a love relationship to Christ as leader) and object choice to identification. The union of identification and object relations constitutes an utter reversal, a complete rejection, of the whole of Freudian metapsychology as it involves the group (and thus the superego), the primal horde (the myth of the primal father), the Oedipus complex, the father complex, libido theory, and the pleasure principle. (Although the unconscious is not directly involved here, it is clear that it can be truly articulated only insofar as identification and object relations are dynamically united.) We can appreciate why it is that Freud concludes his brief paragraph on Christianity as the truth of libidinal relationship with the observation that "this further development in the distribution of libido [uninhibited or inhibited?] in the group [that is not a group!] is probably the factor upon which Christianity bases its claim to have reached a higher ethical level" (168).

Freud also praises the ethics of ancient Judaism for having attained a higher level (than elsewhere in the ancient world) and for continuing to constitute social relationships in modernity. He directly connects ethics with Jewish monotheism, the determination of whose origin is the main purpose of *Moses and Monotheism*. But ethics, as the locus of divine action, also involves Jewish character and the Jewish advance in intellectuality, which, he shows, cannot be accounted for on the basis of the renunciation of instinct (on the basis, in other words, of the father complex, whether primal or Oedipal). Even more fascinating, however, is the distinction that Freud makes between what he calls rational ethics and religious ethics. This distinction is clearly consonant with the difference that appears, as he once again returns to a discussion of totemism as originary religion, between the religious prohibitions stemming from the will of the father and the command of a different motive and the new order that grant equal rights to the primal brothers (and sisters). The distinction between the old order of the father's religious prohibitions and the new motive and order granting equal rights to all human beings as brothers and sisters is captured in the distinction that he draws between "religious ethics" and "rational ethics." He writes that the precepts of ethics are "rationally justified by the necessity for delimiting the rights of society as against the individual, the rights of the individual as against society, and those of individuals as against one another." In contrast to this concept of "rational ethics" is "religious ethics," whose origin is "the will of the father" (370). The irony here, as always, is that it is rational ethics that is consistent with the biblical ethics that Freud has articulated in *Moses and Monotheism*. The religious ethics, which he clearly rejects, is that embodied in the father complex!

Although Freud's concept of "rational ethics" is modest in articulation and would require comprehensive elaboration and amplification if it were to achieve the status of political and social theory, we can say five simple things about it. (1) It is consistent with (as it has its source in) the Hebrew covenant with God, the golden rule. (2) It is unknown in the extra-biblical traditions of the ancient world, including Greece (and Rome). (3) It is the basis of our own modern, social ethics, which, involving a dialectic of individual and society, is generally missing in Freud, given the dualism that he posits metapsychologically between the ego (individual) instincts and the sexual (species or group) instincts. Although he conjures up, in phenomenological terms, the dialectic between individual and society at the beginning of *Group Psychology*, he then sacrifices this phenomenology to the dualistic (hierarchical) relations of father and son and of leader and group as demanded by the metapsychology of his libido theory (the castration complex) and the theory of the primal horde. (4) Like the single paragraph in *Group Psychology* on Christianity, the single sentence in *Moses and Monotheism* on "rational" ethics, which is at once biblical and modern, represents the utter denial or rejection of the metapsychology of the father complex to which Freud tries so hard to assimilate the Bible, even as he proves otherwise in terms of his insight into the basic content of Jewish phenomenology: characterology, mind (the advance in *Geistigkeit*), and ethics. (5) The singular sentence on ethics also represents total failure on Freud's part to account for the relationship between primitive civilization and modern civilization. It embodies his recognition that the Bible or, in other words, Jewish phenomenology, is not primitive, notwithstanding his contradictory claim to address the problem of innovation and difference by reducing Jewish monotheism to Egyptian imperialism. ("It would be in contradiction to the conservative nature of the instincts if the goal of life were a state of things which had never yet been attained" (*Beyond the Pleasure Principle* 310). Indeed, what

Freud stresses is the continuity between ancient Judaism and modern Judaism and between the character, mind, and ethics of ancient Judaism and modern life. In the end, however, Freud does not relinquish belief in his metapsychological god *Logos*, the father complex, as the explanation of both the history of civilization and the manner in which the newborn – boy and girl – become "civilized." Human beings attain sexual and social (cultural) maturity only to find that adulthood is founded on (founders on) the guilt of repudiating femininity and thus masculinity.

Why does Freud adhere to the metapsychology of the father complex, notwithstanding overwhelming evidence to the contrary – the contradictions inherent in his metapsychology, the contradictory gaps that the ontological force and the ontological event create in his argument, and the contradictory evidence of the phenomenology that he adduces? I do not know, if I may paraphrase Rousseau's refusal to be drawn into a (metapsychological) discussion of why it is that "man," although born free, is now in chains. How can the bonds of the father complex be made legitimate, to continue my paraphrase of Rousseau? That is the ontological question to which this study is dedicated. It should be borne in mind that analysand and analyst do not know and will never know *why* the analysand, insofar as he is neurotic, is enslaved to the father complex – except through and as the illegitimate use of, the abuse of, love (freedom) on the part of both self and other. The analysand provides the phenomenology (the associations, including dream material) with all its gaps and conflicts (contradictions), while the analyst provides the interpretation, which, if successful in filling in the gaps, will gain (construct) the analysand's consent and commitment. The construction at which analysand and analyst reciprocally arrive is not archeological reconstruction. The analytical subject is still alive and still freely producing material, which, when it proves to be the creation of a true construction, establishes a pattern of free and loving relations while it breaks the pattern of neurotic dependence and helplessness as embodied in the father complex. When the construction proves to be a "complete result," it no longer generates in the analysand disabling and paralyzing consequences.

As alive and creative, the subject is also indestructible, which is precisely what Descartes discovers when he analyzes doubt (despair) down to the very depths of psychical hell where God is not the creator of our humanity but our most determined, diabolical, and demented deceiver. Like the saintly confessor Augustine before him and the patient Freudian analysand after him, Descartes confirms that there is still one thing that he cannot doubt so long as he is a doubting subject – alive, creative (producing contradictory doubts), and indestructible – and that is his own thought and existence. The one thing that the analysand cannot doubt, so long as he is willing to engage, truthfully, the illusory contradictions of the deceptive father complex, is that he does not desire to be deceived. He desires neither to be deceived by nor to deceive either others or himself, so help him God, however monumentally difficult it is, as Nietzsche says, to will the past "it was," with all of its deceptive contradictions, as one's own and thus to legitimate them as one's bonds to life.

Unlike in archeological reconstruction – whose material is dead and rarely recuperable and whose method is an end in itself – in analytical construction the analysand finds that he is indestructible and alive and that his construction is but a preliminary to life. Construction is provisional and providential, providing the provisions that one desires for life. There is life after analysis, so long as there is life in analysis. Analysis, insofar as it is liberated from and liberates the individual from the father complex and from the pseudo-biological bedrock of the repudiation of femininity and thus of masculinity, is terminable, while life – the love of analysis, like the unconscious itself – is interminable: alive, indestructible, and creative, constantly, of a complete result.

There are two issues here: not only why Freud continues to adhere to the father complex, in face of overwhelming evidence to the contrary, but also what it means to legitimate it. Just as the analyst does not know why the analysand suffers from enslavement to the father complex and can only analyze the neurotic structures of dualism in light of the dialectical structures that give a complete result in the future, so we can analyze Freud's texts solely in light of an ontology that overcomes the dualisms of his metapsychology. Thus the two issues – slavery and freedom, neurosis and liberation, suffering and cure, pathology and health, repetition and working through, dualism and dialectic – are profoundly related to each other. Indeed, the first cannot even be thought, analyzed, or thematized except in light of the second – the dialectic of the relationship of self and other as found in the golden rule: the command to do unto others as you would have them do unto you. It is also the case that the second issue – the legitimation of the bonds of our relationships, both personal and social – can never be undertaken except in and through the overcoming of neurosis (slavery), as both Freud and Rousseau, not to mention Hamlet, Cordelia, and Alyosha Karamazov, know so profoundly.

We cannot say why Freud adheres to the father complex, just as we cannot say why the analysand suffers neurotic impairment. Still, analysis of the father complex gives us what we need to know. With its centre in both the myth of the primal father and the Oedipus complex, the father complex begins in identification with the father('s penis). What results is that originary castration on the part of the female child confirms her in her Oedipus complex and that final castration on the part of the male child smashes his Oedipus complex. The father complex is but one version among innumerable versions of dualism with which dialectic – the loving relationship of self and other – is unavoidably (freely) beset. These versions are interminably psychological, literary, philosophical, theological, social, political. They are profoundly authoritarian, non-democratic, hierarchical, and thus inevitably involve sexism, racism, and class division, even when their author is of the best intentions. (I do not think that Freud intends to be misogynist, anti-Semitic, or anti-democratic; but it is also the case that his metapsychology provides no defense against sexism, racism, or authoritarianism. I mention the issue of Freud's intentionality only in passing, for my focus is ontological.) We cannot say why Freud remains systematically committed to his metapsychological dualisms, notwithstanding the spectacular contradictions and reversals that they constantly produce in his work. But once we have seen through his metapsychology to the ontological depth of his psychology, then we can analyze that metapsychology as an intellectual pathology whose roots are clearly discernible as profoundly embedded in the history and structure of modern (originally biblical and ultimately world) culture.

Notwithstanding the theory embodied in the reciprocal relationship central to the analytic situation and his insight into both Judaism and Christianity, Freud has no concept of desire (but only of the pleasure principle), no concept of reciprocal love as the golden rule (but only of the castration complex), no concept of thought and existence (but only of the dualistic opposition between primary process and secondary process), and no concept of history (but only of the phylogenetic inheritance of acquired characteristics). He continues to hold to a reified, positivistic, and objectivist conception of science. However, in saying that, it is important to see that the alternative metapsychology for psychoanalysis, for depth psychology, generally, is not a refined concept of (biological or physical) science but a concept of interpretation whose principles are consistent with and, indeed, embody the Freudian concept of the unconscious.

The unconscious – together with the attendant notions of repression, resistance, regression – is the one concept of Freud that survives the revelation that the metapsychology of the father complex is riddled with contradictory dualisms that utterly falsify the phenomenological insight of psychoanalysis. But, in order for the unconscious to be made true to its depths, it must be freed from its metapsychological bondage to the father complex and integrated with concepts of desire, reciprocation (the golden rule), and history, with, above all, concepts of origin, beginning, and principle whose structure is paradox, not contradiction. It would be of enormous help to all of us – thinkers, professional and amateur, formal and informal – if we would learn to distinguish between paradox and contradiction. The Greeks (as all extra-biblical peoples) live by the law of contradiction (and the corresponding laws of identity and excluded middle) alone. They – as typified by Socrates and Oedipus – do not know what contradiction is. They know that they are ignorant, but they do not know *what* they are ignorant of. They do not know the law of contradiction as contradiction. In contrast, we moderns, heirs of the Bible, live by the law of paradox alone. It is only when we learn to distinguish contradiction from (i.e., by means of) paradox that we shall be able to understand that there is no concept of the unconscious in the Greek (or extra-biblical) world. It is solely when we see, truly, that there is no concept of the unconscious – or of consciousness, properly comprehended – in extra-biblical life that we can come to understand the unconscious. Then, and only then, are we in a position to conceive of the metapsychology, the ontology, the principle of interpretation that is true to the paradox – that, in the beginning, the unconscious cannot be unaware of beginning unconsciously if its beginning is, in truth, unconscious.

The paradox here is that the Greeks, in living by the law of contradiction alone, are unable to think (about or through) contradiction. It is this that explains the impasse of the Cretan liar, as we saw earlier. In contrast are we moderns who, in living by the one alternative that there is to the law of contradiction, which is the biblical law of paradox, are able to think (about or through) contradiction. In the Greek world, contradiction is unthinkable, precisely because contradiction constitutes the very essence of thought and existence. In the biblical world, we can think (about and through) contradiction precisely because our thinking and existence are not intrinsically contradictory – as we learn in and through the analytic situation, a play like *Hamlet*, and this study (if I may be so bold as to hope). We may recall that Oedipus, King of Thebes, is blinded by the contradictory law that is celebrated by the chorus in the final lines of the play: count no man happy unless he has looked upon his last day and "passed the final limit of his life secure from pain." The fact that the end of contradictory life is the death of contradiction is then celebrated by Oedipus at Colonus. He dies with the secret of his death known only to Theseus, the secret of contradiction that is incommunicable except in death. Death – the contradiction of death – brings the death of contradiction, except that contradiction does not know a natural death. There is no end to natural contradiction, to the contradiction of nature, as the Trobrianders and other primitive peoples who are cited by Freud know so well, for they mortally fear the terrible contradictions that their loved, immortal ones will visit upon them in death. The death of contradiction, embodied in the ambivalence of taboo, metamorphoses into its opposite, the contradiction of death.

It is the same contradiction, of which humans are ignorant, that Plato celebrates not only in the death trilogy of Socrates – *Apology*, *Crito*, and *Phaedo* – but also in the *Gorgias* and *Republic*, which conclude with myths of punishment. Those who in life do evil in ignorance of the good (for no one can knowingly do evil) are punished. Those who are virtuous (for to know the good is to be the good: virtue is its own reward) are rewarded. But even Socrates, in his upward journey, is brought down by the contradictory adages of Heraclitus: the way up is the way down; justice is injustice; and the might of Zeus is right. After a thousand years, Socrates, virtuous in ignorance, not in knowledge – for no one can knowingly do evil, and no one can knowingly do good, for to know the good is to be the good – is also fated to be reversed and to return to earth. Once again he will suffer the karma of contradictory ignorance, consistent with the Upanishads, as Freud so astutely sees (although, as ever, he is unable to account for what he sees).

Is it not uncanny that Freud appeals to one of the Platonic myths of punishment – that of Aristophanes' account of Eros – to explicate the fact that sexual instinct is the inherent tendency to restore an earlier state of things? Three elements stand out in Freud's invocation of Aristophanean Eros. First, he suppresses the central feature in Aristophanes' account of Eros, the fact that Eros – as contradictory wish or seeking – reflects divine punishment. To wish, to seek, to act in the Greek world is to be punished as blindly and ignorantly contradictory. Second, in citing the authority of Plato to demonstrate that Eros seeks to restore an earlier state of things, Freud makes the life (sexual) instincts of Eros indistinguishable from the death instincts. Third, he bases his concept of Eros on Greek myth because he is not able, he points out, to find support in biology for his concept of the instincts.

There are two fundamental points to be noted in Freud's appeal to Greek myth. The first is that, for all of Freud's pseudo-science – not to mention the attack on or the defense of Freud as a competent scientist – the real issue is not (his) science. When the going gets metapsychologically rough for Freud, he turns away from science to myth, and to that degree his intuition is sound, as I indicated earlier. The alternative to Plato and Lamarck is not Darwin, if one intends to found the depth psychology of psychoanalysis on a sound metapsychology or, rather, ontology. The alternative to Freudian metapsychology to which there is no alternative is a concept of myth whose structure is not that of contradiction – and so unable to conceive of origins in a non-contradictory, non-dualistic (non-binary) fashion – but that of paradox. One can overcome the dualism between beginning and end, consistent with Zarathustra, in terms only of a notion of desire (will), which itself rests on the biblical concept of creation from nothing, on the ontological argument. Freud is typically modern not because he attempts to found depth psychology on a science of nature but because, at key moments in his argument, he swerves away from biology to myth. The second point is that Freud is typically modern – again, I can only describe this, I cannot say "why" this is – in that, in turning away from science to myth, he attempts to found the interpretive principles of depth psychology not on biblical myth but on pagan (Greek or extra-biblical) myth. In saying this, I do not mean that he chooses one particular myth over another. I mean that he projects the Oedipal conflict of the modern individual, which cannot be understood in terms of Darwinian science, onto Greek myth – Sophocles, Plato, Empedocles – and then reads this (metapsychological) myth back as the scientific truth of (the phenomenology of) modern Oedipal conflict. Equally, he projects the myth of the primal father onto antiquity and then reads it back as the scientific truth of modernity. What these projections represent, above all, is massive resistance to and massive repression of biblical myth and thus a total distortion of not only the primitive but equally the biblical and (as) the modern.

Freud does not see that biblical myth is unlike all other myth(s). The two great, originary myths of the Bible are creation and "fall," the paradoxical creation of life from nothing in the nature of contradictory myth and the paradoxical fall of man and woman from the contradictory nature of mythology. In beginning with the creation story, the biblical authors engage the reader in the paradox that creation (God) is the cause of itself, the standard of truth to which there is no exception. The undecidable choice is either creation or nothing. Choose life, not death. In beginning, again, with the story of the fall, the biblical authors engage the reader in contradiction. Will the reader construct the contradiction as the father complex? Is God the natural authority whose contradictory command not to eat of the fruit of the tree of the knowledge of good and evil it is sinful to disobey? Or is God the divine authority whose contradictory command not to eat of the fruit of the tree of knowledge of good and evil is the paradox that obligation – to God and neighbour – is unthinkable outside of the human responsibility of knowing good and evil? Is sin contradiction or paradox? Are man and woman banished from paradise as punishment for the sin of contradicting the father complex? Or does the banishment of man and woman from paradise represent the paradox that you cannot live by the natural contradictions of the father complex alone? Is the "fall" contradiction or paradox? There are two traditions in the reading of the story of Adam and Eve. One tradition is idolatrous and contradictory. The other tradition is loving and paradoxical. The idolatrous tradition supports the contradictions of the father complex, whether found in what Kierkegaard calls Christendom (rationalized paganism) or in the metapsychological dualism of Freud. The loving tradition supports the paradox of the golden rule, the equal rights of brothers and sisters. This is what Kierkegaard calls Christianity (the fear and trembling involved in the recognition on the part of Abraham that the father-son relationship involves him in the paradox of being true to the reciprocal love of both son and father, of both Isaac and God). This is what Freud recognizes to be the principles of Hebrew and modern ethics and calls the Christian supplementation of libido (the union of identification and object relations, of self and other).

The difference between Socratic ignorance and biblical knowledge of good and evil – a distinction that Freud himself acknowledges phenomenologically – entails a complexity that we must carefully elucidate if we are to grasp the full implications of the concept of interpretation that is demanded by the dialectic of biblical critique. The difference between contradiction and paradox is one that involves not merely a twofold but rather a threefold distinction. (1) Extra-biblical (pagan) reality (both thought and existence) reflects the primacy of contradiction resulting in the terminable/interminable regress (progress) of opposites: one and many, reality and appearance, immortality and mortality, form and matter. Freud points out that primitive peoples have no understanding of the ambivalent or contradictory nature of taboo; and this is also what Malinowski and Spiro demonstrate, in spite of themselves. Contradiction, in the Greek world, is manifested in Socratic ignorance and Oedipal blindness. The secret of Oedipus at Colonus, as I have indicated, is the secret of contradiction, the fact that contradiction cannot be known in itself, that it is known only in death. The contradiction of death is the death of contradiction. (2) Biblical reality (both thought and existence) embodies the primacy of paradox, whose ontological expression is creation from nothing contradictory and the fall from the paradise of natural contradiction into the paradox that sin (-consciousness) is knowing good and evil. (3) When paradox (biblical reality) is conflated with or reduced to contradiction, the result is dualism, the idolatry to which the Bible is opposed from beginning to end.

The triadic distinction among contradictory opposites, paradox, and dualism (idolatry) is critical. It is only in the biblical (modern) world that contradictions can be seen for what they are, that what is contradictory about contradiction can be seen as contradictory. The only way in which you can see what contradictions are and not be contradicted (blinded) by what you see is if your perspective is subject not to the law of contradiction but to the law of paradox, to the golden rule and its reciprocal relation of self and other. It is important to observe that the distinction between contradiction and paradox represents the point of view of paradox. Paradox does not exist and is unthinkable in the world subject to contradiction, in the world whose subject is contradiction. (Another way of putting this is that contradiction does not exist or cannot be thought outside the world of paradox. It "exists" in appearance and can be "known" only in ignorance.) It is equally important to distinguish between the extra-biblical world of opposites (where contradiction is not *known* as contradictory) and dualism (the biblical world of idolatry). Dualism as idolatry is not found in the Greek, Hindu, or Trobriand world. Dualism is the evasion (the repression) of responsibility, of choice, of desire, of reciprocal relation, of the golden rule, all of which are absent from the world ruled by the law of contradiction.

Because Freud, like all moderns, cannot return to the innocent garden of nature – the way back is eternally blocked by the flaming swords of the Cherubim – what we find in his version of Oedipus, both the classical Oedipus and the modern Oedipal child, is not Oedipal ignorance and blindness but evasion of contradiction, in other words, dualism (idolatry). We also find a dualistic conception of Oedipus in Malinowski and Spiro (but not in the Trobrianders). Notwithstanding the difference that separates the two anthropologists on the question of the universality of the Oedipus complex, they equally fail to account for the fundamental difference between primitive and modern (biblical), between contradiction and paradox (whose opposite is dualism or idolatry). We have no right to criticize and I do not criticize or find fault with Plato or the Trobrianders. The ontological argument for thought and existence, in serving as the paradoxical ground of our critique, of our concept of interpretation, is utterly other than the contradictory premises of Plato, the Trobrianders, and all other extra-biblical peoples. Our criticism, our interpretation, is only of those moderns who, in claiming to appropriate Plato, Sophocles, or Empedocles, distort both them and themselves. They do not see how utterly different is the difference between, on the one hand, paradox (truth as its own standard) and idolatry and, on the other hand, biblical paradox and Greek (extra-biblical) contradiction. Without exception, one finds – and Freud here is exemplary, as we have seen – that when the distinction between paradox and dualism (idolatry), on the one hand, and between paradox and contradiction, on the other hand, is evaded (repressed), then both the primitive (the extra-biblical including the Greek) and the modern (the biblical) are completely misread.

Greek texts are not misread because of their overdetermination, that is, because they express what is supplementary, unconscious, or *unheimlich*. They are misread because they have no concept of overdetermination, the *supplement*, the unconscious, or the uncanny. What we would call overdetermination is, in the Greek world, simply fatal ignorance (blindness, death). There is nothing in the Greek (or extra-biblical) world to overdetermine or to supplement. The secret of ambivalent taboo, of contradiction, is the contradictory secret of Aristotle's unmoved mover. You are moved in your ignorance and blindness by that which is unmoved in its ignorance and blindness: the unmovable law of contradiction (thought thinking itself). Movement (motion, motive, emotion) is forever contradictory in the Greek (or extra-biblical) world, its moving secret known only in the unmoved end, the death, of contradiction. To hold, as it is so commonly, that the Socratic and the Oedipal search for knowledge represents the analytic process results in the utter distortion of both the Greek world and our own. The conflation of Greek philosophy (reason) with our own analysis ([de]construction) fails to take into account the difference between contradiction and paradox, between ignorance and knowledge of good and evil, between myth blind to and ignorant of its own contradictions and myth self-conscious of unconscious paradox, between the unmoved mover and creation from nothing (the creative fall from nothing). To seek knowledge with Socrates or Oedipus, to desire (to love) wisdom, is to demonstrate that you are utterly ignorant of and blinded by that by which you are moved, the law of contradiction, whose happy secret (end) is known only in death. To love, to be a friend of, wisdom – *philo-sophia* – is to demonstrate that the gods are not your friends. For to love or to seek wisdom is to demonstrate, fatally, that you seek in ignorance of, because you are blinded by, that which you seek.

The unaccountable difference between Socratic ignorance (*philosophia*) and analytic insight (depth psychology) is the difference between knowing *that* you are ignorant and knowing *what* you are ignorant of. It is the difference between knowing that you are contradicted (by the fatal other who moves but is not moved by you) and knowing what your contradiction is. To know what your contradiction is means that you have to work through the repetition compulsion of the father complex by becoming your own mover, the *causa sui*. It is to recreate and to redeem the past "it was" as "thus I willed it." There is literally (or symbolically) nothing similar or analogous between the two worlds of contradiction and paradox, except in words – and even then only in the loosest sense. Reasoning by analogy from paradox to contradiction (and vice versa) is a fatal Aristotelian malady – for Thomists and Freudians alike – whose consequence, the unconsciousness of dualism, Kant explicitly makes the subject of his critique of pure reason.

The fact that Freud replaces biology with extra-biblical myth points to a number of critical limitations (contradictions) in his thinking, including his inability to develop a coherent conception of either history (development) or modernity. These are really the same problem; for, just as there is no development from primitive to modern, so the only coherent concept of history is one that recognizes history to be coincident with modernity. Not only, however, are the concepts of history and modernity commensurate, but both are also biblical; and this is the imaginative leap – of reason – that Freud will not take. He cannot imagine that the impasse that constantly results from the contradiction between his metapsychological dualism and his phenomenological insight demands acknowledgment that the contradictions between primitive and modern can be overcome (worked through) solely when it is recognized that the biblical is not only not primitive but is, indeed, modern, from beginning to end. It is here that the problem of origins, of what is originary (original), and along with it the concept of the unconscious, becomes so critically important. Just as there is no development from primitive to modern, from religion to science, from the narcissism of autoerotic identification with the father('s penis, its presence or absence) to object relations (the mutuality of the golden rule), or from (the primitive) unconscious to (modern) consciousness, so modernity, history, and the unconscious are all constituted by the common problem of origins.

I have played upon the paradox that the unconscious cannot be unaware of being unconscious in the beginning and yet be unconscious in the beginning to make it (laboriously) obvious that the unconscious is, as principle (principal), not only beginning but also end, both the internal and the external. Indeed, the unconscious, in uniting past and future, is the activity of desire, shared (split) between self and other. (It makes no difference whether self and other are conceived of as human or divine, for both are properly psychical, and neither is directly a somatic or a natural object.) To redeem, to recreate the past "it was" such that I will it – with Zarathustra – even as I find myself yet in chains, although born free, is to engage and to be engaged by the unconscious. The unconscious is not the past "it was." The unconscious describes, rather, the activity by which I, in transforming the past "it was" into the nothing of creation and redemption, of liberation, historically appropriate the past for the future of self and other. The unconscious, like history, no more belongs to the past than it belongs to the future. Indeed, the unconscious, like history, belongs to the present (but it is *not* presence) as the difference between past and future. This is what Kierkegaard calls the moment, the Cartesian leap of faith whose despair in willing to be itself is so strong that it fuses the bonds connecting self and other, past and future, thought and existence. The unconscious is found in the Kantian practice of willing the paradoxical link between individual and universal, with each always other to, and thus never directly commensurate with, the other, yet always the contemporary of the other, as Kierkegaard puts it. I indicated before that the unconscious is not found outside modernity, history, the moment of the paradox, or coming into existence. It is also the case that "consciousness" – properly, self-consciousness, the consciousness that my self is always other (unconscious, overdetermined, metaphoric, fictional, paradoxical, supplementary, historical) – cannot be thought outside modernity, history, the moment of the paradox, or coming into existence. Consciousness is not immediate awareness but desire, will, love, action, the self-consciousness that, insofar as it is limited – to and by the other – is infinite and unconscious.

Freud has two fundamental insights into the phenomenology of the unconscious. First, he knows that the unconscious does not operate by the law of contradiction, that it knows no negation, and that it is indestructible, unchanging, and eternal. Second, he acknowledges that there is active "communication" between the unconscious and consciousness. (This insight does not rely upon his bogus claim that the unconscious can be proved to exist on the basis of immediate consciousness, as if you could prove the existence of the other on the basis of inference from your own immediate consciousness of self!) But Freud severely compromises these two critically significant, phenomenological insights into the unconscious by making them subject to two dualistic claims stemming from his metapsychology. First, he holds that the unconscious (like the id) is complete in the beginning, both in the beginning of the human race (in the primal sons, if not in the primal father) and in the birth of the individual. But then Freud cannot explain the emergence of consciousness, except as the product of the painful, alien stimulus of the external world, repeating the same contradictory pattern as we find in his account of the pleasure principle. Second, Freud holds that the laws governing the unconscious are completely different from those governing consciousness. But then he cannot explain the active "communication" between the unconscious and consciousness.

The dualism between the unconscious and consciousness repeats the pattern of dualism so fundamental to Freud, that between primary process and secondary process, between internal (the coherence theory of truth) and external (the correspondence theory of truth). As always, Freud never puts himself (as analyst or analysand) into the centre of his metapsychology. He does not ask who it is who knows and how it is that he knows that the laws governing the unconscious are totally different from those governing consciousness. Nor does he ask whether this knowledge is unconscious or conscious. If this knowledge is unconscious, his unconscious beginning will contradict his conscious end. If this knowledge is conscious, his conscious end will contradict his unconscious beginning. Another way of formulating the dire consequences of the dualism between the unconscious and consciousness is to see that, while the unconscious, as primordial and originary, is not bound by the law of contradiction, Freud views consciousness as secondary yet adhering to the (pseudo-)scientific logic of contradiction. But the split between non-contradictory and contradictory logics simply means that the impasse that appears in the relationship between religion (as illusory) and science (as rational) is a reprise of the dualistic relationship between the unconscious (as primary process) and consciousness (as secondary process).

Just as the religious account of the father complex is true, although illusory, so the unconscious is the true psychical reality yet illusion. Science and the logic of consciousness both have their origin in and depend on a beginning, a principle, that is their contradictory opposite. It remains utterly inexplicable, and contradictory, therefore, how science and the logic of consciousness can arise out of their opposite, indeed, how they can become the rational, conscious explanation of that which is their own illusory beginning and principle. How can that which is secondary effect (process) become the explanation of that which is primary cause (process)? The contradictory consequence of the originary dualism between reason and religion and between consciousness and the unconscious is that, while reason is the return of the repressed religious, consciousness is the return of the repressed unconscious. In other words, consciousness has no metapsychological rationale for distinguishing between repression and the unconscious, although Freud properly insists that the phenomenology of the unconscious is not reducible to the repressed. It may also be noted that the unconscious, as the true psychical reality, would appear to be what is primordially religious, in opposition to the science of secondary consciousness. It may further be noted that the dualism between the unconscious and consciousness also dominates Freud's theory of dreams. It is never clear whether the dream

work is the product of consciousness (the censor) or of the unconscious (the censored).

Freud does not see that the non-contradictory phenomenology of the
unconscious is rendered utterly contradictory by his metapsychological
claims that the unconscious is prior to, and governed by laws other
than those of, consciousness. This blindness to contradiction is reflected in his failure to distinguish, metapsychologically, between primitive
and modern, between primitive and biblical. He does not see that, since
the unconscious is not governed by the laws of contradiction, it does
not exist (and is not thought) in the Greek or primitive (extra-biblical)
world, whose first law of thought and existence is the law of contradiction (the ambivalence of taboo). The obverse of his failure to see
that the unconscious is not found in the Greek (or extra-biblical)
world, prior to consciousness, is that he fails to see that the attributes
that he ascribes to the unconscious are those that theologians in the
biblical tradition have traditionally ascribed to God. It is precisely God
of whom it is said that, in not being subject to contradiction or negation, he is indestructible, immutable, and eternal. It is on the basis of
the argument "from the absolute power of God" that William of Ockham, in gathering the fruits of medieval theology in the early four-
teenth century, deconstructs the contradictory logic of the unmoved
mover and the analogistic structure of the Thomistic doctrine that
grace perfects (Aristotelian, rational) nature.[2] What Ockham demonstrates, at least in principle, is that (paradoxical) reason is no less theological than is grace. Reason enacts the theology of divine power.
Reason does not simply reflect the Aristotelian mythology of divine
impotence (thought thinking itself). In other words, Ockham rejects all
analogies between the natural reason of paganism (as found in Plato,
Aristotle, or Virgil) and Christian grace, between reason reflecting the
law of contradiction and reason embodying the paradoxical ontology
of creation from nothing. *All* creation is from nothing, from nothing
natural or contradictory. Because creation is from nothing, the relationship between existence and thought is not natural, subject to the
law of contradiction, but psychical – at once divine and human – subject to the law of paradox.

The unconscious does not know the law of contradiction, but only
the law of paradox. The unconscious does not know negation, but only
affirmation (desire, will, love). The unconscious is indestructible (eternal) precisely because it is psychical and not (directly) subject to the
laws governing physical objects as found in natural time and space. In
showing that reason falls into dialectical (unconscious) illusion insofar
as it views itself as a physical object (soul) subject to space and time,
Kant's critique of the paralogisms (and also the antinomies) of pure

reason is applicable to everything that is psychical, including the unconscious. The dialectical illusion to which reason, or the psychical, is subject, is, in simple terms, its confusion of psychical reality with the reality of physical objects existing in the time and space of nature. The paradox of the psychical is that, although it is found in, and cannot be found outside of, natural time and space, it is not reducible to, and is not explicable in terms of, the time and space of natural objects.

We thus see that, when the psyche is truly understood with Freud to be non-contradictory, ontological consequences of which he is unaware follow directly. The unconscious is not prior to the awareness of beginning unconsciously. Further, in adhering to the law of paradox (and not to the law of contradiction), the unconscious as the psychical is revealed to be biblical and thus modern (historical) and not primitive in origin. Additionally, it can then be understood that the psychical embodies the ontological argument. It is precisely psyche, at once divine and human, that cannot be thought without existing and that cannot exist without being thought. The "necessary," that is, the freely determined, relationship between thought and existence is desire, action, love, will: the golden rule of doing unto others as you would have them do unto you. Just as the subject of thought expresses existence, so the existence of the subject (subjective existence) involves thought. Something cannot be thought unless it exists, and something cannot exist unless it is thought. I paraphrase Spinoza's formulation of the ontological argument as given at the beginning of the *Ethics*, but I also mean to recall the simple, yet revolutionary insight of Hegel that consciousness has an object (which he ultimately shows to be Spirit), to which I referred in the Preface. Consciousness does not merely know that it is conscious (as in the Greek or extra-biblical world), but it also knows what it is conscious of; and what it is conscious of involves and expresses the unconscious other, the other of the unconscious (it unconsciously involves and expresses the other). The "what" (content) of consciousness is the self that is equally the other. The object, that is, the subject of consciousness is never finitely determinable or commensurate but always already infinitely desirable (unconscious). That to which non-contradictory and thus paradoxical affirmation (desire is not mere prohibition), indestructibility, and eternal life apply is psyche: the will to redeem and to recreate the contradictory past "it was" as the paradox that, therefore, I have willed it. The law of the unconscious is to be understood not as other than but as the other law of consciousness, just as the law of God is to be understood not as other than but as the other law of human beings. The dialectic of unconscious-conscious, like the divine-human dialectic, is to be understood as paradoxical and not as contradictory otherness.

There is, naturally, an idolatrous notion of consciousness. It involves reducing either consciousness to the unconscious (one knows nothing) or the unconscious to consciousness (one knows everything). The same reductionism occurs in the self-other relationship when either self is reduced to other or other is reduced to self. A proper concept of consciousness is one profoundly aware that it is unconscious. A proper concept of the unconscious is one that involves and expresses the recognition that, to be creative, it must be truly conscious (it must be the truth of consciousness). It must be self-conscious. The self must be the (dialectical) center at once conscious and unconscious. Because the centre is both conscious and unconscious, at once self and other, it is always ex-centric.[3] Consciousness is no more the end (historical) product of externality (correspondence to reality, conformity to the *Logos* of contradiction) than the unconscious is the beginning (historical) producer of internality (illusory coherence, conformity to the pleasure of non-contradiction). The dualism between the unconscious and consciousness, like that between primary process and secondary process, is always fruitless metapsychology. It is this metapsychology that constantly distorts Freud's insight into the *Unheimlichkeit* of the unconscious, and thus of consciousness.

The sole way to see through the neurotic structures of the father complex and thus of not only the dualism of Freudian metapsychology but also all dualistic structures is on the basis of a concept of interpretation whose ontology is consistent with, as it works through and appropriates, the biblical concept of creation from nothing. Only then can one redeem and recreate, can one construct, the past "it was" as the complete result in the future that I will, not solely for myself but equally and truly for you. This is why I say that there is no alternative to the concept of interpretation that constructs the facts, the history, of life in terms of human right. This means that there is no alternative to determining human right on the basis of the golden rule, the paradoxical relationship of individual and universal. The self, because it is both mine and yours, is the undecidable difference (and unity) of individual and universal, both conscious and unconscious, as I undertake to do unto you as I would have you do unto me. The self, in desiring to be itself, embodies the very structure of self and desire in its relatedness (bondage) to the other as its historical contemporary. As Spinoza and Kant, above all, make clear, the facts of human existence are facts because our desire makes them so.[4] The objects of life are the products of our desire or will; our desire or will is not subordinate to objects, whether external or internal, the two versions of the father complex. Something is good (or bad) not in itself but because we desire it; in desiring it, we make it good (or bad) by our historical action.[5]

It is solely because the facts of the father complex are the products of our desire, and thus nothing in themselves, that we can construct, redeem, and recreate the past "it was" as "thus I willed it." But it is equally the case that it is only because the facts of the father complex are the product of our will that they are so pervasive and perverse in our lives, as they are absent from the extra-biblical world. There is no father complex in the Greek (extra-biblical) world of contradictory opposites, where one is always blind to and ignorant of the other. The father complex bursts into the reality of repression and oppression with and through the Bible. It is only on the basis of the creation of the world of historical relations from nothing that any word, fact, action, fiction, thought, object – anything that we desire – can be projected as natural and viewed as the idolatrous thing-in-itself to which all life is reducible. Idolatry does not exist outside the Bible; and the Bible does not exist outside the story of the fall, the story of idolatry and its paradoxical overcoming through the labour and conception of human desire. In its confrontation with natural death (the death of nature), human desire is revealed as the (unconscious) spirit of life, at once creative and indestructible (eternal).

It is important to see, as Freud realizes, yet does not comprehend, that it is desire – unconscious, primordial wish – that is indestructible, eternal, and "immortal," without contradiction or negation (for even *un*conscious and *in*finite are affirmations, not negations or privations). It is not nature – as it is in the Greek world: *physis* as *telos* that fatally metamorphoses into its opposite, chaos – but spirit, psyche, the psychical apparatus, the (unconscious) primordial wish that is eternal, providential, immutable, that which cannot be thought without eternally existing and that which cannot exist without eternally being thought. Thought eternally has a subject – thought exists; and existence is eternally subject(ive) – existence is the subject of thought. The eternal necessity – the determination – connecting thought and existence is not the causal necessity of objects, as found in time and space. For that necessity, as Spinoza, Kant, Hegel, Kierkegaard, and Nietzsche demonstrate, is always contingent and dependent, ultimately, on the will to power, the will whose power involves and expresses the ontological relationship of existence and thought. The necessary existence of thought and the necessary thought of existence are, rather, expressive of Freud's concept of mind, psyche, and of the unconscious as living, creative, indestructible construction, unlike archeological reconstruction.

It is in light of Freud's inability to see that the living, creative, and indestructible phenomena of life are rendered contradictory by the metapsychology of the father complex that we can properly view his theory of the three scientific blows – cosmological, biological, and psychological – against human egoism as a conventional and altogether illusory reading of modernity. His three blows presuppose the contradictory movement from the unconscious (id) to consciousness (ego), from the internal to the external, from illusion to reality, from primary process to secondary process, from religion to science, from the primitive to the modern. We have seen, however, that it is only on the basis of the dialectic of, and not the dualistic opposition between, the unconscious and consciousness that modernity can be truly comprehended. But, in order for modernity to be understood as the dialectic of unconscious and conscious, it must also be understood as originally biblical and not as originally primitive. The unconscious (as the dialectical other of consciousness), modernity, history, and the Bible are inextricably linked together.

The first scientific blow against human egoism, the Copernican revolution, far from reducing the ego to cosmological insignificance, as Freud conventionally holds, reverses the Greek dependence of "man" on the cosmic contradictions of finite space and time. As understood by Kant, the Copernican revolution strictly adheres to the biblical demand that human beings not live by the natural antinomies of space and time alone. He points out in the *Critique of Pure Reason* that the scientific revolution would never have occurred "if Copernicus had not dared, in a manner contradictory of the senses, but yet true, to seek the observed movements, not in the heavenly bodies [as the Greeks did], but in the spectator" (B xxiii). However inspired Copernicus may have been by advanced observational astronomy in the Greek tradition, the science of astronomy does not exist by observations alone. It presupposes, consistent with the ontology of creation from nothing, an Archimedean point that is located, not outside the world in another contradictory space and time, but in the entirely new world of the psyche. As Kant indicates, it is the psyche that becomes the center of the universe, an infinite center without the presence (pretense) of spatial or temporal analogy.[6]

Contrary to the hoary, textbook accounts, in the tradition of Freud's first blow, Copernicus (when understood by Kant) does not remove "man" from the centre of the universe. Rather, he eliminates, in principle, the closed, finite cosmos of the Greeks, whose centre, man, is split between the opposites of earthly and quintessential, body and soul, appearance and reality, matter and form. Copernicus thus presupposes an infinite universe whose centre – the psychical (divine or human) – is nowhere and whose circumference is everywhere, to recall the paradoxical formulation of Nicholas of Cusa in the fifteenth century.

The encompassing centre of this universe is now the ontological self whose existence and thinking cannot be known on analogy with natural space and time. This centre is not the father complex of contradictory theophallologocentrism but the paradox of interpretive reciprocity, the thing-in-itself that can be thought (willed) only as eccentric, as other than itself: the psyche conscious from beginning to end that it constitutes and is constituted by the unconscious other. Because the human self is not the natural centre of the universe, because it is not *in* the natural cosmos at all, it is not, like Socrates, ignorant of and blindly dependent on the contradictions of finite space and time. The self, rather, is the infinitely psychical centre of the universe. Since the self is not in the cosmos, it is rather the (natural) cosmos that, as Kant puts it, is *in* the (psychical) self. For it is only on the basis of this paradox (at once divine and human, both religious and rational) that the finite antinomies (dualisms) of natural space and time can be resolved, as Kant shows. The reciprocal self of biblical paradox displaces the oppositional self of paganism from the centre as it subjects to critique the antinomies of the contradictory self centred on the father complex.

We have already seen that Freud is not true to Darwin – in either his myth of the primal horde or his phylogenetic theory of the inheritance of acquired characteristics. It is not surprising, therefore, that Freud also misconstrues the significance of the Darwinian revolution as his second blow of science against the privileged position of human consciousness. Typically modern, Freud fails to see that Darwinian theory, in explaining the evolution of organic life according to the principle of natural selection, has nothing to do with the human subject, with the human psyche, with human desire, with human culture and history.[7] Darwin, like Copernicus, is true to the ontology of the Bible according to which the creation of the human psyche is from nothing, from nothing analogous with natural space and time, as distinct from the evolution of the organic forms of nature that conform to the antinomies of space and time.[8] There is no analogy between creation (history) and evolution (generation). Human beings, *qua* animals, are biologically generated. But the paradox of the theory of evolution is that it is not subject to (it is not the subject of) the theory of evolution. The theory of evolution does not constitute the evolution of theory. The theory of evolution does not explain the history of ideas, including scientific ideas and, in particular, the idea of evolution. The theory of evolution cannot explain its own history. There is no analogy between evolution and history. The theory of evolution cannot explain itself. It is not self-referential, for the human being is the only animal that is *causa sui*. As Lord Zuckerman writes at the end of his article "Apes Я Not Us," "there is nothing with which to compare language. Language exists sui generis. That is why we [humans] are what we are. And that is a mystery no less profound than is the origin of life itself" (49).[9]

Because the human species is unlike other species – it is without analogy or comparison: it is self-referential – it cannot be explained by the theory of evolution. Human beings have no reciprocal relationship with animals, with nature, except in and through the human recognition that we are completely dependent on nature; for, although reciprocation cannot be extracted (inductively or deductively) from nature, there is no human reciprocation outside nature. Because the theory of evolution is not an explanation of the theory of evolution, it does not explain mind (psyche) as cultural history. In other words, the evolution of the brain is a *theory* of mind, but it is not a theory of *mind*. The explanation of the brain is an *explanation* of, but not an explanation *of*, the mind; and this proposition is not reversible. The brain cannot explain itself.[10] But the mind can and does explain itself. Indeed, there is no other subject of explanation, or interpretation, for the mind but the mind. The mind, *sui generis* and *causa sui*, is its own interpretation. That which explains the brain – the mind – is not then itself explicable by the brain. The mind is not explicable in terms of the neural sciences.

Religious dogmatists (and skeptics) are mortified and scientific skeptics (and dogmatists) are uplifted by the theory of evolution. But those sophisticated in both science (like Darwin) and religion (like the heirs of Spinoza, Kant, and Hegel) see that there is no conflict between the science of evolution and (biblical) religion. They also see that, to the degree evolutionary science is used to debunk theological dogmatism (skepticism), theology can be used to debunk scientific skepticism (dogmatism).[11] Like Copernican cosmology, Darwinian biology is unthinkable outside of an ontology of creation from nothing. It presupposes a theory of mind – at once conscious and unconscious – that is not itself subject to the theory of evolution, although it cannot exist apart from it.

Freud never recognizes the fundamental difference between causal (scientific) explanation and reciprocal (interpretive) explanation, between what Kant in the *Critique of Pure Reason* calls a question of fact (*quid facti*) and a question of right (*quid juris*). Indeed, Freud distorts not only science but also interpretation by reducing them both to the putative authority of the father complex, which is no more scientific than it is interpretive. With regard to scientific law, he fails to see that that which explains (that is, the cause) cannot be the product (that is, the effect) of that which it purports to explain. For example, science cannot be the rational explanation of religion, when science is, for Freud, the (historical) product of religion. The secondary process (the

342 Depth Psychology, Interpretation, and the Bible

reality principle, reason) cannot explain the primary process (the pleasure principle, illusion) when it is the effect of that which it claims to
be the explanation (cause). The theory of evolution explains the origin
of species. But the origin of species does not explain (account for) the
theory of evolution. The theory of evolution cannot itself be the product of evolution, for the effect cannot be the cause of that by which it
is produced. With regard to reciprocal interpretation – the golden rule
– Freud fails to see that that which explains (interprets) is itself the subject of explanation (interpretation). To explain (interpret) another is to
be subject yourself no less than the other to your explanation (interpretation). The golden rule of reciprocation commands you to interpret
the other as you would have the other interpret you.

We may summarize the difference between science, interpretation,
and Freudian metapsychology in the following fashion. Science argues
from fact to fact – presupposing the question of right. Interpretation
argues from right to fact – presupposing the ontology of creation from
nothing (the facts of nature, being nothing in themselves, are the creation of desire, the will to power). Freudian metapsychology argues
from fact to right – utterly distorting both science and interpretation.
It is the argument that (some) facts are natural, primordial, originary,
and thus the basis of human right that, without exception, lies at the
origin of dualism, contradiction, and idolatry. Perhaps the most spectacular example in Freud of how reversal and distortion – of both reason (science) and religion (interpretation) – results from the conflation
of fact and right, of science and interpretation, is his demonstration
that it is the religious (but illusory) explanation of the father complex
that is true. This demonstration is neither scientific nor interpretive.

We have now seen that the first two scientific blows against the pretense of human consciousness only go to show that, since science is not
master in its own unconscious house, cosmology and biology exist
within the human psyche. It will then be no surprise to find that, when
Freud strikes the third blow for science in the name of his own depth
psychology, he demonstrates that the master of psychology, as the science of the unconscious, is the lord God, not the father complex. The
third displacement of human megalomania is of a piece with the two
earlier blows against human egoism. It both presupposes biblical
ontology – creation *ex nihilo* – and advances it meaningfully (if unconsciously!). It is hardly news to those who are religiously informed to
learn that human beings do not live by bread alone, that they are not
their own centre but that their centre is the unconscious other – the
neighbour and God. But it is here, I think, that Lord Zuckerman himself remains unconvincing. It is not language that is the truly human
(psychical) miracle. If there were only language – the plenitude of

human languages – but no communication, no concept of communication, centred on the notion of the unconscious and thus on history, we would have no consciousness of the significance that language is *sui generis*. Just as language is not reducible to the origin of species, so communication is not reducible to language. Language remains natural in the sense that all human beings (assuming normal physical development) naturally learn to speak the tongues (including sign languages) of those by whom they are acculturated. Where the species *homo sapiens* is, there natural language – of one kind or another, but always perfect and complete – shall be spoken (and perhaps also written). No natural language, as such, is superior or inferior to any other natural language; for all natural languages are fully capable of expressing all that there is to express. (Whether the linguistic capacities are so used, in any given case, by individual or society, is another matter.) But natural language does not entail communication, which is precisely the point of the story of the Babel of languages as told in Genesis 11. The oneness of human beings and the oneness of God cannot be communicated by one or more natural languages. Natural language is not communication. Something else is needed, in addition to natural language, for communication to occur; and that something else is psyche: the ontology of creation from nothing as articulated in and through the golden rule. Just as the mind presupposes the brain yet cannot be explained by the brain – the mind is the brain's limit – so communication presupposes language but cannot be explained by language – communication is the limit of language.

The historical significance of Copernicus, Darwin, and Freud is not in dispute. But I do dispute the canonical version of history as represented in Freud's theory of the three blows of modern science. Freud is typically modern in his failure to see that what is at stake in the historical revolution of modernity is ontology, a concept of communication whose other name is interpretation. Interpretation is not given in the nature of space and time, nor is it given in natural language. It is given only when men and women conceive of themselves, not on analogy with nature, but in the image of the other – God, the neighbour, the unconscious. Structured by desire, by the golden rule, I interpret, I construct the other as I would wish the other to interpret, to construct me, as I argue from the right that we humanly share to interpret the facts in play between us. Interpretation embodies the principle of reciprocation. That which explains the other is also subject to the interpretation of the other. Interpretation acknowledges authorship, authority, creativity, as it deconstructs the father complex with all its attendant, authoritarian concepts of dualism. It is precisely the concept of interpretation that Freud presupposes both in his phenomenology

344 Depth Psychology, Interpretation, and the Bible

and in his concept of psychotherapeutic construction. It is, then, bewildering that Freud fails to discern the contradiction between his concept of reciprocal construction and his metapsychological principle of scientific explanation. When he attempts to explain the other on the basis of the metapsychology of the father complex, what he demonstrates, without fail, is the return of the other as repressed. He shows the contradictory dependence of that which explains on that which is to be explained (the other), of the unconscious on consciousness, of the primary process on the secondary process, of the pleasure principle on the reality principle, of the id on the ego, of the primal father on (the murder by) the primal sons.

In the beginning is interpretation, that act appropriating the ontological argument for the reciprocal relationship of thought and existence. Unless we begin with a concept of existence and thought that is at once theological and philosophical, both faithful and rational, and no less religious than it is secular, we shall, without exception, always end, as Freud ends, in contradiction. We shall end with a concept of reason as the return of the repressed religious and with a concept of religion as the return of the repressed rational. The psychology of religion is no less, and no more, than the religion of psychology. Psychology and religion demonstrate together that, insofar as depth psychology provides insight into religion as the principle (origin) of the secular other, so religion has insight into depth psychology as the principle (end) of the religious other. There is no exception, no alternative to the truth, Freud is right. But what he does not see is that truth is no more rational than it is faithful and no less religious than it is secular. The religous is fully explicable rationally, when reason is (de)constructed on the basis of the desire of the golden rule, consistent with the ontological argument that both thought and existence are created from nothing. The secular is fully explicable in religious terms, when religion is (de)constructed on the basis of the desire of the golden rule, consistent with the ontological argument that both thought and existence are created from nothing. Indeed, it is only in terms of the reciprocal relationship of psychology and religion that the dogmatism (together with the skepticism) of each can be overcome.

The texts of Freud provide us with an extraordinary example of the impasse that occurs when interpretation as the principle of reciprocation – although central to his phenomenology and the presupposition of his analytic practice – does not replace the father complex as the basis of his metapsychology. The reversals and contradictions that emerge everywhere in Freud's thinking and do enormous harm to his phenomenological insight result from his failure to see that depth psychology is not scientific but interpretive. While his metapsychology is neither scientific nor interpretive, his phenomenology is consistent solely with the concept of interpretation whose principle of reciprocation is true to the Bible. The ontological argument for the creation of thought and existence from nothing, from nothing outside their reciprocal relationship, involves and expresses the golden rule of interpretation according to which indestructible desire constructs the other as the complete result of the unconscious self. Where, in the beginning, the ontology of creation *ex nihilo* is, there, in the end, shall the golden rule of interpretation be.

APPENDIX:
Freud and the Upanishads

In the footnote that Freud attaches in 1921 to the summary he gives, in *Beyond the Pleasure Principle*, of the myth of Eros attributed to Aristophanes by Plato in the *Symposium*, he remarks that "what is essentially the same theory is already to be found in the Upanishads." He cites a brief passage from the Brihadaranyaka, one of the ten principal Upanishads in the Hindu tradition, claiming that it is the oldest of the Upanishads and that all competent scholars agree that it cannot be dated later than 800 BCE. *Upanishad*, we may note, means sitting near devotedly and, by extension, secret teaching, knowledge of Brahman (supreme reality: utterly undifferentiated, undivided, selfless identity), the identity of the Atman (Self) with Brahman (in later tradition called nirvana). In the passage cited by Freud, it is said that the Self (Atman) "'made this his Self to fall in two, and then arose husband and wife'" (331). Freud goes on to say that he would hesitate, against the prevailing scholarly opinion, "to give an unqualified denial" to the possibility that Plato's myth is derived, if only indirectly, from the Hindu myth, and he adds that, "even if a derivation of this kind ... were established, the significance of the coincidence between the two trains of thought would scarcely be diminished" (331–2).[1]

Two points may be noted here. (1) Freud is right that, whatever the historical relationship between ancient Greeks and ancient Hindus, there is an essential congruence in their mythical thought. (In other words, even if there were no evidence of Plato's dependence on the Vedas, "the coincidence between the two trains of thought would scarcely be diminished.") It is often not appreciated (either it is not recognized or it is denied) that contradictory opposites equally shape the mythological structures of Hindu and Platonic (Greek, and ultimately all extra-biblical) thinking. The opposition between the one and the many, between reality and appearance, is such that where there is being (Brahman or Form) there is no consciousness, and where there is consciousness (or desire) there is no being. The contrast with the biblical tradition, in which existence and thought are united (yet not immediately identified) through the ontological argument, is absolute. (2) Just as Freud obscures the real significance of the myth attributed by Plato to Aristophanes by failing to indicate that the division of the sexes reflects their punishment (contradiction) for seeking to attain their original or past (finite) wholeness or unity, so he equally obscures the significance of the original unity of the Hindu concept of Self (Atman) by citing only its division into male and female. The fundamental point that the Brihadaranyaka seeks to establish, however – and it is this which Freud fails to note - is that any division in the utter self-identity of Atman reflects a fall into the world of contradictory appearances. In order to attain the nirvana of self-identity, the self must be released from the endless cycle of contradictory ignorance, suffering, and craving, i.e., from all consciousness and desire.

Notes

PREFACE

1 Cahill writes that "the Jews developed a whole new way of experiencing reality, the only alternative to all ancient worldviews and all ancient religions" (246). "All religions *are* cyclical, mythical, and without reference to history as we have come to understand it – all religions *except* the Judeo-Christian stream in which Western consciousness took life" (247–8). Bibliographical information on authors and texts referred to will be found in References.

2 This is the position of Spinoza in his *Theological-Political Treatise*, on which I shall call throughout my study, as I have done in previous studies. I refer the reader to the studies of Fishbane and Levinson who show that the (Hebrew) Bible is interpretive at its very core. Note Akenson's claim that, "to a remarkable degree, the scriptures tell us how to read the scriptures, although these self-contained instructions are now out of fashion among biblical scholars" (7).

3 Aristotle changes the terms but not the structure of Platonic (Greek) thought. He posits the unknowable and the unknown law of contradiction, consistent with Plato's noble lie, as the unknown and the unknowable basis of all life in the *Metaphysics*. He also repeats the Platonic opposition between the determinate one and the indeterminate many, between form and appearance, as the opposition between soul and body, form and matter, and actuality and potentiality. Aristotle then crowns his metaphysics with the contradiction than which none greater can be thought without existing: the unmoved mover, that which, in moving all,

is moved by none – thought thinking itself, thought identical with itself as its own object.

4 I take the distinction between knowing *that* (where consciousness is opposed to, as the contradiction of, its object, and the object is opposed to, as the contradiction of, consciousness) and knowing *what* (where consciousness has an object) from Hegel and Kierkegaard. I have applied it systematically in earlier studies, and I shall elaborate it here in later chapters.

5 It is hard to know where to begin, for two massively pervasive errors are dogmatically embedded here as the received truth of philosophy. First, the standard interpretation of Descartes (from Spinoza, Hume, and Hegel to such disparate thinkers in our century as Husserl, Ryle, and Foucault, not to mention the deconstructionist Mark Taylor) is that he initiates modern thought by reducing it to the fundamental dualism between consciousness and existence. The truth is, however, that Descartes, notwithstanding the primitiveness of his formulations and arguments, inaugurates modern philosophy by being the first thinker to articulate the ontological argument for existence as involving human self-reflexivity while also expressing divine existence. Apel, however, does recognize that self-reflexivity in Descartes involves an object. I shape my *Truth and Interpretation* around the Cartesian dialectic of thought and existence as a means of contesting the received dogma of philosophy. Second, Socrates (together with Plato and Aristotle) is nearly universally viewed as the founder not only of philosophy, notwithstanding the decisive demonstrations of Hegel and Kierkegaard to the contrary, but even (within psychological circles) of psychotherapy. If Socrates proves anything to his fellow interlocutors, however, it is that they are ignorant of the fatal truth of the law of contradiction. To seek (to desire) knowledge is always to lack (to want!) knowledge, for all seeking (desire) is in ignorance of what you seek (just as to know the truth is to be identical with the truth – in the absence of all desire). It is perplexing, therefore, to see such intelligent writers on depth psychology as Lear and Stein severely compromise their insights by claiming that depth psychology is consistent with the Greek logic of contradiction, when, as Socrates demonstrates, to desire is, by the logic of contradiction, to lack, to be ignorant of, the end of your desire (i.e., desire does not exist in the Greek world). Lear and Stein fail to see that the loving difference moving both analyst and analysand, on which the logic of psychotherapy is founded, is completely different from the difference that the law of contradiction imposes in its appearance as the unmoved mover: that which (ignorantly and blindly) moves the other is eternally unmoved by the (ignorant and blind) other.

6 See the recent studies of Freud by Paul and Webster. What is particularly interesting in light of the approach that I take here is that, while both

scholars argue that Freudian metapsychology is biblical, Paul views it as true and Webster as false. Thus each scholar fails to see that it is the phenomenology of Freud, not his metapsychology, that is biblical. His phenomenology is true (because it is biblical), while his metapsychology is false (because it is not biblical). Paul and Webster are thus each right that Freud is true to the Bible. Both, however, are wrong about Freud's metapsychology, the first in claiming that it is true because it is biblical, the second in claiming that it is false because it is biblical. See my "Freud, the Bible, and Hermeneutics." See also Crews and McGinn ("Freud under Analysis") for a sampling of critical evaluations of Freud's thought and Forrester for a standard defense of Freud. Both Yerushalmi (in *Freud's Moses*) and Derrida (in *Archive Fever*) discuss the issue of whether or in what sense psychoanalysis is a "Jewish science." Derrida even writes that "belief, the radical phenomenon of believing, the only relationship possible to the other as other, does not in the end have any possible place, any irreducible status in Freudian psychoanalysis. Which it nonetheless makes possible" (94). But neither Yerushalmi nor Derrida systematically distinguishes between Freud's metapsychology and phenomenology in light of what I call biblical ontology.

CHAPTER ONE

1 Closely related to this passage are two of Nietzsche's aphorisms in *The Gay Science*: #34 "*Historia abscondita*" and #341 "The greatest weight." In "Of Experience" Montaigne views "pastime" (passing the time, time passing) as the time "it was," the time in which one's soul rather loses than finds itself (853–4).

2 It is in this same spirit that one must be critical of both Hegel and Kierkegaard for evading the dialectical identity of theology and philosophy, faith and reason, the religious and the secular. Hegel holds to the hierarchical superiority of philosophy to religion (Christianity), although what he actually demonstrates with incomparable acumen is the undecidability of their difference. Kierkegaard holds to the hierarchical superiority of the religious (Christianity) to secular life (as found, for example, in the family, politics, and art). But what he actually demonstrates with incomparable insight is that love of existence believes all things and yet is never deceived, least of all by his claim that love's upbuilding of existence is any less secular than it is religious. That the relationship between religion and psychology is uncanny is well indicated in the following two testimonies. In the first, Clarence Earl Gideon (a poor prisoner who successfully petitioned the Supreme Court of the United States to find it unconstitutional to be tried in a state criminal court without a lawyer) related his life in a letter written in 1962 (in the precise terms that fol-

low) to the lawyer appointed by the Supreme Court to represent him in his constitutional challenge: "Once hearing a wise old Doctor say that the best thing for a poor person who did not have the money to hire psychiatry, the best thing is to send them to church. So I decided to use the church. I do not like the idea of forcing my children are [or] enticing them to believe in any certain religion but I have always wanted them to learn the moral respect that the people of this country has and of all the great religions I have pick the christian religion because it is based on love" (Lewis, 74). In the second, Robert Lowell stated in a conversation published in 1965 that, having abandoned Protestantism (in which he was raised) and Roman Catholicism (to which he subsequently converted), "when that goes and we look at it another way, Freud seems the only religious teacher ... He's a prophet. I think somehow he continues both the Jewish and Christian tradition, and puts it maybe in a much more rational position ... What I find about Freud is that he provides the conditions that one must think in ... There are very few countries founded on a declaration the way ours was. There's something biblical and Jewish about that – Messianic" (Alvarez, 102–3). I wish to thank Charles B. Smith and Heidi Ronteix, respectively, for bringing these texts to my attention.

3 I discuss Spiro's *Oedipus in the Trobriands* in chapter 3.

4 In separating philosophy from theology, such that the hierarchical subordination of one to the other is eliminated (i.e., the difference between philosophy and theology is demonstrated to be undecidable, not dualistic or binary), Spinoza shows that both are founded on the ontology of the golden rule. He thus shows that reason no less than faith is biblical in origin and structure.

5 In developing a concept of interpretation according to which the Bible is to be interpreted (faithfully) from itself alone, by the reader (rationally) from himself alone, Spinoza deconstructs both the dogmatic rationalism of Maimonides (according to which the Bible is subordinated to a concept of reason external to itself alone) and the skeptical fideism of Maimonides' opponents (according to which the Bible is subordinated to a concept of faith internal to itself alone). See chapter 5.

6 It is important to note, however, that, although Hegel articulates the process of mutual recognition – spirit recognizing spirit – as the structure of (modern) self-consciousness in the *Phenomenology of Spirit*, he suppresses the fact that it presupposes (by resuming) biblical ontology.

CHAPTER TWO

1 Reference will also be made to Freud's general works on psychoanalysis (*Introductory Lectures, New Introductory Lectures*, and *An Outline*), *The Ego and the Id*, and individual, shorter pieces.

2 Freud continued to revise and expand *The Interpretation of Dreams* through the eighth edition of 1930.

3 In *The Interpretation of Dreams* Freud elaborates a concept of mind in terms of what he calls the systems *Ucs.* (unconscious), *Pcs.* (preconscious), *Cs.* (consciousness), and *Pcpt.* (perception). Since he later dropped this system, I shall use the more conventional designations to facilitate communication.

4 See Freud's like statement in the footnote on 186.

5 See also "Some Additional Notes on Dream-Interpretation as a Whole," B: "Moral Responsibility for the Content of Dreams," and the discussion of "lying dreams" in "The Psychogenesis of a Case of Homosexuality in a Woman" (392–3).

6 Freud points out that, while dreaming, we often remind ourselves that it's only a dream (453, 628, 726); that we are conscious of dreaming and that individuals can become skilled in directing their dreams (726–7); and that we often say that "I should never dream of such a thing" (137).

7 I omit all discussion of the analysis of individual dreams, many of them famously his own, to which Freud devotes a large part of *The Interpretation of Dreams*. Our focus in this study is on Freud's theory, not on Freud himself.

8 Freud goes on to say that "it is in any case instructive to get to know the much-trampled soil from which our virtues proudly spring. Very rarely does the complexity of a human character, driven hither and thither by dynamic forces, submit to a choice between simple alternatives, as our antiquated morality would have us believe" (783).

9 Freud further observes that, although this assumption cannot be proved to hold generally, it also cannot be disproved. Three points should be noted in connection with Freud's founding the mechanism of the dream work (of what constitutes dreams) on his theory of neurosis. (1) He argues that the dream work is identical with the irrational psychical processes involved in the formation of neurotic symptoms. (2) He formulates the thesis that he borrows from his theory of hysteria as follows: "*A normal train of thought is only submitted to abnormal psychical treatment of the sort we have been describing if an unconscious wish, derived from infancy and in a state of repression, has been transferred on to it*" (757). I shall discuss the concept of infantile wish and repression in chapter 4 in conjunction with Freud's concept of phylogenesis. (3) In founding the mechanism of the dream work on his theory of neurosis, Freud undercuts (contradicts) his express aim (claim) to develop a concept of the unconscious independent of psychopathology.

10 The passage continues: "The part played by the latter [the preconscious] is restricted once and for all to directing along the most expedient paths the wishful impulses that arise from the unconscious. These unconscious

wishes exercise a compelling force upon all later mental trends, a force which those trends are obliged to fall in with or which they may perhaps endeavor to divert and direct to higher aims" (763).

11 Freud notes further that "a neat example of a psychical system shut off from the stimuli of the external world, and able to satisfy even its nutritional requirements autistically ... is afforded by a bird's egg" (37).

12 "*Education* can be described without more ado as an incitement to the conquest of the pleasure principle, and to its replacement by the reality principle; it seeks, that is, to lend its help to the developmental process which affects the ego. To this end it makes use of an offer of love as a reward from the educators; and it therefore fails if a spoilt child thinks that it possesses that love in any case and cannot lose it whatever happens" (41).

13 Further presentations of the unconscious may be found in "A Note on the Unconscious," *Introductory Lectures* (chapter 18); *The Ego and the Id* (chapter 1); *New Introductory Lectures* (chapter 31), where what Freud says about the id is largely taken from "The Unconscious"; and *An Outline* (chapter 4).

14 After raising objections that this process of inference discloses not an unconscious but a second consciousness, Freud concludes that "we have grounds for modifying our inference about ourselves and saying that what is proved is not the existence of a second consciousness in us, but the existence of psychical acts which lack consciousness" (172).

15 But, Freud adds, "internal objects are less unknowable than the external world" (173).

16 Freud typically sees the problems inherent in the binary opposition between immediate consciousness (perception) and inference. In his study of Rat Man he notes that, according to an astronomer, our knowledge of whether the moon is inhabited possesses the certainty of our knowledge of who our father was but not of who our mother was and comments: "A great advance was made in civilization when men decided to put their inferences upon a level with the testimony of their senses and to make the step from matriarchy to patriarchy" (113).

17 Not to mention by their predecessors, Descartes and Spinoza, and their successors, Kierkegaard and Nietzsche.

18 In fact, he states in the last sentence of section V that "in human beings we must be prepared to find possible pathological conditions under which the two systems alter, or even exchange, both their content and their characteristics" (193).

19 Freud writes in *An Outline* that "the division between the three classes of material which possess these qualities [conscious, preconscious, and unconscious] is neither absolute nor permanent" (391).

20 "Repressions that have failed will of course have more claim on our

interest than any that may have been successful; for the latter will for the most part escape our examination" (153). In *The Ego and the Id* Freud writes that "we obtain our concept of the unconscious from the theory of repression" (353).

21 In the *New Introductory Lectures* Freud writes that "the ego must on the whole carry out the id's intentions, it fulfils its task by finding out the circumstances in which those intentions can best be achieved. The ego's relation to the id might be compared with that of a rider to his horse. The horse supplies the locomotive energy, while the rider has the privilege of deciding on the goal and of guiding the powerful animal's movement. But only too often there arises between the ego and the id the not precisely ideal situation of the rider being obliged to guide the horse along the path by which it itself wants to go" (109–10).

22 "But this in turn is due to the fact," Freud continues, "that the ego, at the time at which it was set the task, was undeveloped and powerless. The decisive repressions all take place in early childhood" (304). Whether it is consistent to explain repression on the basis of the undeveloped, powerless, weak, helpless, and "infantile" ego, situated between developed id and developed reality, given that the ego emerges from the id due to the influence of the external world, will be considered in chapter 4.

23 Freud writes as follows in "Analysis Terminable and Interminable": "the analytic situation consists in our allying ourselves with the ego of the person under treatment, in order to subdue portions of his id which are uncontrolled – that is to say to include them in the synthesis of the ego" (235). "The therapeutic effect of analysis depends on the making conscious what is, in the widest sense, repressed within the id" (256). Although Freud tends to ignore the role of the superego when addressing ego psychology from the point of view of therapy, he does observe in *An Outline* that when the doctor goes to help the ego in its internal civil war, their enemies are "the instinctual demands of the id and the conscientious demands of the superego" (406). The ego's "activity is inhibited by strict prohibitions from the superego, its energy is consumed in vain attempts at fending off the demands of the id" (414–15).

24 "The pleasure principle, then, is a tendency operating in the service of a function whose business it is to free the mental apparatus entirely from excitation or to keep the amount of excitation in it constant or to keep it as low as possible" (336).

25 Freud also notes that "what psychoanalysis reveals in the transference phenomena of neurotics can also be observed in the lives of some normal people. The impression they give is of being pursued by a malignant fate or possessed by some 'daemonic' power" (292).

26 In a footnote added in 1925 Freud warns that "the reader should not overlook the fact that what follows is the development of an extreme line

of thought" – to be corrected when account is taken of the sexual instincts (310).

27 This is consistent with the argument of his later works that the death instincts cannot be found separate from Eros, as we shall see in the next chapter.

28 When Freud observes a few pages later that his theory of the life and death instincts replaces his earlier theory of the sexual and ego instincts, he asserts that "our views have from the very first been *dualistic*, and today they are even more definitely dualistic than before ... Jung's libido theory is on the contrary *monistic*" (326).

29 I follow here the analysis that is found in my study, "Beyond the Pleasure Principle."

30 See the Appendix, "Freud and the Upanishads," for a presentation of what Freud calls "the significance of the coincidence between the two trains of thought," Hindu and Platonic (332).

31 In *An Outline* Freud appears to reject the Platonic basis of instinct. If living things come later than and arise from inanimate things, he observes, "then the death instinct fits in with the formula we have pro-posed to the effect that instincts tend towards a return to an earlier state. In the case of Eros ... we cannot apply this formula. To do so would presuppose that living substance was once a unity which had later been torn apart and was now striving towards reunion" (332), as Freud in fact speculates in *Beyond the Pleasure Principle*. In a footnote Freud adds that "creative writers have imagined something of the sort, but nothing like it is known to us from the actual history of living sub-stance." He goes on to remark that the two instincts, in biologically opposing and combining with each other, produce the whole variety of life. "The analogy of our two basic instincts extends from the sphere of living things to the pair of opposing forces – attraction and repulsion – which rule in the inorganic world." In yet another footnote Freud observes that "this picture of the basic forces or instincts, which still arouses much opposition among analysts, was already familiar to the [ancient Greek] philosopher Empedocles" (380). In "Analysis Ter-minable and Interminable" Freud expresses great delight that his theory of the life and death instincts, although rejected by psychoanalysts, had already been put forth by Empedocles, whom he fulsomely praises for the Faustian breadth of his vision. In holding that both individual beings and the cosmos as a whole are ruled by two antagonistic powers, love and strife, which operate instinctually and not with a conscious purpose, Freud remarks, "Empedocles thought of the process of the universe as a continuous, never-ceasing alternation of periods in which the one or the other of the two fundamental forces gains the upper hand ... The two fundamental principles of Empedocles ... are, both in

name and function, the same as our two primal instincts, *Eros* and *destructiveness*" (246).

32 This seemingly banal observation is revolutionary for Freud. Previously, he had held that the sexual act, in reducing tension, serves the pleasure principle. In *Beyond the Pleasure Principle*, for example, he writes that the pleasure principle is a tendency serving the function of freeing "the mental apparatus entirely from excitation or to keep the amount of excitation in it constant or to keep it as low as possible ... The function thus described would be concerned with the most universal endeavor of all living substance – namely to return to the quiescence of the inorganic world. We have all experienced how the greatest pleasure attainable by us, that of the sexual act [*sic*!], is associated with a momentary extinction of a highly intensified excitation" (336–7). In *The Ego and the Id* Freud even claims (sophistically) that, because the sexual act results in the discharge of tension (unpleasure), the id, by speedily complying with it, serves the pleasure principle (the death instinct). He also notes in the same connection that the satisfaction of the sexual act is equated with death and that copulation in some of the lower animals directly results in their death (388).

33 But, just as Freud always insists upon the quantitative over the qualitative factor, so even here his abandonment of the quantitative (known) factor for the qualitative (unknown) factor is grudging and doubtless indicative of the fact that it does not signal a fundamental reorientation in his thinking: "It appears that they [pleasure and unpleasure] depend, not on this quantitative factor, but on some characteristic of it which we can only describe as a qualitative one" (414).

34 Heraclitus, together with his brilliant follower Protagoras, equally demonstrates that the unchanging one of Parmenides is contradictory. In the concluding paragraph of *Fear and Trembling* Kierkegaard indicates that the wish to go further, the wish to go further than faith, the wish to go further than the faith of father Abraham always demonstrates the canny truth of the Greek logic of contradiction – the truth uncannily unrealizable by the Greeks themselves. To attempt to go beyond Heraclitus is to find yourself back in the unmoving stream of Parmenides, and vice versa.

CHAPTER THREE

1 But see "The Psychogenesis of a Case of Homosexuality in a Woman."
2 It should be noted, however, that Freud concludes his *Three Essays on Sexuality* with this sentence: "The unsatisfactory conclusion, however, that emerges from these investigations of the disturbances of sexual life is that we know far too little of the biological processes constituting the

essence of sexuality to be able to construct from our fragmentary information a theory adequate to the understanding alike of normal and of pathological conditions" (169).

3 For Rousseau, see the earlier sections of the *Social Contract* and the *Second Discourse*, part II. For Spinoza, see the *Theological-Political Treatise*, chapter 16.

4 "While he was still speaking to the people, behold, his mother and his brothers stood outside, asking to speak to him. But he replied to the man who told him, 'Who is my mother, and who are my brothers?' And stretching out his hand toward his disciples, he said, 'Here are my mother and my brothers! For whoever does the will of my Father in heaven is my brother, and sister, and mother'" (Matthew 12.46–50). See Mark 3.31–35 and Luke 8.19–21.

5 I call upon the Gospels here.

6 Freud adds that the fact of bisexuality also complicates the picture. In *Civilization and its Discontents* he notes that "the theory of bisexuality is still surrounded by many obscurities and we cannot but feel it as a serious impediment in psychoanalysis that it has not yet found any link with the theory of the instincts" (295–6).

7 Also see the following for additional discussions of the distinction between active and passive: "The Psychogenesis of a Case of Homosexuality in a Woman" (399–400) and *Civilization and its Discontents* (295–7).

8 In *The Ego and the Id*, chapter V, Freud views the ego as helplessly dependent on three masters – id, superego, and external world – and thus menaced by the dangers they represent.

9 Freud goes on to say that this requirement distinguishes psychoanalysis from other types of therapy.

10 The basic sources for Freud's concept of the Oedipus complex and the superego are all subsequent to 1920: *Group Psychology* (chapter 7), *The Ego and the Id* (chapter 3), *New Introductory Lectures* (chapters 31 and 33), *An Outline* (chapter 7), and the following shorter studies: "The Dissolution of the Oedipus Complex," "Some Psychical Consequences of the Anatomical Distinction between the Sexes," and "Female Sexuality."

11 In the *New Introductory Lectures* Freud describes identification as "the assimilation of one ego to another one, as a result of which the first ego behaves like the second in certain respects, imitates it and in a sense takes it up into itself ... It is a very important form of attachment to someone else, probably the very first, AND NOT THE SAME THING AS THE CHOICE OF AN OBJECT." For a boy to identify with the father is to want "to *be like* his father." For the boy to make the father his object choice is to want "to *have* him, to possess him. In the first case his ego is altered on the model of his father; in the second case that is not necessary. IDENTIFICA-

TION AND OBJECT CHOICE ARE TO A LARGE EXTENT INDEPENDENT OF EACH OTHER" (94–5ᶜ).

12 Freud adds in a footnote that "perhaps it would be safer to say 'with the parents'" (370).

13 In *The Ego and the Id* Freud writes of the identifications formed in the superego as both "a residue of the earliest object-choices of the id" and "an energetic reaction-formation against those choices" (373–4).

14 Freud goes on to write that "the derivation of the superego from the first-object cathexes of the id [*sic*!], from the Oedipus complex, signifies even more for it. This derivation ... brings it into relation with the phylo-genetic acquisitions of the id and makes it a reincarnation of former ego structures which have left their precipitates behind in the id" (389–90). Two comments are in order here. (1) To claim that the superego derives "from the first object cathexes of the id" can only mean that these object choices (active regarding the mother, passive regarding the father) are repressed by the original identification with the father. (2) The fact that the superego repeats the id, which repeats the ego, which repeats the superego ... can only mean that identification with the father('s penis) is a circle closed within the ego of the primal father.

15 Freud goes on to say that, "since the penis (to follow Ferenczi [always dangerous!]) owes its extraordinarily high narcissistic cathexis to its organic significance for the propagation of the species, the catastrophe to the Oedipus complex (the abandonment of incest and the institution of conscience and morality) may be regarded as a victory of the race over the individual. This is an interesting point of view when one considers that neurosis is based upon a struggle of the ego against the demands of the sexual function" (341–2). It is "interesting" precisely because it is false. Narcissism (representing the ego) can hardly be "organic," social, or sexual, compared to the individual; and neurosis cannot be viewed in terms of the opposition between individual and society.

16 Freud continues: "To it itself [libido] we cannot assign any sex; if, follow-ing the conventional equation of activity and masculinity, we are inclined to describe it as masculine, we must not forget that it also covers trends with a passive aim. Nevertheless, the juxtaposition 'feminine libido' is without any justification. Furthermore, it is our impression that more constraint has been applied to the libido when it is pressed into the ser-vice of the feminine function, and that – to speak teleologically – Nature takes less careful account of its demands than in the case of masculinity. And the reason for this may lie – thinking once again teleologically – in the fact that the accomplishment of the aim of biology has been entrusted to the aggressiveness of men and has been made to some extent indepen-dent of women's consent" (165–6). It is clear that biology (when viewed in Darwinian and subsequent genetic terms) has nothing to do with tele-

ology or aims and that here in Freud it is cultural analysis masquerading as science.

17 See Freud's "Observations on 'Wild' Psychoanalysis."

18 One should bear in mind, however, the fierce criticism to which Freud's analyses of Dora and Schreber have recently been subject; and there are also fundamental questions to be asked about his theoretical framework in his studies of both Rat Man and Wolf Man.

19 Freud writes in *An Outline* that, "if we ask an analyst what his experience has shown to be the mental structures least accessible to influence in his patients, the answer will be: in a woman her wish for a penis, in a man his feminine attitude towards his own sex, a precondition of which would, of course, be the loss of his penis" (429).

20 Although, as I have indicated, Freud greatly modifies his instinct theory (from his original theory of ego instincts and sexual instincts through the notion of ego libido and object libido to the instincts of death and life), he never relinquishes as such his adherence to his original position based on what he calls the two fundamental needs of hunger and love. In the *New Introductory Lectures* he writes that, "however jealously we usually defend the independence of psychology from every other science, here we stood in the shadow of the unshakable biological fact that the living individual organism is at the command of two intentions, self-preservation and the preservation of the species, which seem to be independent of each other, which, so far as we know at present, have no common origin and whose interests are often in conflict in animal life. Actually what we are talking now is biological psychology, we are studying the psychical accompaniments of biological processes. It was as representing this aspect of the subject that the 'ego instincts' and the 'sexual instincts' were introduced into psychoanalysis" (128).

21 Freud adds that "this, however, is more easily said than done" (359).

22 Note that near the beginning of chapter 33, on "Femininity," in the *New Introductory Lectures*, Freud cites verses from Heine to illustrate his observation that "throughout history people have knocked their heads against the riddle of the nature of femininity" (146) and that he concludes his chapter, after remarking that what he has had to say about femininity is incomplete, fragmentary, and unfriendly in sound (having described women only "insofar as their nature is determined by their sexual function"), as follows: "If you want to know more about femininity, inquire from your own experiences of life, or turn to the poets, or wait until science can give you deeper and more coherent information" (169).

23 Although Freud is here discussing the taboo of virginity in primitive peoples, he goes on to observe: "In all this there is nothing obsolete, nothing which is not still alive among ourselves" (271).

24 Freud writes in a footnote added in 1910 to *Three Essays on Sexuality*: "The most striking distinction between the erotic life of antiquity and our own no doubt lies in the fact that the ancients laid the stress upon the instinct itself, whereas we emphasize its object. The ancients glorified the instinct and were prepared on its account to honor even an inferior object; while we despise the instinctual activity in itself, and find excuses for it only in the merits of the object" (61).

25 Freud writes a few pages later that "the program of becoming happy, which the pleasure principle imposes on us, cannot be fulfilled; yet we must not – indeed, we cannot – give up our efforts to bring it nearer to fulfillment by some means or other" (271).

26 Freud returns to this on 274.

27 Freud repeats this on 290–1.

28 Freud indirectly mentions the golden rule at this point and anticipates his critique of it in the second half of *Civilization and its Discontents*. I shall discuss that critique in section IV of this chapter.

29 "Family Romances" opens with this ringing declaration: "The liberation of an individual, as he grows up, from the authority of his parents is one of the most necessary though one of the most painful results brought about by the course of his development. It is quite essential that that liberation should occur and it may be presumed that it has been to some extent achieved by everyone who has reached a normal state. Indeed, the whole progress of society rests upon the opposition between successive generations" (221).

30 But Freud is by no means consistent here when he attempts to assimilate the neurotic and the infantile to the primitive, as we shall see in chapter 4. Later in *Civilization and its Discontents* Freud argues that, while primitive peoples originally did not know the restrictions of instinct to which civilized peoples were bound, they also had few prospects of enjoying their happiness. But then he points out that it was only the primal father who originally enjoyed this instinctual freedom, while the primal horde "lived in slavish suppression." As for primitive peoples living today, he says that research shows that "their instinctual life is by no means to be envied for its freedom. It is subject to restrictions of a different kind but perhaps of greater severity than those attaching to modern civilized man" (306). In the third "Contribution to the Psychology of Love" Freud observes that the taboos against women in primitive society are so extensive that "we have every reason to doubt the reputed sexual freedom of savages" (271).

31 Freud writes a bit later that "even in its caprices the usage of language remains true to some kind of reality. Thus it gives the name of 'love' to a great many kinds of emotional relationship which we too group together theoretically as love; but then again it feels a doubt whether this love is

real, true, actual love, and so hints at a whole scale of possibilities within the range of the phenomena of love. We shall have no difficulty in making the same discovery from our own observations" (141).

32 Freud goes on to say that two errors must be avoided, those of underestimating the importance, for psychopathology, of the repressed libidinal impulses remaining in the unconscious and "of judging the normal entirely by the standards of the pathological. A psychology which will not or cannot penetrate the depths of what is repressed regards affectionate emotional ties as being invariably the expression of impulses which have no sexual aim, even though *they are derived from impulses which have such an aim*" (172ᵉ).

33 The ambiguity of speaking of the aim-inhibited instincts as a "diversion of," and not as (in earlier passages) a "derivation from," the purely sexual instincts allows Freud to point out the complexity of aim-inhibited instincts. They not only can retain their "original sexual aims" but also "are capable of *any degree of admixture* with the uninhibited; they can be transformed back into them, just as they arose out of them." In the same fashion that a "religious tie can revert to ardent sexual excitement," so "it is also very usual for directly sexual impulses, short-lived in themselves, to be transformed into a lasting and purely affectionate tie; and the consolidation of a passionate love marriage rests to a large extent upon this process" (172-3ᵉ). Our quarrel is not with Freud's phenomenology but with his metapsychology, which does not conform to his phenomenology and constantly falsifies it.

34 Freud writes that "by being born we have made the step from an absolutely self-sufficient narcissism to the perception of a changing external world and the beginnings of the discovery of objects" (163). We have seen that male identification with the penis, when faced with castration, is narcissistic and that castration for the female is a narcissistic wound that never heals. It is, therefore, not surprising, as we shall see, that the monopoly that the primal father enjoys over all the primal women, at the expense of their primal sons, is not so much sexual as narcissistic. He not only has but is a big prick. But thus it is also not surprising that non-libidinal (narcissistic) identification with the penis on the part of the primal father leads to his castration (murder) at the hands of the primal sons.

35 Freud goes on to say (representing the male point of view) that this is true with regard to both sexual love of women (because of the obligations incurred) and to "desexualized, sublimated homosexual love for other men, which springs from work in common." In a latter passage he writes that "we know that love puts a check upon narcissism, and it would be possible to show how, by operating in this way, it became a factor of civilization" (156).

36 In his extraordinary account of love and hate in "Instincts and their Vicissitudes," Freud claims that love and hate spring from different sources *and* that love becomes the opposite of hate only at the genital stage. At the same time, however, he derives both from narcissism. "The true prototypes of the relation of hate are derived not from sexual life, but from the ego's struggle to preserve and maintain itself ... Love ... is originally narcissistic, then passes over on to objects ... Hate, as a relation to objects, is older than love. It derives from the narcissistic ego's primordial repudiation of the external world with its outpouring of stimuli" (136–7). If the original response, on the part of an infant, to the world (of its mother) is that of narcissistic hatred, it is hardly surprising that love will begin and end with the castration complex, with the narcissistic contradiction of identifying with the (father's) penis.

37 See the formulations that Freud gives on 144, 147, 161, and 167. In the *New Introductory Lectures* he writes that "in 1921 [in *Group Psychology*] I endeavored to make use of the differentiation between the ego and the superego in a study of group psychology. I arrived at a formula such as this: a psychological group is a collection of individuals who have introduced the same person into their superego and, on the basis of this common element, have identified themselves with one another in their ego" (99).

38 See chapter 7 on "Identification."

39 In his essay on "Fetishism" Freud explains that, when a man's sexual (object) choice is dominated by a fetish, "the fetish is a substitute for the penis ... The fetish is a substitute for the woman's (the mother's) penis that the little boy once believed in and ... does not want to give up" (351–2).

40 In his presentation in section V Freud claims that army and church are similar in that the head of each loves its members equally. "This equal love was expressly enunciated by Christ: ['Truly, I say to you,] as you did it to one of the least of these my brethren, you did it to me' [Matthew 25.40]. He stands to the individual members of the group of believers in the relation of a kind elder brother; he is their substitute father. All the demands that are made upon the individual are derived from this love of Christ's. *A democratic strain runs through the church*, for the very reason that before Christ everyone is equal, and that everyone has an equal share in his love. It is not without a deep reason that *the similarity between the Christian community and a family* is invoked, and that believers call themselves brothers in Christ, that is, brothers through the love which Christ has for them. There is no doubt that the tie which unites each individual with Christ is also the cause of the tie which unites them with one another. The like holds good of an army. The Commander-in-Chief is a father who loves all soldiers equally, and for that reason

they are comrades among themselves" (123ᵉ). Notwithstanding the claim on the part of Freud that army and church are similar, the description that he gives of the church here in section V is consistent with his analysis of how the church differs from the army in section XII.

41 In *Civilization and its Discontents*, when Freud suggests that St Francis went further than anyone in transforming sexual love into aim-inhibited love, he remarks that "what we have recognized as one of the techniques for fulfilling the pleasure principle has often been brought into connection with religion; this connection may lie in the remote regions where *the distinction between the ego and objects or between objects themselves is neglected*" (291ᵉ).

42 See 144 and 148 for Freud's expression of dissatisfaction and note 37 for the location of these earlier formulations.

43 See, for example, *Introductory Lectures* (chapters 19, 27–28), "Remembering, Repeating, and Working Through," "Observations on Transference Love," and "Negation."

44 See "Constructions in Analysis."

45 See 271, 291, 301, 304–5, and 337.

46 Freud makes it clear that, although he is on the side of those who protest the inequality of wealth and its social consequences, he also believes that "to base this fight upon an abstract demand, in the name of justice, for equality for all men," as socialists and communists do, is to ignore the fact "that nature [*sic*], by endowing individuals with extremely unequal physical attributes and mental capacities, has introduced injustices against which there is no remedy" (304). In "Why War?", immediately after remarking that psychoanalysis need not be embarrassed in appealing to love as an indirect method of combating war, given that religion uses the same words in the golden rule (see section III), he writes that "one instance of the innate and ineradicable inequality of men is their tendency to fall into the two classes of leaders and followers. The latter constitute the vast majority; they stand in need of an authority which will make decisions for them and to which they for the most part offer an unqualified submission ... The ideal condition of things would of course be a community of men who had subordinated their instinctual life to the dictatorship of reason. Nothing else could unite men so completely and so tenaciously, even if there were no emotional ties between them. But in all probability that is a Utopian expectation" (359–60).

47 In introducing a summary of the changes that his instinct theory has undergone, Freud writes: "Of all the slowly developed parts of analytic theory, the theory of the instincts is the one that has felt its way the most painfully forward. And yet that theory was so indispensable to the whole structure that *something had to be put in its place. In what was at first my utter perplexity*, I took as my starting-point a saying of the poet-

philosopher, Schiller, that 'hunger and love are what moves the world'"
(308ᵉ). (Freud repeats this appeal to Schiller several times is his work.) I
should modify my earlier comment about Freud's failure to call upon the
humanistic tradition for the principles of his metapsychology (ontology)
by saying that he fails to call upon its strong representatives. Rather, he
takes ideas from, or claims affinity with, weak thinkers like Schiller and
Schopenhauer (or projects ideas upon ancients like Plato). But it is Freud,
not Schiller, who is to blame; for even if we say that hunger and love are
the powers that move the world, there is no reason to divide them
between ego instincts and sexual instincts, as Freud constantly demonstrates phenomenologically.

48 Freud adds a bit later that, "since the assumption of the existence of the
[death] instinct is mainly based on theoretical grounds, we must also
admit that it is not entirely proof against theoretical objections" (313).

49 Freud observes parenthetically: "(The desire for destruction when it is
directed *inwards* mostly eludes our perception, of course, unless it is
tinged with erotism)" (311).

50 "And," he adds, "it is this battle of the giants that our nurse-maids try to
appease with their lullaby about Heaven" (314).

51 Freud writes slightly later that "through its work of identification and
sublimation it [the ego] gives the death instincts in the id assistance in
gaining control over the libido, but in so doing it runs the risk of becoming the object of the death instincts and of itself perishing" (398).

52 Freud adds in a footnote that "all that has been said above about conscience and guilt is, moreover, common knowledge and almost undisput-
ed" (317).

53 See his letter to Fliess, 21 September 1897, and his accounts in *On the
History of the Psychoanalytic Movement* (74ff) and *An Autobiographical
Study* (216ff).

54 Freud acknowledges that, since the two classes of instincts rarely appear
in unmixed form, the clinical material is equivocal.

55 It is not really the case, however, that the mother has or that her daughter develops a significant superego. The idea that the child's superego is
constructed out of its parents' superego is consistent with the passage in
"On Narcissism" where Freud remarks that parents project their unfulfilled dreams (*sic*) upon their child, "His Majesty the Baby." "Parental
love, which is so moving and at bottom so childish, is nothing but the
parents' narcissism born again, which, transformed into object love,
unmistakably reveals its former nature" (85).

56 Freud goes on to say that "in spite of all these difficulties, we may expect
that one day someone will venture to embark upon a pathology of cultural communities" (338–9). Freud is conventionally called a cultural pessimist. But he typically foresees a utopia of scientific knowledge or opts

for pacifism, notwithstanding his claim that life begins in and with violence, as we saw in "Why War?". He is, in fact, as much an optimist as a
pessimist; and his attitudinal dualism is, like his theory of the instincts of
Eros and death, an accurate reflection of his metapsychology: identification with the father('s penis), as castrated by the absent cultural woman
in her sexual, asocial sphere.

57 In the previous paragraph Freud notes that the therapeutic treatment of
neurosis leads him to oppose the superego on two grounds. "In the severity of its commands and prohibitions it [the superego] troubles itself too
little about the happiness of the ego, in that it takes insufficient account
of the resistances against obeying them – of the instinctual strength of the
id and of the difficulties presented by the real external environment. Consequently we are very often obliged, for therapeutic purposes, to oppose
the superego, and we endeavor to lower its demands. Exactly the same
objections can be made against the ethical demands of the cultural superego. It, too, does not trouble itself enough about the facts of the mental
constitution of human beings. It issues a command and does not ask
whether it is possible for people to obey it. On the contrary, it assumes
that a man's ego is psychologically capable of ... unlimited mastery over
his id" (337).

58 Freud continues: "It may be that in this respect precisely the present time
deserves a special interest. Men have gained control over the forces of
nature to such an extent that with their help they would have no difficulty in exterminating one another to the last man. They know this, and
hence comes a large part of their current unrest, their unhappiness and
their mood of anxiety" (340).

59 Freud writes in *Civilization and its Discontents* that the "struggle
between the individual and society is not a derivative of the *contradiction*
– probably an irreconcilable one – between the primal instincts of Eros
and death. It is a dispute within the economics of the libido, ... and it
does admit of an eventual accommodation in the individual, as, it may be
hoped, it will also do in the future of civilization" (335ᵉ). Freud thus
evades the question of how his theory of neurosis – involving the reconcilable (because falsely posed, as he himself shows us) conflict between
sexuality and civilization – is embedded in the irreconcilable *contradiction* between the opposed instincts of death and Eros. It is this contradiction that, in representing the originary ambivalence of identification with
the penis, underlies the Oedipus complex, the root of all neurosis!

60 Dependence on an exalted Father as providential "is so patently infantile,
so foreign to reality," Freud writes in *Civilization and its Discontents*,
that "it is painful to think that the great majority of mortals will never be
able to rise above this view of life. It is still more humiliating to discover
how large a number of people living today, who cannot but see that this

religion is not tenable, nevertheless try to defend it piece by piece in a series of pitiful rearguard actions" (261). What is truly astonishing, however, is that it is precisely this belief that identification with the penis involves (for, even if the penis does not appear providential, it is certainly what *provides* children, both male and female, with their future).

CHAPTER FOUR

1 See "Obsessive Actions and Religious Practices" and "Notes upon a Case of Obsessional Neurosis" (Rat Man).

2 The claim that violence (the regime of taboo) is inexplicably imposed by the earlier (prior), which is not subject to taboo, on the later (posterior) is characteristic of the non-historical claims that Freud typically makes, including his argument in favour of the myth of the primal father, as we shall see. There are two fatal flaws in this hermeneutic, one general, the other specific. The general flaw is that Freud leaves his beginning (principle) inexplicable (unanalyzable). The specific flaw is that, in the myth of the primal father, as we shall see, the taboo or prohibition forbidding incest is not instituted by the (prior) father but by the (posterior) sons.

3 Also see 106, 117, and 152 for Freud's additional reflections on the taboo structure as based upon unconscious desire and conscious fear.

4 Freud has already remarked that "the differences between the situation of a savage and of a neurotic are no doubt of sufficient importance to make any exact agreement impossible and to prevent our carrying [out] the comparison to the point of identity in every detail" (84–5).

5 Freud states in the next paragraph that "the ceremonials and inhibitions of obsessional neurotics show these same characteristics [as found in primitive prohibitions] and are nevertheless derived only from psychical reality – from intentions and not from their execution" (223).

6 "Primitive men and neurotics ... attach a high valuation – in our eyes an *over*-valuation – to psychical acts" (147).

7 I am not concerned here with Frazer and will treat his statement as expressing Freud's own views.

8 Freud, not unlike Joseph K., nervously asks the reader not to expect exactitude or certainty from him (204).

9 Freud prudently adds "without prejudice to any other sources or meanings of the concept of God, upon which psychoanalysis can throw no light" (209). He is generally quite defensive in *Totem and Taboo* about how his views on religion might be taken. Also see 159, 208, and 220, not to mention his famous preface to the Hebrew translation of the work.

10 "Fantasies of being seduced are of particular interest, because so often they are not fantasies but real memories. Fortunately, however, they are

nevertheless not real as often as seemed at first to be shown by the findings of analysis. Seduction by an older child or by one of the same age is
even more frequent than by an adult ... A fantasy of being seduced when
no seduction has occurred is usually employed by a child to screen the
autoerotic period of his sexual activity ... You must not suppose, however, that sexual abuse of a child by its nearest male relatives belongs
entirely to the realm of fantasy. Most analysts will have treated cases in
which such events were real and could be unimpeachably established"
(417).

11 Freud adds: "I have repeatedly been led to suspect that the psychology of
the neuroses has stored up in it more of the antiquities of human development than any other source" (418).

12 It should be borne in mind that, while the subject of the case study is the
Wolf Man's childhood neurosis, the subject of analysis, for more than
four years, is the (return of the) Wolf Man's neurosis as a young man.

13 Freud, like so many readers (imitators) of Kant, fails to see that the Kantian distinction between freedom (thought, practice) and nature (knowledge, experience) means that "the categories of philosophy" (i.e., the categories of possible experience) apply to the objects of nature (appearances), *not* to the content of human practice (history). The "categories"
that are applicable to human "experience" are desire, will, and thought.
They properly constitute what Freud calls psychical reality.

14 In the inverted Oedipus complex the boy is not only hostile to the father
but also seeks with him a relationship like the one his father enjoys with
his mother. I.e., he wants to sleep with and have a child by his father.

15 Freud adds the following comment: "The significance of the traumas of
early childhood would lie in their contributing material to this unconscious which would save it from being worn away by the subsequent
course of development" (364).

16 I shall not take into account Freud's opposition to and critique of
Adler.

17 "What is left over, however, and rejected as false," Freud observes, "is
precisely what is new in psychoanalysis and peculiar to it. This is the eas-
iest method of repelling the revolutionary and inconvenient advances of
psychoanalysis" (287).

18 He remarks that "many people will certainly think that this single admission decides the whole dispute. I am anxious not to be misunderstood"
(284).

19 In a later addition Freud considers the possibility that the boy (in his
dream) transfers a scene of copulating animals onto the scene of his parents lying together. But it is clear that this is not his preferred opinion.

20 Freud cites Jung's *The Psychology of the Unconscious Processes*, 1917
(the title is left in German in the Standard Edition!), and comments

(defensively): "This was published too late for it to have influenced my *Introductory Lectures*" (337).

21 Freud pursues the same analogy between mental and archeological preservation in *Civilization and its Discontents* and concludes with the same disavowal of the analogy (chapter 1).

22 Freud is careful to add that the fact that construction is a preliminary work does not mean that it is completed before the next stage begins. Construction is both means (beginning) and end, both hypothesis and history. He writes: "The analyst finishes a piece of construction and communicates it to the subject of the analysis so that it may work upon him; he then constructs a further piece out of the fresh material pouring in upon him, deals with it in the same way, and proceeds in this alternating fashion until the end [when the construction is no longer preliminary but the whole story of the cure]" (260–1). In his study of Rat Man Freud writes that "the scientific results of psychoanalysis are at present only a by-product of its therapeutic aims, and for that reason it is often just in those cases where treatment fails that most discoveries are made" (88).

23 Freud remarks that he prefers "construction" to "interpretation" as more properly describing the fact that what the analyst does is to lay before the analysand the interconnectedness of all the parts of his history (261).

24 Freud adds: "I can assert without boasting that such an abuse of 'suggestion' has never occurred in my practice" (262).

25 See the topographical diagrams of the mental agencies that Freud gives in *The Ego and the Id* (363) and the *New Introductory Lectures* (111).

26 See *The Ego and the Id* (chapter 5) and *New Introductory Lectures* (111).

27 Freud also writes that "the impressions of this [infantile] period impinge upon an immature and feeble ego, and act upon it like traumas. The ego cannot fend off the emotional storms which they provoke in any way except by repression and in this manner acquires in childhood all its dispositions to later illnesses and functional disturbances ... The difficulty of childhood lies in the fact that in a short span of time a child has to appropriate the results of a cultural evolution which stretches over thousands of years, including the acquisition of control over his instincts and adaptation to society ... He can only achieve a part of this modification through his own development; *much must be imposed on him by education.* We are not surprised that children often carry out this task very imperfectly. During these early times many of them pass through states that may be put on a par with neuroses" (182ᵉ).

28 Freud adds: "It may be that the aetiology of neurotic illnesses is more complicated than we have here described it; if so, we have at least brought out one essential part of the aetiological complex" (436).

29 Freud goes on to say that the damming up of sexual instinct, which follows from the preference that the young ego gives to the external over the internal world, results in the prohibition of infantile sexuality and the consequent desexualization of original instincts. This allows him, he writes, to "anticipate the thesis that many of the highly valued assets of our civilization were acquired at the cost of sexuality and by the restriction of sexual motive forces" (437). In thus holding to the opposition between civilization (repression) and sexuality, Freud returns to his early dualism between ego instincts and sexual instincts, as he evades the more sophisticated conception of the relationship between sexuality and civilization as found in both *Group Psychology* and *Civilization and its Discontents*, as we saw in chapter 3. The regression on the part of Freud is consistent with his claim that the modern child's sexual life is neurotic compared with the free sexual life of the primitive child. This conception of primitive life is, as Freud well knows, inconsistent with available anthropological data, with the structure of taboo as ambivalence, and with his own metapsychology (involving phylogenesis).

30 This is consistent with *Three Essays on Sexuality*, as I indicated earlier.

31 Freud's discussion of Oedipus is found in the section on "Typical Dreams." He had already written to Fliess about his interest in Oedipus in 1897 and 1898.

32 Kierkegaard himself abets this interpretation in his polemic against the Hegelianism that he associates with Christendom (i.e., paganism rationalized as Christianity).

33 Marx also possesses deep insight into history. But his concept of history is irremediably compromised by his inability to see that the dialectical spirit central to history is biblical and thus by his claim that history is "scientific."

34 For Hegel's comments on Socrates see especially his *Lectures on the History of Philosophy* and *Lectures on the Philosophy of History*. For Kierkegaard's comments on Socrates, see *The Concept of Irony, with Particular Reference to Socrates*; *Philosophical Fragments*; *Concluding Unscientific Postscript*; *Sickness unto Death*; and *Works of Love*.

35 After his act of self-blinding in *Oedipus the King*, Oedipus tells the chorus:

It was Apollo, friends, Apollo,
That brought this bitter bitterness, my sorrows to completion.
But the hand that struck me
Was none but my own. (1329–33)

36 Jocasta tells Oedipus in *Oedipus the King*:

Why should man fear since chance is all in all
For him, and he can clearly foreknow nothing?
Best to live lightly, as one can, unthinkingly.
As to your mother's marriage bed, – don't fear it.
Before this, in dreams too, as well as oracles,
Many a man has lain with his own mother.
But he to whom such things are nothing bears
His life most easily. (977–84)

Two comments are in order here. (1) In the German translation used by
Freud (who cites lines 981–3) and in the English version, there are no
"oracles"; and "oracles" are absent from the Greek text. (2) Freud's
heavy-handed commentary is hardly consistent with the unthinking, easy
attitude that Jocasta has towards incest: "Today, just as then, many men
dream of having sexual relations with their mothers, and speak of the
fact with indignation and astonishment. It is clearly the key to the
tragedy and the complement to the dream of the dreamer's father being
dead. The story of Oedipus is the reaction of the imagination to these
two typical dreams. And just as these dreams, when dreamt by adults, are
accompanied by feelings of repulsion, so too the legend must include horror and self-punishment" (*The Interpretation of Dreams*, 366).

CHAPTER FIVE

1 In the *Theological-Political Treatise* Spinoza distinguishes philosophy
   from theology such that each, in teaching the charitable doctrine of the
   golden rule, is true only in so far as both are true. In the *Critique of Pure
   Reason* Kant shows that the dualistic opposites of dogmatism and skepticism (rationalism and empiricism, the transcendent and the imminent)
   result whenever reason is not understood as the paradoxical practice,
   consistent with the golden rule, of uniting individual and universal.
2 This is the form of the name used by Strachey in his English translation.
   See "A Note on the Transcription of Proper Names" (241–2).
3 Because I am not here directly concerned with Freud's theory of neurosis,
   I shall not take up his rich reflections on religion in his case studies,
   above all, those of Rat Man and Dr Schreber.
4 Freud also dismisses the claims that science is not qualified to judge religion and that religion is too sublime to be criticized by other disciplines.
   He points out that what he is concerned with is not the invasion of the
   religious field by science "but on the contrary an invasion by religion of
   the sphere of scientific thought. Whatever may be the value and importance of religion, it has no right in any way to restrict thought – no right,
   therefore, to exclude itself from having thought applied to it" (206).

5 In a note to "Dostoevsky and Parricide," the translator points out that the phrase a "knife that cuts both ways" derives from Constance Garnett's translation of the Russian phrase (which is also found in the German translation): "a stick with two ends" (455).

6 Freud also notes that psychoanalysis shows "how religion originated from the helplessness of children" and traces "its contents to the survival into maturity of the wishes and needs of childhood" (203).

7 Freud later remarks that science attempts "to take account of our dependence on the real external world, while religion is an illusion and it derives its strength from its readiness to fit in with our instinctual wishful impulses" (211).

8 In *The Future of an Illusion* Freud also develops the analogy between the religious neurosis of the childhood of humanity and the "phase of neurosis" through which the individual, modern child passes. As infantile neuroses are outgrown or cleared up by psychotherapy, so it could also be said, Freud indicates, that "humanity as a whole, in its development through the ages, fell into states analogous to the neuroses, and for the same reasons – namely because in the times of its ignorance and intellectual weakness the instinctual renunciations indispensable for man's communal existence had only been achieved by it by means of purely affective forces ... Religion would thus be the universal obsessional neurosis of humanity; like the obsessional neurosis of children, it arose out of the Oedipus complex, out of the relation to the father" (226). Also see 237.

9 In *Civilization and its Discontents* Freud notes that "in my *Future of an Illusion* I was concerned much less with the deepest sources of the religious feeling than with what the common man understands by his religion – with the system of doctrines and promises which, on the one hand, explains to him the riddles of this world with enviable completeness, and, on the other, assures him that a careful Providence will watch over his life and will compensate him in a future existence for any frustrations he suffers here. The common man cannot imagine this Providence otherwise than in the figure of an enormously exalted father. Only such a being can understand the needs of the children of men and be softened by their prayers and placated by the signs of their remorse. The whole thing is so patently infantile, so foreign to reality, that to anyone with a friendly attitude to humanity it is painful to think that the great majority of mortals will never be able to rise above this view of life" (261). See chapter 3, note 60.

10 Freud adds that "it is asking a great deal of a person who has learnt to conduct his ordinary affairs in accordance with the rules of experience and with a regard to reality, to suggest that he shall hand over the care of what are precisely his most intimate interests to an[y religious] agency which claims as its privilege freedom from the precepts of rational think-

ing." He remarks on the repressive role that religion has played in practical life – forbidding women "to have anything to do with their sexuality even in thought" and inhibiting "thought in the life stories of nearly all eminent individuals in the past" (207).

11 In *The Future of an Illusion* Freud writes that "scientific work is the only road which can lead us to a knowledge of reality outside ourselves" (214).

12 At the end of *An Enquiry Concerning Human Understanding* Hume claims to disprove the ontological argument for existence with the demonstration that "whatever *is* may *not be*. No negation of a fact can involve a contradiction" (183). But he conveniently forgets that there is one negation of fact that involves a contradiction, the fact of his own existence. I.e., Hume evades seeing that his claim, rather than disproving, presupposes the ontological argument. In presupposing his own existence, his argument involves the paradox of self-referentiality. It is Hume's evasion that woke Kant up from what he calls his dogmatic slumber.

13 Freud is suspicious that such arguments serve the end of eliminating science in order to reinstate the old religious *Weltanschauung* (212).

14 Freud, in fact, proceeds to discuss the implications of Marxism and Russian Bolshevism for a scientific *Weltanschauung*.

15 In claiming that the slave initiates the process of mutual recognition, Hegel falsifies the phenomenology of the master-slave dialectic. His ontology, however, is flawless.

16 Consistent with his observation in *Civilization and its Discontents* that what he writes is common knowledge, Freud points out in *The Future of an Illusion* that his critique of religion as illusory only repeats what others have said before him and better. "All I have done – and this is the only thing that is new in my exposition – is to add some psychological foundation to the criticisms of my great predecessors. It is hardly to be expected that precisely this addition will produce the effect which was denied to those earlier efforts" (218).

17 I take up the only contradiction that is relevant here. Already earlier the opponent had observed that people's affective needs "'can never be satisfied by cold science; and it is very strange – indeed, it is the height of inconsistency – that a psychologist who has always insisted on what a minor part is played in human affairs by the intelligence as compared with the life of the instincts – that such a psychologist should now try to rob mankind of a precious wish fulfillment and should propose to compensate them for it with intellectual nourishment'" (217).

18 It is clear that Freud, in locating the origin of neurosis in an external event, ultimately never relinquishes the trauma theory of neurosis, which, in being utterly unanalytical, completely falsifies his psychoanalytic insight, even as it is demanded by his metapsychology.

19 Freud views the biblical text as providing "invaluable historical data" that are "distorted by the influence of powerful tendentious purposes and embellished by the products of poetic invention." He suggests that it is easier to accept the history of King David as "genuine historical writing, [produced] five hundred years before Herodotus," on the basis of the hypothesis of Egyptian influence. He holds that the biblical text betrays two traditions, one which revises, falsifies, mutilates, and even reverses its original aims, and the other which piously preserves everything, no matter how inconsistent or contradictory. The Bible's resultant gaps, repetitions, and contradictions are "indications which reveal things to us which it was not intended to communicate. In its implications the distortion of a text resembles a murder: the difficulty is not in perpetrating the deed, but in getting rid of its traces" (281–3). Also see 265, 272, and 290 for further comments by Freud on the biblical text as tendentious and distorted.

20 See note 9. Macmurray notes that "the God of the traditional proofs [as deconstructed by Kant in *The Critique of Pure Reason*] is not the God of religion" (*Persons in Relation*, 207).

21 Freud writes in *The Future of an Illusion* that "I have said nothing which other and better men have not said before me in a much more complete, forcible and impressive manner. Their names are well known, and I shall not cite them, for I should not like to give an impression that I am seeking to rank myself as one of them" (217–18). See note 16.

22 This is the hypothesis of Sellin, for which there is no evidence and no scholarly support.

23 This is the hypothesis of Meyer.

24 Freud adds that "genius is well known to be incomprehensible and irresponsible, and we ought therefore not to bring it up as an explanation till every other solution has failed us" (307). See 259 and 329 for additional claims that it is Egyptian imperialism that explains Jewish monotheism.

25 Freud adds: "Ordinarily god and people are indissolubly linked, they are one from the very beginning of things. No doubt we sometimes hear of a people taking on a different god, but never of a god seeking a different people. We may perhaps understand this unique event better if we recall the relations between Moses and the Jewish people. Moses had stooped to the Jews, had made them his people: they were his 'chosen people'" (285–6).

26 He adds: "To my critical sense this book, which takes its start from the man Moses, appears like a dancer balancing on the tip of one toe. If I could not find support in an analytic interpretation of the exposure myth [of Moses] and could not pass from there to Sellin's suspicion about the end [the murder] of Moses, the whole thing would have had to remain unwritten" (299).

27 Freud adds that the writings of Smith, a genius, "have given me valuable points of contact with the psychological material of analysis and indications for its employment. I have never found myself on common ground with his opponents" (380).

28 Freud adds that "in this way the compass as well as the importance of the archaic heritage would be significantly extended" (345).

29 In an earlier passage Freud also writes about "the universality of symbolism in language" as an "original knowledge" in children that is probably ubiquitous in all peoples and that provides what would appear to be "an assured instance of an archaic heritage." But in this passage Freud goes on to say that the universality of symbolism may only be "a case of the inheritance of an intellectual disposition similar to the ordinary inheritance of an instinctual disposition – and once again it would be no contribution to our problem" (343–4). See the long section on "Representation by Symbols in Dreams – Some Further Typical Dreams" in chapter 6 of *The Interpretation of Dreams*, nearly all of which is added from 1909 on. Freud utters (in an addition made in 1909) what he calls "an express warning against overestimating the importance of symbols in dream-interpretation, against restricting the work of translating dreams merely to translating symbols and against abandoning the technique of making use of the dreamer's associations." He points out that while the two techniques of dream-interpretation are complementary, first place, in both practice and theory, is held by the technique of making use of the dreamer's associations, "which attributes a decisive significance to the comments made by the dreamer" (477). Also see lecture 10, "Symbolism in Dreams," in the *Introductory Lectures*.

30 Freud also fails to connect the role of construction in metapsychology with the role of either construction in the analytic situation or reconstruction in archeology.

31 Freud adds that his "greatness as the founder of a religion is unequivocally established" (357). Whatever the justice in this statement, the religion of Akhenaten bears no historical or ontological relation to ancient Judaism.

32 In an earlier passage Freud writes that "the efforts of the prophets had a lasting success; the doctrines with which they re-established the old faith became the permanent content of the Jewish religion. It is honor enough to the Jewish people that they could preserve such a tradition and produce men who give it a voice – even though the initiative to it came from outside, from a great foreigner" (292). Also see 306.

33 Freud adds: "and perhaps for some other prizes of a similar degree" (358).

34 Freud suggests that an unbeliever might understand how belief in a great God confers self-esteem on analogy with the British traveller whose feel-

ing of superiority reflects "pride in the greatness of the British Empire ...
This may resemble the conception of a grand God. And, since one can
scarcely claim to assist God in the administration of the world, the pride
in God's greatness fuses with the pride in being chosen by him" (359).
Interestingly, just prior to this, Freud observes that, while primitive people depose or castigate their gods, as they do their kings, when they are
not satisfied with them, "the people of Israel, however, clung more and
more submissively to their God the worse they were treated by him"
(358–9).

35 Freud will shortly dissociate the advance in intellectuality from the renunciation of instinct.

36 Freud notes that "immediately after the destruction of the Temple in
Jerusalem by Titus, the Rabbi Jochanan ben Zakkai asked permission to
open the first Torah school in Jabneh" (362).

37 Freud adds that "the pre-eminence given to intellectual labors throughout
some two thousand years in the life of the Jewish people has, of course,
had its effect. It has helped to check the brutality and the tendency to
violence which are apt to appear where the development of muscular
strength is the popular ideal. Harmony in the cultivation of intellectual
and physical activity, such as was achieved by the Greek people, was
denied to the Jews. In this dichotomy their decision was at least in favor
of the worthier alternative" (362–3).

38 Freud adds: "Taking sides in this way with a thought-process in
preference to a sense perception has proved to be a momentous step"
(361).

39 Freud observes that "the renunciation of the instinct would lead to a lasting tension owing to unpleasure, if it were not possible to reduce the
strength of the instinct itself by displacements of energy" (363).

40 Freud arrives again at the same negative conclusion a little later when he
notes that "the cause [the father complex] does not, so to speak, match
the effect [the "intellectual and emotional wealth" of the Jews: "a new
idea of God," having "been chosen by this great God" and given "his
special favor," and "an advance in intellectuality"]; the fact that we want
to explain seems to be of a different order of magnitude from everything
by which we explain it" (371). Also see 376.

41 Freud goes on to say that this intellectuality is later "overpowered" by
Christian faith and that it leads to ethical development within Judaism
(365), topics that I shall take up later.

42 Freud repeats a bit further on that "the command in favor of exogamy,
of which the horror of incest is the negative expression, was a product of
the will of the father and carried this will on after he had been removed"
(369).

43 324–6, 379–80.

44 See note 34, where I indicated that Freud points out the remarkable fact that, unlike other ancient peoples who, when things go badly for them, replace their gods, the Jews continue to adhere to their God while blaming themselves.

45 Freud reviews the motives for anti-Semitism on the basis of two different grounds. First, there are motives that derive from reality and do not call for interpretation: the reproach against Jews for being aliens, for living as minorities, for being different, and, finally, for not only defying oppression ("the most cruel persecutions have not succeeded in exterminating them") but also succeeding in commerce and, when admitted, in every form of cultural activity. Second, there are hidden and deeper motives that operate "from the unconscious of the peoples." He mentions three. (1) People are jealous of the Jews for viewing themselves as specially chosen "as though they had thought there was truth in the claim." (Also see 352.) (2) People fear circumcision as dreaded castration. (3) Today, those who excel in hatred of the Jews became Christians late in history, often due to coercion. Their "misbaptism" leaves them, "under a thin veneer of Christianity, what their ancestors were, who worshipped a barbarous polytheism." They displace their grudge against Christianity "on to the [Jewish] source from which Christianity reached them ... Their hatred of Jews is at bottom a hatred of Christians" (335–6).

46 Freud discusses Christianity and its relationship to Judaism in two major passages: 330ff and 384ff.

47 "He was a man of an innately religious disposition: the dark traces of the past lurked in his mind, ready to break through into its more conscious regions" (331).

48 Freud speculates on the fact that, since the one who sacrificed himself for the murder could not himself be innocent, "the 'redeemer' could be none other than the most guilty person, the ringleader of the company of brothers who had overpowered their father." Whether or not there was such a ringleader, he says, it is clear that each brother in the primal horde had the *wish* to kill the father. "If there was no such ringleader, then Christ was the heir to a wishful fantasy which remained unfulfilled; if there was one, then he was his successor and his reincarnation" (331). Whether or not this is fantasy or the return of forgotten reality, Freud observes further, the hero always rebels against his father and kills him. One is curious, however, to understand how Freud's model of the hero is applicable to Moses and Jesus, given the fact that, while it is the heroes Moses and Christ who would have had the murderous intention to kill their father, it is they, rather, who are killed!

49 Earlier, Freud views the *credo quia absurdum* as analogous to psychotic delusion (328–9).

50 This is a profoundly radical judgment whose implications Freud fails to pursue systematically. We could view it as follows. Christianity absorbs into its heritage of Jewish monotheism the polytheism of antiquity. Modernity would then be understood as the progressive deconstruction of Christianity in light of its Jewish monotheism. Freud, like most writers, fails to see that Greek "philosophy" (not to mention the myths of Aristophanes and Empedocles and the Oedipus story) is shown by Jewish (and Christian) monotheism to be no less "superstitious, magical, and mystical" than the primitive religions of the ancient near East.

51 See note 48, where I summarize the passage in which Freud indicates that Jesus is heir to the guilt of the primal sons. Freud also points out that, although Christianity emphasizes "reconciliation with God the Father, atonement for the crime committed against him," it is equally the case that the son "became a god himself beside the father and, actually, in place of the father. Christianity, having arisen out of a father-religion, became a son-religion. It has not escaped the fate of having to get rid of the father" (385).

52 In the context of noting that his work is full of (compulsive) repetitions, Freud comments that "unluckily an author's creative power does not always obey his will: the work proceeds as it can, and often presents itself to the author as something independent or even alien" (350).

53 See Bloom (*Shakespeare*) and Girard for important (if different) claims about the significance of Shakespeare.

CHAPTER SIX

1 It will be recalled that identification in group psychology is reversed from what it is in the Oedipal model. In group psychology, identification is with fellow group members, while group members look upon the leader as their ideal. Nevertheless, Freud holds that both group psychology and the Oedipus complex have their origin in the myth of the primal father. The primal sons do not identify with the father but only with themselves. In contrast, the Oedipal son's primal relationship is (non-libidinal) identification with the father.

2 See Oberman, *The Harvest of Medieval Theology*.

3 It may be recalled that Jung directly relates the concepts of self, the unconscious, and God.

4 Spinoza writes in the *Ethics* (III.9: Scholium) that something is good because we desire it (the good is what we desire). We do not desire something because it is good. In the *Critique of Practical Reason* Kant shows that it is the will that determines the good object. The will is not determined by the object (62, 66). The distinction between the will (freely) determining the object and the object (tyrannically) determining the will

represents the Kantian distinction between autonomy (freedom) and heteronomy (the father complex of idolatry).

5 Macmurray writes as follows in the final chapter of *The Self as Agent*: "To think the Self as agent is to think the unity of the world as a unity of action" (217). "We shall act as though our own actions were our contributions to the one inclusive action which is the history of the world" (221).

6 See the studies of Foster and Barfield, each of whom demonstrates that natural science presupposes the creation of mind from nothing.

7 Actually, Darwin equivocates here, while Wallace, the stricter Darwinian, holds that the theory of evolution, because it applies solely to the natural world, cannot explain the emergence (the history) of mind. I.e., the theory of evolution is the product of mind. Mind is not the product of evolution. See his *Darwinism*. Today, Neo-Darwinians typically hold that, because mind is caused by brain, mind can (in principle, in the future) be explained by (reduced to) brain. The monism of these Neo-Darwinian positivists is the mirror reflection of Freud's metapsychological dualism. See Webster for a defense of Neo-Darwinism and McGinn ("Can we Ever Understand Consciousness?") for a critique of it.

8 Kant points out in the *Critique of Practical Reason* that "creation" concerns human beings only insofar as they are things-in-themselves (i.e., persons) and not insofar as they are natural objects (subject to the theory of evolution). Things, *qua* created, are noumena, not phenomena. God is the creator of noumena, not of phenomena (106).

9 He also notes that "whatever scientific merit attaches to the study of monkeys and apes in the wild, it cannot be that it will tell us more about our evolutionary past than zoologists have long known" (49).

10 Kant writes in the *Critique of Pure Reason*: "Now it is, indeed, very evident that I cannot know as an object [of nature, e.g., the brain] that which I must presuppose [the mind: myself] in order to know any object" (A 402).

11 In the *Critique of Pure Reason* Kant demonstrates that the dogmatism of rationalism is indistinguishable from the dogmatism of empiricism and that the skepticism of empiricism is indistinguishable from the skepticism of rationalism. In other words, dogmatism and skepticism are but dualistic opposites, blind projections on and of the other. See Lightman for a presentation of these issues.

APPENDIX

1 Carse shows that the concept of life and death held by both ancient Greeks and Hindus is distinct from the biblical concept of life and death as articulated by, above all, Kierkegaard and the ancient Jewish rabbis.

References

WORKS BY FREUD

All works cited are from *The Penguin Freud Library*, 15 volumes, based on *The Standard Edition of the Complete Psychological Works of Sigmund Freud [SE]*, 24 volumes, trans. James Strachey et al. (London: Hogarth Press 1953-74), unless otherwise noted. The year given in round brackets refers to the date of both writing and publication. When a year is additionally given in square brackets, it refers to the date of writing as distinct from the date of publication.

"Analysis of a Phobia in a Five Year Old Boy" (Little Hans) 8 (1909)

"Analysis Terminable and Interminable" SE 23 (1937)

"An Autobiographical Study" 15 (1925 [1924])

Beyond the Pleasure Principle 11 (1920)

Civilization and its Discontents 12 (1930 [1929])

The Complete Letters of Sigmund Freud to Wilhelm Fliess. Trans. J.M. Masson. Cambridge: Harvard University Press, 1985

"Constructions in Analysis" SE 23 (1937)

"[Three] Contributions to the Psychology of Love" 7 (1910, 1912, 1918 [1917])

"The Dissolution of the Oedipus Complex" 7 (1924)

"Dostoevsky and Parricide" 14 (1928 [1927])

"The Economic Problem of Masochism" 11 (1924)

The Ego and the Id 11 (1923)

"Family Romances" 7 (1909)

"Female Sexuality" 7 (1931)

"Fetishism" 7 (1927)
"Formulations on the Two Principles of Mental Functioning" 11 (1911)
"Fragment of an Analysis of a Case of Hysteria" (Dora) 8 (1905 [1901])
"From the History of an Infantile Neurosis" (Wolf-Man) 9 (1918 [1914])
The Future of an Illusion 12 (1927)
Group Psychology and the Analysis of the Ego 12 (1921)
On the History of the Psychoanalytic Movement 15 (1914)
"Instincts and Their Vicissitudes" 11 (1915)
The Interpretation of Dreams 4 (1900)
Introductory Lectures on Psychoanalysis 1 (1917 [1915–17])
"Leonardo da Vinci and a Memory of His Childhood" 14 (1910)
Moses and Monotheism 13 (1939 [1934–38])
"The Moses of Michelangelo" 14 (1914)
"Negation" 11 (1925)
New Introductory Lectures 2 (1933 [1932])
"A Note on the Unconscious in Psychoanalysis" 11 (1912)
"Notes Upon a Case of Obsessional Neurosis" (Rat Man) 9 (1909)
"Observations on Transference Love" SE 12 (1914)
"Observations on 'Wild' Psychoanalysis" SE 11 (1910)
"Obsessive Actions and Religious Practices" 13 (1907)
"On Narcissism: An Introduction" 11 (1914)
An Outline of Psychoanalysis 15 (1940 [1938])
"Psychoanalytic Notes on an Autobiographical Account of a Case of Paranoia
    (Dementia Paranoides)" (Dr Schreber) 9 (1911 [1910])
"The Psychogenesis of a Case of Homosexuality in a Woman" 9 (1920)
"The Question of Lay Analysis" 15 (1926)
"Remembering, Repeating, and Working Through" SE 12 (1914)
"Repression" 11 (1915)
"Some Additional Notes on Dream Interpretation as a Whole" SE 19 (1925)
"Some Psychical Consequences of the Anatomical Distinction Between the
    Sexes" 7 (1925)
Studienausgabe. 11 vols. Frankfurt am Main: S. Fischer Verlag, 1989
Three Essays on the Theory of Sexuality 7 (1905)
*Totem and Taboo: Some Points of Agreement Between the Mental Lives of
    Savages and Neurotics* 13 (1913 [1912-13])
"The Uncanny" 14 (1919)
"The Unconscious" 11 (1915)
"Why War?" 12 (1933 [1932])

OTHER WORKS

Akenson, Donald Harman. *Surpassing Wonder: The Invention of the Bible and
    the Talmuds.* Montreal and Kingston: McGill-Queen's University Press,
    1998

Alvarez, Alfred. "A Talk with Robert Lowell." In *Robert Lowell, Interviews and Memoirs*. Ed. Jeffrey Meyers. Ann Arbor: University of Michigan Press, 1991

Apel, Karl-Otto. "The Problems of Philosophical Foundations in Light of a Transcendental Pragmatics of Language." In *After Philosophy: End or Transformation?* Ed. K. Baynes, J. Bohman, and T. McCarthy. Cambridge: MIT Press, 1987

Aristotle. *The Complete Works*. 2 vols. Ed. Jonathan Barnes. Princeton: Princeton University Press, 1984

– "The Poetics." In *On Poetry and Style*. Trans. G.M.A. Grube. Indianapolis: Bobbs-Merrill, 1958

Aquinas, St Thomas. *Summa Theologica*. Trans. Fathers of the English Dominican Province. 3 vols. New York: Borziger Brothers, 1947–48

Augustine, St. *The City of God*. Trans. Marcus Dods. New York: Modern Library, 1950

Barfield, Owen. *Poetic Diction*. Middletown, CN: Wesleyan University Press, 1973

– *Saving the Appearances: A Study in Idolatry*. New York: Harcourt, Brace & World, 1965

Bible: Authorized Version (1611). Revised Standard Version (1952). The New Revised Standard Version (1989)

Bloom, Harold. *Agon: Towards a Theory of Revisionism*. Oxford: Oxford University Press, 1982

– *The Anxiety of Influence: A Theory of Poetry*. Oxford: Oxford University Press, 1973

– "Freud's Concepts of Defense and Poetic Will." In *The Literary Freud: Mechanisms of Defense and the Poetic Will*. Ed. J.H. Smith. New Haven: Yale University Press, 1980

– *Ruin the Sacred Truths: Poetry and Belief from the Bible to the Present*. Cambridge: Harvard University Press, 1989

– *Shakespeare: The Invention of the Human*. New York: Riverside Books, 1998

Brown, Norman O. *Life Against Death: The Psychoanalytic Meaning of History*. Middletown, CN: Wesleyan University Press, 1959

Buber, Martin. *I and Thou*. Trans. R.G. Smith. 2nd ed. New York: Charles Scribner's Sons, 1958

Cahill, Thomas. *The Gifts of the Jews: How a Tribe of Desert Nomads Changed the Way Everyone Thinks and Feels*. New York: Nan A. Talese/Anchor Books, 1998

Carse, James P. *Death and Existence: A Conceptual History of Human Mortality*. New York: Wiley, 1980

Crews, Frederick, ed. *Unauthorized Freud: Doubters Confront a Legend*. New York: Viking Press, 1998

Darwin, Charles R. *The Origin of Species*. London: Dent, 1963

Derrida, Jacques. *Archive Fever: A Freudian Impression*. Trans. Eric Prenowitz. Chicago: University of Chicago Press, 1996

– "Before the Law." In *Acts of Literature*. Ed. Derek Attridge. New York: Routledge, Chapman, and Hall, 1992

– *Dissemination*. Trans. Barbara Johnson. Chicago: University of Chicago Press, 1981

– "The Force of Law: The Mystical Foundation of Authority." Trans. Mary Quaintance. *The Cardozo Law Review* 11 (1990): 919–1045.

– *Of Grammatology*. Trans. G.C. Spivak. Baltimore: Johns Hopkins University Press, 1976

– "Hospitality, Justice and Responsibility: A Dialogue with Jacques Derrida." In *Questioning Ethics: Contemporary Debates in Philosophy*. Ed. Richard Kearney and Mark Dooley. London: Routledge, 1999

– *Margins of Philosophy*. Trans. Alan Bass. Chicago: University of Chicago Press, 1982

– *The Post Card: From Socrates to Freud and Beyond*. Trans. Alan Bass. Chicago: University of Chicago Press, 1987

– *Writing and Difference*. Trans. Alan Bass. Chicago: University of Chicago Press, 1978

Descartes, René. *The Philosophical Writings*. 3 vols. Trans. John Cottingham, Robert Stoothoff, and Dugald Murdoch. Cambridge: Cambridge University Press, 1984

Dostoevsky, Fyodor. *The Brothers Karamazov*. Trans. Richard Pevear and Larissa Volokhonsky. San Francisco: North Point Press, 1990

Euripides. In *The Complete Greek Tragedies* 3–4. Ed. David Grene and Richmond Lattimore. Chicago: University of Chicago Press, 1959

Fishbane, Michael. *Biblical Interpretation in Ancient Israel*. Oxford: Oxford University Press, 1989

Forrester, John. *Dispatches from the Freud Wars: Psychoanalysis and its Passions*. Cambridge: Harvard University Press, 1997

– *The Seductions of Psychoanalysis: Freud, Lacan and Derrida*. Cambridge: Cambridge University Press, 1990

Foster, M.B. "The Christian Doctrine of Creation and the Rise of Modern Natural Science." *Mind* 43 (1934): 446–68.

– "Christian Theology and the Modern Science of Nature." Parts I and II. *Mind* 44–5 (1935–36): 439–66 and 1–27

Foucault, Michel. *The History of Sexuality*. 3 vols. Trans. R. Hurley. New York: Pantheon Books, 1978

– "Sexuality and Solitude." In *On Signs: A Semiotics Reader*. Ed. Marshall Blonsky. Oxford: Basil Blackwell, 1985

Girard, René. *"To double business bound": Essays on Literature, Mimesis, and Anthropology*. Baltimore: Johns Hopkins University Press, 1978

Hegel, G.W.F. *The Encyclopaedia Logic*. Trans. T.F. Garaets, W.A. Suchting, and H.S. Harris. Indianapolis: Hackett Publishing Company, 1991

– *Lectures on the History of Philosophy.* 3 vols. Trans. E.S. Haldane and Frances H. Simson. London: Routledge and Kegan Paul, 1955

– *Lectures on the Philosophy of History.* Trans. J. Sibree. London: Dover Publications, 1956

– *Lectures on the Philosophy of Religion.* 3 vols. Ed. Peter C. Hodgson. Berkeley: University of California Press, 1984–87

– *The Phenomenology of Spirit.* Trans. A.V. Miller. Oxford: Oxford University Press, 1977

– *The Philosophy of Mind* [Part III: *Encyclopaedia of the Philosophical Sciences*]. Trans. William Wallace. Oxford: Oxford University Press, 1971

Hillman, James. *The Myth of Analysis.* Evanston: Northwestern University Press, 1972

– *Revisioning Psychology.* New York: Harper & Row, 1975

Hobbes, Thomas. *Leviathan.* Ed. J. Plamenatz. London: Collins, 1972

Hume, David. *An Enquiry Concerning Human Understanding.* La Salle, PA: Open Court, 1966

Husserl, Edmund. *The Crisis of European Sciences and Transcendental Philosophy.* Trans. David Carr. Evanston: Northwestern University Press, 1970

Jung, C.G. *Collected Works.* 18 vols. Trans. R.F.C. Hull et al. Princeton: Princeton University Press, 1953–73

Kafka, Franz. *The Trial.* Trans. Willa and Edwin Muir. New York: Schocken Books, 1968

Kant, Immanuel. *Critique of Practical Reason.* Trans. Lewis White Beck. Indianapolis: Bobbs-Merrill, 1956

– *Critique of Pure Reason.* Trans. Norman Kemp Smith. New York: St. Martin's Press, 1965

– *Grounding for the Metaphysics of Morals.* Trans. James W. Ellington. Indianapolis: Hackett Publishing Company, 1981

Kierkegaard, Søren. *The Concept of Irony, with Particular Reference to Socrates.* Trans. H.V. and E.H. Hong. Princeton: Princeton University Press, 1989

– *Concluding Unscientific Postscript.* Trans. H.V. and E.H. Hong. Princeton: Princeton University Press, 1992

– *Fear and Trembling.* Trans. H.V. and E.H. Hong. Princeton: Princeton University Press, 1983

– *Philosophical Fragments.* Trans. H.V. and E.H. Hong. Princeton: Princeton University Press, 1985

– *Purity of Heart is to Will One Thing.* Trans. Douglas V. Steere. New York: Harper & Row, 1956

– *The Sickness Unto Death.* Trans. H.V. and E.H. Hong. Princeton: Princeton University Press, 1980

– *Works of Love.* Trans. H.V. and E.H. Hong. Princeton: Princeton University Press, 1997

Küng, Hans. *Freud and the Problem of God.* Enlarged ed. Trans. Edward Quinn. New Haven: Yale University Press, 1990

Lacan, Jacques. *Écrits: A Selection.* Trans. Alan Sheridan. New York: Norton, 1977

– *The Four Fundamental Concepts of Psychoanalysis.* Trans. Alan Sheridan. New York: Norton, 1981

– "Seminar on 'The Purloined Letter.'" Trans. Jeffrey Mehlman. In *The Purloined Poe.* Ed. John P. Miller and William J. Richardson. Baltimore: Johns Hopkins University Press, 1988

Lawrence, D.H. *Fantasia of the Unconscious* and *Psychoanalysis and the Unconscious.* London: Heinemann, 1961

Lear, Jonathan. *Love and Its Place in Nature: A Philosophical Interpretation of Freudian Psychoanalysis.* New York: Farrar Straus Giroux, 1990

Leibniz, G.W. von. *The Monadology and Other Philosophical Writings.* Trans. R. Latta. London: Oxford University Press, 1965

Levinson, Bernard M. *Deuteronomy and the Hermeneutics of Legal Innovation.* New York: Oxford University Press, 1997

Lewis, Anthony. *Gideon's Trumpet.* New York: Vintage Books, 1964

Lightman, Bernard. *The Origins of Agnosticism.* Baltimore: Johns Hopkins University Press, 1987

Macmurray, John. *Persons in Relation.* London: Faber and Faber, 1970

– *The Self as Agent.* London: Faber and Faber, 1969

Malinowski, Bronislaw. *Sex and Repression in Savage Society.* New York: Harcourt, Brace, 1927

Marcuse, Herbert. *Eros and Civilization: A Philosophical Inquiry into Freud.* New York: Random House, 1962

Marx, Karl. *The Marx-Engels Reader.* Ed. Robert C. Tucker. New York: W.W. Norton and Company, 1978

McGinn, Colin. "Can we Ever Understand Consciousness?" *New York Review of Books* (10 June 1999)

– "Freud under Analysis." *New York Review of Books* (4 November 1999)

Meissner, W.W. *Psychology and Religious Experience.* New Haven: Yale University Press, 1984

Milton, John. *Paradise Lost.* Ed. Alastair Fowler. London: Longman, 1971

Montaigne, Michel de. *The Complete Essays.* Trans. Donald F. Frame. Stanford: Stanford University Press, 1965

Nicholas of Cusa. *On Learned Ignorance.* Trans. A. J. Hopkins. Minneapolis: J. Benning Press, 1981

Nietzsche, Friedrich. "*The Anti-Christ.*" In *The Portable Nietzsche.* Trans. Walter Kaufmann. New York: Viking Press, 1954

– *The Gay Science.* Trans. Walter Kaufmann. New York: Vintage Books, 1974

– *On the Genealogy of Morals.* Trans. Walter Kaufmann. New York: Vintage Books, 1969

- *"Thus Spoke Zarathustra."* In *The Portable Nietzsche.* Trans. Walter Kaufmann. New York: Viking Press, 1954
Oberman, Heiko A. *The Harvest of Medieval Theology.* Cambridge: Harvard University Press, 1963
Ockham, William of. *Philosophical Writings.* Trans. P. Boehner. Edinburgh: Nelson, 1957
Pascal, Blaise. *Selections from The Thoughts.* Trans. A. H. Beattie. New York: Appleton-Century-Crofts, 1965
Paul, Robert A. *Moses and Civilization: The Meaning Behind Freud's Myth.* New Haven: Yale University Press, 1996
Plato, *Five Dialogues: Euthyphro, Apology, Crito, Meno, Phaedo.* Trans. G.M.A. Grube. Indianapolis: Hackett Publishing Company, 1981
- *Gorgias.* Trans. Donald J. Zeyl. Indianapolis: Hackett Publishing Company, 1987
- *Phaedrus.* Trans. W.C. Helmbold. New York: The Liberal Arts Press, 1956
- *The Republic.* Trans. G.M.A. Grube. 2nd ed. rev. C.D.C. Reeve. Indianapolis: Hackett Publishing Company, 1992
- *Symposium.* Trans. Alexander Nehamas and Paul Woodruff. Indianapolis: Hackett Publishing Company, 1989
- *Theaetetus.* Trans. F.C. Cornford. In *Plato's Theory of Knowledge.* New York: The Liberal Arts Press, 1957
Polka, Brayton. "Beyond the Pleasure Principle: A Speculative Essay on Freud." *The American Journal of Psychoanalysis* 49, 4 (1989): 297–309.
- *The Dialectic of Biblical Critique: Interpretation and Existence.* London and New York: The Macmillan Press and St. Martin's Press, 1986
- "Freud, the Bible, and Hermeneutics." *The European Legacy* (forthcoming).
- "Freud, Science, and the Psychoanalytic Critique of Religion: The Paradox of Self-Referentiality." *Journal of the American Academy of Religion* 62, 1 (1994): 59–83.
- "Interpretation and the Bible: The Dialectic of Concept and Content in Interpretative Practice." In *Hermeneutics, the Bible and Literary Criticism.* Ed. A. Loades and M. McLain. London: The Macmillan Press, 1992
- "Nietzsche and the Meaning of History." In *Between Memory and History.* Ed. D. Paycha and B. Zelechow. Cergy-Pontoise, France: Les Cahiers du CICC, 2000
- "Psychology and Theology in *The Brothers Karamazov*: 'Everything is Permitted' and the Two Fictions of Contradiction and Paradox." *Journal of Literature and Theology* 5, 3 (1991): 253–76
- "Spinoza and Biblical Interpretation: The Paradox of Modernity." *The European Legacy* 1, 5 (1996): 1673–82
- "Spinoza's Concept of Biblical Interpretation." *Journal of Jewish Thought and Philosophy* 2 (1992): 19–44

- "Spinoza and the Separation between Philosophy and Theology." *Journal of Religious Studies* 16, 1–2 (1990): 91–119
- "Thinking – Between Kant and Kierkegaard – Modernity and the Bible." In *Cult & Culture: Studies in Cultural Meaning.* Ed. D. Paycha and B. Zelechow. Cergy-Pontoise, France: Les Cahiers du CICC, 1999
- *Truth and Interpretation: An Essay in Thinking.* New York: St. Martin's Press, 1990

The Presocratic Philosophers. Trans. G.S. Kirk and J.E. Raven. 2nd ed. Cambridge: Cambridge University Press, 1983

Richardson, Samuel. *Clarissa.* Ed. Angus Ross. Harmondsworth, England: Penguin Books, 1985

Ricoeur, Paul. *Essays on Biblical Interpretation.* Ed. Lewis S. Mudge. Philadelphia: Fortress Press, 1980
- *Freud and Philosophy.* Trans. Denis Savage. New Haven: Yale University Press, 1970
- "A Philosophical Interpretation of Freud." In *The Philosophy of Paul Ricoeur: An Anthology of His Work.* Ed. Charles E. Reagan and David Stewart. Boston: Beacon Press, 1978
- "The Question of Proof in Freud's Psychoanalytic Writings." Ibid.

Rousseau, J.-J. *Social Contract* and *Discourse on the Origin and Foundation of Inequality Among Mankind.* Ed. Lester G. Crocker. New York: Washington Square Press. 1967

Ryle, Gilbert. *The Concept of Mind.* London: Hutchinson, 1949

Sade, Marquis de. *The Complete Justine, Philosophy in the Bedroom and Other Writings.* Trans. R. Seaver and A. Wainhouse. New York: Grove Press, 1966

Sartre, Jean-Paul. *Being and Nothingness.* Trans. Hazel E. Barnes. New York: Washington Square Press, 1966

Shakespeare, William. *Hamlet* et al. In *The Pelican Shakespeare.* Ed. Alfred Harbage. Baltimore: Penguin Books, 1957

Sophocles. In *The Complete Greek Tragedies* 2. Ed. David Grene and Richmond Lattimore. Chicago: University of Chicago Press, 1959

Spinoza, Baruch. *"Ethics."* In *The Collected Works of Spinoza* 1. Trans. Edwin Curley. Princeton: Princeton University Press, 1985
- *Opera.* 4 vols. Ed. Carl Gebhardt. Heidelberg: Carl Winters Universitäts Buchhandlung, 1972
- *Theological-Political Treatise.* Trans. Samuel Shirley. Indianpolis: Hackett Publishing Company, 1998

Spiro, Melford E. *Oedipus in the Trobriands.* Chicago: University of Chicago Press, 1982

Stein, Robert. *Incest and Human Love: The Betrayal of the Soul in Psychotherapy.* New York: Third Press, 1973

Taylor, Mark C. *Alterity.* Chicago: University of Chicago Press, 1986

- *Erring*: *A Postmodern A/theology*. Chicago: University of Chicago Press, 1984

Thucydides. *The Peloponnesian War*. Trans. S. Lattimore. Indianapolis: Hackett Publishing Company, 1998

The Upanishads: *The Principal Texts*. Selected and Trans. Swami Prabhavananda and Frederick Manchester. New York: New American Library, 1957

Vico, Giambattista. *The New Science*. Rev. Trans. T.G. Bergin and M.H. Fisch. Ithaca: Cornell University Press, 1968

Wallace, Alfred Russel. *Darwinism*. New York: AMS Press, 1975

Webster, Richard. *Why Freud Was Wrong: Sin, Science, and Psychoanalysis*. New York: Basic Books, 1995

White, Victor. *God and the Unconscious*. London: Harvill Press, 1952

- *Soul and Psyche*. London: Collins and Harvill, 1960

Yerushalmi, Yosef Hayim. *Freud's Moses: Judaism Terminable and Interminable*. New Haven: Yale University Press, 1991

Zuckerman, Lord. "Apes Я Not Us." *New York Review of Books* (30 May 1991)

Index

Note on the use of the Index:
Given the interdependence of the basic concepts of Freudian thought examined in this study, and also of the interrelationship of key concepts used here to explicate Freud's thought, it is not practicable to include every mention of each concept in the Index. When searching for any particular concept, the reader should check related concepts. This is particularly true with regard to the following clusters of concepts: castration complex, identification, libido, Oedipus complex, and superego (autoerotism, ego, id, narcissism); contradiction (dualism, idolatry) and paradox; Eros (life instinct) and death instinct; father complex and myth of the primal father; golden rule and reciprocity; interpretation and hermeneutics; metapsychology and phenomenology; pleasure principle (primary process, Nirvana principle, illusion, religion) and reality principle (secondary process, science); and unconscious and consciousness. In some cases, the Index favors one concept over another (i.e., when one concept constantly implies or is contrasted with another concept or when it is basically identical with it). It should be further noted that when particular concepts or works are the subject of an entire chapter or sub-chapter, the Index directs the reader to the chapter(s) in question.